The Novel in the Age of Disintegration

Northwestern University Press
Studies in Russian Literature and Theory

The Novel in the Age of Disintegration

DOSTOEVSKY AND THE PROBLEM OF GENRE IN THE 1870s

Kate Holland

NORTHWESTERN UNIVERSITY PRESS / EVANSTON, ILLINOIS

Northwestern University Press
www.nupress.northwestern.edu

This book has been published with the support of the Andrew W. Mellon Foundation

Printed in the United States of America

ISBN: 978-0-8101-4449-1

The Library of Congress has cataloged the original, hardcover edition as follows:

Holland, Kate.
The novel in the age of disintegration : Dostoevsky and the problem of genre in the 1870s / Kate Holland.
p. cm.—(Studies in Russian literature and theory)
Includes bibliographical references and index.
ISBN 978-0-8101-2926-9 (cloth : alk. paper)
1. Dostoyevsky, Fyodor, 1821–1881—Criticism and interpretation. 2. Russia—Social conditions—1801–1917. 3. Social change in literature. I. Title. II. Series: Studies in Russian literature and theory.
PG3328.Z6H59 2013
891.733—dc23

2013011156

Contents

Acknowledgments

This book would not have been possible without the help and support of people in four countries: the United Kingdom, the United States, Russia, and Canada. Parts of it were conceived at the University of Cambridge; it took shape at Yale University and was completed at the University of Toronto. At Yale, a Whiting Graduate Fellowship and a Morse Junior Faculty Fellowship helped to provide much-needed writing time, while grants from the MacMillan Center for International and Area Studies helped to fund research trips to St. Petersburg. I am extremely grateful to Mike Levine and to Northwestern University Press for their enthusiastic support of this manuscript.

I would like to begin by expressing warm thanks to Dr. Aileen Kelly, my undergraduate supervisor at King's College, Cambridge, and the person responsible for my introduction to Dostoevsky. My deepest debt of gratitude is to Robert L. Jackson for his intellectual mentorship, comradeship, and friendship over the years. He led this project from its embryonic beginnings in my undergraduate thesis through its intermediate stage in my doctoral dissertation and beyond. He was the intellectual inspiration behind my migration to the New World, and for that, as well as for his limitless kindness and unwavering support, I thank him from the bottom of my heart. I am grateful to the Department of Slavic Languages and Literatures at Yale University for being such a comforting home to me for so many years, first during graduate school and then for my first job. I would like to thank Katerina Clark, Irina Dolgova, Hilary Fink, Harvey Goldblatt, John Mackay,Tomas Venclova, and especially Vladimir Alexandrov for their stimulating conversation, company, and support during the decade I spent in New Haven. This book was completed after my move to the Slavic Department at the University of Toronto and has profited immensely from the wonderfully warm and welcoming environment of my new home department. I would like to thank Veronika Ambros, Christopher Barnes, Leonid Livak, Taras Koznarsky, Julia Mikhailova, Pia Paivio, Joseph Schallert, Maxim Tarnawsky, and Tamara Trojanowska for their collegiality and enthusiasm and for the rich intellectual exchange that takes place every day on the fourth floor of Alumni Hall. Especially warm thanks go to Christina Kramer and Donna Orwin for their support, mentorship, and friendship. My understanding and appreciation of Dostoevsky has become so much deeper and richer as a result of the brilliant insights and encouragement of the many undergraduates and graduate students I have had the immense pleasure to teach for the last ten years. Particular thanks go to Chloe Kitzinger and Keside Ugoji, two subtle and sophisticated readers of Dostoevsky, and to Olha Tytarenko, whose insights during the last three years have helped greatly as I have sought to structure my ideas.

I have presented parts of this project at many conferences, colloquia, and symposia. Special thanks go to the Slavic Departments of Yale, UC Berkeley, UCLA, Stanford, New York University, and Toronto for inviting me to present my work and for the many helpful suggestions I received, many of which have been incorporated into this final version. I am grateful to Irina Paperno for invaluable help and advice with an earlier version of this project. Ilya Kliger and Lina Steiner have read chapter drafts and have cheerfully served as sounding boards for my ideas over the years. I am immensely grateful for that and for their friendship and collegiality. I would like to thank the manuscript readers at Northwestern University Press for their helpful suggestions and corrections.

Some of the ideas in chapters 4 and 5 were originally presented in articles in the following publications, and I would like to gratefully acknowledge their permission for republication: "The Fictional Filter: 'Krotkaia' and *The Diary of a Writer,*" *Dostoevsky Studies*, n.s., 4 (2000): 95–116; "The Legend of the *Ladonka* and the Trial of the Novel" in *A New Word on "The Brothers Karamazov,"* ed. Robert Louis Jackson, 192–200 (Evanston, Ill.: Northwestern University Press, 2004); and "Novelizing Religious Experience: The Generic Landscape of *The Brothers Karamazov,*" *Slavic Review* 66, no. 1 (Spring 2007): 63–81.

This book could never have been written without the comradeship, loyalty, support, and affection of friends and colleagues all over the world. On the other side of the Atlantic, Jane Adshead, Rodie Akerman, Alice Fox, Frances Forsyth, and Rachel Smith have always found time in their busy schedules for an emergency phone call or a last-minute get-together. From my graduate school cohort, I would like to thank Ioana Drutu, Lilach Gilady, Laura Heins, Hiba Hafiz, Masha Salazkina, and Emma Wasserman for so many happy New Haven memories. Research in St. Petersburg would not have been the same without the hospitality and friendship of Marina Kruglova, Vadim Goloubev, and Ildar and Katya Ibraguimov. Special thanks go to the Yale Junior Faculty drinks crowd for so many stimulating conversations and late nights at the Blue Pearl: Alex Beecroft, Seth Brodsky, Anne Dunlop, Eckart Frahm, Milette Gaifman, David Greven, Justin Isenhart, Gundula Kreutzer, Barry McCrea, Karin Melnick, Corinne Pache, Youval

Rotman, Kathryn Slanski, and Jude Stewart. Key parts of this book were written in Memphis, where we were fortunate to enjoy the company and intellectual fellowship of Teresa Delfin and William Dolphin. In Toronto, I am fortunate to count on the friendship of Dragana Obradovic, Alison Smith, and Lis Pimentel.

I owe an enormous debt of gratitude to my family, without whose love and support this book could never have been completed. Thanks to my siblings, Tom and Jude, and their partners, Clare and Andy, for always providing safe harbor during a storm, and to my parents-in-law, Angel Fernandez and Maria-Angeles Pelaez, for their kindness and warmth in accepting me into their family. After a very long gestation period, this book was born only days before my son, Daniel Holland-Fernandez, and it is thanks to his sweet nature that its final days were so uneventful. I lack the words to express the extent of my debt to my husband and partner-in-crime, Ivan Fernandez Pelaez, without whom my life would be considerably more Dostoevskian. I dedicate this book to my parents, Jon and Pat Holland, from whom I inherited my love of literature and who first encouraged my early Russophilia.

A Note on Transliteration and Sources

The main body of this book follows a modified Library of Congress transliteration system. To make the text more readable for a general audience, I use the common anglicized versions of Russian names and surnames in the body of the work: Fyodor Dostoevsky rather than Fedor Dostoevskii, Leo Tolstoy rather than Lev Tolstoii, Alexander rather than Aleksandr, Alyosha rather than Alesha, and Mitya rather than Mitia. In the notes and bibliography I use the standard Library of Congress transliteration system. References to Dostoevsky's works appear in parentheses in the main text and refer to the volume and page number of the Academy Edition of the *Complete Works* of Dostoevsky: F. M. Dostoevskii, *Polnoe sobranie sochinenii v tritsati tomakh*, ed. V. G. Bazanov et al., 30 vols. (Leningrad: Nauka, 1972–90).

The Novel in the Age of Disintegration

Introduction

AT THE END OF 1872, following the end of the publication of his most controversial novel, *Demons,* Fyodor Dostoevsky became editor of Prince Meshchersky's conservative weekly journal, *The Citizen,* returning to the world of journalism for the first time in almost a decade. Sitting down to plan one of his first articles for the publication, he wrote the following notes:

> Article about the diversity of modern society, people have lost their forms; they have been obliterated all at once, and the new ones are still in hiding. The gentry, the hereditary serf-owners, gave the government service in exchange, and the shaping of a tradition; gentry literature, concepts, suddenly chaos, people without forms—there are no convictions, no science, no points of special emphasis, they preach some secrets of socialism. People, like Kirillov, using his own intellect, suffering. The main thing is that they do not understand each other. This entire jellied mass was seized by cynicism—the youth, lacking guidance, welcomes it with open arms. How could it be that Nechaev could have been successful. Meanwhile, a few preconceived ideas, the feeling of honor—a false concept of humaneness. The pettiest vanity. Look at literature, with what restraint it expresses its goals, its rage, its abuse, its haste . . . The Citizen must present the picture . . . There is absolutely no one to respect (that's the present day plague), how the enlightenment of the past is not taken seriously today amongst us Russians. Faces without forms.[1]

Despite their fragmentary status, these notes provide a comprehensive insight into the concerns and preoccupations that drove Dostoevsky throughout the final decade of his literary career and helped to shape the last great works of his life: the two novels *The Adolescent* (1875) and *The Brothers Karamazov* (1878–80) and the two incarnations of the groundbreaking journalistic venture *A Writer's Diary:* the column in *The Citizen* (1873) and the monojournal (1876–77 and 1880–81). The 1872 projected article is devoted to a theme that was both to serve as the central subject of Dostoevsky's contributions to the journal and to shape his own thinking about literary and journalistic representation for the rest of his life: the transformation of society as a result of the sustained modernization brought by the reforms of Tsar Alexander II in the 1860s and early 1870s. The reforms, which began with the emancipation of the serfs in 1861 and included the large-scale restructuring of the realms of the judiciary, local government, army, education, and censorship, constitute the most significant sustained period of social and political transformation in nineteenth-century Russia.[2] Dostoevsky concerns himself not with concrete details of the reforms and their legacy, but rather with the modernization of Russian society as a crisis of form. He examines the tempest of modernization, which has fractured society's image into a multiplicity of fragments, so that it can no longer be imagined or visualized. Dostoevsky believes that the old artistic forms are no longer capable of representing society in all its multiplicity and complexity. The world has taken on a new appearance that can no longer be captured by the old lenses; it requires a new way of seeing.

The notes situate the cause of this crisis of form in the experience of social transition, conjuring up a vision of a world that has outgrown one historical phase but has not yet grown into the next. They provide a historical contextualization for the current crisis, explaining it in terms of the waning influence of the gentry as the form-shaping force in Russian society. The noble estate has provided society with its values, its modes of expression, and its inward and outward forms. The reforms have led to the decline of the gentry, precipitating the disintegration of Russian society's self-image: "suddenly chaos, people without forms." In a later notebook entry, Dostoevsky invokes one conservative social commentator's view that the contemporary moment is characterized by "the complete annihilation of the gentry and the gentry spirit through the squeezing out of their rights or the loss of land of small landowners, the very people in whom the old noble families and the spirit of the gentry found refuge" (21:271). The notes connect the decline of the gentry with the spiritual and moral bankruptcy of the intelligentsia, embodied here in the image of Dostoevsky's own fictional creation, the character of Kirillov from *Demons* (1872), the nihilist engineer who seeks to conquer God and overcome death by killing himself. The nobility's declining role at the helm of Russian culture and the intelligentsia's monstrous ideological fantasies have led to a widespread crisis of belief: "There are no convictions, no science . . . people do not understand each other"; instead there are "preconceived ideas," "a false concept of humaneness." Russian society is riven by mutual incomprehension, the breakdown of values leading to a vacuum in which divisive figures such as the infamous nihilist Nechaev can exert malign influences over the young and the weak. Social disintegration has brought about a communication breakdown that has affected all levels of society. The notes emphasize the continuing importance of literature in this moment of social transition, yet they express an underlying anxiety about what shape it might take. "Gentry literature" has disappeared, along with the estate with which it is associated, yet a new literature has not yet emerged.

The crisis of form expressed in these notes is the central problem of this book, *The Novel in the Age of Disintegration: Dostoevsky and the Problem of Genre in the 1870s.* I argue that Dostoevsky's works of the 1870s are characterized by two contradictory formal impulses that reflect two different readings of Russian modernity. The first, which is summed up in the original title of *The Adolescent,* "Disorder," is an impulse toward fragmentation. It seeks to represent on a formal level the sense of disintegration and atomization that is fundamental to the experience of modernity. It assumes the world to be radically contingent and seeks to replicate this contingency with as open and unfinished a structure as possible. It borrows from the old in order to demonstrate its own experimental ambitions, and insists on a continual fidelity to the flux of life, even when such fidelity threatens formal coherence. This impulse represents an acceptance of Russian modernity in all its social and spiritual disintegration. It emerges out of a conservative reading of modernization as leading to social, political, and hermeneutic breakdown, yet leads to an approach to form that is experimental and innovative. This fragmentation impulse is countered by an opposing impulse toward formal unity. This approach seeks to reintegrate the fragments of a world shattered by modernity. It strives toward narrative totality. It posits the idea of the transfiguring power of harmonious ideal form, which is embodied in the ideal figure of Christ. This approach seeks to deny the concept of fragmentary modernity and its implications, replacing it instead with a vision of social and spiritual unity modeled on the imagined harmony of the pre-Petrine nation. It invokes a dream of national salvation and of a future society redeemed by the faith of the Russian people and transfigured by the image of the Orthodox Christ.

The Novel in the Age of Disintegration argues that this conflict between fragmentation and unity plays out in every work of Dostoevsky's last decade. It leads to diverse experimentation in the realm of genre. It cuts across genre boundaries, determining the forms of both novels and journalistic genres, and leads to two contradictory approaches toward the novel as a genre. Sometimes Dostoevsky perceives it as a fragmentary literary form that expresses post-Petrine Russian modernity through the prism of its alienated heroes; at others he recognizes in it a possible vehicle of national literary and spiritual accord and regeneration. The fragmentation impulse is reflected in his attempt to remake the novel as maximally open to the diversity of modern experience. It inspires the formal peculiarities of *The Adolescent,* a proto-modernist work within a work, the fragmentary autobiographical "notes" of a quintessentially divided modern subject framed by a fictional critical commentary on the generic status of those "notes." The unity impulse is reflected in Dostoevsky's dream of redeeming the novel, of imbuing the genre with the aesthetic experiences and religious beliefs of the Russian people. It inspires the tightly orchestrated novelistic symphony of *The Brothers Karamazov*, in which medieval and modern popular religious genres are embedded in the structure of the novel itself, allowing a normally secular genre to become permeated with religious experience. The conflict between the opposing impulses structures both works: unifying associations such as the symbolic connections between Arkady's two fathers, Makar and Andrei, undergirded by hagiographic and iconic associations, place a break on the poetics of disintegration in *The Adolescent*. Unanswered questions regarding the suffering of children and the nature of sin and redemption, never completely addressed within the novel's ideological scheme, threaten to fragment the formal unity of *The Brothers Karamazov*. This book argues that, in Dostoevsky's novels at least, the conflict between fragmentation and unity is never resolved and continues to trouble, provoke, and inspire readers of Dostoevsky's late works up to the present day.

The impulses of fragmentation and unity also structure Dostoevsky's journalistic works of the 1870s. The two different incarnations of his heterogeneous and structurally complex work, the 1873 column published in *The Citizen* entitled "A Writer's Diary," and the 1876–77 and 1880–81 monojournal of the same name, constitute two attempts to give shape to Russian social life in the postreform period. They combine fiction, journalism, autobiography, literary criticism, and other genres less easy to categorize. The diverse stories of modern life they represent, the range of contradictory voices and ideas they invoke, and the array of different genres they employ all reflect the fragmentation impulse. Their frequent appeals to a principle of aesthetic and spiritual harmony enshrined in the image of Christ and the search for signs of a coming national salvation reveal the presence of the unity impulse. The formal conflict between fragmentation and unity finds its ideological counterpart in *A Writer's Diary* in a conflict between two attitudes toward the word. Sometimes Dostoevsky recognizes the heteroglossia of contemporary Russian life; he represents a full range of voices with different political and social orientations and allows these diverse perspectives to reveal and reflect postreform Russia's diversity and heterogenousness.[3] At other times he takes on a monologic voice that brooks no authority and denies the polysemic nature of many of the images he chooses to highlight.[4] By 1877 the monologic principle begins to dominate the monojournal as Dostoevsky insists ever more dogmatically on the absolute power of the final word he is offering to the world, a word that will overcome the linguistic and social differentiation of the modern age. It is only in Dostoevsky's journalism, as well as in his letters and notebooks, that the unity impulse and its ideological counterpart, monologism, are ever permitted the final word.

Generic experimentation was nothing new for Dostoevsky. He had been experimenting with the novelistic form ever since his first novel, *Poor Folk* (1846), which combines the already outmoded form of the epistolary novel with the subject of the lowly St. Petersburg civil servant made famous by Nikolai Gogol. In *Notes from the House of the Dead* he remade the memoir form. *Crime and Punishment, The Idiot,* and *Demons* all expand the purview of the novelistic form, including diverse kinds of narrative experimentation. Yet the question of genre took on a special urgency for Dostoevsky in the context of the social, historical, and hermeneutic dislocation of the postreform era. In the 1870s literary form became a way to convey and contain, but also sometimes to overcome, his perception of the fragmentary nature of contemporary Russian reality. Choosing the right genre became a matter of paramount importance for Dostoevsky: nothing less than the future of Russia was at stake. In the works of the 1870s Dostoevsky dramatizes his own generic choices, opening up each of his creative projects to the reader and revealing his motivations, demonstrating in the process the divided nature of his own vision of Russian modernity. *The Brothers Karamazov* stages a trial of genres that mirrors on a formal level the murder trial of Dmitry Karamazov. In *A Writer's Diary,* genres struggle with one another in a rhetorical war, as each seeks to achieve dominance on the level of individual diary sections and within the work as a whole. In *The Adolescent,* the titular hero, Arkady, plunders the generic legacy of his father, the nobleman Versilov, for generic models on which to base his own autobiography. By providing form to a society threatened with formlessness, genre becomes both the key to humanity's salvation and the instrument of its demise.

THE STRUCTURE OF *THE NOVEL IN THE AGE OF DISINTEGRATION*

This book is arranged in two parts, the first of which lays the groundwork for the second. The first part, divided into two chapters, examines the background and buildup of Dostoevsky's anxiety about Russian modernity in the decade of Alexander II's reforms, the 1860s; the culmination of those anxieties in the novel *Demons;* and the development in the early 1870s of the two distinctive and very different perspectives on Russian modernity that would play a central role in shaping the aesthetic and especially the formal vision of his last decade. The first chapter deals with the process of gradual disillusionment that marked the evolution of Dostoevsky's views on Russian history, society, literature, and culture during the 1860s. I argue that this disillusionment forms the basis of the complex and contradictory vision of Russian modernity that informs the experiments in genre which characterize the works of the 1870s. It examines how, in the space of just over ten years, from his return from exile to Siberia on the eve of the emancipation of the serfs, to the publication of *Demons,* Dostoevsky's views on Russian modernity were transformed from the optimistic embrace of social and political change that we find in the journal *Time,* which he founded with his brother Mikhail, Nikolai Strakhov, and Apollon Grigoriev in 1860, to the dark and pessimistic vision that permeates his 1872 novel *Demons.* My examination of the generic aspirations and configurations of *Demons* focuses not so much on the completed novel as on the project as process, from its beginnings in Dostoevsky's unwritten work, *The Life of a Great Sinner,* to its transformation after the Nechaev affair, to the addition of its tragic hero, Stavrogin. I also examine the circumstances under which Dostoevsky worked on *Demons* during the four years he spent with his family in Europe. Much of the planning and writing took place in the shadow of the looming Franco-Prussian war. Crucial sections of the novel were written in May 1871, while the Paris Commune was being suppressed. Dostoevsky read these historical events as the final proof of Western Europe's decline and of the cultural, social, and political bankruptcy of the Russian Westernizers who had shaped Russian politics and history since Peter the Great's reforms. The chapter traces the roots of Dostoevsky's discontent with the "gentry literature" of his contemporaries Leo Tolstoy and Ivan Turgenev, and his association of the traditional Russian novel with the Russian Westernism that was born out of the Petrine reforms. This interpretation of the history of the Russian novel would play a crucial role in Dostoevsky's works of the 1870s, beginning with *Demons.* It would lead, I argue throughout, to the urgent impulse to remake the Russian novel for a new historical moment. What that moment and the resulting novel would look like are questions I deal with throughout the rest of the book.

The second chapter examines Dostoevsky's editorship of Prince Meshchersky's conservative weekly journal, *The Citizen.* I argue that the author struggles to reconcile two mutually incompatible views of Alexander II's reforms and two very different interpretations of contemporary Russia's social and political development. On the one hand, he shares the view of Meshchersky and his conservative colleagues that in destabilizing and dismantling Russia's post-Petrine social and political system, the reforms have paved the way for a widespread social and cultural collapse. Its symptoms include the disintegration of the nobility, social breakdown in the countryside, the erosion of religious beliefs, and the collapse of family life. On the other, he celebrates the radical possibilities that the reforms have brought. By liberating the peasants from their economic oppression at the hands of the nobility, the reforms have overcome the social and cultural rift between the two groups that was the legacy of the Petrine reforms. They have created the conditions for the possibility of national spiritual renewal based on the Russian people's Orthodox faith. I show how these two visions of Russian modernity found their expression in two different approaches to form in Dostoevsky's regular column for *The Citizen*, "A Writer's Diary." The columns were the scene of the struggle between, on the one hand, his recognition of the social fragmentation that modernization had brought and the need to represent this fragmentation on the level of form and narrative, and, on the other, his journalistic commitment to overcoming that fragmentation and presenting Russian society with a "new word," a vision of the possibility of national spiritual renewal.

The book's second part provides readings of *The Adolescent*, the monojournal version of *A Writer's Diary*, and *The Brothers Karamazov* as literary articulations of the two approaches to Russian modernity outlined in the first part. The third chapter analyzes Dostoevsky's most structurally problematic novel, *The Adolescent* (1875). I read the work not only as an attempt to represent the social transition of the postreform era in all its fragmentation, but also as a novelistic meditation on whether and how such representation can be possible within the form of the novel. Consciously setting itself up against the "noble family novels" of Tolstoy and Ivan Goncharov, *The Adolescent* makes the case for a fundamental rethinking of novelistic representation following changes in the institutions that have traditionally been most central to the Russian novel: the nobility and the family. The work's narrative framing creates a complex interplay between the perspectives of narrator and hero and of narrator and implied author, an interplay that provides two parallel processes of narration with very different narrative motivations and leads to a multilayered novel of education, in which a young man's search for self-fulfillment becomes the narratological pretext for a meditation on the past, present, and future of the Russian novel. Inscribed into the novel's basic bildungsroman narrative, the adolescent Arkady's education in the world, is the search for a literary form capable of expressing the fragmentary reality that has formed his own conflicted identity and ambiguous social status. As Arkady learns to negotiate his own relationship to the family and society to which he belongs, and to the historical moment he occupies, he also learns how to express himself in narrative. Representing the process of Arkady's narratological education allows Dostoevsky to dramatize his own attempts to find a novelistic form to express the social disintegration of the 1870s, that is, to include within the novel an account of his own authorial *Bildung*. The earlier novelistic models employed in this novel provide Arkady with the possibility of exploring his father's narrative legacy and his own narrative inheritance and provide Dostoevsky with the possibility of inscribing into *The Adolescent* the history of the Russian novel as a genre, of representing in his own novel the models he is writing against. Dostoevsky figures his own departure from tradition in Arkady's rebellious overcoming of his father's generic legacy. Yet like the illegitimate adolescent who must first explore the past certainties of which he has been deprived before he can reject them, Dostoevsky recognizes that without genre memory, literary experimentation is impossible.

In the fourth chapter, I shift my theoretical focus from an examination of a particular subgenre of the novel to a discussion of the ways in which novelistic narrative interacts with and stands apart from other generic discourses within Dostoevsky's 1876–77 monojournal version of *A Writer's Diary.* I examine the work in the context of the rich processes of literary and hermeneutic exchange between the novel and journalism that characterized 1870s Russian literary life. Dostoevsky's return to journalism allowed him to renew his generic experiments within a new framework, to combine the principles of novelistic and journalistic representation in a completely new genre, an encyclopedic work that sought to model the heterogeneous narratives of the postreform era within its very structure. The *Diary* is born out of the dialogue of the novel and journalism and shares many of the novel's formal devices: a tension between particular and universal perspectives, a dynamic hierarchy of narrative voices, and an ability to embody within narrative itself the hermeneutic confusion of social transition. Yet the coexistence of novelistic and journalistic representation in the work creates bewilderment in many of its readers, projects contradictory sets of hermeneutic assumptions, and results in textual lacunae and sometimes even narrative collapse. In my examination of the *Diary,* I show how the tensions between novelistic and journalistic representation play out on two particular levels within the work: in the shifting identity of the Diarist himself, and in the attitude toward dialogue. At times resembling a novelistic narrator, and at other times coinciding with the voice of Dostoevsky himself, the Diarist remains the key to the work's dissonant poetics. Focusing on the *Diary*'s October, November, and December 1876 issues, I demonstrate how the bewildering combination of broken narrative contracts, contradictory generic conventions, and differing narrative perspectives constitutes a profoundly appropriate literary response to the ferment of different social discourses that clamored for attention in the Russia of the mid-1870s.

The fifth and final chapter of the book, which represents the culmination of my argument, explores the work that comes closest to realizing Dostoevsky's dream of a regenerated novelistic form, *The Brothers Karamazov.* In its own way, this last of Dostoevsky's novels reflects the anxieties and preoccupations of its epoch as much as *The Adolescent* and *A Writer's Diary,* yet the terms of the novelistic experiment could not be more different. Whereas the earlier works engage with the question of how to represent the experience of social and historical transition in literary form, Dostoevsky's last novel is concerned with the problem of how to represent the sacred within a genre rooted in a secular narrative tradition, how to infuse a genre born out of the Russian nobility's Westernizing tendency with the cultural and religious memory of the Russian people. At the heart of *The Brothers Karamazov*'s generic project is the attempt to find a way to incorporate religious experience into the novel. Rather than searching within the canon of the contemporary European novel for his generic prototype, Dostoevsky borrows from earlier, more traditional genres, such as Christian legend, and particularly from hagiography, apocrypha, and folk legend. Importing the metaphysical, aesthetic, and ethical landscapes of legends into his novelistic universe allows him to extend the possibilities of novelistic representation. Conversely, novelistic narrative provides him with many possibilities for examining and comparing the aesthetic and ethical principles of different kinds of legend. I argue that Dostoevsky incorporates the worldviews of hagiography, apocrypha, and folk legend into the novel through the generic identities of the Karamazov brothers, as each brother expresses himself in interpolated narratives structured according to the assumptions of a different kind of legend. Alyosha is associated with hagiographic legend, Ivan with apocryphal legend, and Mitya with folk legend, the genre that most closely shares the novel's aesthetic and ethical temperament. Similarities and differences on the level of character are informed by and in turn inform the conflict between genres. This conflict leads to an examination of the generic assumptions of the novel itself and the revelation of the genre memory of medieval religious and vernacular works. I locate this interest in the novel's generic past within critical and theoretical debates on the nature of the novel that were taking place in Russian academic and literary circles at the time Dostoevsky was writing *The Brothers Karamazov*. The heterogeneous nature of the religious worldviews Dostoevsky models takes us beyond the conventional view of the novel as an expression of his Orthodox faith. It demonstrates an engagement with the complex ethical and narrative potentiality of Christian legend in all its forms and constitutes yet another kind of radical experiment in novelistic form.

One of the central claims of this book, and the main reason for its specific temporal focus, is that the formal conflict which structures Dostoevsky's late works, and the two views of modernity which lie behind it, emerge out of the specific discursive context of the Russia of the 1860s–1880s. I argue that, although the struggle between fragmentation and unity comes to the fore in the works of the 1870s, its roots lie in Dostoevsky's engagement with the problem of Russian modernization in the 1860s, during and immediately following the period of Alexander II's reforms, sometimes called the Great Reforms.

THE REFORMS OF ALEXANDER II AND THEIR LEGACY

The reforms carried out by the government of Tsar Alexander II between 1861 and 1874 were frequently compared by those who lived through them to the reforms of Peter the Great.[5] Though Alexander's reforms did not immediately carry the same volcanic significance as Peter's, which effectively catapulted Russia from the medieval into the modern world in the space of only a few years, they did fundamentally transform the Russian state and its relationship to its citizens. The reformers, motivated by Russia's humiliating defeat in the Crimean War to replace the rusty machinery of the centralized autocratic state with a more efficient bureaucracy, sought to transform Russia from an ancien regime based on arbitrary and unchecked autocratic power (*samoderzhavie*) with a system that united all the disparate classes of society under the universal rule of law (*zakonnost'*). They hoped to change a social order stratified by estate privileges into a citizen society. Whereas earlier efforts at reform had been largely piecemeal, the emancipation of the serfs and the institutional reforms that followed were characterized by an unprecedented thoroughness, a larger vision of unity and organization that extended into the very details of the reforms themselves. The reformers saw their task as the integration of all the inhabitants of the Russian Empire into one efficient bureaucratic apparatus. They were inspired by the idea of the organization and stratification of the inchoate phenomena of Russian social life.[6]

W. Bruce Lincoln has described the period from the mid-1870s to the death of Alexander II as the phase when the reforms moved from the sphere of administration to the field of politics and social action, the epoch of the testing of the reforms, when the Russians "sought to define the limits within which *glasnost'* [openness], *proizvol* [arbirtrariness] and *zakonnost'* [the rule of law] could function."[7] The development of *glasnost'* encouraged the growth among the intelligentsia and wider public of ambitions and projects that went far beyond what the autocratic regime was willing to condone. Fears of having gone too far caused the autocratic government to cut short the consultation process at the very moment when the emerging civil society or *obshchestvennost'* had already gained its own momentum, and the resulting loss of faith in the reform process radicalized those whose hopes had been disappointed. In the middle 1860s idealist youth had concentrated on advocating changes in the domestic and economic order, reordering sexual and emotional relations on the one hand, and promoting new kinds of economic organization on the other; but the 1866 assassination attempt on the tsar marked the beginning of a new phase of political unrest. The failure of the 1874 attempt to incite revolution among the peasantry and the resulting split within the populist movement tore the intelligentsia asunder.[8] The newly constituted People's Will chose the path of terror, and assassinations became more and more frequent during the final years of the decade. Meanwhile, once it had opened the Pandora's box of public opinion, the regime could not easily close it again, and attempts to use the reformed legal system to manipulate verdicts to deter the revolutionary Left backfired spectacularly, leading to high-profile acquittals such as that of Vera Zasulich, the young revolutionary who shot the governor of St. Petersburg in 1878 but was acquitted by a sympathetic jury.[9] Such acquittals in turn led to claims that the reformed institutions themselves contributed to the process of social breakdown.

At the same time, as Russian society learned more about itself, the sense of the reforms as introducing order and organization gave way in the public consciousness to new perceptions of disorganization and disorder. The observation surveys and statistical research that accompanied the reforms revealed an ever more complex variety and multiplicity of social experiences on the part of the empire's inhabitants.[10] The explosion in print journalism, precipitated by censorship reforms, economic growth, and migration to the cities offered expanding opportunities for discussion of the social and political diversification that modernization had triggered. A wide variety of newspapers and journals with diverse political perspectives provided a platform for discussing the strengths and weaknesses of the reform process itself.[11] While the growth of newspapers offered society the chance to look at itself in the mirror for perhaps the first time, the new open jury trials provided it with the opportunity to witness and to analyze its darker side, to consider crime and its causes from many perspectives.[12] All these factors meant that a much more diverse collection of narratives made their way into the public realm. New and contentious issues such as incest, child abuse, infanticide, suicide, and domestic violence entered into the public consciousness through the press and through the publicity generated by controversial court cases.[13] Traditional institutions such as the family and the church came under public scrutiny in the courtrooms and in the press.[14] Through their very act of integration, the reforms had opened up new vistas of disintegration, as uncharted territories of experience came into public view. As the extent of the diversity of different models of social life began to emerge, conservative newspapers and journals began to recast modernization as a process of social disintegration and societal breakdown.[15]

BETWEEN DISINTEGRATION AND REINTEGRATION

Dostoevsky shared conservative fears that Russia's modernization might bring social disintegration. The image of disintegration enters his notebooks in the 1860s and recurs throughout his writings for the rest of his life. It serves as the expression of his fears about the effects of modernization on Russian society, the family, the peasantry, and the nobility, and on religious beliefs and social values. Dostoevsky's fears of social disintegration are always countered by hopes of social reintegration. These dual concepts of disintegration and reintegration are later realized in formal terms as the impulses toward fragmentation and unity.

The image of disintegration is the corollary of a Christian interpretation of history and its lapsarian view of human society. In September 1864, in a notebook passage entitled "Socialism and Christianity," Dostoevsky envisages a model of history that posits humans' fall from a spontaneous communal state into a differentiated world of isolated, atomized individuals (20:191–94).[16] This explanation, clearly shaped both by the biblical account of the Fall and the quintessential modern Fall narrative, Rousseau's *Discourse on the Origin and Basis of Inequality Among Men,* argues that at the beginning of history humans lived collectively and spontaneously in primitive patriarchal communities. As the modern age dawned, this state of existence gave way to a transitional period that saw the development of human consciousness, the disappearance of spontaneous ideas and laws, and the loss of faith in God. This in turn led to the disintegration of communities, the state known as "civilization" but in fact characterized by the atomization that marks modern societies, particularly in the West.[17] For Dostoevsky, civilization is a transitional state. The process of atomization can be reversed by belief in the ideal embodied in Christ. This ideal represents the only possibility of return to wholeness, because Christ's self-sacrifice represents the overcoming of humanity's original fall from grace. The embrace of Eastern Orthodoxy will allow humans to return to their previous, spontaneous collective life, because Eastern Orthodoxy has maintained a sense of brotherhood, or *sobornost',* which is akin to the collective community of primitive societies.[18] This belief in the ideal of Christ and the attendant return of community is the only alternative to the social disintegration of modern life.

Dostoevsky and many of his contemporaries in the Slavophile camp saw this Fall narrative instantiated in modern Russian history. They looked back to an epoch of lost unity before the reforms of Peter the Great, when the Russian people had maintained a common identity and sense of community. They believed that the Petrine reforms, which had reshaped Russian institutions according to Western European models, caused a rupture in Russian history and society, a division between the educated classes, who had followed the Westernizing path of Peter and his reformers, and the Russian people, or *narod.* This division had defined Russian life for the 150 years following the Petrine reforms, as the two halves of Russian society developed in isolation from each other, each evolving its own cultural and philosophical models, growing gradually further apart. While the educated classes developed an ever greater dependency on Western European models, becoming estranged from Russian national life and values, the Russian people became involved with heretical cults and sects and developed misshapen and superstitious ideologies that bore little relation to church teachings. The post-Petrine rupture incarnated the very same differentiation and alienation that constituted the state of "civilization." In this lapsarian reading, the Petrine reforms became associated with other historical ruptures in Russia's past and present, such as the Nikonian reforms, which divided the population between those who went along with the reforms and those who rejected them. In the 1870s, conservatives inscribed Alexander II's reforms into the same lapsarian grand narrative.

For Dostoevsky, returning from Siberian exile in 1859 to a St. Petersburg rife with rumors of reform, the imminent emancipation seemed to finally offer the possibility of overcoming this transitional state of social and cultural division. The emancipated peasants would be reintegrated into Russian social and political life, and the educated classes would be reintegrated into Russian national life (18:35–40). Each would learn from the other, thereby enabling Russians to return to the pre-Petrine sense of community. However, far from providing signs of reintegration, Russian political and social life of the 1860s seemed only to offer evidence of the opposite process: the social and political unrest in both the cities and the countryside seemed to further splinter the divided estates. Universal and unshakeable moral values were becoming relativized in the disembodied rationalist ideologies of the radical intelligentsia, while traditional institutions such as the church, the family, and the gentry were disintegrating. Nowhere was the rapid progress of this process more evident than in the so-called Nechaev affair of 1869, the murder of a student in Moscow by a group of conspirators led by the nihilist revolutionary Sergei Nechaev.

By the early 1870s Dostoevsky had become increasingly concerned by this process of disintegration. In his 1872 "Writer's Diary" column for *The Citizen* he wrote, "We are living through the most troubled, the most awkward, the most transitory, and the most fateful moment, perhaps, in the whole history of the Russian people" (21:58). Two years later, in his notebooks for *The Adolescent,* he wrote, "The foundations of society are cracking under the pressure of the revolution brought by the reforms. The sea has become troubled. The borderlines of good and evil have disappeared and become obliterated" (16:7). This process of social disintegration receives the most systematic treatment in his 1876–77 monojournal version of *A Writer's Diary,* where it is called *obosoblenie,* which Kenneth Lantz translates as "dissociation."[19] *Obosoblenie* is one of the underlying themes of the *Diary,* a topic to which the Diarist returns again and again. In a March 1876 entry entitled "Obosoblenie," he refers to the present as the "the epoch of universal dissociation," which he explains as follows:

> All are dissociating themselves, isolating themselves from everyone else, everyone wants to invent something of his own, something new and unheard of. Everybody sets aside all those things that used to be common to our thoughts and feelings and begins with his own thoughts and feelings. Everyone wants to begin from the beginning. (22:80)

In Dostoevsky's eyes this rejection of traditional spiritual and cultural commonality and consensus in favor of the new and the original took shape in the grand social and political theories expounded by the intelligentsia, theories that led not only to the disintegration of ethical awareness, but also to a sense of absolute egotism, in which the individual was no longer aware of anything outside him- or herself:

> There is scarcely anything about which we can agree morally; everything has been or is being broken up, not even into clusters, but into single fragments. (22:80)

The image of fragmentation, such a universal expression of the experience of modernity, crops up with extraordinary frequency throughout Dostoevsky's works in the 1870s. We find it repeatedly in the notebooks for *The Adolescent;* it is a central preoccupation of the *Diary;* and it recurs throughout Dostoevsky's letters of the period.

Dostoevsky's fears about Russia's social, spiritual, and moral disintegration were nonetheless always tempered by the view that reintegration remained possible. As early as 1860, in the announcement to subscribers of *Time,* the journal he founded together with his brother Mikhail, he expressed the idea that the coming emancipation might bring a social and cultural reconciliation to Russia's divided population. Although the social unrest and violence of the first half of the 1860s quickly dampened his hopes for an imminent reconciliation, he subsequently began to develop a more abstract, utopian vision of national regeneration. During the 1860s, Dostoevsky's reading of Russian history became suffused with an Orthodox millenarian nationalism. The return to community that constituted the final stage in his model of the history of humanity in the diary entry "Socialism and Christianity" was reconfigured as a belief in the salvatory power of Orthodox Christianity. He continued to believe that the reforms represented the possibility of bringing to an end that which he called, at the end of *The Adolescent,* the "Petersburg period of Russian history," the Western-influenced era of the estrangement of the educated classes and the people initiated by the Petrine reforms; however, now he envisioned deliverance not as the reconciliation of two different sets of traditions, but as the triumph of the Christian ideal preserved in the religious worldview of the Russian people (13:455). This ideal, he believed, would bring about national salvation and spiritual renewal. It would eventually come to save even Western Europe from the processes of social disintegration and atomization. Dostoevsky came to see the disintegration of the contemporary moment as a necessary precondition for the spiritual redemption, social regeneration, and national reintegration that would result from the wholehearted embrace of the image of the Russian Christ. This salvatory vision can be seen as an attempt to bypass and deny modernity itself; it sees in premodern Russia a unique spiritual and cultural organic entity that can inspire a new path for the country in the postreform era.[20]

Dostoevsky expressed this vision of reintegration throughout his works, letters, notebooks, and diaries from the early 1860s up to his death in 1881. In his "Writer's Diary" column for *The Citizen,* he provided examples of the unquenchable Orthodox faith of the *narod,* like the peasant he calls Vlas, after Nikolay Nekrasov's poem of the same name, who is on the point of committing the terrible blasphemy of shooting the Eucharist when he falls unconscious, struck down by horror at his act (21:31–41). He argued that such examples were evidence of the coming national salvation and of the Russian people's role in the nation's sacred mission. This idea of the *narod's* moral potentiality and its salvatory significance plays a negligible role in *Demons,* but an increasingly central role in the works of the later 1870s. In *The Adolescent* the promise of social reintegration can be found in the person of the hero Arkady's legal father, the peasant Makar, whose symbolic identity preserves Arkady from the fate of his biological father, Versilov. In *The Brothers Karamazov* it plays the most significant role of all. Folk and vernacular genres that reflect the belief system of the Russian people punctuate the novel's own structure, offering a vision of reintegration that goes to the structural as well as the ideological heart of the work.

Dostoevsky insists that true reintegration can take place only by embracing the ideal of the Orthodox Christ. Yet he is also sensitive to the power and appeal of what he sees as false visions of reintegration, particularly the idea of collective community offered by socialism. In the diary passage on "Socialism and Christianity" quoted above, he warns, "Socialists go no further than the belly" (20:193): the socialist vision of wholeness speaks only to material needs as the whole future basis of the world. It offers community through coercion and materialism, not through voluntary self-renunciation. He is keenly aware of the enticing nature of the ideal of paradise on earth, and this ideal inspires the dreams of two of the most compelling characters in his novels of the 1870s: Stavrogin and Versilov. Nikolai Stavrogin recounts his "dream of the Golden Age" in the suppressed chapter of *Demons,* "At Tikhon's," and Andrei Versilov recounts a very similar vision to his son Arkady in *The Adolescent.* To these could be added the unfinished "poem" of Ivan Karamazov, "Grand Inquisitor." All three visions offer a promise of reintegration for a society that has deserted, or has been deserted by, God. In all three cases Dostoevsky represents these visions as false simulacra of the true sense of collective community offered by Orthodoxy. He negates the moral force of Stavrogin's dream by juxtaposing it to a sin of unimaginable seriousness, the rape of a child, thereby negating its moral force.[21] Versilov is briefly accorded the status of chief spokesman in Dostoevsky's words for the grandeur of the so-called Genevan idea of virtue without Christ, but he subsequently collapses within the novel, as though torn apart by his own internal contradictions. And Ivan Karamazov's vision of a collective community without God is juxtaposed to the message of brotherhood and *sobornost'* with which the novel ends.

DISINTEGRATION AND LITERARY FORM

The two contradictory explanatory paradigms of disintegration and reintegration influenced Dostoevsky's thinking about form from the late 1860s. *The Novel in the Age of Disintegration* considers the implications of these paradigms for both his novels and journalism. In recent years much attention has been paid by scholars to the relationship between Dostoevsky's fiction and his journalism.[22] My focus is on the different creative pressures the fragmentation and unity impulses brought to each sphere of Dostoevsky's writing. I do not seek here to establish formal or ideological primacy for either Dostoevsky's novels or his journalism; rather, I compare the formal implications of disintegration for each. At first sight, it might be seen to present less of a threat to the hermeneutic coherence of print journalism. Though journalists such as Dostoevsky bemoaned what they saw as a disintegrating society, their complaints can be viewed with more than a little irony, since they themselves contributed more than anyone else to the delineation and perception of that very social disintegration.[23] In the arena of journalism it was reintegration, rather than disintegration, which offered Dostoevsky the greatest formal challenges. In both incarnations of *A Writer's Diary* he created a cacophonous chorus of disembodied voices expressing contradictory views to represent the disintegrated society of postreform Russia. He used a bewildering variety of genres, narrative personas, themes, and references to draw a "guiding thread" through chaos, as he himself put it in the *Diary* (25:35). For the novelist, on the other hand, the task of representing the process of disintegration was a far more daunting prospect. Since the concept of disintegration goes right to the heart of the question of the novel's formal and thematic mission, we must turn to a brief examination of the Russian novel and its generic history.

The Russian novel developed in a social landscape very different from that of its French and German counterparts. Whereas the continental European novel had emerged out of the historical rupture of the French Revolution, its formal dynamism shaped by the sense of social fragmentation that came with the beginnings of the transition to capitalism, the Russian novel came of age in a period of relative historical stability, shaped exclusively by the social and cultural activity of one estate, the nobility. In the West the novel articulated the desires and fears of the newly emerging bourgeoisie; in Russia the genre drew its themes and preoccupations from the nobility. The different circumstances of their rise created very different formal trajectories for these two novelistic traditions. Having emerged in an era of rapid social transition, the continental European novel was forced from the very beginning to respond to the challenges of modernity. Its socially mobile heroes were poised on the boundary of old and new worlds, their ambitions shaped by the new possibilities brought into play by the French Revolution, but their achievements curbed by the remnants of the old world still in place. In the tension between social constraints and individual aspirations the genre formally embodied the longing for a world before social disintegration, differentiation, and dynamism, and the simultaneous awareness that such a world was lost forever. It was, in Georg Lukács's words, "the epic of an age in which the extensive totality of life is no longer directly given, in which the immanence of meaning in life has become a problem, yet which still thinks in terms of totality."[24] By contrast, the Russian novel was shaped by the centuries-long alienation of a social estate that knew little of the cultural traditions and religious practices of its compatriots because its social values and political beliefs were largely inherited from the West. It articulated the political and social aspirations of the alienated nobility and intelligentsia and represented the displacement of these aspirations onto the closed world of the domestic sphere. Rooted in the patriarchal society of the country estate or in city salons frequented by the cosmopolitan gentry and the deracinated intelligentsia, the Russian novel in its mid-nineteenth-century incarnation knew nothing of the social mobility that came with mass migrations from the countryside to the city. Yet early in the period of its generic ascendency, it was called upon to respond to a period of intense social change unparalleled in modern Russian history.

Dostoevsky was keenly aware of the Russian novel's history. At the end of the 1860s, when he had already written *Crime and Punishment* and *The Idiot* and was becoming known for the dark and misshapen protagonists who would inspire the nickname given to him by critics, "the poet of the underground," he began to criticize his fellow novelists Tolstoy and Turgenev for creating Westernized aristocratic heroes who were alienated from their Russian identity. He came to associate the Russian novelistic tradition with the worldview of the Westernized Russian nobility who had dominated the period of Russian cultural and social life up to the 1860s, but whose outlook and style of life had now become increasingly outmoded and irrelevant for postreform society. Neither his vision of social disintegration and spiritual collapse nor his hopes for a society redeemed and unified by the religious faith of the people offered any room for the alienated Russian aristocrats of the traditional Russian novel. His own novels represent a society in transition, focusing on moments of struggle, flux, development, and change. They recognize the shortfall between the ideal and the reality and chronicle the hero's failure to achieve his dream, even while insisting on the continuing potential of that dream to fire up the hero's imagination and ambition. The fragmentation impulse is always insistently present.

Of all Dostoevsky's works of the period, *The Adolescent* deals most directly with the experience of social transition in the postreform era and its effects on novelistic representation. A novel that started out with the title "Disorder," *The Adolescent* deals with the problem of fragmentation and form head-on. Like the rest of Dostoevsky's literary projects, *The Adolescent* went through many changes during the process of writing, and the notebooks for the novel reveal many narrative and thematic blind alleys, novelistic seeds that were never brought to fruition. Of all the ideas and images that found expression in the notebooks, perhaps the most tenacious is the image of disintegration, or *razlozhenie.* It enters the notebooks during the first few days of planning and provides both a formal and a thematic impetus for the novel throughout the period of writing. In the first few pages of the notebooks, we find the following lines:

> *Most important.* The idea of disintegration [*razlozhenie*] is present everywhere, for everything is falling apart, and there are no remaining ties not just in the Russian family, but even simply between people in general,
>
> "The tower of Babel," he says. "Here we are, for example, a Russian family. We speak different languages and cannot understand one another. Society is decomposing [*razlagaetsia*] chemically." (16:16; italics in the original)[25]

A few lines later, Dostoevsky adds the following line, "Disintegration is the principal visible idea of the novel." (16:17) Alongside the image of disintegration is the idea of disorder, which also recurs throughout the notebooks as one of the novel's primary themes:

> Title of the novel: "Disorder [*Besporiadok*]."
>
> The whole idea of the novel is to demonstrate that we now have general disorder [*besporiadok*], disorder everywhere and wherever you go, in society, in business, in guiding ideas (of which, [for that very reason,] there aren't any, in <our> convictions (which [for the same reason,] we don't have), in the dis-

> integration of the family unit [*razlozhenie semeinogo nachala*]. If there are any passionate convictions, they are all destructive (socialism). There aren't any moral ideas; suddenly not a single one is left, and above all," he says, "one has the impression that there never were any." (16:80–81)

Disintegration and disorder might seem at first sight interchangeable concepts with identical implications for the novel. However, the etymological differences between the words *razlozhenie* and *besporiadok* reveal semantic differences that are crucial for an understanding of the novel's structural dynamics. *Razlozhenie* denotes the chemical process of decomposition or dissolution, the breaking down of a whole, or, as Dal' puts it, the division of a body into its component parts.[26] The prefix *raz-* indicates the diffusion of these component parts. The semantic emphasis is on the process of breakdown. Thus, while a previous sense of wholeness is implied—something must be being broken down—the emphasis is on the diffusion. There is also an implication of inevitability, of necessity, of the occurrence of a chemical process. *Besporiadok* expresses the absence of an order that was there to begin with and is still locked within the signifier itself. If it does not always signify violent upheaval, *besporiadok* at the very least implies a transgression of the normal structures of existence. If *razlozhenie* implies a process, *besporiadok* suggests a state. In the extended meaning of social dislocation, these semantic differences become significant, since we ask whether or not a previous social harmony existed at all. In the matter of novelistic form the differences become crucial. Whereas disintegration can be formally represented, disorder proves more challenging, since representation requires some sort of order.

The conflict between *razlozhenie* and *besporiadok* animates *The Adolescent* on both formal and thematic levels. In this novel Dostoevsky sought to narrate the processes of social fragmentation that threatened to destabilize institutions such as the family and the nobility, which had been the bedrock of social and political order for centuries. Moreover, he made it his aim to structure disintegration into the novel itself, to represent the process of breakdown on the level of language and literary form. Yet as he tried to model *razlozhenie,* he continually ran the risk of merely creating *besporiadok.* There was no more than a hair's breadth between the novelistic model of disintegration and the disintegration of the novelistic model. Yet this hair's breadth was of absolute importance for the novel's status as an intelligible artistic text. If the form of the novel fell into disorder, then the idea of disintegration could not be conveyed. Dostoevsky's task was an extraordinarily complex one. Since artistic texts are based on a model of integration rather than disintegration, creating meaning through juxtaposition, comparison, and repetition, he had to find a way of maintaining the novel's textual integrity even while using it to represent the effects of disintegration on the novel itself. Given the fact that modernity characterizes itself by its transitional nature, chaotic diversity, and refusal to be categorized, how can it be translated into literary form? This paradox of representation lies at the root of *The Adolescent* as a novelistic project and animates the work's narration.

The tension between disorder and disintegration that plays out in *The Adolescent* is foreshadowed in *Demons.* In contrast to *The Adolescent,* the process of disintegration in *Demons* takes place during the novel's prehistory, when Stavrogin undergoes his circuitous ideological journey from liberalism to nihilism to Orthodoxy to the liberation of man from God and back again, attracting the acolytes who will come to embody his abandoned ideological obsessions. This fits in with Dostoevsky's ideological and historiographic intentions, which see the source of disintegration as the Westernizing path taken by post-Petrine educated Russian society. The main plot of the novel is characterized by disorder: events take place mysteriously as the normal rules of causality break down; the narrator is both ignorant of many events taking place and willfully blind toward their consequences. Unlike in *The Adolescent,* where an ideal of harmonious order can be found in the character of Makar Dolgoruky, in *Demons* there are no characters who symbolize hope for a reintegrated society. That hope is instead conveyed on a structural level, through an invitation to an allegorical reading which suggests that Stavrogin's collapse and disintegration could renew and regenerate the sterile generic material of the novel of alienation.

THE DREAM OF REINTEGRATION

While *The Adolescent* and many other works of the 1870s reflect Dostoevsky's sensitivity toward the demands made on novelistic form by the fragmented nature of contemporary reality, several of his works reflect the opposing formal impulse: the desire to redeem the fallen novelistic form and remake it into a vehicle for representing Dostoevsky's utopian vision of messianic nationalism and of the Russian people's salvatory faith. This tendency first makes itself felt in his unfinished projects of 1868–71, *Atheism* and *The Life of a Great Sinner,* in which Dostoevsky takes an archetypal Russian man "of middling social status" and launches him on a moral and spiritual journey set against a historical background of one thousand years of Russian Christianity populated by figures as diverse as the eighteenth-century elder Saint Tikhon Zadonsky, Petr Chaadaev, and Vissarion Belinsky. By this means, he seeks to infuse the structure of the bildungsroman with the genre conventions of hagiography and epic and to regenerate the novelistic form with genres taken from the *narod.* These aspirations also provide the impulse behind the powerful allegorical tendency within *Demons,* which portrays the novel's events against the backdrop of a tableau of seventeenth-century Russian history.

In *The Brothers Karamazov,* Dostoevsky's dream of regenerating the novel comes closest to fulfillment. He brings religious experience into the novel not merely through pious characters, as in *The Adolescent,* but also by embedding medieval and modern popular religious genres such as hagiography, apocrypha, and folk legends into the structure of the novel itself. Here genre becomes the arena within which Dostoevsky can express his utopian messianic vision. As alienated, rootless characters such as Dmitry Karamazov and Grushenka become aware of the possibilities of their own moral spirituality as expressed within the formal contours of genres such as the folk legend, they are able to liberate themselves from their own tragic trajectories and voluntarily embrace an open future. It is here that the third stage of human evolution outlined in "Socialism and Christianity," the successful reintegration of the human into a sense of oneness with God, is finally and fully represented in Dmitry Karamazov's voluntary renunciation of the ego. At the same time the full generic potentialities of the novel itself become realized as it becomes the vehicle for representing the human moral freedom and potentiality in an open-ended world rather than for expressing the alienation and apotheosis of the ego that are the side effects of modernity's atomizing processes.

While many of Dostoevsky's statements about his novels declare his intention to dispense with past traditions and with the traditional Russian novel, close readings of *Demons, The Adolescent,* and *The Brothers Karamazov* reveal the persistence of past models and the force of their influence on all of Dostoevsky's works. In my analysis of the generic structures of each of Dostoevsky's novels, I will use and slightly adapt the concept of genre memory, first put forward by Mikhail Bakhtin in his 1963 *Problems of Dostoevsky's Poetics.*[27] Bakhtin argues that although genres change over time, like any system of laws and structures, they carry within themselves memories of their own past incarnations and birth. Accordingly, modern incarnations of genres can carry allusions to past incarnations, irrespective of the author's familiarity with that tradition. Echoes of genre memory may reverberate through texts, perhaps even independently or in contravention of the author's intentions. Bakhtin's primary example of genre memory is the influence on Dostoevsky's works of the memory of Hellenistic dialogic genres such as Menippean satire, works of which Dostoevsky can have known nothing. Although I find Bakhtin's original definition useful, I also extend it to describe relationships between Dostoevsky's works and groups of texts and genres with which he himself was familiar, but which in the context of his novels take on a status above and beyond those of individual texts. For instance, when Dostoevsky invokes the noble family novels of Tolstoy, Turgenev, and Goncharov as works against which he is writing in *The Adolescent,* he conceives of those novels not just as texts, but as works that share and project a particular worldview against which he reacts. Intertextual relations may be, and often are, part of this relationship; he does quote and parody particular works, but what is important is not so much the works themselves as what he sees as their shared generic assumptions. Those assumptions enter Dostoevsky's works as images of genres, analogous to the images of languages about which Bakhtin writes in "Discourse in the Novel."[28] But often Dostoevsky shows those generic worldviews as broken or fragmented. They have disintegrated in the face of the modern world's complexity and diversity. In the projects of the late 1860s, such as *The Life of a Great Sinner,* Dostoevsky borrows conventions from genres such as hagiography and epic as an alternative to the traditional Russian novel's Europeanized models. In both *The Adolescent* and in *The Brothers Karamazov,* Dostoevsky invokes a variety of genres in order to then deconstruct their assumptions and worldviews, breaking them down in order to reuse their fragments in new constructions of his own making.

Genre memory serves a central function in Dostoevsky's novels of the 1870s. Genre becomes the contested space of engagement with past traditions. Where Dostoevsky himself rejects the gentry family novels of Tolstoy and Turgenev in his letters, within his novels their memory carries an unmistakable hint of nostalgia that belies his intent. In *The Adolescent,* with its first-person adolescent hero undergoing an education in narrative by learning about the literary models that have helped to form the social identity of his biological father, Versilov, genre memory plays a crucial role in allowing that protagonist to forge his own literary way in the world. The noble family novel here is overcome, but remains persistently present in the genre fragments that attach themselves to the figure of Versilov. In *The Brothers Karamazov* an appeal to the memory of vernacular genres such as apocryphal and folk legends opens up new potentialities within the novelistic form itself and reveals the novel's own pre-Petrine history within the heterogeneous genres of legend that proliferated in the Middle Ages. Genre memory serves as an important accessory to the dream of reintegrating the fragments of Russian literature and art shattered and dispersed by the pressures of modernization.

PART I

Context

Chapter One

From *Time* to *Demons:* Genre, History, and Modernization, 1861–1871

IN THE MIDDLE OF DECEMBER 1859, Dostoevsky returned to St. Petersburg from his ten-year exile in Siberia. A new tsar, Alexander II, had been on the throne since 1855, and limited consultation regarding changes to the system of serfdom and censorship reform had already begun. A spirit of great optimism reigned among the intelligentsia and found voice in the plethora of new journals that opened following a relaxation of censorship policy after 1857. Even Nikolai Chernyshevsky, later to be imprisoned by Alexander in the Peter and Paul Fortress, shared in the hopeful mood, writing in 1858, "With the reign of Alexander II, there begins a new era for Russia, just as one had begun with Peter."[1] Almost immediately following his return to Petersburg, Dostoevsky began to make plans with his brother Mikhail to join the burgeoning journalistic scene by setting up a journal, to be called *Time*. The Dostoevskys' collaborators on the journal were the literary critic Apollon Grigoriev and the philosopher Nikolai Strakhov.[2] In September of the following year an announcement was circulated inviting subscriptions to the new journal. This announcement lays out *Time*'s general aims and provides a foretaste of the journal's program. Seeking to justify *Time's* presence in the already crowded marketplace of new journals, its editors underline the extreme importance of the present moment in the social life of the nation (18:35–40). Russia is on the threshold of a new historical epoch, which will be brought into being by the imminent resolution of "the great peasant problem, the solution of which has begun in our time," that is, the emancipation of the serfs (18:35).[3] Though the Emancipation Proclamation would not be signed into law by Tsar Alexander II until a few months later—on February 19, 1861, by the Julian calendar—the *Time* announcement is filled with heady excitement about the coming emancipation movement.[4] The announcement refers to a "prodigious change which is about to take place peacefully and with the consent of our entire nation," a change "equivalent to the most outstanding events in our history and even to the great reforms of Peter the Great" (18:35). The journal envisioned this change as the reintegration of a nation whose educated classes and *narod* had split apart 170 years before, following the Petrine reforms. While the nobility and the educated classes had gone along with Peter's efforts to impose Western European cultural and political models onto Russian life, embracing modernization and in the process becoming estranged from Russian national life or "soil," the *narod* had recoiled from the effects of modernization and maintained their old beliefs and traditions, their connections to the Russian soil (18:36). Ever since, the two groups had lived separate and independent lives. Now, at last, they would come together again as a result of the coming emancipation, which would at last allow the *narod* to fully enter Russian life and contribute to Russian society, bringing new ideas and values to an intellectual discourse that had been too dependent on Western European models and structures for too long (18:36). This process of reconciliation would give rise to a new Russian national consciousness as the two groups shared the ideas and beliefs they had developed during the years of their separate evolution and growth. The ensuing knowledge and insight would allow Russia to rediscover her inner national strength and creativity, to create new indigenous forms and ideas, and ultimately to offer Europe a great new "Russian Idea," an idea that would reconcile the disparate European nations, just as it had reconciled Russia's own divided society (18:37).

It is difficult to imagine a more enthusiastic response to the modernization about to take place under Russia's new reforming tsar than this rousing announcement and its glorious vision of the nation's future. According to Strakhov, the piece, written in the spirit of profound hopefulness about the future that marked the public discourse of the early 1860s, was written by Dostoevsky himself.[5] It introduces the principles that will guide *Time* and its readership through the exciting and turbulent times ahead. Its central rallying cry, mission statement, and program is the idea of reconciliation. Whereas Dostoevsky recognizes that the Petrine reforms had brought the kinds of effects we usually associate with modernization (i.e., a sense of separation, social breakdown, and atomization), he asserts that this time the effects of reform will be different. The modernization set into motion by Alexander II's regime will bring about unification, reintegration, and the reestablishment of common beliefs, ideas, hopes, and dreams among two groups separated by the Petrine reforms. These reforms will create in the nation's reintegrated body the desire to rediscover old national forms of life and create new national social and cultural models. *Time* will help foster the process of reconciliation, reveal the values and beliefs common to the two previously estranged groups, and advocate for institutions and processes that will hasten reconciliation, such as the spread of literacy. The journal will also deal extensively with Russian literature, one of the most important tools of reconciliation (18:38–39). Dostoevsky and his colleagues argued that even during the darkest days of mutual separation Russian literature served as a mediating force between the estranged halves of Russian society, taking ideas and models from the Westernized nobility but also drawing upon the values and beliefs of the Russian soil maintained by the *narod.*

Barely ten years later, in the notebooks for *Demons* and then in the novel itself, Dostoevsky depicted the modernization of the 1860s in far darker terms. Centering on a fictionalized depiction of the infamous Nechaev affair, the novel shows the social and moral chaos and disintegration into which a small town is plunged after the arrival of Nechaev's fictional counterpart, Petr Verkhovensky.[6] Dostoevsky makes clear, both in his extensive notebooks for the novel and in the novel itself, that Verkhovensky's reign of destruction and violence is a direct result of Petrine modernization, of educated society's estrangement from the values of the Russian soil. His name ties him to the tsar; Dostoevsky had characterized the nihilists in an article for *Time* as "tiny little [*kroshechnye*] Peter the Greats" (20:58).[7] Petr Verkhovensky himself declares, "We are a consequence of Peter the Great" (11:272).[8] In the notebooks a prototype of the same character explains that the vagueness and weakness of the reforms and the irresolute approach taken by the government has "produced in our society that unsteadiness [*shatost'*], that vagueness, that confusion, that debility of conviction and of faith . . . By rejecting the old they have confounded the reactionaries; while by failing to give the necessary reassurance, they have discouraged the progressives" (11:148). He later continues, "Unsteadiness, confusion, the fall of the idol, the decline of our faith and of our morality which, though they may have been fantastic, yet had been standing firm and were supported by our entire social structure. This unsteadiness will penetrate into the lower classes and will leave the whole ocean of our common people agitated" (11:148). These, he argues, are the perfect conditions for him and his fellow conspirators, since the frightened lower classes will join his conspiracy: "All we need to do is destroy; anything will come in handy for destruction, any material" (149). Although Nechaev was anything but a spokesman for Dostoevsky, this description of the destruction of beliefs and values and social instability caused by modernization and the effects of the reforms is very similar to some of Dostoevsky's own views expressed soon afterward in articles published in *The Citizen* and in the notebooks for *The Adolescent.* By 1869, when the Nechaev circle carried out their murder, Dostoevsky already saw Russia as trapped in a downward spiral of social and political disintegration and decline. The Nechaev affair seemed to illustrate this decline.

By the time of the serialization of *Demons* in 1871, Dostoevsky also seemed to have lost faith in the ability of Russian literature to respond to and represent the contemporary sense of crisis. In a May 1871 letter to his friend and former colleague Strakhov, he wrote that the works of his contemporaries Turgenev and Tolstoy were "all gentry literature [which] has said everything that it had to say" and bemoaned the fact that there was as yet no "new word to replace that of the gentry" (29:I:216).[9] He saw the Russian novelistic tradition as having emerged out of the intellectual current of Russian Westernism. He viewed it as predicated on an adoption of Western European models and values and a rejection of the beliefs and practices of the *narod.* Now that Russian Westernism had taken on the distorted features of Nechaev and his ilk, the time had come to rethink the Russian novel and its relationship to the nation.

How and why, in the space of just over ten years—from his return from Siberian exile on the eve of the serfs' emancipation to the publication of *Demons*—were Dostoevsky's views on Russian modernity transformed from the optimistic embrace of social and political change that we find in *Time* to the dark and pessimistic vision that permeates *Demons*? How and why did he go from envisioning Russian literature as a cultural and aesthetic force that would help heal the Petrine schism between the Russian educated classes and the *narod* to seeing the Russian novel as a form born out of that schism, a form that belonged to the epoch that had ended with the 1861 Emancipation Act?

Without a doubt, the 1860s was a decade of profound political and social upheaval in Russia, and like many of his contemporaries, Dostoevsky responded to that instability by retreating into a conservative critique of modernization. Yet he continued to maintain faith in the idea, first articulated in the 1860 announcement of *Time,* of Russia's ultimate ability to withstand the storms of modernity and bring to bear on Europe the principle of universal reconciliation that was the legacy of her own divided history. What became stronger and more explicit in his vision was the role of Orthodoxy in shaping the Russian national mission. At the same time his reading of Russian history took on an apocalyptic tinge and he began to view the Petrine reforms as akin to the biblical Fall. This change of heart can be seen as Dostoevsky's response to a particular set of Russian and European political events. Shaped first by the particular conditions of the journalistic world of the mid-1860s and its fierce ideological and literary polemics, and then by a series of ideological dialogues and engagements with such figures as Strakhov and Danilevsky that took place against the backdrop of the Dostoevsky family's extended stay in Europe from 1867 to 1871, Dostoevsky's views of the role of Westernism in Russian cultural, political, and social life hardened considerably.

This changing perspective on Westernism affected Dostoevsky's attitude toward the Russian novel, a form synonymous with that movement's influence. He began to view it as a fallen genre, a form in need of redemption. The messianic nationalistic historiographic vision that had begun to infuse his worldview brought with it an urgent formal imperative, the impulse to remake the novel. In this chapter and those that follow, I will argue that this desire to redeem or remake the novel coexisted in Dostoevsky's creative vision with a grudging awareness of the genre's inability to escape its own past. First in *Demons,* and then in *The Adolescent,* his attempts to resist or escape the fallen history of the novel as a genre prove futile; both novels dramatize his problematic relationship with Russian Westernism. I argue here that *Demons* marks the transition to the final stage of Dostoevsky's literary career, a phase marked by two fundamentally contradictory views of Russian modernity with very different formal demands and impulses. The work comes into being on the boundary between two very different creative projects; it is both an allegorical representation of the decline of Russian Westernism and a work replete with nostalgia for that legacy. The extensive notebooks for the novel testify to a long and complicated period of creative gestation during which Dostoevsky's shifting ideas about Russian and European history took the form of a struggle between epic and novelistic tendencies within the project. This testifies to the endurance in his fiction of the ideal of reconciliation that seemed to have long disappeared from his letters and diaries. As a developing project as well as a finished work, *Demons* brings to light those very problems of form, genre, history, and modernity which Dostoevsky would spend the rest of the 1870s trying to solve.

TIME AND *EPOCH:* RECONCILIATION IN HISTORY, SOCIETY, LITERATURE, AND JOURNALISM

Time, which became the de facto organ of the "native soil" movement (*pochvennichestvo*) was nominally founded by Dostoevsky's brother Mikhail, because of Fyodor's status as a former political prisoner, but the dominant voices in the journal belonged to Grigoriev, Strakhov, and Dostoevsky himself.[10] Established in January 1861, on the eve of the emancipation, *Time* joined a rapidly increasing chorus of new publications adding their voices to the social ferment that accompanied the beginning of Alexander II's reign.[11] It tried to steer a middle way between radical publications such as *The Contemporary* and *The Russian Word,* for which the reforms were just the beginning of what they hoped would be the total transformation and modernization of Russian society and institutions; Slavophile publications such as *Day,* which believed that the reforms would do nothing to repair the post-Petrine chasm between the educated classes and the *narod;* and conservative publications such as *The Russian Messenger,* which turned against the reforms at the first indication of social or political unrest. In the 1860 announcement to subscribers, Dostoevsky claimed that the divisions between the Slavophiles and the Westernizers were no longer relevant, yet he borrowed ideas from both groups for *Time*'s opening salvo (18:35–40). In articles such as "Two Camps of Theoreticians" from 1862 he attacked both *Day* and *The Contemporary* for their views on the Petrine reforms, the *narod,* and Russian literature, playing them off against one another as two extremes and advocating a middle way on these three issues (20:5–22). It was not long before *Time* found itself attacked by radicals, conservatives, and Slavophiles alike, its program denounced as vague, naive, or unpatriotic.[12]

In its reading of Russian history *Time* attempted to reconcile the positions of the Slavophiles and the Westernizers. It shared the Slavophile view that the Petrine reforms had led the educated classes to abandon national ideals and modes of living and to adopt Western trends and beliefs, thereby precipitating the divisions within Russian society. At the same time it viewed the reforms as necessary, since the intellectual and cultural horizons of the Russian state had been far too narrow, suffocating any possibility of contributing to European civilization (18:36–37).[13] The reforms had allowed the Russian educated and noble classes to grow and develop, nurtured by the rich cultural influences from Western Europe. Through the reforms, Russians had come "to understand our future importance in the great family of nations" (18:37). Yet the very rapidity and success with which Russians assimilated European ideas had deepened the social, cultural, and spiritual divisions between those who accepted Peter's Europeanizing path and those who did not. As Dostoevsky argued in "Two Camps of Theoreticians," though Peter had responded to Russian society's need for cultural expansion, he had gone too far (20:5–22). The Petrine transformation had been too precipitous. Following the reforms the educated classes had become too infatuated with Western cultural models and strayed too far from Russian traditions and values, while at the same time the *narod* had rejected the new European influences. The gap between the groups opened up by Peter had broadened in the subsequent century into a gulf. Retrenchments on each side following the brief moment of unity in the 1812 campaign against Napoleon had led to ever-widening divisions that were exacerbated by the intellectual conflicts between Slavophiles and Westernizers, two groups equally ignorant of the values and beliefs of the Russian people.

For *Time* the Emancipation Act of February 1861 marked the final collapse of the phase of Russian history that had begun with the reforms of Peter the Great, a phase marked by the estrangement of the increasingly Westernizing nobility and later the Europeanized intelligentsia from the vast body of the Russian people, the *narod.* In March 1861 *Time* published the Emancipation Act in its entirety.[14] The journal's founders believed that the emancipation would at last provide the possibility for the social, political, and cultural reconciliation of the estranged groups. The *narod* would benefit from the cultural leadership of the nobility and intelligentsia, while the latter would be redeemed by the spiritual and religious faith and beliefs of the people. As the *narod* came to play a more full and active role in the nation's social life, Russian culture would be renewed by its faith, beliefs, and ideas. *Time* referred to the set of essential beliefs and ideas that formed the basis of the *narod*'s life as the *pochva* or soil, from which they took the name for their movement, *pochvennichestvo*. Strakhov wrote, "Under the term soil are meant those basic and distinctive powers of a people which are the seeds of all its organic manifestations."[15] This could include songs and stories or customs and traditions. *Time* saw the supposed "spirit of reconciliation," the defining spirit of the emancipation period, as providing a way out of the bitter Slavophile-Westernizer conflicts that had further divided Russian society for the previous three decades.

The *pochvenniki* argued that the contemporary moment, with its potential reunification of the Russian nation, was also a crucial period for Western Europe. While Western European nations were rife with class divisions that had riven their societies apart, causing social and political instability, Russia had never developed economic divisions of this kind; the only divide in Russia was between the educated classes and the *narod* (18:41–53). Russia was thus in a position to help bring Europe out of this age of conflict. In fact, the very diversity of social and historical experience the two sectors of Russian society had lived through since the Petrine reforms gave Russia a unique ability to completely understand Europe while remaining outside it. On the one hand the educated classes had come to understand European social and cultural models, to speak to Europeans in their own languages, while on the other the *narod* had maintained traditional values of community, religion, and morality, their links with the Russian soil. This duality of experience gave rise to the special role *Time* believed Russia was destined to play in the world, the role of synthesizing, mediating, and reconciling all of the separate ideas that had arisen in diverse parts of Europe (18:37). The union of the two estranged halves of the Russian population was thus all the more urgent, since the future not just of Russia, but of all Europe depended on it.

The founders of *Time* saw Russian literature as one of the most important tools for the social and cultural reconciliation of the intelligentsia and the *narod*. As one of the only spheres of culture that had maintained an independent and autonomous life during the decades of estrangement, it now carried the potential for leading the way in bringing them back together. Bringing literature to the people through the spreading of literacy would help to extend the intellectual and cultural gains and insights of the previous decades, while Russian literature's return to the soil would help liberate it from an overreliance on the foreign models that had helped to sustain it during the years when it was cut off from the *narod.* In 1861 Dostoevsky wrote a series of five articles on Russian literature in which he weighed in on a whole series of topics related to literature and literacy, from the question of what texts to use in teaching peasants how to read to contemporary debates about art's utility (18:41–103; 19:5–66).[16] By this time Chernyshevsky had already been in charge of the literature section of *The Contemporary* for a year, and debates over literature and aesthetics had been fiercely dividing the world of the thick journals since at least 1856.[17] Dostoevsky jumped into the fray with his "Mr. –bov and the Question of Art," a polemic against Dobroliubov that drew furious rejoinders from the radicals (18:70–103).[18]

As Wayne Dowler has persuasively shown, *Time*'s aesthetic philosophy was derived in large measure from ideas formulated by Apollon Grigoriev in the late 1850s.[19] Grigoriev posited an organic connection between a nation's art and the life of that particular nation, arguing that national literatures expressed their nations' underlying forms of national life.[20] The history of the Russian literary tradition was irrevocably bound up with the recent history of Russia itself, and above all with the cultural turmoil of the Petrine reforms. Produced by writers who belonged mainly to the educated classes, which had gone along with the Petrine reforms, Russian literature had flourished in the age of Western European influence, becoming enriched by the new models and influences imported from the West. Yet at the same time Russian writers had soaked up a national consciousness from the *narod;* they had served as the unconscious instruments through which national ideas, threatened by the modernization of the post-Petrine period, could be expressed. In contrast to the Slavophiles, who believed that Russian literature had fallen under the Western influence of the Europeanized educated class, Grigoriev and his colleagues were enthusiastic about the Russian literature of their own day, arguing that literature had remained a unifying force in Russian society even after the Petrine reforms. Like Russia itself, Russian literature had learned to reconcile European and homegrown forms and ideas.

For Grigoriev and Dostoevsky no writer embodied Russian literature's potential for reconciliation more than Alexander Pushkin. In an article published in 1859, Grigoriev had asserted that only Pushkin had been able to mediate between the foreign literary models brought into Russian culture in the eighteenth century and the national forms of the folk tradition: he was "the complete sketch of our national personality, a man of natural gifts who assimilated . . . everything that should have been assimilated and who discarded everything which should be discarded"; he was "the full and complete form of our national essence."[21] Only Pushkin had been able to synthesize foreign trends and translate them into Russian artistic types.

Grigoriev saw Russian literature as the main expression of the country's recent historical experience. The main tools literature used to convey the basic features of a particular historical, social, and cultural moment were character types, sets of dynamic features symbolized within characters in literary works. In the 1840s and 1850s Grigoriev had formulated a theory of types in Russian history and culture. He saw Russian culture as constantly playing out a dynamic that could be traced back to the very foundation of Rus' itself, when the meek (*smirennyi*) Slavic tribes had invited the predatory (*khishchnyi*) Varyngian nobles to rule over them.[22] The opposition between meek domestic types and predatory foreign ones had been replayed throughout Russian history, especially during the reign of Peter the Great. The Petrine reforms had served as the Russian nation's lapsarian moment, bringing into being the consciousness of national specificity engendered by differentiation and conflict with other, foreign ideas, values, and modes of life. In the years following the reforms, Russian literature had responded to the encroachment of foreign models in contradictory ways. The satirical mode, practiced by writers such as Denis Fonvizin, provided the possibility of criticizing imported types and models while serving as the basis for a new national tradition. Nikolai Karamzin had taken Russian literature in a different direction, privileging foreign forms and rewriting Russian history according to a common European narrative.[23] The conflict had been given true artistic form only by Pushkin. His works embodied this basic historical-cultural conflict through the interplay of meek and predatory types, two opposing types that represented the two poles of Russian national identity, the two halves of Russian society divided by the Petrine reforms.[24] The meek, humble type was embodied by Pushkin's Belkin, the narrator of *Tales of Belkin,* who represented and recognized the values of the Russian people. In the language of *Time,* Belkin maintained his connection with the soil. The opposing figure was the predatory type, born out of Western cultural and intellectual influences and distilled by the experiences of the Russian educated classes. The predatory type, alienated from life and love, cut off from the soil, blinded by ego, and trapped in the realm of reason, could be most clearly identified in the figures of Pushkin's Eugene Onegin and Aleko from *The Gypsies.* Other Russian writers, most notably Turgenev, followed in Pushkin's path and conveyed the persistent divisions between the educated people and the *narod.*[25] Through these two types, Russian literature was able to unify in itself the polarities of the Russian national character, foreshadowing or prefiguring the reconciliation of the intelligentsia with the *narod.*

Dostoevsky took Grigoriev's ideas further, arguing in the introduction to his 1861 series on Russian literature that Pushkin represented the essence of Russian nationality, the ability to comprehend and to reconcile foreign cultures (18:66–70). This argument would later underlie his 1880 Pushkin speech, but it was already a major preoccupation of *Time.*[26] Pushkin became the potent symbol of Russia's contribution to the world. Just as Pushkin had been able to take on the voices of French aristocrats and German engineers, Russian counts and Russian peasants, so Russia would be soon in a position to understand the differing positions of her European neighbors, to reconcile them to one another and to help create a new world order. Then all the historical ruptures of the previous centuries would be healed and all the European countries brought together under a universal set of models and values borrowed from Russia. It was Pushkin, according to Dostoevsky, "who made us understand that the Russian ideal is complete integrity, complete universality and complete reconciliation" (18:69).

Yet *Time* struggled to reconcile the paradoxes of its own perspective on Russian literature, and Dostoevsky in particular was forced to defend a national literary historical narrative that he had not yet fully thought through. The Slavophiles and their sympathizers argued logically that since Pushkin was the quintessential product of the Westernized intelligentsia and his works were the generic epitome of cultural and literary borrowings from the West, he could not be a truly national poet. He was the representative of only the Westernized part of the populace. His greatest creation, Onegin, was not a national type, but a portrait of the alienated gentry. *Time*'s rejoinder, voiced by Dostoevsky, was that the educated class represented the principle of Russian nationality as much as the *narod* (19:5–20). Onegin embodied a particularly dark moment in Russian history, when the Russian gentry, alienated from its own people, had begun to recognize that its own ideas and values, borrowed from Europe, were nonetheless different from those of Europe. His inner struggle reflected this historical conflict (19:10–12). Dostoevsky argued in the same article that the Russian people had not developed sufficiently in cultural and intellectual terms to provide a national poet from within their ranks. Besides, in works such as his "Songs of the Western Slavs," Pushkin demonstrated his sensitivity to the national tradition (19:15–16). In the light of Dostoevsky's ideas about genre and nationality as they developed in the 1870s, his robust defense of Russian literature's Westernized gentry roots is far more unexpected than his adulation of Pushkin. Whereas his admiration of Pushkin would remain continuous and peak in his 1880 speech, his thinking about the value and role of Westernism in the development of Russian literature would harden significantly by the end of the 1860s. The contorted arguments Dostoevsky uses in Pushkin's favor seem to undermine his own increasing sense of *narodnost'* as the preserve of the *narod,* revealing structural flaws in his reasoning that hint at the ambivalence with which he would soon begin to view the history of the Russian literary tradition.[27]

From its beginnings *Time* steered a precarious course between recognition and frank discussion of the yawning chasm that separated the cultural values and political priorities of the educated classes and the *narod* in Russia and a utopian vision of Russian nationality as offering a new sense of universalism for a Europe that was losing its way. During the second year of its publication, the latter vision prevailed, and as the Russian journalistic scene became increasingly polarized, *Time* found itself embroiled more and more in polemics with the radicals. The journal's April 1862 involvement in the "Pirogov affair" marks the beginning of a decline in relations with the radicals that would come to a head in 1862 after Chernyshevsky's arrest and the suspension of *The Contemporary*.[28] Dostoevsky's notebooks for 1862 reveal that following the Pirogov affair he had begun to categorize the radicals of *The Contemporary* together with the conservatives of *The Russian Messenger* as "Westernizers," who were overly dependent on European ideas and ignorant of the rich potential of the Russian soil. He wrote of Chernyshevsky and his friends, "You tie onto what is true in abstraction, and remove everyone from earth, from the native soil. Why the complex—our youth does not understand the simplest phenomenon of our Russian soil, they have completely forgotten how to be Russians. But this is really old-fashioned, this is really backwardness, this is only the most extreme Westernizing trash" (20:170). He remained insistent that the radicals had called the first shot: "You began first. We did not want to begin, although we have been squirming in place for a long time. But you were dear to us, we sympathized with you, and we decided that it was better to be silent . . . But now you have begun, and now we would very much wish to say everything to you, not as before, just a bit" (20:155). By the end of 1862 the idea of reconciliation with *Time*'s journalistic opponents had collapsed completely.

Meanwhile, in early 1862 the political and intellectual atmosphere was rapidly changing. In the wake of the publication of the emancipation manifesto and peasant confusion about what the new order would mean, uprisings in the countryside had become widespread. Anonymous leaflets and proclamations had been circulating throughout the previous year, and their tone and programs grew increasingly radical. In spring 1862 the pamphlet entitled *Young Russia* called for "a revolution, a bloody and pitiless revolution, a revolution which must change everything down to the very roots, utterly overthrowing all the foundations of present society and bringing about the ruin of all who support the present order," and many in the government and in educated society at large perceived it as the greatest threat yet.[29] Responsibility for the series of fires that broke out in St. Petersburg at the same time was attributed to the pamphlet's authors. Both the fires and the pamphlet stirred up sentiments against students. Two articles on the fires and proclamations, written by either Dostoevsky or his brother for *Time* but rejected by the censor, warned against blaming students for the disorders. *Time* thus continued to advocate reconciliation between those impatient with the gradualism of the reforms and those alarmed by their rapidity. Concerned over the social unrest, Dostoevsky paid a visit to Chernyshevky and urged him to use his influence over the radical youth to dissuade them from extreme acts. He had not yet come to view social disorder as an inevitable by-product of modernization and was still willing to view its architects as isolated and deluded individuals who were far outside the radical mainstream. However, following the rejection of the two articles on the fires, *Time* came under increasing pressure from the authorities.

Chernyshevsky's arrest in June 1862 and the suspension of *The Contemporary* and *The Russian Word* dramatically raised the stakes in the debates between the journals. When *The Contemporary* reopened, hostilities between the journals intensified, with Schedrin and Dostoevsky trading increasingly personal insults.[30] At the same time, partly as a result of the perceived nihilist threat, many journals, including *The Russian Messenger,* moved further to the right. *Time* began to concentrate its attacks on the radicals rather than the Slavophiles, and though Dostoevsky remained committed to maintaining an independent position, Strakhov's residual Slavophilism had more opportunities to express itself.[31]

In May 1863 the authorities closed *Time* down because they perceived Strakhov's article on the Polish Rebellion as too sympathetic to the Poles and thus proof of the journal's "harmful tendency." At the year's end, Mikhail Dostoevsky received permission to open a new journal, this one called *Epoch.*[32] Since the journal received the blessing of the censorship committee so late, it did not open until April 1864, thus missing the opportunity to gain new subscribers at the beginning of the year. At the same time, the cooling political climate brought a falloff in journal subscriptions. From the outset, *Epoch* was a commercial failure. Despite claims to consistency made in the 1864 announcement to subscribers, the journal's political orientation differed from that of *Time.* Its announcement is much sharper and more polemical than *Time*'s in 1860, and it centers on a defensive claim of Russia's right to follow its own autonomous path, without pressure to conform to outside (European) standards and norms (20:217–21). It declares, "In our view, no nationality in the world, no state that is any way stable, has hitherto ever been formed in accordance with a program recommended and adopted from outside" (20:218). It poses the rhetorical questions, "Is not the idea that we are a distinct, separate, historic entity still considered as something shameful and reactionary by many people in our country? Do not the same people consider nationality, in the highest sense of the word, as something like a disease of which all-leveling civilizations will rid us?" (20:217). In its infancy *Time* had attempted to balance the idea of national renewal with the idea of reconciliation between Russian indigenous models and the productive cosmopolitan influence of Europe. *Epoch* viewed the European influence as superfluous and insisted that national renewal would be sustained by the Russian soil alone. *Time* had struck a delicate equilibrium between recognizing the ways in which the Petrine reforms had allowed for a broadening of the definition of Russianness through the infusion of outside influences and arguing that European influence had gone too far. Reflecting Strakhov's dominating influence, *Epoch* claimed that by absorbing any ideas from the West the educated classes had completely betrayed their national instincts; since the Petrine reforms only the *narod* could be considered instinctively Russian.[33]

DOSTOEVSKY'S CHANGING VIEWS ON RUSSIAN WESTERNISM

By the time he had become editor of *Epoch,* Dostoevsky's views on Russia's relationship with Europe had evolved noticeably. As early as his introduction to the series of articles on Russian literature published in *Time*'s very first issue, he had argued that Russia had a unique role to play in the world; that because of its complex cosmopolitan history, it represented a kind of universalism, the ability to comprehend and reconcile other nations (18:54–61). A trip taken to Western Europe in 1862 which subsequently served as the starting point for his polemical travelogue *Winter Notes on Summer Impressions* confirmed his suspicions both that European societies were fragmenting under pressures such as the social and economic differentiation of the classes and that Western influences were the cause of rather than the solution to Russia's educated classes' shiftless discontent.[34] In London he saw the Crystal Palace as the symbol of the West's rationalist utilitarianism, and in Paris he saw how the isolationist individualism of the bourgeoisie necessitated socialism's attempts to instill in the alienated masses an artificial sense of brotherhood (5:68–74, 74–82). *Winter Notes* as well as some of Dostoevsky's diary entries for 1863–65 also demonstrate his increasing hostility toward both Protestantism and Catholicism; he thought the first was shaped by Northern European utilitarianism and the second defined by materialism and hunger for power. These religions in turn contributed to the fragmentation of European social life and the rise of socialism and social atomization.[35]

In contrast, Dostoevsky saw Orthodoxy as the source of a sense of natural brotherhood, or *sobornost',* that insulated the Russians against the social and economic differentiation of the West.[36] His notebooks for 1864–65 demonstrate both an increasingly Christian interpretation of individual and collective human existence and a strengthening conviction as to Orthodox Christianity's centrality to Russia's historical mission. In a famous passage written following his first wife's death in April 1864, he meditates on the paradoxical nature of Christianity's central tenet, the commandment to love one another as oneself (20:172–75).[37] Such love devoid of egoism was possible only for Christ, who was immortal. For mortals the ego impedes such selfless love, yet Christ's example stands forever before them as an inspiration. The highest goal of humans as individuals and as a whole is the annihilation of the self for the sake of the other, yet this remains an impossible ideal on earth. The afterlife remains the only realm where individual egoism can finally be relinquished and the individual can merge with the whole. Man is condemned to spend his earthly existence embroiled in a Sisyphean struggle for an ideal that lies beyond his grasp. The immortality of the soul is the telos of human earthly existence, yet it is an ideal beyond the comprehension of human consciousness. Human existence is defined by the striving for an ideal that, he insists, is opposed to human nature: "All history whether of humanity or of each man individually is only development, struggle, striving and attainment of [the] goal [of immortality]" (20:172). The realization of Christ's example thus becomes for Dostoevsky the engine that drives history. He comes to read national and international events as part of a grand design.

In a notebook passage from September 1864 entitled "Socialism and Christianity," Dostoevsky sketches out a degenerative model of human history that posits humankind's fall from a spontaneous communal state into the differentiated world of isolated, atomized individuals, outlined above (20:191–94).[38] Ultimately belief in the ideal embodied in Christ is the only genuine solution that will allow humans to return to their previous, spontaneous collective life. Dostoevsky contrasts the voluntary return to collective life that comes with Christianity to the coercive power of the artificial collective that exists in socialism. Socialism, he argues, is only possible in a fragmented society where individuals have lost their connection to the collective. It emerges out of Catholicism, a religion built on the principle of papal power. Catholicism is a religion of coercion, rather than of faith, and has adapted itself to the atomized state of civilization. Orthodoxy, on the other hand, has maintained a sense of brotherhood, or *sobornost'*, which is akin to the collective community of primitive societies. It thus creates a more fertile environment for the return to the collective through the ideal of Christ.

This evolution in Dostoevsky's thinking about the social costs of Western ideas was reflected in his literary works of 1864–66, all of which took as their main subject the ways that European intellectual models such as rational utilitarianism, socialism, and positivism had been absorbed and developed by the radical Russian intelligentsia. Continuing with the thought processes first articulated in *Winter Notes*, he represented in fictional form the effects on the human consciousness and conscience of the apotheosis of reason and egoism espoused in such works as Chernyshevsky's *What Is to Be Done?* In *Notes from Underground* (1864) he showed the transition from European-derived Romantic egoism of the 1840s to the hyperconscious individualism of the

1860s.[39] The textual evidence points toward an original conception of the work that would have depicted the underground man as fumbling toward a realization of the Christian ideal as an alternative to these ideologies; the censorship of the passage in question means that we cannot be sure of Dostoevsky's endgame.[40] In *Crime and Punishment* (1866) he showed through the figure of Raskolnikov how abstract theorizing and a formulaic approach to human life could affect an impressionable young radical mind. Here he included a clear alternative to Raskolnikov's ideas in Sonya's Orthodox self-renunciation and the process of expiation and redemption through which she is eventually able to guide Raskolnikov.

By 1867 Dostoevsky had turned his thoughts from the Westernism of the radical intelligentsia to that of the gentry. His letters for 1867 reveal a renewed interest in the role of aristocratic Westernism in Russia's historical development. He wrote to a friend, the poet Apollon Maikov, of his time in Dresden, "I read Russian newspapers and relieved my heart. I sensed that enough material had accumulated for a whole piece about Russia's relations to Europe and about the whole Russian upper stratum" (28:II:205–6). This material helped to shape the two great novels of the period, *The Idiot* and *Demons*. These two novels mark a significant shift away from the world of the *raznochintsy* in which *Crime and Punishment* was set; together with *The Adolescent* they form a loose trilogy representing the symbolic history of the Russian gentry. They offer two radically different visions of the symbolic identity of the Russian nobleman. Myshkin and Stavrogin, both curiously absent central characters, both dramatically at odds with the worlds they inhabit, serve as symbolic doubles, two absolutely conflicting yet inextricably connected figurations of the Russian landowning estate. Whereas Myshkin represents the ancient (and foreign) roots of the Russian gentry and the moral burden of leadership borne by the noble estate since their distant ancestors were, according to legend, first invited from the north by the Eastern Slavs to rule Kievan Rus' in the ninth century, Stavrogin symbolizes the moral and philosophical depths to which the estate had sunk by the second half of the nineteenth century. Where Myshkin first articulates some of the dominant themes of Dostoevsky's nationalist messianic philosophy of history, which would later find expression in *A Writer's Diary*, *Demons* serves as its most powerful allegorical expression, staging a vision of the decline of post-Petrine Russian Europeanism or Westernism in the character of Stavrogin. How can we explain the shift from the sympathetic portrayal of Prince Myshkin, scion of an ancient Russian aristocratic family, to the depiction of Stravrogin as spirit of destruction, whose annihilating force is linked explicitly to his status as "barin," or aristocrat, in the novel by Shatov and in the notebooks by Dostoevsky himself?

The Idiot and *Demons* were both written during the Dostoevskys' extended sojourn to Western Europe from 1867 to 1871, a period of great instability not only in the lives of the family themselves but also in the history of both Russia and Europe. Dostoevsky began work on *Demons* against the backdrop of the Franco-Prussian War. The war slotted neatly into his developing nationalist messianic master narrative of Russian history, as it marked the end of Western European political, cultural, and spiritual ascendency and opened up a space for renewed Russian influence in Europe that would, he believed, eventually lead to the continent's resurrection through its embrace of the Russian Christ (29:I:161–62). These historical circumstances, as well as a series of debates with Nikolai Strakhov and an extensive engagement with the work of Nikolai Danilevsky, helped to develop Dostoevsky's views on the legacy of Russian Westernism.

DOSTOEVSKY, DANILEVSKY, AND A NATIONALIST HISTORIOGRAPHY

During this period Dostoevsky renewed correspondence with Strakhov, who was in the process of founding *Dawn*, a journal of a loosely Slavophile orientation.[41] He was excited to hear from Strakhov about the 1869 publication in *Dawn*'s first issue of *Russia and Europe,* a work by Nikolai Danilevsky, a passionate Fourierist from the Petrashevsky circle, who had, to Dostoevsky's delight, reinvented himself as a Pan-Slavist (28:II:328, 460, 469, 485, 488, 491; 29:I:17, 19, 25, 30, 36, 46). Dostoevsky had eagerly anticipated it but had failed to get hold of a copy (28:II:273). *Russia and Europe* is at once a philosophy of history, a work of cultural anthropology, and a Pan-Slavist manifesto.[42] It analyzes the meaning of the Westernizing path taken by Russia since the reign of Peter the Great within a world historical context and examines the place of both modern Western European and modern Russian civilization within world history. For Dostoevsky, going through his own crisis over Russian Westernism, it offered an inviting model for thinking more broadly about Russia's cultural and historical mission in the face of the West's cultural and political corruption.

The exploration and indictment of Western influence on Russian elites and on policy since the era of Peter the Great that so interested Dostoevsky was just one part of *Russia and Europe*'s realm of exploration. As Robert McMaster has pointed out, Danilevsky's work is written with two distinct aims that frequently function at cross-purposes to one another within the text. On the one hand, it claims the status of scientific inquiry, presenting a philosophy of history, culture, and anthropology that claims to break away from the Hegelian model of linear historical progress that had dominated

Russian thought throughout the previous three decades. On the other it is a political tract advocating for a Pan-Slav union with Russia as its head and for the warfare necessary to carry out this political goal.[43] McMaster insightfully demonstrates that the work contains two different historical models at odds with one another, one progressive and one cyclical, one accepting of modernity and its possibilities, couched in a language that is "secular, Promethean, and innovative," the other holding up the unchanging values of peasant and gentry life as they had been lived for generations, evoked in "sacerdotal, receptive, traditional" terms.[44] Dostoevsky stumbled on the contradictions between these two visions, but they found their counterparts in his own paradoxical response to Russian modernity.

It was Danilevsky's historiography that most influenced Dostoevsky. Historians had traditionally divided world history into three stages—ancient, medieval, and modern—with modern Europe marking the culmination of historical progress. In the first part of *Russia and Europe* Danilevsky turned this schematization on its head, arguing that it was based on an outdated conception of classification.[45] He proposed instead to apply a taxonomy taken from the work of the French biologist Georges Cuvier, which formed the model for a cyclical model of history in which successive civilizations or cultural-historical types evolve separately, according to different conditions and with different characteristics.[46] The evolution of these historico-cultural types had, he argued, taken place at different speeds and at different periods in world history. Nine previous historico-cultural epochs had succeeded one another before the present age of the decline of the Germano-Roman or European type and the rise of the Slavic one, led by Russia.[47] He argued against the idea that contemporary European civilization marked the culmination of cultural and intellectual achievement. He saw evidence of its decline in the European revolutions of 1848 and the materialism and cultural stultification of France's Second Empire. The triumph of the Slavs over this dying civilization had long been obstructed by their imitation of Europe and, in particular, the European-inspired reforms of Peter the Great.

Astonished at the extent to which he found his own ideas reflected in *Russia and Europe,* Dostoevsky wrote to Strakhov:

> It so coincides with my own conclusions and convictions that on certain pages I am even amazed at the similarity of conclusions; for a long, long time, two years now, I've been writing down a lot of my ideas, specifically because of preparing a piece, practically with the same title, with just the same sort of idea and conclusions. Imagine how joyous my amazement when I now come across nearly the same thing that I had wanted to write in the future already written, in an orderly and harmonious manner, with an uncommon force of

> logic and with the kind of scholarly approach that I, of course, in spite of all my efforts, would never be able to achieve. (29:I:30)

Danilevsky's historical and anthropological model provided a supposed scientific rationale for understanding the European cultural decline about which Dostoevsky himself had written. It demonstrated both that the Slavs constituted a civilization in their own right, distinct from that of Europe, which he had been arguing in *Time* and *Epoch* since the early 1860s, and that Western Europe was a dead civilization which had long ago ceased to contribute to the world any productive political, cultural, or spiritual ideas. This was a theory he had been pondering since *Winter Notes.* Implicit in Danilevsky's model was another proposition that also overlapped with Dostoevsky's own thoughts: while Russian Westernism could have claimed some legitimacy in the eighteenth century, when Europe was still an active civilization, contributing to the world ideas such as the political principle of liberty, by the middle of the nineteenth century its attempts to foist old, dead European ideas onto a vibrant young Slavic civilization was suffocating Russia.

Nevertheless, *Russia and Europe* failed to confirm Dostoevsky's explicitly Orthodox vision of Russia's current and future mission in Europe. He wrote to Strakhov, "I'm still not certain that Danilevsky will indicate *to the full extent* the ultimate essence of the Russian mission, which consists of revealing to the world the Russian Christ, who is unknown to the world and whose principle is contained in our native Orthodoxy. In my opinion, that is the entire essence of our mighty future being" (30). Danilevsky's endgame differed sharply from Dostoevsky's. He was more interested in the geopolitical aspect of Russia's future role in the world, specifically her leadership of a new Pan-Slav union whose capital would be Constantinople. For Dostoevsky *Russia and Europe* did not ultimately outline the eagerly anticipated Slavophile teleological narrative leading to world salvation.

Russia and Europe shares some of the paradoxes and self-contradictions that characterize the editorial line of *Time* and *Epoch.* Like Dostoevsky and his journalistic colleagues, Danilevsky contradicted himself on the topic of Peter the Great. Though he condemned Peter's role in sending Russia on its European path, he welcomed the cultural interactions that had enriched Russia's possibilities and germinated new cultural forms. *Russia and Europe*'s idiosyncratic interpretation of world history would eventually help to shape Dostoevsky's own far-from-systematic vision of Russia's past, present, and future relations with Europe as they developed in the next few years, first in *Demons* and later in the monojournal incarnation of *A Writer's Diary.* Dostoevsky's reading of *Russia and Europe* provided the opportunity for the meditations on Europe prompted by his 1864 trip to crystallize into a systematic interpretation of the negative role played by Westernism in Russia's history.

Toward the end of the Dostoevskys' four years in Europe, political events seemed to bear out Danilevsky's predictions about Western Europe. In July 1870, war broke out between France and Prussia. Prussia, aided by a number of other German states, quickly proved militarily superior, and the unification of Germany in January 1871 helped cement victory. France's humiliating defeat led to a period of political instability that culminated in the uprising of Parisian workers and led to the two-month-long Paris Commune. The commune was crushed by the government in a week of violence and mass executions. Danilevsky wrote an appendix to *Russia and Europe*'s 1871 edition in which he argued that the Franco-Prussian War was the final proof of his theory. Dostoevsky's letters are full of references to these events, frequently couched in Danilevskian terms, but with the addition of his own messianic nationalist interpretation. He sees the Franco-Prussian War as the culmination of the materialism, intellectual bankruptcy, and atomism of Western Europe's last century of development. He tells Maikov that the war has allowed him to reflect on the "revulsion, to the point of hatred, Europe has stirred up in me against her in these four years" (29:I:161), but he sees the war as a kind of expiation for France that will lead first to a humiliating defeat and destruction but finally to enlightenment and the rejection of the last century's false values. He senses God's hand at work in the unfolding scenario in Europe and believes that out of the destruction of the old Europe, a new Europe will arise, one that will recognize the destructive nature of Catholicism and its political legacy and will embrace the truth of the Orthodox faith (29:I:137–38).

While Danilevsky responded to the European crisis by arguing that a weakened France would attempt to ally with Russia against Germany, Dostoevsky disagreed, referring to the coming civil war and predicting the total collapse of France. His readings of the war and its aftereffects vacillate between predictions of collapse and destruction and intimations of rebirth and resurrection. In his last letter from Europe, written to Strakhov on the eve of his return to Russia, Dostoevsky reflects on the end of the war and the destruction of the Paris Commune that had taken place two days earlier. He sees the ultimate explanation of the conflict as the fact that "in the West Christ has been lost (through the fault of Catholicism), and because of that the West is declining, exclusively because of that." He believes that the collapse of France and her Catholic allies will ultimately lead to the collapse of papal power, and he connects the destruction of the commune to the collapse of the nineteenth-century European radical dream of building paradise on earth that had sustained Russian Westernizers. Imagining Belinsky or Timofei Granovsky trying to argue against the inevitability of the commune's collapse, he argues that "once you have set out on that road [advocated by the Russian Westernizers] there's no place you can arrive at other than at the Commune and Felix Pyat. The burning of the Tuileries also marks the end of the road for Russian Westernism" (29:I:214).

Both Dostoevsky's growing belief in Russia's messianic role in Europe and his radical reevaluation of the destructive part played by Westernism in post-Petrine Russian history and culture contributed to a shift in his thinking about the past, present, and future of the Russian literary tradition, particularly the novel. In 1861 he had embraced Grigor'ev's view of Russian literature as the expression of the duality of Russian historical experience, the conflict between Westernism and traditionalism represented and neutralized by the clash of the meek and predatory types. But as his views hardened, he began to question the dominance of the alienated figure of the predatory type in Russian literature, especially in the Russian novelistic tradition, and worry about what this might mean. His letters and notebooks from 1868 onward demonstrate an increasing skepticism about the Russian novel as a vehicle for the reconciliation of Russian society and an increasing concern about the genre's slavish dependence on foreign models. In an 1868 letter to Strakhov he insisted that "our own true Russian and original word . . . ceased to exist with the death of Gogol," grudgingly admitting that in Tolstoy's works "there's something of *ours* there, but little" (28:II:334). Had Russian literature really moved on since Pushkin's depiction of Onegin? Was contemporary literature not in fact resisting including the *narod*'s voice within its realm of influence? What examples could be found of contemporary literature representing the union of the estranged halves of Russian society? Where in contemporary literature was the wisdom of the soil or evidence of the ideal of universal reconciliation? The sphere of the contemporary Russian novel as practiced by such writers as Tolstoy and Turgenev was becoming more and more restricted to the experiences of alienated gentry heroes. Perhaps on one level this was not surprising. The novel, after all, was a genre the Russians had inherited from Western Europe. How could a genre that had developed as a vehicle for communicating the experience of Russian Westernism serve as a conduit for conveying Russia's "new word" to Europe?

THE RUSSIAN NOVEL AS "GENTRY LITERATURE"

Dostoevsky's meditations on the Russian novel were motivated in part by the publication and reception of Tolstoy's *War and Peace* in 1869 and the publication of a series of essays written by Strakhov on Tolstoy and Turgenev published in 1870 in *Dawn*. These essays were explicitly framed as a continuation of the narrative of Russian literature articulated by Apollon Grigoriev at the end of the 1850s. In articles published first in *The Library for Reading* and *The Russian Word* and then in *Time,* Grigoriev conceived of Russian literature as a force of cultural reconciliation between the Westernized Russian intelligentsia and the people. Dostoevsky and Strakhov shared this vision. In the mid-1860s, when they were working on *Epoch,* both had begun to read the history of Russian literature since Pushkin and Gogol as a betrayal of the aesthetic and ethical reconciliation offered by those writers, as a story of the creeping dominance of Western European literary preoccupations, modes, and postures.

But in the late 1860s Dostoevsky's and Strakhov's views on the Russian novel began to markedly diverge. Strakhov saw the publication of *War and Peace* as marking the end of Russian literature's alienated phase. In his extended essay on Tolstoy's work he argued that it marked the appearance at last of an authentic Russian epic.[48] The military conflict between the French and the Russians could be seen in world historical terms, with the Russians defending their nation and values against French cosmopolitanism. Strakhov uses the term "epic" rather loosely; he is concerned not so much with the work's representation of historical events as with its portrayal of the Rostov and Bolkonsky families. It is this, he argues, which constitutes its artistic center of gravity. Strakhov viewed *War and Peace* as a family chronicle, a literary tradition that he saw as having emerged out of Pushkin's idealized vision of the Russian family saga (*predani[e] russkogo semeistva*) invoked in book 3 of *Eugene Onegin.* Pushkin himself had embodied this ideal in "The Captain's Daughter," his depiction of the Pugachov rebellion and its effects on the Grinov family. Strakhov argued that *War and Peace* followed in the generic footsteps of Pushkin's novella and of Sergei Aksakov's *Family Chronicle,* which had provided the emerging genre with a name.[49] He saw the family chronicle as a characteristically Russian literary genre, one that had enriched the nineteenth-century tradition with its truthful representation of everyday life, its embodiment of national values, and its harmony of form. The genre was focused not on the adventures of a separate individual but on the life of a whole family and its development over time. Strakhov viewed *War and Peace* as the apotheosis of the genre, a work in which Russian history, Russian life, domestic life, beauty, and heroism were all synthesized in the harmonious image of the Rostovs and the Bolkonskys. He saw in the work's combination of epic and family chronicle a new, uniquely Russian genre.

Dostoevsky could not agree. In letters to Strakhov written in 1869 and 1870, he offered a muted response both to *War and Peace* and to his friend's reading of the work (29:I:16–17, 109, 114). He objected to Strakhov's placing Tolstoy beside Pushkin in the Russian literary pantheon, yet he did not fully articulate this objection until the very last letter he wrote to Strakhov from Europe (29:I:214–17). It was only then, as he was completing work on *Demons,* that Dostoevsky expressed his criticism of Strakhov's articles on Tolstoy and Turgenev. Strakhov had attacked Turgenev for his complete lack of interest in Russian life and literature, arguing that it had marred his latest works, yet he continued to defend the writer's artistic insight.[50] Dostoevsky responded:

> If you recognize that Turgenev has lost the point and is hedging, and doesn't know what to say about certain phenomena of Russian life . . . then you ought also to have recognized that his great artistic ability has weakened . . . But you know—it really is all gentry literature. It has said everything that it had to say (superbly in the case of Lev Tolstoy). But that word—a gentry one to the highest degree—was the last one. There has not yet been a *new word* to replace that of the gentry, and besides, there's no time for it. (The Reshetnikovs haven't said anything. But the Reshetnikovs nevertheless express the idea of something new in the artistic word, something no longer gentry, though they express it in a hideous form.) (29:I:216)

This response reveals the extent of Dostoevsky's skepticism regarding the Russian novelistic tradition in the early 1870s. He sees the novel of Tolstoy, Turgenev, and Goncharov as "gentry literature" and associates it with the corrupt legacy of Russian Westernism. He views it as the literary manifestation of Petrine assimilation, a tradition forged by the estrangement of the gentry from the *narod.* He characterizes its central characters as rootless gentry and intelligentsia whose cultural, social, and spiritual values are shaped by their alienation from their own nation. Dostoevsky's developing vision of the Petrine reforms as an analogue to the biblical Fall further inscribes the Russian novelistic tradition into a narrative of cultural betrayal, designating it as a fallen tradition through its association with Russian Westernism. He views it as part of the Petrine cultural inheritance and characterizes it as a foreign form, loaned from the West. He also sees it as a tradition that belongs to the past, because of its association with the gentry and with Westernism. Because it arose in a particular historical moment, the era of the cultural and political ascendancy of the nobility, the Russian novel is, for Dostoevsky, a tradition that has seen its day; it is unsuited to and incapable of representing the social and historical transformation wrought by the emancipation. He comes to see the Russian novelistic tradition as the expression of what he calls in "Vlas" the Petrine period of Russian history, the era that has just ended with the Emancipation Act (21:41).[51]

Implicit in these meditations on the Russian novelistic tradition was the need for a new kind of genre, one capable of representing both the Russian Idea of universal reconciliation and the complexity and diversity of Russian history and culture, including the rich pre-Petrine period. If the Russian novel was a fallen tradition, born of and into a lapsarian moment, then the historical and social redemption of the reform period, which had ended the Petrine period, required a parallel redemption of the novel. A new "redeemed" novel was needed for the new historical moment. Yet how could a genre that was defined by its origins in the alienation and uprootedness of Russian Westernism adapt or be adapted to what Dostoevsky now viewed as the new circumstances of Russia's privileged position in Europe? It could happen only if the novel relinquished the alienated, fragmented narrative perspective that had characterized its outlook on the world since its conception in favor of a totalizing, even epic perspective that placed the post-Petrine epoch into the larger context of the nation's thousand-year history. The genre must be infused with forms and ideas taken from the *narod,* reclaiming the generic and religious traditions of the pre-Petrine period, shaped by the polymorphous forms of Russian spirituality and religious faith that had long been forgotten by the practitioners of the Russian novel.

The idea of a "redeemed" literary genre to replace the novel lies behind a series of projects Dostoevsky undertook between 1868 and 1871. In *The Idiot* (1868–69), he attempted to regenerate the novel with the addition of a "positively beautiful" hero, the Christ-like Prince Myshkin, a figure whose virtue and selfless compassion would serve as a challenge to the alienated heroes of Tolstoy and Turgenev. Yet though Myshkin is closer to the soil than Dostoevsky's other protagonists of the time, he is unable to understand or be understood by the conflicted, fallen characters who share his novelistic existence. Ambitions of a different kind of generic redemption lie behind *The Life of a Great Sinner,* the unfinished novel that gave way to *Demons* but also shaped *The Adolescent* and *The Brothers Karamazov.* They also enter into plans for *Demons,* but their role in shaping that novel's finished version is far more complicated and limited in scope. *Demons* testifies instead to the difficulties Dostoevsky had in relinquishing Russian Westernism's hold over his imagination. *Demons* is both the apotheosis of Dostoevsky's criticism of Russian Westernism and a proof of the persistence of its hold both on Russian society and on the novelist himself. The dream of a redeemed genre would continue to serve as a guiding idea throughout the rest of Dostoevsky's literary career, coming to the forefront once more as he worked on *The Brothers Karamazov* in 1878–80.

THE GENERIC PREHISTORY OF *DEMONS*

The work that became *Demons* emerged out of Dostoevsky's plans for a multivolume novel or set of novels where the biography of a paradigmatic Russian hero would be staged as a drama of national, spiritual, and religious reconciliation played out against the backdrop of a thousand years of Russian Christianity. The first reference to this project appears in a December 1868 letter to Maikov, in which Dostoevsky describes "an enormous novel called *Atheism*," which would center on an ordinary Russian man of middling social status who suddenly loses his faith and then undergoes a series of spiritual interactions with Catholics, atheists, Orthodox believers, and schismatics before finally finding "Christ, the Russian land, the Russian Christ and the Russian God" (29:I:11, 20–21, 24–25). The structure of the project, the idea of an unformed seeker who embarks on a journey of discovery and is transformed by his interactions with the world, is structured as a bildungsroman. Like the archetypal protagonist of the bildungsroman, the hero of *Atheism* lacks a proper education and is thus shapeless clay ready to be fashioned by the spiritual and social influences he encounters. Yet *Atheism*'s religious historical backdrop sits uncomfortably with this most European and secular of genres.[52] Moreover, *Atheism*'s triumphally redemptive ending elides the ambivalence with which the traditional bildungsroman regards its hero's reconciliation with the social world. The conflict between individual desire and the constraints of the world which Lukács saw as the formal motivation of the bildungsroman as a genre, and which Dostoevsky had depicted so memorably in both *Crime and Punishment* and *The Idiot,* is resolved in a kairotic moment when its hero recognizes his oneness with God.[53] The bildungsroman is transformed into something more akin to a hagiographic legend. The process of national social reconciliation led by the intelligentsia which Dostoevsky had advocated in *Time* is supplanted by a messianic nationalism that finds formal embodiment in an exploration of premodern genres such as hagiography.

The project's next incarnation was conceived in explicitly hagiographic terms. *The Life of a Great Sinner,* on which Dostoevsky worked from the end of 1869 until the spring of 1870, concurrently with the initial plans for *Demons,* preserves largely the same narrative shape as the embryonic *Atheism.* This work was to begin with the illegitimate titular hero's neglected childhood and his participation in the murder of an escaped convict, after which he was to confess (9:125–39). As part of his punishment he was to be sent to a monastery, where he would find his spiritual confessor, a monk called Tikhon, based on the eighteenth-century elder Saint Tikhon Zadonsky, as well as a whole series of Russian historical figures such as Petr Chaadaev, Belinsky, Granovsky, and Monk Parfeny. Under Tikhon's tutelage he would learn to control his anger and bend his self-will to asceticism. He would set off on a pilgrimage through Russia and would be recognized everywhere for his humility, all the while continuing to battle his pride and arrogance. He would die confessing his crimes. Dostoevsky imagined the Great Sinner as representative of the *narod,* as "a primitive type, subconsciously agitated by his own primitive strength, a strength which is completely spontaneous and ignorant of any base of support" (9:128). He emphasizes the "extraordinary, innate power" of this type, "a power which asks for and seeks a foundation to stand on and a cause to lead, a power which greatly suffers if it is exposed to the storms of life, yet cannot help stirring up storms before it finds its peace." Like the hero of *Atheism* before him, the Great Sinner was finally to "come to rest in Christ" (9:128).

The hagiographic overtones of *The Life of a Great Sinner* are clear. Yet even its title suggests generic mixing. As Linda Ivanits has pointed out, Dostoevsky takes the motif from a group of folk legends that deal with the exploits of a sinner who gives himself up to repentance after a life of transgressions.[54] The title thus evokes not so much the highly conventionalized generic territory of the *zhitie,* the canonical hagiographic legend, as the hybridized territory of folk legend, which reworks the narrative traditions of hagiography within the heavily syncretistic world of popular religion.[55] Dostoevsky's own allusions to hagiography in the notes to *The Life* suggest a syncretistic approach to genre, an enthusiastic impulse toward mixing the worlds of hagiography and secular novelistic genres. In a note he wrote to himself in the plans for the work he emphasized the particular tone that he wished to convey:

> Tone (the narrative is a *vita*—i.e., even though it comes from an author's pen, it is concise, not sparing of explications, yet presenting some things in scenic form. (Here, harmony is of the essence.) Matter-of-factness of the narrative, sometimes to the point of Gil Blas. At spectacular and scenically impressive junctures, it may appear that there is little reason to attach much value to this trait.
>
> Yet it is also important that the dominant idea of the *vita* be apparent, i.e., even though the whole dominant idea may never be explained in so many words, and though it may remain something of a mystery, the reader still ought to know at all times that this idea is a pious one, also that the vita is deemed to be a work of importance, so much so that it was worth starting it with the childhood. (9:132–33)

The hagiographer's authoritative and yet sometimes abstract and imagistic tone would be combined with the picaresque narrator's down-to-earth tone (invoked here through the reference to the French picaresque novel *Gil Blas*) to create a colorful and lively impression of events that carried a deeper signification. The episodic plot borrowed both from the picaresque and the bildungsroman, but in starting with the sinner's childhood, Dostoevsky saw himself as following the traditional narrative arc of hagiographic legend. In its depiction of a life, hagiography is always directed toward the moment of conversion, the moment when the life will have achieved divine meaning. Here that moment is the resurrection following the Great Sinner's fall. *The Life of a Great Sinner*'s intended hagiographic tone and narrative arc suggest that it was conceived as a work directed toward the ineffable, a work that gestured toward the possible overcoming not merely of the fallen nature of the protagonist, but of the fallen nature of narrative itself. The work's central idea lies in the Great Sinner's eventual transfiguration. Yet the plan does contain seeds of doubt concerning this final resurrection. Dostoevsky writes that the moral vacillations the Sinner experiences "give substance to the novel," thus giving intimations of the Sinner's moral freedom and moral choice, mechanisms that do not occur in hagiography's end-determined moral trajectory (9:130).

In characterizing the Great Sinner, Dostoevsky specified that he was to be "a type contrary to the scion of that noble family of Counts, degenerate to the point of swinishness, which Tolstoi has depicted in *Childhood* and *Adolescence*" (9:128). This reference to Tolstoy's *Childhood* trilogy provides another key to *The Life*'s generic identity. It reveals the extent to which Dostoevsky conceived of its generic perspective as radically different from that of the traditional Russian novel as practiced by his contemporaries Tolstoy and Turgenev. The invocation of Irteniev, the alienated hero of Tolstoy's trilogy *Childhood, Boyhood, Youth,* in the notebooks for *The Life of a Great Sinner* points toward his conscious attempt to distance his work from the alienated Westernized heroes not merely of this quintessential Russian bildungsroman but from the Russian novelistic tradition more generally. For Dostoevsky Irteniev epitomized the alienated Russian noble novelistic hero, the symptom of the Russian novel's Westernism and fragmentary subjectivity; he symbolized its fallen state.[56] *The Life* was his challenge to the novel of Russian Westernism, his attempt to resurrect the Russian novelistic form through the infusion of hagiography and epic. The project would share the external form of Tolstoy's trilogy, dealing first with his hero's childhood and his youth, but then it would overcome the trilogy's fragmented post-Petrine alienated subjectivity in favor of the totality of perspective claimed by hagiography and epic. It would borrow from hagiography the convention of illustrating its ideas through example, in scenic form, and revealing through its hero the man of the future (9:132–33). Like national epic, *The Life of a Great Sinner* would project through its hero the perspective of the nation. His moral and spiritual resurrection would serve as a figure for the nation's overcoming of the Petrine schism (128). *The Life of a Great Sinner* can be seen as the generic counterpart of *Time*'s political fantasy of the reconciliation between the two halves of Russian society, Dostoevsky's attempt to create what Strakhov had seen in Tolstoy's *War and Peace:* an authentically Russian epic.[57] It represented Dostoevsky's most serious attempt yet to escape from the novel of alienation and sidestep the fragmentation of Russian modernity.

Although *The Life of a Great Sinner* is rooted in the historiographic assumptions of Dostoevsky's messianic utopian nationalism, those assumptions are not the work's central focus. In another embryonic project conceived at the same time as *The Life,* he addressed historiographic questions more explicitly, reflecting on the question of what a Russian historical epic might look like. The outlines of such a work emerge in his May 1869 letter to his friend the poet Apollon Maikov, in which he sketched out a project (to be realized by Maikov) for a series of *byliny* or folk epics depicting significant moments in Russian history (29:I:38–46). He envisages such moments as instances of an almost cosmic insight, points at which Russia's destiny appears "to be concentrated and expressed wholly, suddenly, in its entirety." These points provide a panoramic view of Russia's historical and spiritual mission, serving as hermeneutic keys opening up an epic vision of Russian history. Perhaps the most important of these historical episodes is the fall of Constantinople to the Turks and the corresponding transfer of the power and significance of Orthodoxy to the Russia of Grand Prince (later Tsar) Ivan III. This episode's centrality reveals Dostoevsky's vision as based within the doctrine of Moscow as the third Rome, the process of *translatio imperii* from Rome to Constantinople to Moscow.[58] He even invokes one of the central images of the *translatio imperii,* the icon of the Blachernitissa virgin, the intercessory protectress of Constantinople, which reappeared centuries after the city's fall and was taken to Moscow and later enshrined in the Dormition Cathedral. Dostoevsky imagined that the Grand Prince would be depicted in a wooden hut, rather than a palace, "and the great idea of Russia's significance for all of Orthodoxy is transferred to this wooden hut and the first stone of its leadership in the East is laid" (29:I:40). The idea is then infused with a Danilevskian pan-Slavic triumphalism as Dostoevsky predicts the regeneration of Christianity with the pan-Slav Orthodox idea after the triumph first of Catholicism and then of atheism has precipitated the West's decline. This vision of simplicity pregnant with messianic promise would be counterposed to a ballad representing the artistic splendor of Western Europe during the Renaissance and the Enlightenment. This ballad would carry dark intimations of the social and spiritual degeneration that lay ahead for the West. Having originally planned the series to end with Peter the Great, Dostoevsky decided instead that it should continue on to the emancipation of the serfs, to the self-imposed European exile of the Russian nobility and the infection of Western Europe with the ideas of socialism and atheism. Taken together these scenes are supposed to demonstrate the divine intentionality that Dostoevsky was beginning to believe governed the unfolding of world history.

The totality of perspective that Dostoevsky envisioned as possible from the viewpoint of these particular historical moments was matched by what he perceived as the idea's unmediated and direct translation from the poet's soul into poetic form. The poet would "seize those points and narrate them in a folk epic, to each and everyone . . . to seize the main point and so convey it that it is plain with what idea it was shaped, with what love and torment this idea was obtained" (29:I:39). The genres Dostoevsky envisaged for the verses include ballads, songs, short narrative poems, and romances: in other words, those premodern folk genres transmitted through the oral tradition. It is rather ironic that he specifically chose genres which in the Romantic nationalist tradition were thought to embody the people's collective consciousness (*Volksgeist*) and yet at the same time conceived of the actual verses being written by an experienced writer such as Maikov. The way he described the form's emergence from the poet's soul borrowed directly from the discourse of Romantic inspiration: "The essence and even the meter of the verses here depend on the poet's soul and appear suddenly, completely ready in his soul, even independently of him" (29:I:39). This description conveys Dostoevsky's unspoken desire for a *narod* capable of transmitting such verses without the mediation of a poet from the intelligentsia but at the same time suggests his inability to really imagine such an entity. It also reveals his anxiety about his own ability to find a genre to convey a seamless and nonfragmented vision of Russia's historical and religious mission. All too conscious of his own creative temperament as "poet of the underground," he here sketches out the outlines of the utopian generic and historiographic fantasies and dreams of hermeneutic totality that were integral to *The Life of a Great Sinner* and would continually emerge during the writing of *Demons* to offer resistance to the fragmented novelistic account of an alienated Russian noble protagonist.[59]

This embryonic plan for a Russian historical epic and the *Life of a Great Sinner* project both attempt to overcome the historical and cultural alienation of the Russian novel, to reinvigorate or even resurrect the form. The religious and folk genres informing both projects open up the Russian people's worldview, a perspective that Dostoevsky believed had disappeared from post-Petrine Russian literature. Both projects are organized according to the assumption of a divine plan structuring Russian history. Both broaden the normal scope of Russian history from the post-Petrine period to one thousand years of Russian Christianity. Both depict visions of a chaotic present that enacts this divine plan, whether the Great Sinner's moral vacillations finally giving way to his final transfiguration, or the seminarists preaching atheism to nomadic rootless Russian nobles signaling the providential fulfillment of Russia's spiritual mission of replacing atheism with the Orthodox idea. This vision of a utopian future and its corresponding projects were interrupted by a set of events that took place in Russia at the end of 1869.

In November 1869, a student at the Petrovsky Agricultural Academy in Moscow, I. I. Ivanov, was murdered by a group of conspirators led by the nihilist revolutionary Sergei Nechaev (29:I:107). The murder was generally viewed as a stark indication of the social and political unrest that was threatening Moscow and St. Petersburg. The murder proved the tipping point in Dostoevsky's gradual change of heart regarding the modernization of the 1860s. Following the social unrest of the mid-1860s, this heinous crime far outweighed the student demonstrations and Petersburg fires in its social and political significance. It clearly exemplified the chaos to which the reform period had led. The dream of social and spiritual reconciliation between the *narod* and the intelligentsia had sustained Dostoevsky's writings throughout the 1860s, but the Nechaev affair changed everything. Dostoevsky saw Nechaev not so much as a danger in his own right, but as a symptom of Russia's post-Petrine social and historical development and a symbol of all that had gone wrong in the previous three decades.

In February 1870 Dostoevsky wrote to Maikov that he had begun to tackle a new project which would engage with "the most direct contemporary issue" that had "great resonance with the public" (29:I:107). References to the Nechaev affair began to make their way into his notes for *The Life of a Great Sinner* in late 1869 (9:121). The project developed a more ideologically loaded aspect, and by early February a figure based on Nechaev himself (originally called "the student") had entered the notebooks (11:66). From the very beginning Dostoevsky's depiction of the Nechaev affair had a deeper ideological purpose: it explored the legacy of Russian Westernism and examined Nechaev's political genealogy against the broad backdrop of Russia's historical development during the previous few centuries. Nechaev served as the perfect pretext for Dostoevsky to explore the transformation, chaos, and fragmentation of Russian modernity. He was interested in Nechaev as a symptom, rather than the cause, of Russia's contemporary malaise. He held the generation of Belinsky, Alexander Herzen, and Mikhail Bakunin responsible for the intellectual development that had created the conditions for the Nechaev affair. He began his project, appropriately enough, with the conflict of the fathers and the children. This was the governing topos of the Russian antinihilist novel, the figure for generation conflict that had been exploited to such effect by Turgenev. From the very earliest pages of the notebooks for *Demons*, Dostoevsky's Nechaev figure, later Petr Verkhovensky, was depicted as the son of a Westernizer par excellence. He was modeled after Timofei Granovsky, a historian and a member of the Stankevich circle (11:65). Making the Nechaev figure the son of the Granovsky figure allowed Dostoevsky to demonstrate on a formal level that responsibility for Nechaev and his conspiracy lay with the entire rotten edifice of Russian Westernism. Answering his own question about Granovsky's role in his project, Dostoevsky wrote, "He is there for the purpose of letting two generations of what really are the same Westernizers, those of pure vintage and the nihilists, meet each other" (11:68).

At first sight this "novel-pamphlet" seems to bear little relation to earlier works such as *The Life of a Great Sinner*, with their allegorical ambition, dynamic, developing hero, and dialectical teleology. Yet as plans progressed, the project's original structuring idea, the fathers and sons model, was gradually replaced by a radically different generic model, which emerged out of the embryonic plans for *The Life*.[60] This model, which we might call the epic, found its locus in the mysterious character of the Prince, later to become Stavrogin, who was identified as a rootless and alienated aristocrat (11:68). He initially formed part of the novelistic attack on Russian Westernism, but eventually came to serve as a generic catalyst in the work's transformation into tragedy, as Dostoevsky himself was quick to recognize (29:I:142). The ensuing clash of these two different models made of *Demons* a generic hybrid, a work uneasily balanced on the boundary between epic, tragedy, and novel, between narrative totality and fragmentation.

THE NOTEBOOKS FOR *DEMONS*: THE CLASH OF TWO MODELS

The two generic models that shape the 1870 plans for *Demons* appear most clearly as two distinct character constellations which remain remarkably constant throughout the notebooks until the late summer.[61] The first is the father-son pairing of Granovsky and Nechaev. Stepan Trofimovich (Granovsky) is the character who changes least throughout the writing process. The traits that define Stepan in the novel—his inflated sense of self, wounded pride, aimlessness, tendency toward abstraction, and persecution complex—are present at the very inception of the Granovsky character. The nihilism of his son, who appears first as the Student, then as Nechaev, is initially refracted through Granovsky's own perspective; his failure to recognize his own intellectual culpability in the development of his son's nihilist beliefs underscores the irony of this refraction. Stepan Verkhovensky is to be "a portrait of a pure and idealistic Westernizer in his full splendor," in other words, alienated and uprooted from the Russian soil (11:65). This is the core structure of the pamphlet-novel, which tells the story of the decline of Russian Westernism and remains more or less unchanged in the completed novel.

The dominance of the Granovsky-Nechaev character axis within the notebooks is challenged by another character constellation centering on two characters originally known as the Teacher and the Prince, later to become Shatov and Stavrogin.[62] The Teacher/Shatov is initially conceived as the murder victim of Nechaev and his fellow conspirators, while the Prince is a follower of Nechaev's ideas. The Teacher/Shatov and the Prince are first brought together in an early variant of the plot entitled "Envy." They compete for the love of the Ward (later Dasha), and the slap that Shatov eventually gives to Stavrogin in the final version of the work is first delivered to the Teacher by the Prince as part of their romantic rivalry (11:58–64). This romantic plot serves primarily as the structuring mechanism that reveals the social, spiritual, and ideological connections and antagonisms between the two characters. True doubles throughout much of the planning process, they are interchangeably analogous to one another as well as opposites. In "Envy" both characters are initially identified as ideal figures, although the Prince's moral sensitivity is often tempered with hatred for his rival (11:63).

In notes for January 1870, the Teacher, now called Shaposhnikov, is identified as "a truly native type" (11:66). He becomes the mouthpiece for Dostoevsky's own ideas, associating the nihilists with Russian Westernism and viewing the current social and political impasse as a result of the forced Europeanization of the Petrine reforms (11:85, 97). Later he is described as "the restless type, the product of a collision between a bookish world and reality, a man who has embraced his faith with passion, yet does not know what to do" (11:131). In the February notes Shapostnikov is placed more frequently in opposition to Granovsky, with whom he argues about Europe's role in Russian history and with whom he is involved in a complicated romantic plot involving the latter's marriage to his sister, and to Nechaev, with whom he becomes involved politically and who plots his assassination. Yet by March the same character, now sometimes called Shatov, was already taking on the role of the Prince's principal interlocutor, as the latter began to move to the center of Dostoevsky's conception of the project. As the figure of the Prince gradually becomes the novel's hero, it is Shapostnikov-Shatov who emerges as his main sparring partner.

From his initial conception, the Prince shares many of the traits of the Great Sinner, though his moral and spiritual trajectory is characterized by vacillation between moral extremes rather than by a journey toward enlightenment. Early in the notes he becomes identified with the rootlessness and alienation that Dostoevsky associated with the Westernized gentry. It is Shaposhnikov who diagnoses the social phenomenon he represents, just as it is Shatov in the novel who ties Stavrogin's spiritual disorder to his social and cultural origins. Both Shaposhnikov and the Prince are described at various points as "new men," associating them with a redemptive and regenerative narrative within the embryonic project.

In notes written in the spring of 1870, the Prince, who has previously appeared as both an atheist and a passionate believer, comes to resemble the figure of the Great Sinner even more, undergoing spiritual and political *Bildung* that encompasses atheistic nihilism, 1840s-style liberalism, pan-Slavism, and Slavophilism (11:127–44). These ideas are embodied by four ideological representatives, Nechaev, Granovsky, Shaposhnikov/Shatov, and a new character called Golubov, who does not appear in the novel and whose espousal of Orthodox *sobornost'* is ideologically most akin to Dostoevsky's own position. Dostoevsky writes, "It turns out that the Prince is a romantic and mysterious figure. He visits with everybody, listens to everybody—in order to grow firmer in his own convictions" (11:131). The notebook iterations of his character are marked by ideological vacillation rather than development. Sometimes his rage concerning his own social background and everything that it represents leads him to embrace Nechaev's doctrine of destruction, while at others his urgent desire for redemption, his "persistent desire to become a new man," leads him to reach out to Shaposhnikov/Shatov and Golubev. Vacillating constantly between nihilism and Orthodoxy, the Prince sometimes embraces the Russian Idea and bitterly denounces the Western liberalism of his youth. What remains consistent in his character is his rootlessness, which is recognized and exploited both by Nechaev and by Shapostnikov/Shatov. The Prince undergoes a parallel process of romantic formation in his love affairs with the Beauty (Liza), the Lame Woman (Maria Lebyadkina), and the Ward (Dasha). Alongside these romantic entanglements arise rumors of a child's rape, which will only be given psychological motivation later in the year (11:136).

By May and June the Prince's search for spiritual redemption has led him to embrace Slavophilism and the idea of Russia as the defender of Orthodoxy before the great powers of Europe. He envisions the relationship between the tsar and his people as "natural brotherhood," with the tsar as the incarnation of the soul or spirit of the *narod.* He believes that

> Russia is no more and no less than the embodiment of Orthodoxy . . . We have reached the last stage of our submission to Europe, to civilization, to the curse of Peter's reform . . . We shall smash those European fetters which have been clinging to us for so long, and they will break like cobwebs; and we shall all realize, finally, that the world . . . has never seen such a gigantic idea as the one which is now taking shape here, in the East, and moving to take up the place of the European masses to regenerate the world. Europe will flow into our waters as a living stream, and the part of it which is dead and doomed to die will serve as ethnographic material for us. We are bringing the world the only thing we can give it, which is, however, the only thing it needs: Orthodoxy, the true and glorious, eternal creed of Christ, and a full moral regeneration in his name. We are bringing the world the first paradise of the millennium. (11:167)

More than any other character in the notebooks, the Prince expresses Dostoevsky's utopian vision of the Russian mission to the world. This ultimate overcoming of the Prince's alienation stages Dostoevsky's continuing desire to redeem not merely his character but also his social origins, to show that the reconciliation that the *pochvenniki* yearned for is still possible, that an ideal can still be salvaged out of the historical detritus of Russian Westernism. Dostoevsky indicates his own awareness of the utopian nature of this ideological and narrative scenario by means of several sections of the notebooks that he titles "fantastic pages" (11:173, 177, 185). After the first fantastic page, dated June 23, 1870, Dostoevsky wrote, "The Prince is seeking a great moral feat, some true accomplishment, something by which Russia would manifest her strength to the whole world. His idea is true, genuine, active Orthodoxy." The fantastic pages serve as potential spaces of utopian realization, but they also indicate the difficulty, even impossibility, of establishing psychological motivation or narrative impetus for the Prince's transformation into an active representative of the Russian Idea. It is as though once the barrier is breached between the Prince's abstract beliefs and concrete activity, the project must leave the realm of realism and enter the domain of the fantastic. Not only is Dostoevsky unable to articulate the specifics of the fantastic pages, but he is also always forced by narrative logic into making the Prince admit the difficulty, even impossibility, of belief (11:186). The scenarios always end with the Prince either shooting or hanging himself, buckling under the weight of his own symbolic history (11:132, 136, 144, 151, 154, 175, 201).

Finally, by the end of the summer, the Prince morphs into a character we can recognize as Stavrogin and is even sometimes now given that name. The child rape is now central to his character; he gives his tacit ideological support to Nechaev; and romantic intrigues have replaced ideological conflict. Why, despite Dostoevsky's ideological and aesthetic aspirations, is the figure of the Prince incapable of true belief in Orthodoxy? There are a number of clues in the notebooks and in the completed novel. In the second half of the year another refugee from *The Life of a Great Sinner* reappears in the notebooks: the monk (later bishop), Tikhon, who had served as the Great Sinner's confessor and who now reappears as the Prince/Stavrogin's confessor. Like Shatov, Tikhon recognizes and unmasks the Prince/Stavrogin, but whereas the former explains his lack of belief in terms of his social and historical origins, the latter reveals his failure to believe as a result of his deep-seated individualism and inability to repress the demands of his ego. The Prince reproaches Tikhon for his lack of individualism (11:267). We see repeated here in an almost identical formulation Dostoevsky's own idea regarding the necessary surrender of the ego expressed in April 1864 after the death of his wife: Tikhon tells the Prince, "The notion to surrender one's own I has been confirmed to the point where there exists an urge to surrender it" (11:190). The renunciation of individuality is the core of Christ's lesson to the world, and as one who values his ego, originality, individuality above all else, the Prince is incapable of such a surrender. In notes for mid-June, the Prince tells Shatov that Orthodoxy demands self-perfection, which he understands as the aggrandizement rather than the renunciation of the self. He asks Shatov, "Do you actually know how strong 'one man' is? Raphael, Shakespeare, Plato, Columbus or Galileo? He stays alive for 1000 years and regenerates the world—he does not die" (11:168). Here the Prince seems to advocate a combination of the ideas of Raskolnikov and those of Kirillov. Orthodoxy becomes a philosophy of the apotheosis of the ego. Like Raskolnikov, the Prince seeks to demonstrate the power of his ego by liberating himself from all moral and social constraints. In the notebooks and in the chapter of the completed novel entitled "At Tikhon's," suppressed by Mikhail Katkov and never subsequently reinstated by Dostoevsky, he attempts to prove his individualism and liberation from all constraints by raping a young girl.[63] Tikhon proves that the manner of Stavrogin's self-presentation following the rape shows that he, like the underground man, is still taking into account the perspective of others, and thus incapable of complete autonomy. Had the chapter been included in the novel, this unmasking would have helped explain Stavrogin's suicide as his acknowledgment of the failure of his life's project. As Joseph Frank and others have pointed out, the removal of this chapter from the novel obscures the presentation of Stavrogin's character and its function in the novel's ideological structure.[64] Only his perverse marriage to Maria Timofeevna and other acts of self-debasement suggest his goal of liberation from social and moral norms.

The paradoxical coexistence of two opposing ideological strains or scenarios within the notebooks for *Demons* can be more clearly explained if we conceive of them as representing different generic impulses within Dostoevsky's evolving literary project. The utopian dream of reconciling the worldviews of the Westernized nobility/intelligentsia and the *narod,* long since renounced in Dostoevsky's letters, coexists in his literary imagination with a sense of the stubborn inescapability of the Prince's alienated Romantic individualism, his inability to renounce his own ego. These two ideas find expression in the conflict between the two generic impulses that structure the embryonic project. The drive toward epic is expressed in the all-embracing perspective of the Russian Idea and its dynamics of resurrection and regeneration and in the coincidence of the Prince's heroic personality with the world he occupies. Dostoevsky's statements "The whole pathos of the novel lies in the Prince; he is the hero. All the rest moves around him like a kaleidoscope . . . A boundlessly lofty figure" and "Everything is contained in Stavrogin's character. Stavrogin is everything" reveal his conception of the Prince/Stavrogin as an epic hero, indistinguishable from the world he inhabits (11:136, 207). This epic impulse conflicts with the generic hallmarks of the Russian bildungsroman and the character traits of the self-conscious Russian novelistic hero. Dostoevsky writes,

> The Prince is a person who is easily bored. A product of this Russian century . . . He looks down on people and knows how to remain independent, i.e., he keeps away from the gentry, as well as from the Westernizer, and from the nihilists, and from Golubov. Yet there remains for him the question: what is he himself? The answer for him is "Nothing." (11:134)

He is shown as estranged from the world he inhabits, self-conscious, seeking above all else to retain his own individual autonomy, the composite of all the social and psychological attributes of alienated novelistic protagonists from Onegin to Bolkonsky.

Dostoevsky aims to reconcile the mutually exclusive generic tendencies of epic and novel (or perhaps bildungsroman). By making the Prince, who is as much of a nobleman as any of Tolstoy's heroes, not merely into a spokesman for his Russian Idea but into an active Orthodox believer, he hopes to stage the redemption both of Russian Westernism and of the Russian novel itself. The fantastic pages, with their unwritten content, represent the mute redemptive climax of the marriage of these two generic impulses. The stubborn narrative iteration of the Prince's act of hanging himself demonstrates the project's internal resistance to Dostoevsky's attempt at generic reconciliation. The notebooks express both the extent of Dostoevsky's generic ambitions and the impossibility of fulfilling them at this stage in his literary career. The finished novel contains very little trace of either the epic vision of Stavrogin or the psychological structure of the bildungsroman. Dostoevsky seems in the end to have accepted the logic of his characterization of the Prince/Stavrogin and made him an existential adventurer cut from the same cloth as preconversion Raskolnikov, the victim of his own alienated and attenuated individualism. The finished work remains highly ambivalent toward the ideological and generic legacy of Russian Westernism.

DEMONS AS ALLEGORY OF RUSSIAN WESTERNISM

Many recent critical treatments of *Demons* regard the work as generically unstable or hybridic, identifying one set of generic features with the plotline of the Verkhovenskys, father and son, and another with the figure of Stavrogin. Significantly, these two generic strands map exactly onto the character constellations present in the notebooks. Frank sees the two models as the source of inconsistencies between the work's symbolic-historical and ideological structures.[65] He argues that Stavrogin lies at the center of the symbolic-historical framework, lending a tragic aspect to the novel that fits uneasily with the ideological drama enacted by the Verkhovenskys. W. J. Leatherbarrow sees the novel as projecting two demonic orders, one embodied in the carnivalistic chaos brought about by Petr Verkhovensky, and the other in the apocalyptic motifs that accompany Stavrogin throughout the novel.[66] For Russell Valentino the work straddles the generic boundaries of satire and allegory, the first constituting the generic field occupied by Stepan Verkhovensky, the second the one occupied by Stavrogin, two characters who, significantly, never meet in the novel.[67] All of these scholars are right in seeing a fundamental structural, symbolic, and ideological dissonance within the completed novel. *Demons* contradicts itself on many different levels and defies a consistent reading. At the root of this dissonance is Dostoevsky's conflicted vision of Russian Westernism and his ambivalent attitudes toward the novel, the compromised literary vehicle through which he chose to express this vision.

Dostoevsky's original goal of ideologically equating the two generations of Westernizers, "those of pure vintage and the nihilists," dominated his conception of the novel's final version. When he sent a copy of the finished novel to Grand Prince Alexander Romanov, he explained that the work was intended to show that phenomena such as the Nechaev affair "are the direct consequences of the age-old divorce of all Russian enlightenment from the native and distinct principles of Russian life" and that "it is precisely that kinship and continuity of thought from the fathers to the children that I wanted to express in my work" (29:I:260). The "fathers and sons" model is strongly established at the opening of the book through the parodic representation of Stepan Verkhovensky, the 1840s liberal par excellence. The meaningless liberal chatter of Stepan and his friends creates a rhetorical, spiritual, and intellectual void that is filled by Petr Verkhovensky and his ideology of destruction. Yet the model breaks down with Stavrogin. Valentino is right in asserting that he occupies a completely different generic field from the Verkhovenskys.[68]

The Stavrogin of the completed novel bears little resemblance to the evolving figure of the notebooks. It is only in the main plot's projected prehistory that he lives through the ideas expressed in the notebooks; in the main plot they remain as residue in the ideas of his disciples, Petr Verkhovensky, Shatov, Kirillov, and Shigalev. The completed Stavrogin is the eroding imprint of the dynamic figure of the notes, capable only of isolated acts of madness or desperate self-abasement. For most of part I he is present only through rumor and hearsay, appearing almost a third of the way through the novel. He is revealed only through analeptic references in conversations with his disciples; traces of his former intellectual and spiritual struggles remain only in their ideological deformities. He serves as the novel's empty center, a specter with a mask instead of a face.[69] His last remaining connection to the Prince of the notebooks is broken when Maria Lebyadkina, who calls him Prince, realizes her mistake and reveals him as an imposter. The great seducer of the notebooks ultimately becomes an impotent figure unable to respond to Liza's ardor, an indifferent lover who sends his would-be mistress off to be killed by the mob.

Stavrogin's inability to develop within the novel is shown to be a consequence of his role in the work's symbolic historiography as a Europeanized Russian nobleman. From his first appearance in the notebooks as the Prince, his aristocratic status defines his identity: he is referred to by a series of different titles, including Count, before his name is finally fixed, quite late in the writing process.[70] Shatov recognizes in Stavrogin's identity as a nobleman the locus of his corruption: "You're an atheist, because you're a nobleman's son [*barin*], the last nobleman's son [*poslednii barich*]. You've lost the distinction between good and evil because you've ceased to know your own people" (10:202–3). This emphasis on Stavrogin's social status along with the trajectory of his development from the notes through the prehistory of the novel's main events and into the vacant figure of the main plot reveals the world historical symbolic underpinnings of his identity, undergirded by Dostoevsky's reading of *Russia and Europe*. This Europeanized Russian nobleman whose ideas have all been absorbed during his travels abroad embodies the amorality and apotheosized individualism that both Dostoevsky and Danilevsky saw as the legacy of the "Petersburg period of Russian history" (13:455).[71] In Danilevskian terms, Stavrogin, as a Europeanized Russian, is the disintegrating representative of a dying historical-cultural type. The vestiges of the dying civilization that has created him are symbolized in his intellectually deformed acolytes.

If the novel holds liberal, radical, and aristocratic representatives of Russian Westernism directly responsible for the breakdown and fragmentation of Russian society, it paints an equally pessimistic picture of the state of the *narod*. The novel's main representatives of the *narod* and its beliefs are the ruthless convict Fedka; the holy fool Semon Yakovlevich (based on a real historical figure, the Muscovite holy fool Koreisha); the faintly heretical, hysterical, and victimized Maria Timofeevna; and the Gospel seller Sofia Matveevna, who, as the redeemer of Stepan Verkhovensky, is the only positively marked character among these examples. Ivanits points out that the novel does offer some positive characterizations of the *narod*'s beliefs, such as Liza's nanny and the peasants who help Stepan Verkhovensky at the end of the novel, but they are all marginal to the plot, melting into the novel's darker background of rioting factory workers and lynch mobs.[72] She suggests that Dostoevsky seems here to be presenting a *narod* in need of enlightenment rather than the self-sufficient and spiritually cohesive people to which he refers in his nationalist outpourings.[73] In fact, this representation of the *narod* recalls the description in *Time*'s 1860 announcement to subscribers of the state of the post-Petrine condition of the Russian people: "They walked in darkness, but they went on their separate way regardless . . . They tried to create their own views on life, their own philosophy, broke up into all sorts of mysterious, ugly sects" (18:36). Dostoevsky is here creating a novelistic picture of the failure of the very reconciliation he had looked forward to in the early 1860s. The effects of the failed postemancipation integration are shown to be as destructive for the *narod* as they are for the intelligentsia and the nobility.

With the excision of Tikhon from the completed novel, there are no representatives of mainstream Orthodoxy to bring the *narod* back into the fold. There is only Stavrogin. Maria Timofeevna's identification of Stavrogin as Prince underlines the need for the Prince of the notebooks, for a heroic figure who represents the Russian Idea and who can unite the town and the townspeople and save them from the chaos and violence of Petr Verkhovensky and his associates. But in the end Maria recognizes Stavrogin as the imposter he is, identifying him with the seventeenth-century monk-pretender Grigory Otrepev and anathematizing him, thereby breaking the last remaining connection to the salvatory Prince of the notebooks and any hope for reconciliation. Maria Timofeevna's unconsummated carnivalesque marriage to Stavrogin represents both the potentiality for reconciliation and its grotesque parodic distortion.[74] As Ivanits points out, Stavrogin's wasted potentiality is underlined by negative associations with Saint Nicolas the Wonderworker.[75] Dostoevsky inserts Stavrogin into a profoundly complex symbolic economy in which nothing less is at stake than his own once dearly held vision of Russian social and spiritual reintegration.

Demons thus presents a highly ambiguous picture of Russian Westernism's legacy. Stavrogin ends his life as the putative citizen of the canton of Uri, hanging in the attac at Skvoreshniki, his suicide apparently marking the failure of the reconciliation of Russia's divided society. Stepan Trofimovich, on the other hand, finally recants on his deathbed, under the influence of the meek Gospel seller, Sofia Matveevna. He embraces the Russian Idea and the Russian Christ in his own way and fulfills the epigraph's role of the man formerly possessed by demons sitting at the feet of Jesus. This moment of redemption seems to rehabilitate the possibility of the social and spiritual reconciliation of the educated classes and the *narod* that was previously associated with Stavrogin. How are we to understand these contradictory outcomes?

Dostoevsky's indictment of Russian Westernism in *Demons* is not merely thematic; it is also symbolic, structural, and hermeneutic. The breakdown of the bildungsroman model in the notebooks and in the novel's prehistory presages the introduction at the novel's outset of a mode of reading very different from that of the bildungsroman or other secular genres. This mode is expressed in the metaphor of possession introduced by the novel's dual epigraphs, Pushkin's poem "Demons" and Luke 8:32–36, with its account of demons leaving a possessed man and entering a herd of swine. Pushkin's poem, which conveys the mounting terror of being lost on a ride through a snowstorm, opens with a secular perspective, positing the idea of demonic possession only as a last resort to explain a situation that has become incomprehensible within normal terms of reference. Dostoevsky chooses to quote two partial stanzas consisting of four lines each, separated by a set of parentheses. The first conveys the speaker's final conclusion that only a demon can be responsible for the calamity in which he finds himself. The second depicts his resigned acceptance of this state of affairs: he only questions the number of demons and their motivation. Thus the parentheses represent not merely the omitted verses but also the speaker's acceptance of the demonic as an explanation, the suspension of ordinary secular causality. Dostoevsky's presentation of Pushkin's poem paves the way hermeneutically not only for the biblical passage, which we must accept on faith, but also for the novel's own realization of the metaphor of possession.[76] This realization indicates Dostoevsky's rejection of the psychological novel's structures and the causal relations of secular historiography alike. It introduces a perspective of narrative totality that takes the form of allegory.[77]

The possession metaphor, first mentioned in a letter to Maikov in October 1870, takes different forms to penetrate all levels of the text (29:I:145). The novel can be seen as representing the antics of the possessed swine (both Stavrogin's multiple deluded doubles, Kirillov, Shatov, et al., and the townspeople as a whole) after the demons have left the body of the possessed man (Stavrogin). Yet on his deathbed Stepan Trofimovich claims the status of the formerly possessed man, and as the father of Peter and the teacher of Stavrogin, he certainly has justification for this view (10:499). Like the speaker of Pushkin's poem, the narrator of *Demons* participates in a descent into chaos that defies ordinary explanations. Demonic possession is suggested first by Stavrogin's strange antics; he leads Gaganov by the nose, literalizing the latter's metaphorical declaration that he "won't be led around by the nose." These semiotically unreadable acts, traceable only to episodes in the novel's veiled prehistory, prepare the way for the destruction wreaked upon the town by Petr Verkhovensky and his minions, destruction that ultimately leads to the deaths of the Lebyadkins, Liza, Shatov, Kirillov, and Stavrogin. These acts foreshadow a novelistic universe in which nothing will be clear or comprehensible. The possession metaphor marks the intrusion of an older, religious hermeneutic code into the secular world of the realist novel. It suggests a very different way of reading the world from that of the narrator, Stepan Verkhovensky, and their liberal friends.

Harriet Murav highlights the novel's profuse references to seventeenth-century Russian history, which indicate Dostoevsky's deliberate parallels between the political and social turmoil of his own time and the breakdown in legitimacy and internecine conflict of the Time of Troubles.[78] This network of references provides a connection to the plan for a historical epic that Dostoevsky had pitched to Maikov a few years earlier and demonstrates the partly concealed epic ambition within *Demons*. It broadens the novel's historical and generic horizons from the limits imposed by Russian Westernism to those of Christian epic.

As many scholars have noted, the generic aspirations of *Demons* reach back beyond the Petrine reforms into the realm of chronicle. The narrator, who is referred to repeatedly in the notebooks as the "Chronicler," introduces his narrative as a chronicle in the novel's very opening paragraph, yet is himself very far from understanding the significance of this designation. There is a strange disjuncture between the possession metaphor's claims to hermeneutic totality and the fragmentary nature of the narrator's perspective. His perspective is fragmentary both on a narrative level, because of his own ignorance of events and contexts, and on an ideological and metaphysical level, because of his political and spiritual affinities to the alienated Westernism of Stepan Verkhovensky.

Murav has convincingly argued that these generic and historical markings function as an invitation to figural interpretation of the kind that Erich Auerbach sees as characteristic of the way history is presented in patristic texts.[79] Events that do not seem to be connected on a secular historical level are shown to be connected on a sacred or symbolic level. Here not only history seems to be transfigured, but also the novel itself. One can extend Murav's point and argue that not only secular historical causality but also novelistic causality is here superseded by a divine intentionality that is shown to function outside human space and time. The apparently chaotic and senseless events taking place in the provincial town are ultimately incorporated into the sacred history prefigured by the biblical epigraph and finally understood by Stepan Trofimovich. The model of biographical development, of the developing personality, which still structures the plans of *Atheism* and *The Life of a Great Sinner*, has here been jettisoned. Instead it is the epigraph that structures the novel as a kind of biblical thematic motif. This is Dostoevsky's first attempt to replace the fragmentary perspective of the novel with hermeneutic totality, with an allegorical suprahistorical framework that can potentially overcome the novel's lapsarian condition.

The Christian historiography that had begun to shape Dostoevsky's worldview in the mid-1860s here becomes the hermeneutic engine of *De-*

mons as the crisis of Russian society is presented as part of a divine plan. The generic structure of *Demons* is predicated on a rejection of the model of development of the Russian bildungsroman as part of the legacy of that very Europeanized Russian culture that has shaped Stavrogin and his ilk. Premodern figural chronicle structures are grafted onto a nationalist messianic philosophy of history to create a symbolic indictment not merely of the ideology of post-Petrine Russian culture, but also of its forms.

And yet there are enough gaps in the novel's symbolic structure to suggest that Russian modernity cannot be so easily exorcised from *Demons*. The position of Shatov constitutes one key problem. One of the most significant shifts in emphasis from the notebooks for the final novel is the diminution of his place in the work's ideological system. From serving as the Prince's/Stavrogin's main interlocutor in the notebooks, he comes to represent little more than one of the stages of Stavrogin's ideological development. This helps to explain his death sentence in the novel, yet why does such a character give voice to the very messianic nationalism that Dostoevsky himself shared? In fact, Shatov reflects most directly the vision of Danilevsky, rather than of Dostoevsky, and Stavrogin's allegation that he "reduces God to an attribute of nationality" articulates precisely the accusation that Dostoevsky made against Danilevsky in the notebooks for *Demons*, in his later letters to Strakhov, and in *A Writer's Diary* (10:199). For Dostoevsky Orthodoxy was not just a mark of Russian nationality, a religion shaped according to the needs and values of the Russian nation, to which the Russian people had access and for which they were responsible for sharing with the world, but also a universal truth. Yet this alone does not seem like enough to account for his intellectual debts to Stavrogin. Shatov himself explains his failure to fully embrace the Russian faith through the fact that he too is a nobleman's son (10:202–3). His beliefs emerge out of the very Westernism that created Stravrogin; he is, like every other Russian of the intelligentsia and the nobility, including Dostoevsky himself, a creature of the Petrine legacy. The rich ideological and spiritual vein that Shatov leaves behind in the text points toward the ambiguities of Dostoevsky's treatment of Russian Westernism and in the direction of another model within which Westernism is conceptualized within the novel, one in which Russia's disintegrated post-Petrine history is not rejected outright but rather assimilated into a vision of the future.

This model enacts the biological metaphor taken from Cuvier and used by Danilevsky in *Russia and Europe* to explain the continuing influence of dead and dying civilizations on those which come after them. Just like decomposing matter in the natural world, argued Danilevsky, decaying civilizations disintegrate into the ground occupied by subsequent ones, providing a cultural residue that serves them as a kind of nutrient, contributing to an ongoing process of renewal as the fragments of the old are regenerated into the achievements of the new.[80] For Danilevsky this process was embodied by the Romano-German idea of liberty being extended further into the social realm by the Slavs through the uniquely Slavic institution of the commune after the decline and decay of the Romano-German civilization. Dostoevsky seems to be alluding to the model in the notebooks for *Demons* when the Prince declares that the part of Europe "which is dead or doomed to die will serve as ethnographic material for us" (11:167). In *Demons* the dream of European Westernism, in which Dostoevsky had found much good in his writings on the Petrine reforms in the early 1860s, is figured in the active elements of the cultural residue from Stavrogin's "productive phase," which persist in the novel long after his own deterioration. Shatov's ideas, flawed though they are, are part of this residue.

The transformation of the project of *Demons* is informed by historical events—the Paris Commune and its bloody suppression in May 1871—which are then assimilated into a millenarian vision of European and Russian history supported by Dostoevsky's reading of Danilevsky. Dostoevsky was writing *Demons* during the Franco-Prussian War and the creation and destruction of the Paris Commune. As mentioned above, his last letter written from Europe to Strakhov before the family's return to Russia in the summer of 1871 begins with an attack on the commune. For Dostoevsky the destruction of the commune marked the end of the nineteenth-century European radical dream of paradise on earth, a dream that began with the phalanstery, took in the revolutions and uprisings of 1848 and 1849, and ended with the burning of Paris by the communards (29:I:214). The commune is invoked in the notebooks in the plans for the speech that Stepan Verkhovensky makes at Yulia von Lembke's ball attacking the corruption of Russian modernity, which include a reference to the burning of the Tuileries as marking the abolition of history (11:287). It is worth remembering that the most powerful image that Stavrogin inherits from the collective past of the Westernized intelligentsia, his dream of a Golden Age, articulated in the expurgated chapter "At Tikhon's," is ultimately banished from the finished novel. But perhaps the Nechaev affair marked the end of another dream for Dostoevsky: the necessary renunciation of his own vision of the reconciliation of the representatives of Russian Westernism with the *narod. Demons* became the staging for a symbolic history of Russia's post-Petrine European path, with Stavrogin as the repository of these broken hopes, hopes that are present in the final novel only as prehistory, as the forgotten motivations for inexplicable acts that manifest themselves as evidence of demonic possession.

This final letter written to Strakhov from Europe also contains the clearest of Dostoevsky's warnings against the Russian novel. At first sight Dostoevsky seems in *Demons* to have heeded his own warnings. The "gentry literature" against which he inveighs, with its model of biographical development and its roots in post-Petrine alienation, seems at first to have been cast off in the notebooks for *Demons,* in the novel's prehistory, and in the exclusion of the chapter "At Tikhon's." It has seemingly been replaced by an insistent allegorical narrative that relies on a Christian messianic historiography and an appeal to the sacred. Yet ultimately the novel is saturated with the generic residue of the gentry novel of alienation, and with the cultural residue of Russian Westernism. Implicit in its Danilevskian model is a justification of the novel itself, a genre that is, after all, part of the heritage of Russian Westernism and will form part of the ongoing process of cultural renewal. This genre memory of the gentry novel of Tolstoy and Turgenev is not fully realized in *Demons,* but in *The Adolescent* it will prove to be a crucial model for conceiving of the complex relationship between the utopian future, the present in all its disorder, and the divided legacy of the post-Petrine past.

The contradictory generic impulses that we find in the projects that precede *Demons* continue to influence the plans for Dostoevsky's "novel-tragedy," exerting a persistent pressure on the work right up to its completion.[81] The finished novel is structured by two competing hermeneutic impulses: one claiming that unity and totality of perspective are possible, indeed necessary, inviting the novel to be read as national allegory, even as scripture, which we might call the epic impulse; and the other taking into account fragmentation, recognizing the ruptures of history, accommodating the past, and accepting modernity and the challenges and imperatives of individuality, which we might call the novelistic impulse. These contradictory impulses will persist and develop in Dostoevsky's next venture, his editorship of *The Citizen,* and their juxtaposition and troubled coexistence will shape his works for the rest of the decade.

Demons stands as a structural testament to Dostoevsky's problematic engagement with modernity and to his concerns over the Russian novel as a genre limited by the circumstances of its development within a particular historical moment and resistant to development within a new one. Genre becomes the contested space of engagement with past traditions.[82] The totalizing perspectives of Russian epic and of allegory clash with the fragmented and fragmentary perspective of Russian Westernism that finds its greatest representation in Stavrogin. The redemptive ending of Stepan Trofimovich's story coexists with the traumatic ending of Stavrogin's, giving rise to multiple readings of the novel itself. *Demons* testifies both to the total transformation that has taken place in Dostoevsky's thinking about Russian social and historical progress since his preaching of reconciliation in *Time* and to the beginnings of his search for a genre which would break with the old yet still reflect the generic and cultural memories of the age that had come to an end.

Chapter Two

Dostoevsky as Editor: Conflicting Visions of Russian Modernity in *The Citizen*

AT THE END OF 1872, following the end of the serialization of *Demons,* Dostoevsky returned to the world of journalism for the first time since the closure of his journal *Epoch* in 1865, becoming the editor of Prince Meshchersky's weekly journal *The Citizen.* He edited sixty-five issues of the journal, from January 1, 1873, to April 22, 1874.[1] Sitting down to plan one of his first articles for the publication, he wrote a set of notes detailing the problems he saw as besetting contemporary Russia: the social and spiritual collapse of the gentry and the cultural forms and values they represented; the moral degradation of the intelligentsia; the loss of any common beliefs and values; the loss of respect for institutions such as the gentry and the church; and, perhaps most importantly, the loss of a common understanding or language among the citizens of the country.[2] In his notebooks and in the journal itself, these problems are presented as a result of the modernizing Great Reforms of the 1860s. Where *Time* had begun optimistically in 1861, calling for the reconciliation of the intelligentsia and the *narod, The Citizen,* coming out a decade later, took the social breakdown caused by the modernization of the previous decade as a given. Its twofold task was to represent and respond to that collapse, to seek out the positive values among the social and intellectual debris of the reform era.

The notes conclude with Dostoevsky's announcement that the journal will present a picture of this breakdown of beliefs, values, and forms. The journal's mission will be not merely to inform its readers of the social and political events of the day but to build up a picture of the underlying currents that produced these events, to examine their connections with one another and with the historical evolution of the nation. It must identify the outlines of the emerging social forms of this new epoch in Russian history. It must find a way of counteracting the communication breakdown of the contemporary moment so as to communicate those outlines to its readership. It must provide society with an image of itself. This will involve restoring respect to the values of the past, even while recognizing the changed social conditions of the new historical moment. An editorial statement entitled "A Wish" that appears in the first issue of *The Citizen* published under Dostoevsky's editorship suggests how the journal might overcome the communication breakdown to which most other newspapers and journals had contributed.[3] Where other newspapers and journals concentrate on depicting Russian society's scandal and disorder, *The Citizen* will celebrate the positive values that still exist among those living in society's dark corners, honest workers who have devoted their lives to serving the public good. It concludes with the comment that "the story of a beautifully fulfilled life, a life of noble exploits—isn't this in our time of doubt and negation the best weapon against all our social ills?"

The fragmentary notes from the end of 1872 hint at *The Citizen*'s crucial role in staging Dostoevsky's multiple conceptions of Russian modernity. Because he took on the editorship at a moment when the journalistic world was focused on the ten-year anniversary of the Great Reforms, he was called upon to participate in the widespread public discussion about the reforms, about their place in Russian history and their significance for Russia's present and future. His editorial responsibilities required him to keep up with press coverage of contemporary social and political issues, which brought him into contact with many different voices and interpretations of the state of contemporary society. His participation in journalistic dialogues both engendered a sense of frustration over the way other journals contributed to the communication breakdown afflicting Russian society and redoubled his sense of the urgency of finding a way to bypass this breakdown, of bringing his readers an image of the new society of which they were part and of cementing their citizenship in this new society. Dostoevsky's 1873 notebooks reveal the underlying historical, social, and literary preoccupations that find expression in *The Citizen* and testify to the development of two competing historical interpretations of the meaning of the Great Reforms and their legacy. Alongside the representation of the 1870s as characterized by social fragmentation and hermeneutic collapse emerges a vision of the present as full of utopian possibility, as offering the possibility of widespread social and aesthetic renewal. Dostoevsky's involvement in *The Citizen* encouraged him to think about new ways of representing the present, new modes of literary and journalistic expression for the emerging historical moment. It precipitated his participation in several important literary polemics that helped to sharpen his thinking about genre, representation, and literary technique. The journal became a kind of creative laboratory within which Dostoevsky began to formulate his own varied literary responses to the challenges of modernization and to explore those of his contemporaries.[4] It served as the forum where he began to meditate on many of the formal problems that would preoccupy him until his death and would lead to the generic experimentation of his final three works.

Dostoevsky's own regular column, "A Writer's Diary," was the central space for the formal articulation of his response to Russian modernity, his attempt to create a literary image out of the "flux of contemporary life."[5] The column was the scene of the struggle between his recognition of the social and hermeneutic fragmentation that modernization had brought and his journalistic commitment to overcoming that fragmentation and presenting Russian society with a "new word," a vision of the possibility of national spiritual renewal. These two conceptions of Russian modernity and its literary and journalistic demands were manifested in Dostoevsky's two different approaches to the chaotic narratives of contemporary life told in the columns. On the one hand, "A Writer's Diary" allowed the narratives to speak for themselves, seeking out the connections between them to establish a picture of the inner workings of contemporary society. On the other, it trawled them for evidence of the utopian future that Dostoevsky saw as the end point of the prophetic vision unleashed by the liberation of the reforms. "A Writer's Diary" serves as a prologue for the struggle in the works of Dostoevsky's last decade between a grudging acceptance of Russian modernity and an emphatic denial of its social and spiritual fallout, between a recognition of the inescapability of the fragmentation of modern life and an insistence on the possibility of healing that fragmentation through the cultural and spiritual reintegration of Russian society.

THE CITIZEN AND THE GREAT REFORMS

In his memoirs, the conservative aristocrat Prince Meshchersky claimed to have founded *The Citizen* in 1872 in order to counteract what he perceived as the harmful effect on Russian society of the radical and liberal journals and newspapers that dominated the journalistic sphere.[6] Yet he chose as the journal's first editor the well-known liberal Gradovsky, who later worked as a feuilletonist at *The Voice.* When he inevitably grew dissatisfied with the resulting liberal editorial line, he courted Dostoevsky as Gradovsky's replacement. Meshchersky saw in Dostoevsky a conservative whose political beliefs dovetailed with his own, an impression compounded by the outrage generated in radical and liberal journalistic circles by the publication of *Demons,* with its fictional representation of the Nechaev affair and its perceived indictment of the liberal intelligentsia as the political progenitors of Nechaev and his followers.[7] As Dostoevsky testifies in a letter to Pogodin, he saw in Meshchersky's offer the possibility of fighting back against what he saw as the corrosive effects of socialism on Russian society, as well as the opportunity to engage with a wider readership on the topic of contemporary social and political developments (29:I:261). As Irene Zohrab points out, there seems also to have been a clear expectation on the part of both men that Dostoevsky would contribute to the journal some new long fictional works, even a novel.[8]

Dostoevsky took over the editorship of *The Citizen* in January 1873, in the midst of a turbulent press discussion of the historical, social, and cultural legacy of the Great Reforms that had been sparked by the ten-year anniversary of the emancipation, in 1871.[9] The following year, 1872, marked another landmark that was extensively discussed in the press: the two-hundred-year anniversary of the birth of Peter the Great.[10] This jubilee was the catalyst for many comparisons between the Petrine reforms and the Great Reforms and their respective importance in Russia's transition to a modern society.[11] Then 1873 began with the trial of Nechaev, who had been extradited from Switzerland, a political event that was covered extensively both by the newspapers and the journals and seemed to epitomize the "social disorder" into which Russian society appeared to have descended.[12] The same year saw the enactment of Count Dmitry Tolstoy's proposals for the reform of secondary education, which included the replacement of "modern" disciplines with instruction in classical languages and generated much journalistic discussion of the merits of a technical versus a classical education and of the wider social and political implications of this change in educational policy.[13] It also saw finalization of the military reform legislation which would mean that on January 1, 1874, Russia's serf army would be replaced by a citizen army, removing some of the nobility's last estate privileges. This legislation received extensive press coverage; it was perceived by many journalists as the herald of the social and political decline of the noble estate and the final stage in the reform process that would bring Russia into the modern age.[14] Meanwhile famine in Samara province drew press attention to the relatively new institutions of the *zemstva* and their problematic integration into the apparatus of central government.[15]

In October 1873 a note from *The Citizen*'s editor to subscribers for the following year announced that the journal would include

> a weekly commentary on life within Russia i.e., domestic affairs; also foreign and Petersburg news; continual reviews of Moscow life; the publication of novels, short stories, longer tales, dramatic works and poems; articles on all aspects of political and social life; critical and bibliographical reviews; contributions from correspondents, both domestic and foreign, and a continual record of anything especially characteristic, unusual, or surprising in the flux of contemporary life.[16]

Other than the final sentence, this description could fit almost any of the thick journals of the 1870s.

A supplementary note in the subsequent issue promised subscribers that the aim of the journal would be "to study, as far as possible, Russia and the country's domestic affairs, to research questions connected with the Church, questions relating to our day to day social and family life, the business of the zemstva and the peasants' communes and at the same time to follow constantly developments in our contemporary literature—such is our continuing task."[17] This invocation of old and new institutions reveals the journal's concerns with Russia's transitional historical state and its intention to deal with the legacy of the reforms.

The Citizen's owner, Prince Meshchersky, did not share its editorial commitment to representing social transition. He was a well-known opponent of the reforms, frequently alluded to in the press by his nickname "Prince Full-stop" because of his wish to bring the reforms to a full stop.[18] Nonetheless, *The Citizen* projected a more nuanced perspective on the reforms and their aftermath than is implied both by Meshchersky's own later statements and by the political opprobrium heaped on *The Citizen* by its opponents on the left. Contributors to the journal included both prominent defenders of the autocracy and the Church, such as Konstantin Pobedonostsev, and conservatives with a more Slavophile bent, such as the literary critic and philosopher Nikolai Strakhov, the historians Mikhail Pogodin and Sergey Soloviev, and the latter's son, the future philosopher Vladimir Soloviev.[19]

In the very first issue of *The Citizen* under Dostoevsky's editorship there appeared a brief review of A. A. Golovachev's *Ten Years of Reform: 1861–1871,* a book of articles on the reforms that had been originally published in 1872 in the liberal journal *The Messenger of Europe.*[20] In addition, the journal promised that this "extremely important" work would be reviewed at greater length in a subsequent issue, a promise that was kept in the fourth issue. Focusing on the financial, administrative, and judicial sectors, the book criticizes the piecemeal nature of the reforms.[21] It argues that the reforms were not systematic enough or sufficiently integrated with one another to fulfill the promise of an enlightened new Russia that had been heralded by the emancipation. Golovachev himself had actively advocated rapid enactment of the emancipation and increased gentry involvement in the emancipation movement and had grown more cynical of the gradualism of the reform process as it unfolded in other areas.[22] His book bemoans the public apathy toward the reform process, the sense of satiation with political progress that has developed in the informed public. He claims that far from advancing, Russian society has in fact regressed in this period of transition. In the postemancipation countryside, within the apparatus of reformed local government, remnants of the old systems remain, stymieing the new institutions and preventing the wholesale advance of society. The *Citizen* reviewer disagrees with Golovachev's opinion that society's transitional regression results from the piecemeal nature of the reforms. He argues that such a transitional phase is an inevitable part of top-down reform, in which the government must inevitably drag the people behind it on the path of progress. The old must necessarily coexist with the new:

> When such an enormous construction as our fatherland must be broken in order to be rebuilt, then one cannot expect that such a breakdown [*lomka*] will bring extraordinary order and complete harmony . . . Only with the creation of the new on the ruins of the old can complete harmony reign, but not if the old is just broken! The breaking or destruction of the old is, so to speak, an inconsistency and a contradiction.[23]

The reviewer also criticizes Golovachev's view that the reformers should have paid more attention to the overarching principles of reform. He disagrees that systematic reform, the integration of the parts into the whole, would have transformed society more convincingly. This book review reveals the outlines of *The Citizen*'s perspective on contemporary society, its sense of the reforms as having precipitated a process of social breakdown in Russia, of old forms and institutions having been fragmented rather than supplanted. The examination of this process of social breakdown was the central theme of the journal under Dostoevsky's editorship and the underlying topic of *A Writer's Diary*.

In December 1873 *The Citizen* weighed in on a topic that was to become a central preoccupation of the Russian press for the next few years: the nobility's future role in Russia's social and political life. If the emancipation had begun the process of divesting the nobility of their historical rights and privileges, then the military reforms proposed by the Russian war minister, Nikolai Miliutin, in 1873 were widely seen as the final phase of that divestment. The reforms proposed universal conscription in wartime, a restructuring of the military hierarchy to allow for a more meritocratic system of promotion, and a relinquishment of the special rights and exclusions that had been the privilege of the nobility since the time of Peter the Great.[24] The most significant advocate of the rights of the nobility and opponent of the reforms was General Rostislav Fadeev. In response to the proposed reforms he wrote a social treatise on the mystical role of the Russian nobility in Russian history, *Russian Society in the Present and the Future,* which was published in article form in *The Russian World* in 1874. Fadeev argued that every society requires the leadership of a "superior cultural group" that has evolved organically over time.[25] In Russia that role had been taken on by the nobility. He further claimed that the bureaucratic reforms of the 1860s had already begun to dissolve the nobility as an estate, and the current military reforms went further still, threatening the very future of the Russian state. The social and spiritual reconciliation of Russia depended on the restoration of the nobility as a ruling estate.

The Citizen jumped into the debate with a December 17 article titled "The Russian Nobility Before Military Reform."[26] The anonymous article was probably written by Meshchersky. The author begins by attacking those who see the military reforms primarily as leveling the differences between the social classes in the army and introducing a meritocratic system to determine promotion to the officer rank. He argues that the Russian nobility has always taken seriously its historical responsibilities, never putting personal profit before country, even in the days of serfdom. Despite their exclusion from the military service requirement, Russian nobles have always stepped up to defend their nation in its moment of need and successfully led their subordinates to victory. The victory of 1812 was a result of the joint efforts of the noble officers and the peasant privates and testifies to the strength of the spiritual unity of the nobility and the *narod.* He is profoundly skeptical of whether officers from the "classless" intelligentsia will be able to do any better.

Dostoevsky himself gave much thought to the question of the nobility's decline. His notebooks for 1873 and 1874 invoke Fadeev repeatedly, and the general's vision of the Russian nobility served as a wellspring for the ideas and character traits of Versilov in *The Adolescent.*[27] In the notebooks Dostoevsky cites the main theme of Fadeev's brochure as "the complete annihilation of the gentry and the gentry spirit through the squeezing out of their rights or the loss of land by small landowners, the very people in whom the old noble families and the spirit of the gentry found refuge, fat-bellied merchants who hoard petty estates will drift in and replace the gentry" (21:271). He agrees with the general on the important leadership role bequeathed to the nobility by Peter the Great, arguing, "The gentry and its preservation are essential, for its very establishment expressed a kind of vital bond between the tsar and the *narod,* and the gentry class had within itself all the possibilities for the further social development of the land. It preserved the spirit of this bond, which it understood as civil obligations" (21:265). He seems also to share Fadeev's sense of the danger posed to Russian autocracy by the gentry's dissolution: "Without a devoted class (the gentry), supreme power that rests only upon indifferent predators and lazy bureaucrats who have no political ideas, with the *narod* and upon those whose feelings have been corrupted by seminarians—will not last very long or go very far. The autocracy, in destroying the gentry, struck a blow against itself" (21:256–66). Yet Dostoevsky differs profoundly from Fadeev in the latter's view of the threat posed to Russia's spiritual and ethical well-being by the nobility's decline. According to Dostoevsky, Fadeev believes the gentry held the key to "the unification of spiritual forces . . . Without that unification, everything goes poof, all honest men are at a loss over what to do" (21:271). Dostoevsky did not believe that the nobility's decline would result in a social, spiritual, and cultural decline. In his view, the gentry had already compromised its own creativity and betrayed the *narod* through its adoption of Western cultural values.[28] He saw that unification of spiritual forces as a lost opportunity. It was rendered impossible by two hundred years in which the gentry had turned down the opportunity of building and developing a uniquely Russian culture in favor of adopting European cultural and social models.

Notwithstanding the accounts of social breakdown that appear throughout *The Citizen,* Dostoevsky's treatment of the reforms and their legacy in the columns and in his preparatory notebooks diverge significantly from the conservative criticism of Meshchersky and Pobedonostsev. Though he shared his conservative colleagues' nostalgia for a lost sense of unity and fears about the threat of social breakdown that the reforms had wrought, Dostoevsky still cherished a very different vision of how the reforms fitted into Russia's past and future. For Meshchersky and Fadeev, the harmony shattered by the reforms was identified with the Petrine and Catherinean periods of Russian history, the age of the nobility's cultural and social dominance, when its strength and prosperity guaranteed Russia's unity, stability, and progress.[29] In their view, transferring the burden of Russian state administration from the ancient noble estate to the new bureaucracy created by the reforms had led to political unrest, social instability, and cultural decline. Dostoevsky had by this point modified his views on the contribution of Peter the Great to Russian history, and like the Slavophiles of the 1840s, he had come to view the decisive moment of historical, social, and cultural rupture not in the modernizing projects of the Great Reforms, but in the Petrine adoption of Western institutions and modes of governance, which in his view had ripped apart the social tissue of ancient Russia, split the nobility off from the people, and prevented Russia from pursuing an independent role in history (21:266).[30] He believed that following the Petrine reforms the nobility had rejected the opportunity to unify Russia spiritually and culturally and had for the intervening two hundred years rejected every opportunity to build and develop a uniquely Russian culture in favor of the adoption of European cultural and social models. In the process they had betrayed the *narod,* the true guardians of Russia's contribution to world culture, the Orthodox idea.[31]

Dostoevsky had therefore come to see the disintegration of the postreform period as further fragmenting a society that had already been divided in two by the Petrine reforms. He located the epoch of lost unity in the moment before the Petrine reforms, seeing in premodern Russia a unique spiritual and cultural organic entity that could inspire a new path for the country in the postreform era.[32] As early as the announcement of *Time* in 1860, he laid the blame for the "great peasant problem, the solution of which has begun in our time," and its legacy, the rift between educated society and the *narod,* firmly at the feet of the Petrine reforms. In "A Writer's Diary" and in the notebooks for 1873 Dostoevsky repeatedly refers to the Great Reforms as representing the negation of the Petrine reforms, as marking the end of the "Petersburg epoch of Russian history."[33] While the intervening thirteen years had demonstrated social and political costs of transition which Dostoevsky could not have envisaged in 1860, he continued in 1873 to see in the reforms a potentially cathartic destructive force that had the potential to sweep away the false foundations of the Petrine era and pave the way for a new era of spiritual and cultural integration between the nobility and the *narod.* Splintering the false order of the "Petersburg period," an order characterized by the nobility's and intelligentsia's betrayal of the *narod,* the reforms had liberated the *narod,* opening the way for them to take the spiritual leadership which was, for Dostoevsky, their destiny. Thus the very splintering of the Petrine order represents the possibility of healing the social, cultural, and spiritual schism that had proved to be the legacy of the earlier modernizing efforts.

The notebooks reveal Dostoevsky's struggle to reconcile two mutually incompatible views of the reforms and two very different interpretations of contemporary Russia's social and political development. On the one hand he shares the view held by Meshchersky and his conservative colleagues that the reforms have paved the way for a widespread social and cultural collapse. They have led to the disintegration of the noble estate, the only social class capable of leading Russian society through the current impasse; to poverty and social breakdown in the countryside; to loss of faith among young people; and to the collapse of family life. On the other, by liberating the peasants from their economic oppression at the hands of the nobility, the reforms have created the conditions for the possibility of a process of national spiritual renewal that will be led by the *narod.* By reintegrating the two lost halves of Russian society under the same laws and institutions, they have created the potential for healing the Petrine rift. Only through the disintegration brought by the reforms can the reintegration of a transcendent future become possible. Yet at the same time the processes of disintegration themselves threaten the very course of national renewal which the emancipation has enabled as the *narod* are confronted with the social, spiritual, and political challenges of modernization and the intelligentsia become the victims of the hermeneutic dislocation that the reforms have wrought.

These two contradictory perspectives on the reforms and their significance for Russian society both find expression in Dostoevsky's notebooks for

1873; this private context provides them with unproblematic accommodation. However, in "A Writer's Diary" their mutual antagonism leads to a rich and complex dialogue, out of which will emerge two different creative visions that will prove central to his literary production for the remainder of his life.

REPRESENTING THE "FLUX OF LIFE" IN "A WRITER'S DIARY"

The 1873 incarnation of "A Writer's Diary" comprises sixteen columns published in *The Citizen.*[34] These columns address many different topics, from Dostoevsky's acquaintance with such luminaries of the Russian intelligentsia as Belinsky, Herzen, Nekrasov, and Chernyshevsky to the conditions in the Russian countryside after emancipation, from the frequent acquittals granted by Russian juries following the judicial reforms of the 1860s to the nature of Nikolai Leskov's fictional representation of the Russian clergy in his story "The Sealed Angel." They are written in a variety of different modes, from the biographical to the feuilletonistic, from the fictional to the analytical and the polemical, and incorporate the generic realms of literary and art criticism, historical and historiographical analysis, reflections on Dostoevsky's own previous literary works, and commentary on contemporary journalism and on Russian and European social and political affairs.

"A Writer's Diary" originates in a project Dostoevsky first conceived in the mid-1860s and articulated more fully in *Demons* as Liza Tushina's plan for an annual publication that would select all the essential events taking place in a particular year to produce "a picture of the spiritual, moral, inner Russian life of a whole year" (10:104).[35] The project, as Liza describes it, would require her to read through all the newspapers of a particular time period and choose the news items that seemed most typical, the events and occurrences that seemed to carry within them the fundamental historical dynamic of the age. Whereas Liza's plan merely entails the compilation of these items, Dostoevsky's own project included commentary on the items and analysis of the reasons behind his choice and their significance. Dostoevsky proposed to distill the essence of the social and political forms that characterized this new era. In the crimes and misdemeanors, the wars and famines, the suicides and diplomacy reported in the daily newspapers, he would trace the underlying movements of a society in flux. This plan finds its fullest realization in the 1876–77 monojournal incarnation of *A Writer's Diary,* but its basic aim, the gathering of heterogeneous material to create an image of the "inner life" of Russian society, is central to the columns in *The Citizen.*

Scholars differ on the relationship of the 1873 columns to the 1876–77 monojournal. Igor Volgin points out that the vast majority of critics did not make any connection between the 1873–74 columns and the 1876–77 monojournal.[36] Viktor Vinogradov sees in Dostoevsky's editorship of *The Citizen* the potential realization of a grand literary plan, a format created by Dostoevsky himself, in which the "Diary" forms part of the journal's poetic whole.[37] Though this theory is attractive and conceivable in view of Dostoevsky's own revolutionary approach to literary genre, the fact remains that Dostoevsky chose to include materials under the rubric "A Writer's Diary," while other materials were included elsewhere in the journal, either in his other series of columns, "Foreign Affairs," or as stand-alone articles that often lacked attribution. Zohrab examines the connections between the themes that emerge in the "Diary" columns and the rest of the journal, arguing that the playful, feuilletonistic tone of the columns served as a bridge to draw the reader into the rest of the journal.[38] Vladimir Tunimanov treats the 1873–74 "Diary" as a series of feuilletons that happen to bear the same name as the monojournal but actually constitute a different work.[39] Pavel Fokin sees Dostoevsky's editorship of the journal as indicating that his attitude toward the columns was fundamentally different from his attitude toward the monojournal; the poetics of the *Diary* can be seen only in the 1876–77 version.[40] Gary Saul Morson makes the point that the end of the 1877 *Diary* refers to the second year of its publication, thus excluding the columns in *The Citizen*.[41] As will become clear from what follows, I believe that while the two projects emerge out of a single generic vision, they differ somewhat in their artistic and historical contexts and therefore merit separate treatment in any close analysis of Dostoevsky's creative trajectory.

The 1873 columns centered on the reforms and their social aftershocks. This brought a sense of urgency to the project of creating a picture of Russian society's inner life. As Anna Grigorievna's reminiscences attest, the desire to finally carry out the project of "A Writer's Diary" was one of Dostoevsky's main reasons for accepting the editorship of *The Citizen*.[42] The columns return again and again to the question of the reforms, their historical meaning, and their social significance. In the second column, "Old People," Dostoevsky reflects on the Petrine cultural legacy and the Russian intelligentsia's split from the people. He finds its embodiment in the alienated intellectuals Herzen and Belinsky (21:8–12). In "Dreams and Musings" he connects this rupture between the intelligentsia and the people to the problem of social breakdown in the countryside following the emancipation and the failure of the intelligentsia and upper classes to assuage the people's sufferings (21:91–96). In "Apropos of a New Play" and "Little Pictures," he deals with the dark reality of postemancipation peasant life, examining such issues as poverty, immigration to the cities, alcoholism, and the breakdown of the family. And in "One of Today's Falsehoods," he examines the radicalization of young people and the source of Nechaevism, arguing that the idealism of Russia's youth has been thwarted by the influence of European socialist ideas and the alienation of the educated class from their native soil (21:125–36).

"A Writer's Diary" locates itself within the communication breakdown that has afflicted Russian public life following the social revolution brought by the reforms. The introduction tackles head-on the problem of the breakdown and the ways in which Dostoevsky will respond to it (21:5–8). The column begins with an analysis of how the traditional modes of interaction have turned in on themselves. Common phrases such as "I don't understand a thing" have come to mean the opposite of their conventional definition, columnists have begun to be judged on the basis of the inches they fill, and ready-made ideas are bought and sold by the press (21:6–7). Such is the situation within which *The Citizen* must communicate with its readership. Meditating on his editorship, Dostoevsky recalls the wedding of the Chinese emperor, which is covered in the *Moscow News* on the very same day. He imagines publishing *The Citizen* in China, with all the attendant ceremony implied by a thousand years of tradition, and speculates that this would be a far easier task there than it is in Russia, where the norms of communication are currently in flux, where ignorance is seemingly considered a virtue, but where, paradoxically, each is secretly convinced of his or her own superior understanding of the world.

The introduction both explains and embodies the principles of communication that will form the basis of Dostoevsky's journalistic project. Against the radicals' "ready-made ideas," he sets the principle of *zadumchivost'* or sober thought, repeating the noun *zadumchivost'* and its variants six times in just two paragraphs (21:7). The word implies a state of being long in thought, being weighed down by thought. This is a particular kind of thought, one that is necessary in an age where ready-made ideas abound and contribute to the "same old disorder." Order is currently possible only in China, with its traditions. The only path open to Russia, argues Dostoevsky, is a thousand years of such thought. The repetition of the verb *zadumyvat'sia* almost imperceptibly introduces one of the column's main aims and principles: to find a new way of thinking that can challenge the ready-made ideas with which the intelligentsia is intoxicated.

This principle of sober thought structures the introduction and by extension the "Diary" itself, bringing together such diverse and heterogeneous material as a fable about a pig, his own reminiscence of Herzen, and a conversation between Herzen and Belinsky. Dostoevsky's declaration that the subject of the "Diary" will include "everything that strikes me and sets me to thinking [*zadumyvatsia*]" explains the variety of different material (21:7). These anecdotes, personal reminiscences, historical accounts, and news items are examined as clues to the multifaceted nature of the Russian present. Unlike the traditional newspaper, which, as Walter Benjamin points out, contributes to the fragmentation of modernity by isolating the phenomena it reports, concealing the connections between the news items it presents, and splitting information off from experience, the "Diary" works against that fragmentation by seeking out connections between its parts.[43] The reader is invited to participate as the Diarist observes the phenomena of contemporary life, bringing his or her experience to the fragmentary narratives that trigger Dostoevsky's reflections.

The "Diary's" relationship to its heterogeneous narratives emerges clearly in the column "Environment," in which Dostoevsky examines the strange fact that the jury trials introduced with the 1860s judicial reforms seem to be generating a large number of acquittals. He remarks, "The universality of this tendency in itself presents a most curious topic for reflection and leads one to diverse and sometimes even strange surmises" (21:13). He considers various lines of reasoning for these acquittals: one newspaper article interprets them as the jurors' arbitrary exercise of their own power as citizens, while another theory suggests that an indigenous Russian compassion is the cause. Dostoevsky creates a dialogue about the acquittals, taking on different voices to represent a range of perspectives. One voice points out that civil rights such as trial by jury excessively burden the Russian people. Another points to the Russian people's humility, suggesting that such acquittals are linked to their form of Christianity. Dostoevsky connects the acquittals with the fashionable radical doctrine of "environment" as a mitigating circumstance, yet admits that such a doctrine is unlikely to have swayed the peasants. In fact, he points out, the peasants' habit of calling criminals "unfortunates" suggests another possible cause: the fundamental incompatibility of the religious worldview of the peasants, with their conception of sin, compassion, expiation, and redemption, and the enlightened reason of the new courts, with their conception of a society of citizens under the rule of law, dealing with the problems of crime and punishment. Perhaps, Dostoevsky suggests, pity could account for the acquittals. Yet his conclusions are far from firm: "At least pity provides some sort of explanation; at least it leads you out of the darkness and without it we comprehend nothing and see only gloomy blackness inhabited by some madmen" (21:20).

Each possible reason for the acquittals must be analyzed and new examples brought forth; the process of reflection requires that the disparate fragmentary narratives be brought together before any general observations can be made. Dostoevsky brings up the press reports of two prominent acquittals, the first concerning a peasant who beat his wife for many years until she hanged herself, the second a peasant mother who burned her child's hand with a samovar to stop it from crying (21:20–22). Stories such as these have entered the public consciousness for the first time through new institutions such as the press and the courts. They illustrate the diversity of the models of social life that the reforms have uncovered. When Dostoevsky attempts to analyze them, they seem to collapse into fragments before he can put them together to form a lucid picture of contemporary Russian life. He interrogates the stories themselves, imagining the suffering of the beaten wife and the psychological steps that might have led to her suicide and the reasoning of the jurors who offered clemency to the woman who burned her own child. But extrapolating any clearer meaning out of these incidents proves increasingly difficult, even impossible. The narratives themselves multiply, giving rise to a present that is continually expanding and becoming forever more complex and uncertain as new phenomena enter the Diarist's purview. The scope and complexity of this all-pervasive present prevent access to any kind of future perspective. The only certainty is that "long ago we entered into a period of complete uncertainty" (21:41).

Alongside this presentation of news stories as evidence of an ever-fragmenting present, Dostoevsky begins to read them as signs of national salvation. He presents them not as examples of modernity's infinite diversity, but as the embryonic beginnings of a divinely preordained narrative leading to a transfigured future society. This approach emerges out of a reading of the reforms and their legacy that views them as opportunities for escape from the Petrine legacy. In "A Troubled Countenance," Dostoevsky recognizes the emancipation as the catalyst for Russia's spiritual regeneration. Freed from bondage, the newly emancipated serfs will be able to take on their divinely determined role as the guardians of Russia's spiritual renewal: "Since the Emancipation of February 19, 1861, the light of a new life has been shining on [the Russian peasant]." That new life, Dostoevsky explains, is "the principal, preordained mission of the Russian people, within the destiny of humanity as a whole" (21:58). It is the Russian people's mission "to preserve within itself this divine image of Christ in all its purity, and when the time comes, to reveal this image to a world that has lost its way" (21:59). This millenarian vision, which inscribes the Great Reforms into a mythical account of Russian history, achieves its fullest expression in the monojournal of 1876 and 1877 in articles such as "The Utopian Conception of History," where Dostoevsky envisions the Petrine reforms as a symbolic analogue to the biblical Fall, a moment of radical rupture, when Russia's subsequent development was transformed by Peter's decision to impose Western political and social norms and practices (23:46–50). According to Dostoevsky's vision, this Fall was manifested in the split between the nobility and the *narod*. Destroying the Petrine order, the Great Reforms opened up the possibility for Russian society to overcome its fallen state and eventually achieve salvation. They thus hold the promise to heal the two-hundred-year social and spiritual schism and to regenerate and redeem society. In the 1873 incarnation of "A Writer's Diary," this prophetic narrative initially emerges as Dostoevsky interrogates news items for signs of social and spiritual regeneration. As a journalist he is always on the lookout for signs of the coming new order.

These two alternative ways of reading and interpreting contemporary phenomena frequently coexist within the columns of "A Writer's Diary." A clear example can be found in the column "Vlas," which is structured around a story Dostoevsky claims to have heard from a monastery elder, one peasant's confession of his participation in a contest with another to commit the most shocking act (21:31–41). The other peasant proposes that he should shoot the Eucharist. On the point of committing sacrilege, the peasant has a vision of Christ on the cross, falls into a dead faint, and, sure of his own damnation, comes to the elder to confess. Dostoevsky uses this story both to meditate on the Russian people's capacity for redemption and to explore the fictional mode as he imagines the peasants' psychological motivations.

Any straightforward interpretation of "Vlas" as a simple illustration of the salvific power of the *narod* is complicated and destabilized by the column that precedes it. In "Something Personal," Dostoevsky relates the story of how a certain editor (Nekrasov) informs him that his journal has published a critical review of *Crime and Punishment* because of a satirical attack Dostoevsky was supposed to have made on Chernyshevsky in his short story "The Crocodile" (21:23–31). Bemoaning this incident, Dostoevsky uses it to explore the problem of misreadings and imagined allegories in general. Allegory, he argues, is in the eye of the beholder, and he offers allegorical interpretations of a series of famous literary works and events. Works are read according to their readers' social and political views, views that have formed as a result of a complex series of events, experiences, and emotions, both personal and political. The unfortunate writer can hardly be held responsible for interpretations conditioned by such a complex concatenation of circumstances. Indeed, his own previous column, "Environment," has been misinterpreted as a call for the abolition of the jury system. After suggesting that such "misreadings" are generally restricted to the radicals ("This was the voice of a man who was most impartial and who stood outside any parties and allegories"), Dostoevsky falls into a utopian meditation: "Even if this national decadence . . . were to cause some sort of real, indisputable calamity among the People, some sort of monumental collapse, some great disaster—even then they would save themselves, themselves and us as well, as they have already done more than once; their whole history can testify to that. That is my idea" (21:30). This expression of the salvific power of the Russian people would seem at first sight to provide "Vlas" with an unambiguously utopian context. However, "Something Personal" ends with the ambivalent lines, "How many different ways can one's words be interpreted. You might even stumble on an allegory here" (21:31). By using the same word, "allegory," that he had used for the misreading of "Crocodile" by the radicals, he immediately undermines the allegorical power of the story he is about to relate.

At first "Vlas" itself seems to belie this ambiguous context. Dostoevsky opens the meditation with an image of the Russian people's thirst for redemption taken from Nekrasov's poem "Vlas," in which a reprobate peasant has a vision of hell that leads him to embark on a lifelong path of repentance (21:31). He wonders, with more than a little irony, if the power and grandeur of the *narod's* faith suffice to awe even this atheistic liberal, whose poetry normally expresses the contempt of the radical for whom love for the universal man has replaced love for the individual. He remembers the similar story of the peasants' contest. He begins with a utopian explanation, couched in the insistent tone of future perfectives: "I still hold that these very same Vlases, repentant and unrepentant, will say [*skazhut*] the last word; they will say it and will show [*ykazhut*] us a new path and a new way out of those apparently insoluble tangles we find ourselves in" (21:34). A close analysis of this sentence reveals typical linguistic features of the utopian voice: a tendency to identify disparate individuals as one and the same, whether repentant or unrepentant; the idea that there is such a thing as the last word; the use of the future perfective to imply inevitability; and the idea of a single direct path that can lead out of the chaos. Such prophetic certainty would at first sight seem to corroborate the idea of "Vlas" as a straightforward allegory. The Diarist then reiterates and extends this utopian reading by discussing the psychological aspect of the case: in the two Vlases of the anecdote, he sees the Russian people in their entirety. Once he has shifted to the allegorical utopian plane, Dostoevsky resorts to maxims and generalizations couched either in the insistent authority of future perfectives or the matter-of-fact, a priori tone of the present tense (21:35–36).

After Dostoevsky's generalizations on the subject of national attributes, it would seem as though the matter was settled, with no room for doubt. But then he opens up the interpretation again by questioning the motivation behind the peasants' contest: "Who provided the impulse to set both these peasant lads to disputing which could commit the most brazen sin? What were the reasons for such a contest? These things remain a mystery, but there can be no doubt that both lads suffered—one by accepting the challenge, the other by offering it" (21:37). In his utopian tone Dostoevsky asks questions only to provide ready-made stock answers; here they signal a return to an open sense of the world, for he acknowledges that the answers "remain a mystery"—ready material then, for the speculations of a fiction writer. He begins to surmise, to conjecture: perhaps there was a concealed enmity between the two peasants that had been there since their earliest childhood? His speculations do not claim the status of truth, however; through the use of disclaimers such as "either . . . or" and "probably" he is able to retain a sense of time as open. As he follows one path into his own imagined scenario, he is careful to emphasize that it is only one of many possible readings. As the realist voice supersedes the utopian voice, the future perfectives and present-tense verbs are replaced by the open-endedness of the conditional tense, suggesting the unrealized potential of many possible paths and the multiple possibilities suggested by the word "perhaps." He speculates that "they could have found some other deed—something very shocking—for their contest: a robbery, a murder, open rebellion against some powerful person," but then stops short. "But no. The tempter thinks the most dreadful acts are too ordinary. He invents some unthinkable sin, unprecedented and inconceivable, and his choice reveals the People's whole outlook on life" (21:37). The apparent intransigence of the "no" seems to hold within it the assumption of the truth of the particular path taken, and Dostoevsky does indeed seem to shift back to a claim of allegorical significance for the choice of the crime. However, the utopian voice dominates only for a minute. Dostoevsky imagines the horror rising up in the peasant's soul at the sinister beauty and appeal of his act. But although his use of past perfectives implies a sense of closed time, he opens it up by triggers of the conditional, such as "it could have been [*mozhno bylo*]," and by the repetition of "perhaps" and "is it possible [*razumeetsia*]," all of which subvert the allegory's single insistent path.

Through the open sense of time and presentation of multiple narrative scenarios that Morson has called "sideshadowing," Dostoevsky attempts to show the peasant's moral freedom.[44] There were any number of moments when he could have drawn back from the action. But does the idea of this openness, freedom, agency, not violate the universal significance of this emblematic representation of the *narod*'s salvific potentiality? The allegorical vision is most fundamentally undermined at the point where Dostoevsky turns the tables and asks us to suppose that really the other peasant was a homegrown atheist, a village Mephistopheles. If so, then for every Vlas there is a Mephistopheles, gleefully devoid of remorse. The repentance Dostoevsky has claimed as central to the spiritual mission of the Russian people is only one side of the coin.

The anecdote of the contest becomes the focal point for the struggle between the "Diary"'s competing worldviews. On the one hand, Dostoevsky the utopian sees it as proof of the coming national salvation, the present as already defined by the future, already circumscribed by its role in the enactment of a grand design. He sees the contest as evidence of the *narod*'s unquenchable Orthodox faith, which will redeem the sins of Russian society. On the other hand, Dostoevsky the psychological realist presents it as a unique phenomenon, able to "speak" only for itself, a source of endless imagined scenarios, proof of nothing more than the endless narrative possibilities open to the creative mind. This narratological cross-fertilization fleshes out the original narrative, rooting it in a fictional world, but also projects onto it a particular worldview, a sense of the present as open-ended, unknowable, leading to an infinite number of possible futures. The anecdote becomes enmeshed within a web of possible narratives that paradoxically make it more real to the reader, even while removing it from the possibility of the universal, transcendent signification that Dostoevsky has claimed for it. The utopian voice is thus undermined, but that voice itself undermines the pessimism of the Meshcherskian conservative view, which sees the present as consisting entirely of disorder.

"Vlas" is succeeded by two columns that, taken together, constitute both the darkest vision of contemporary Russian reality and the most determined effort to represent social and hermeneutic disintegration in "A Writer's Diary": "Bobok" and "A Half-Letter from a Certain Person" (21:41–54, 60–68). Both works are fictional framed narratives consisting of an editor's introduction and a text written by the same "certain person," named in "Bobok" as Ivan Ivanovich. The "certain person" is presented as a journalist who has been contributing articles to *The Citizen,* leading both works into a complex and ambiguous structural relation to the column and to the journal itself.[45] "Bobok" is a confessional narrative in which Ivan Ivanovich relates how he witnessed a conversation among a group of corpses in a cemetery. The "Half-Letter" is presented as an extract from a letter sent by the "certain person" to the editor after *The Citizen* has failed to print the articles he has been submitting. Both works are fragmentary, the literary articulations of the vision of a society without forms found in the December 1872 notebook entry. Both express Dostoevsky's deepest anxieties about his failure to communicate with the public in *The Citizen* and "A Writer's Diary."

Bakhtin considers "Bobok" Dostoevsky's defining work, a work of Menippean satire that expresses its author's profoundest concern over the impossibility of life without belief in immortality, the idea that "contemporary dead men are as sterile seed, cast on the ground, but capable neither of dying . . . nor of being renewed."[46] Robert Louis Jackson sees it as a grotesque drama of disintegration that "explores the darkening world of a despiritualized reality."[47] Ilya Vinitsky reads the work as a "programmatic mystery play" of Swedenborgian ideas in which Dostoevsky uses provocative irony and the fantastic to explore the complexities of the soul in a positivist and realist age.[48] To the rich interpretations of these critics I would add a consideration of the work's immediate context, its place within "A Writer's Diary" and within *The Citizen.* "Bobok" transposes into the fictional mode the journal's representation of the social and spiritual disorder of postreform Russia. Just as Ivan Ivanovich functions as Dostoevsky's own parodic double, so his nightmare vision of the cemetery's sepulchral society serves as a fictional recapitulation of *The*

Citizen's vision of the social and spiritual wreckage of contemporary society. The disembodied voices Ivan Ivanovich hears at the graveyard bring to mind the voices Dostoevsky himself hears in "Environment" and, by extension, the myriad overheard conversations that can be found throughout "A Writer's Diary." The cacophony of the dead parodically invokes the chaotic heteroglossia of the columns themselves. The corpses' "liberation" from all moral and spiritual values reflects Dostoevsky's own sense that "the foundations of society are cracking under the pressure of the revolution brought by the reforms . . . The borderlines of good and evil have disappeared and become obliterated" (16:7). The corpses celebrate their arrival into a "new order," but the social hierarchies among them are clear, with tensions erupting between a baron, several bureaucrats, a shopkeeper, and a general, tensions that seem to replay the social frictions of postreform Russia. The philosopher Platon Nikolaevich's explanation that the corpses are experiencing "a continuation of life through inertia" reveals their status as figures representing postreform Russia's ambiguous historical moment, its transitional state between the old world of the Petrine order and the new world still to come. "Bobok" serves as Dostoevsky's own nightmare vision of the Petrine order's sepulchral afterlife in the postreform era, its continuing existence despite its supposed destruction by the Great Reforms themselves.

Yet sandwiched as it is between "Vlas" and "A Troubled Countenance," both of which address the problem of representing the regenerative faith of the Russian people, "Bobok" also functions as a warning of the dangers of perceiving nothing beyond that disorder, the perils of disregarding the hidden redemptive possibilities that are often ignored by the journalistic world, even by *The Citizen* itself. Dostoevsky warns not only the readership of "A Writer's Diary," but himself as well; he must not get lost in Meshcherskian pessimism when confronting Russian society. The sepulchral nightmare of "Bobok" represents only one side of the fragmented present. It is virtually devoid of any reference to that transcendent future which for Dostoevsky represents the other side of contemporary reality. The only signs of hope within "Bobok" are the simple shopkeeper's continuing religious belief and the general's plaintive rejoinder to Baron Klinevich that when serving his emperor he was "part of the whole" (21:53). The horrified Ivan Ivanovich does not pick up on these signs, but they lead into the textual realm of the "Diary" itself and into the ambiguously redemptive visions of its subsequent columns.

CHALLENGING FRAGMENTATION

As 1873 wore on, "A Writer's Diary" began to address more explicitly the question of how artists and writers should respond to the social and spiritual turmoil of the transitional period. Its competing narratives of Russian modernity suggested different solutions to the problem of how to represent a world in perpetual motion. "Bobok" and "A Half-Letter from a Certain Person" represent social breakdown through formal fragmentation, but "A Troubled Countenance," "Apropos of the Exhibition," "An Impersonator," and "Little Pictures" challenge that fragmentation and demonstrate to the readers of "A Writer's Diary" that firm social and spiritual anchors could be discerned in the contemporary chaos. In these later columns Dostoevsky advocates for the regeneration of secular realist representation with aesthetic and spiritual values and traditions taken from Orthodoxy. These columns explore the possibilities of a new mode of artistic representation that could express Dostoevsky's sense of a utopian future made possible by the chaos of the Great Reforms and allow him to better convey this vision to the readers of *The Citizen.* Such a mode of representation is sustained by the dream of reintegrating the fragments of Russian literature and art shattered and dispersed by the pressures of modernization and of returning to the perfect forms of the pre-Petrine, pre-Nikonian era.[49] Of course Dostoevsky himself neither truly wished for a return to these forms nor believed it to be possible, and he was also aware that such forms were not really perfect, but he needed a repository for his free-floating nostalgia for a time before fragmentation. The utopian promise of a regenerating mode of representation is always undercut by Dostoevsky's sense of fidelity to the demands of the fractured present: "Vlas" is followed by "Bobok," "A Troubled Countenance" is followed by "A Half-Letter," and the pleas for the representation of the ideal in "Apropos of the Exhibition" and "An Impersonator" are followed by Dostoevsky's sympathy for the darkly naturalistic dramatic universe of the playwright Kishensky in "Apropos of a New Play" and his depiction of the disorder of modern urban life in "Little Pictures."

In "Apropos of the Exhibition," Dostoevsky uses a discussion of the Russian genre paintings at the Vienna International Exhibition to question the place of the ideal in representations of the contemporary moment. He admires genre painters such as Ilya Repin and Vladimir Makovsky for their fidelity to the depiction of that same all-pervasive presentness that is the main subject of "A Writer's Diary," as well as their embrace of humble, everyday subjects (21:68–77). But he criticizes their rejection of the ideal, claiming that "the ideal is also reality, after all, and just as legitimate as immediate reality" (21:75–76). As Jackson has observed, the ideal plays a multivalent role in Dostoevsky's artistic philosophy, relating to the realms both of form and of content.[50] It sometimes refers to the form-shaping power of aesthetic vision, the artistic containment of chaotic reality; it sometimes suggests the artist's way of looking, a way of sifting through the extraneous masses of phenomena to get to the essence, the truth beneath. At other times it suggests the defining image, the moment, caught by the artist, when a person looks most like herself. It can be a synonym for *poema,* which he understands as the essence or core of the artistic text, and for *idea,* which he understands as that which organizes poetic form.[51]

In "A Writer's Diary" the ideal is conceived in much more specific terms. In "A Troubled Countenance" Dostoevsky asks, "Has not Orthodoxy alone preserved the divine image of Christ in all its purity? And perhaps the principal, preordained mission of the Russian People, within the destiny of humanity as a whole, is simply to preserve within it this divine image of Christ in all its purity, and when the time comes, to reveal this image to a world that has lost its way!" (21:59). The image of Christ is the aesthetic and spiritual expression of the regenerating faith of the Russian people, which will heal the Petrine rift and the social and moral disintegration of the postreform period.[52] Just as Orthodox Christianity will serve as the conduit for the resurrection of both Russian society and the whole world, so the image of Christ expresses an ideal form that could reinvigorate the Russian literary tradition if Russian writers and artists take as their subjects the regenerating faith of the Russian people rather than the fragmentation of modern life.

It is no accident that Dostoevsky's aesthetic ideal takes the form of a visual rather than a literary image. The image of Christ constitutes an ideal form partly because it is free from the pressures of temporality or the pitfalls of language. It is always easier for Dostoevsky to envisage the possibility of ideal form in the plastic arts, where the problem of temporality does not arise directly. If "A Writer's Diary" attests to Dostoevsky's confidence in the signifying power of Christ's image, it also testifies to his difficulties in reconciling the concept of ideal form as epitomized in the visual image of Christ with the genre of the newspaper column. The columns express the conflict between a philosophy of representation governed by a commitment to the fierce urgency of the contemporary moment and one governed by the atemporal concept of ideal form. In "Apropos of the Exhibition," his call for a return to the ideal falters as it encounters the problem of temporality. He observes how the Russian artists' fear of idealization manifests itself in their reluctance to tackle historical subjects, since they recognize that the past can be depicted in art only as unitary, completed, and closed, and therefore lends itself more to seamless idealized representation than the present, in all its open-endedness.[53] Though he yearns for what he sees as the integrated world before the Fall of the Petrine reforms—its unified faith and its atemporal forms, epitomized by the image of Christ in medieval icons—he cannot evade the pull of temporality, the temptation of narration.

As the author of "A Writer's Diary," Dostoevsky is concerned with the rich store of narrative possibilities opened up by the phenomena of the postreform period but is also committed to attempting to find and capture the defining ideal image of the present moment and recognize in it the promise of the future. If the ideal seamless perfection of Christ's image left nothing to be narrated, the same could not be said of the Russian people's efforts at emulating Christ and the shortcomings of those efforts. Making the ideal of Christ narratable meant bringing it down to earth and embedding it in the soil of 1870s Russia, analyzing its reflections in the Orthodox Christian worldview of the Russian peasants and the challenges posed to their faith by a modernizing world. Dostoevsky's earlier efforts at creating the novelistic image of a perfectly beautiful man in *The Idiot* had focused on the gap between the Christ-like perfection of Myshkin and the fallen world that he occupies; in "A Writer's Diary" he argued for the narrative possibilities of the gap between the real and the ideal in contemporary Russian life. As we have seen in "Vlas," when these images enter the richly contradictory world of the columns and of *The Citizen* they become embedded in a web of conflicting readings, informed by opposed interpretations of phenomena as either proofs of the infinite, open-ended, unknowable nature of contemporary life and its narrative possibilities or signs of the imminent salvation of the world.

Despite (or perhaps because of) Dostoevsky's difficulties in reconciling his utopian vision of the present with his own realist perspective, he was quick to criticize his literary contemporaries for their refusal to acknowledge and represent the Russian people's faith in their works. Aware of the dangers of himself succumbing to the power of disintegration, he was continually sensible to its traces in the works of others. In "A Troubled Countenance" and "An Impersonator," Dostoevsky plunges into a journalistic dispute with his literary contemporary Leskov over the question of how the Russian people's religious worldview might be represented in literary form (21:54–60, 91–96). In "A Troubled Countenance," which, significantly, is located between the two fragmentary texts of "Bobok" and "A Half-Letter from a Certain Person" and which sets itself strenuously against their disintegrating visions, Dostoevsky uses a reading of Leskov's short story "The Sealed Angel" to argue for the accommodation of the concept of the miraculous in contemporary realism.[54] The story, narrated by a former Old Believer, depicts the conversion to Orthodoxy of a whole cartel of Old Believers after they have witnessed what they believe to be a miracle. A bureaucrat who wishes to bribe the dissenters confiscates the icon they worship and places a wax seal over the face of the angel it depicts. The dissenters commission a copy to be made of the icon so that the original can be unsealed. As they are substituting the copy for the sealed icon, the seal disappears. This miraculous occurrence leads to their conversion to Orthodoxy. Dostoevsky is complimentary about Leskov's literary style and notes that the conversation on the subject of icon painting between the Old Believers and the Englishman who helps them is the strongest part of the tale. However, he harshly criticizes Leskov for the story's ending. He objects to the revelation that the "miracle" which provokes the conversion is nothing more than a sleight of hand: the seal turns out to have been attached by a piece of paper to the mounting of the icon. The dissenters do not retract their conversion despite the explanation of the "miracle." Dostoevsky observes, "It seems he got frightened of being accused of favoring superstitions, so he made haste to demystify the miracle" (21:55). For Dostoevsky this "demystification" lacks verisimilitude: those instilled in the deep convictions of the Old Believer tradition would be unlikely, he argues, either to meekly accept the actions of the corrupt bureaucrat or to voluntarily submit to the authority of a church whose pastoral representative has been unable to defend the sacred icon from sacrilegious treatment by the corrupt secular authorities.

In Dostoevsky's view the revelation of the miracle as a sleight of hand constitutes more than a breach of verisimilitude; it marks a deeper ethical and aesthetic betrayal of the dissenters and the rich spiritual tradition they represent. The fact that the conversion to Orthodoxy is predicated on deceit devalues the "thirst for truth" that Dostoevsky sees as an essential characteristic of the Russian peasantry and as the means by which Russian society as a whole will be redeemed. Leskov's story undermines the "firmness and purity" of their beliefs and betrays the complexity of their worldview, which constitutes a window onto the Russian past. For Dostoevsky the symbolic significance of the spiritual and cultural traditions of the schismatics far outweighs their theological transgressions. Through their rejection of the modernization of the Nikonian reforms, they represent an unbroken connection to an indigenous tradition of spiritual and cultural unity. In his 1860 announcement of the publication of *Time,* he identified the schismatics with the best of the traditions and values of the *narod* torn asunder by the rupture of the Petrine reforms: "Coming out of the reforms, the people were not spiritually broken: they sank into themselves and their situation, tried to create their own outlook, their philosophy . . . sought new avenues for their lives, new forms . . . And meanwhile they were called the preservers of old Petrine forms, dim-witted Old Believers."[55] When Leskov has his Old Believers give up their faith in response to a fake miracle, he undermines the rich thousand-year history of their faith, a history that is of particular importance in the contemporary climate, "the most troubled, the most awkward, the most transitory and the most fateful moment, perhaps, in the whole history of the Russian People" (21:58). At the same time he undermines the sustaining promise of a return to that world symbolized for Dostoevsky in the faith of those Old Believers.

In the article's second half, Dostoevsky challenges Leskov's representation of the conversion of the Old Believers with his own representation of the *narod*'s spiritual psychology. He begins by invoking the appearance of the Stundists, a German Protestant sect whose successful proselytizing had been covered by *The Citizen*.[56] He brings up the story of a Stundist pastor who has been schooling the peasants of Kherson province in Orthodoxy rather than his own Protestant faith. Instead of accepting the pastor's concession, the peasants have been converting wholeheartedly to Protestantism and joining the Stundist sect, dismissing Orthodox fasting as "ritual." Dostoevsky contextualizes this tendency within the spiritual disintegration of the postreform period: it results from "the fact that since the Emancipation of February 19, 1861, the light of a new life has been shining on [the Russian peasant]. He might have stumbled and fallen when he took his first steps on the new road, but there was no doubt that he would recover; and when he recovered he saw at once how 'poor and wretched, naked, blind and base' he was" (58). He sees in the Stundist conversion the peasant's thirst for the truth, which must be pursued at all costs. He speculates on what would happen if the Stundist conversions took place all over Russia:

> What if the entire People, having sunk to the depths of their degradation and perceived their own wretchedness, should suddenly say to themselves: "I do not want degradation; I do not want to drink liquor, I want truth and the fear of God; but truth most of all, truth above all." That the thirst for truth will come upon him, of course, is cause for joy. And yet instead of truth the result may be the most outlandish lies, as in the case of the Stundists. (59)

This invocation of Stundism provides a countermodel of the Russian people's turbulent spiritual psychology to stand against Leskov's two-dimensional representation of the converts' pliant gullibility in "A Troubled Countenance." It depicts the psychology of the Russian people as characterized by extreme volatility, making them capable, like the peasant in "Vlas," of the deepest degradation one moment, and the most profound spiritual thirst the next.

Dostoevsky presents the Stundist phenomenon as evidence of the unpredictability of the *narod*'s spiritual force, a force that cannot be harnessed either by the forms and formulas of institutionalized religion or by the naturalistic strategies of secular narration. For Dostoevsky, the Russian people's "thirst for truth" reflects an uncontainable moral freedom and volatility that demands literary recognition and representation. This volatility threatens to undermine his utopian dreams of the *narod*'s salvific power. His monologic outburst "Isn't everything, everything they are seeking, to be found in Orthodoxy? Does not Orthodoxy, and Orthodoxy alone, contain the truth and salvation of the Russian people, and in ages yet to come the salvation of the whole of humanity?" does not preclude his conclusion that teaching the peasants the superiority of Orthodoxy to Lutheranism is an almost impossible task: "The peasants are a dark people, after all: they will understand nothing, and probably will not be swayed by this" (21:59–60). His belief in the implacable moral freedom of the Russian people is always accompanied by anxiety over the social and spiritual obstacles that modernization has brought.

Joseph Frank points toward the significance of Dostoevsky's criticism of Leskov's insistence on explaining away the miracle of the icon for the later thematization of miracles in *The Brothers Karamazov*.[57] Leskov himself mocked this criticism in his response to the review, and Dostoevsky then brought it up again in his later column "An Impersonator." Frank argues that Dostoevsky does not differ significantly from Leskov in his use of miracles in the later novel; instead of revealing them as a sleight of hand, he exposes them as a false prop for faith. Nonetheless, Frank's discussion does not explore the rich aesthetic and ethical chain of connections that tie *The Brothers Karamazov* to "A Troubled Countenance." The column decouples the idea of the miracle from the arena of folk superstition and presents it instead as associated with human freedom and potentiality, as a product of faith rather than a reason for it. In *The Brothers Karamazov*, the miracle will become the means by which the religious worldview of the Russian people can transform and transfigure the secular genre of the novel through the absorption of folk genres. In "A Troubled Countenance," the miracle becomes a source of faith in the spiritual and aesthetic regeneration of Russia in the face of "the most awkward, the most transitory, and the most fateful moment in the whole history of the Russian People." In "Something about Lying," Dostoevsky writes a passage that could almost be addressed to Leskov:

> In Russia the truth almost always has an entirely fantastical character. In fact, people have finally reached the point where all those things the human mind is forever and ever lying to itself about are much more understandable than the truth itself; and this is the case all over the world. The truth can lie on the table right in front of people for a hundred years but they won't pick it up; they go chasing after fabrications precisely because they consider the truth to be fantastic and utopian. (119)

In rejecting the idea of a miracle outright, Leskov has, according to Dostoevsky, also rejected the mystery of humanity's higher moral potentiality and simplified the complexity of religious psychology. In *The Brothers Karamazov* Dostoevsky will inscribe miracles into a novelistic context, revealing the miraculous as the human capacity for spiritual regeneration even at the last possible moment. The Russian people's unpredictability and moral freedom, which finds expression here in the conversion to Stundism, will later be represented in the figure of Dmitry Karamazov and his experience of a novelistic miracle.

ART IN A TIME OF TRANSITION

Despite Dostoevsky's defense of the importance of the ideal in art and despite his advocacy of an aesthetic spiritually regenerated by the faith of the *narod,* his "Writer's Diary" shows an enduring commitment to representing the fragmentary experiences of Russian contemporary social life. This commitment is revealed clearly in Dostoevsky's 1873 dispute with Goncharov over the problem of types, found in their correspondence over Dostoevsky's contribution to *The Collection* (*Skladchina*), a volume of works edited by Goncharov and sold to raise money for the victims of the Samara famine. Dostoevsky contributed a feuilletonistic companion piece to "Little Pictures" titled "Little Pictures (on the Road)."[58] The work includes the character of a foppish priest inclined toward nihilist ideas who speaks out in favor of civil marriage. Goncharov objects to the priest's characterization, arguing that he did not seem realistic, "although, perhaps there are such people (I hardly know anyone of this kind). You say yourself that 'such a type is being born'; forgive me if I permit myself to note a contradiction here: if it is being born, then it is not a type."[59] To be a type, argues Goncharov, a figure must have "formed through long and frequent repetitions or accumulations of phenomena and persons in which the images of all and sundry participate over a period of time, and finally the type becomes established, hardened, and grows familiar to the observer."[60] Unfortunately Dostoevsky's reply to Goncharov is not extant, but it provoked Goncharov to elaborate: "By type I understand something very rooted, established for a long, long time, and forming sometimes a series of generations." He then praises Alexander Ostrovsky as a master of type through his creation of well-worn tyrannical merchants and his rejection of any embryonic new social phenomena or personages.

Dostoevsky adamantly opposed this prohibition on representing new social types that were coming into existence. "Little Pictures (on the Road)" and its companion piece, "Little Pictures," constitute a twin rebuke against Goncharov's ossified conception of contemporary Russian reality (21:105–13, 159–76). The former depicts a quintessentially modern scene, the fleeting encounter and incidental conversation of groups of strangers on a series of different modes of transport, including a train and a steamer. The latter adapts a traditional journalistic genre to analyze some of the new social phenomena of the postreform era. Employing the conventional feuilletonistic form, with its flaneur-narrator and street setting, Dostoevsky observes the habits of the urban poor in St. Petersburg. Beginning with a traditional feuilletonistic topos, the city's European architectural pastiche, the flaneur extends his gaze to the habits and mores of peasants uprooted from the land by the emancipation who have migrated to the city for work. He studies the language of a group of drunken tradesmen, recounting their endless repetition of an obscene word, a word that expresses the violence of their displacement, another version of the meaningless iteration of "Bobok, bobok, bobok." The flaneur gradually finds some shreds of hope within the disorder and urban decay. Training his gaze on the ragged children of these migrants, he sees amid their material deprivation the warmth and affection of their family ties, not completely unraveled by the move to the city. Yet the flaneur is met with mistrust and suspicion, and his unwilling subjects seek to evade his unflinching gaze, as though aware of the provisional nature of their generic status, their failure to conform to feuilletonistic type (or to Goncharov's understanding of literary legitimacy). These transplanted peasants with their shy children seem to Dostoevsky himself to suggest that a kind of order can be discerned within the social turmoil of the modernizing city. Though they have not yet coalesced into a recognizable "type," they seem to represent the possibility of new kinds of aesthetic subjects for the age of transition.

In "Apropos of a New Play," Dostoevsky praises another work of literature that violates Goncharov's dictates, a new play by Dmitry Kishensky, a peasant playwright about whom not much is known (21:96–105). *Strong Drink Every Day Keeps Fortune Away* is set in a small factory town and deals with the social costs of industrialization. The main characters belong to the younger generation who grew up in the wake of the reforms: "In early childhood they encountered a family that was already disintegrating and without ideals; they found wholesale drunkenness; then, directly, they found themselves in the factory" (21:98). The play depicts a relentless orgy of drunkenness, sexual violence, and social collapse. Even the peasant commune, "the only thing that has remained solid and fundamental in Russian peasant life," "its main link with the past and its main hope for the future," has been infected with the seeds of its own destruction: "Its inner spirit and age-old inner truth have been shaken, shaken along with the shaky people who participate in it" (21:100). Dostoevsky sees the play as a powerful and truthful depiction of the shattered foundations of postreform Russian society:

> We find reflected here the whole extraordinary economic and moral trauma that followed the wide-ranging reforms of the current reign. The old world and the old order—which, as bad as it was, was still an order—have disappeared forever. And the strange thing is that the dark, moral aspects of the old order—egoism, cynicism, slavery, disunity, venality—have not only not disappeared with the abolition of serfdom but seem to have grown stronger, developed and multiplied; on the other, of the good moral aspects of the old way of life—which certainly existed—scarcely anything remains. All this is reflected in the picture represented by Mr. Kishensky, at least in my understanding of

> it. Everything here is transitory, everything is unstable, and, alas, provides not even a hint of something better to come. (21:96–97)

Dostoevsky sees Kishensky's play as the fictional realization of the postreform era as characterized in Golovachev's *Ten Years of Reforms.* Dostoevsky here adopts a perspective of social disintegration and moral collapse that seems discursively redolent of Meshcherskian or Fadeevian conservatism, yet at the same time he recognizes the inevitability of historical development and argues for a new kind of art for the new historical moment. This new art takes inspiration from the very uncertainty, ugliness, and formlessness of the present; it depicts a fallen, broken world, and its characters and language reflect this world's postlapsarian nature. Here there is no evidence of the ideal he had called for in "Apropos of the Exhibition." It looks forward instead to Dostoevsky's next project, *The Adolescent,* which at one time bore the title "Disorder" (16:16).

The internal conflict in "A Writer's Diary" between its two readings of the Russian present may well have contributed to Dostoevsky's gradual abandonment of the columns during the second half of 1873, though his disillusionment with *The Citizen* as a project was probably a more significant factor in that abandonment. He wrote only a few columns during the summer, and after "Something about Lying," published in *The Citizen*'s August 27 issue, he wrote only one more, "One of Today's Falsehoods," published in the December 10 edition. Dostoevsky was increasingly weighed down by the responsibilities of his column on foreign affairs and preoccupied with ideas for stories and novels that he had no time to realize.[61] He strenuously objected to the idea that he write a column on internal political affairs (29:I:385–86). The politically precarious tightrope of his editorship became progressively more frayed. The chasm between his own hybridic views on the reforms and Russia's future and those of Meshchersky manifested itself in their clashes over editorial policy.[62] Dostoevsky grew more and more disillusioned with his own attempts to engage his readers in his paradoxical vision of the reforms and their aftereffects. His hopes that *The Citizen* could heal Russia's political rifts and inspire its readers with accounts of lives filled with noble exploits were betrayed by the journal's developing reputation as an ultraconservative publication defending the rights of the nobility while championing government surveillance of students.[63]

The final columns of "A Writer's Diary" reflect Dostoevsky's growing disillusionment. In "To a Teacher" he voices frustratration at having to defend "Little Pictures" from the insinuation by a columnist in *The Voice* that its description of the deprivation and debasement of peasant migrants to St. Petersburg constitutes an attack on the emancipation (21:113–17). In "Something about Lying," he returns to the same theme of communication breakdown with which he had opened the introduction to "A Writer's Diary," but here the sober thought that *The Citizen* was supposed to set against what he saw as the meaningless babble and self-aggrandizing lies of the liberal press has largely disappeared, though he claims that Russian women represent the main hope for the future, since they are less given to lying than men (21:117–25). And he uses the final column, "One of Today's Falsehoods," to set the record straight on *Demons* and point out the differences between his own political views and those of more conventional conservative publications (21:125–36). A claim by the conservative journal *The Russian World* that only idle and undeveloped young people could follow a fanatic like Nechaev provides Dostoevsky with the opportunity to remind readers of his own status as a former political prisoner and to point out that many young radicals are motivated by high idealism and by elevated dreams of a regenerated society. This defense of radical youth allows him to show the clear blue water between his own political views and those of *The Russian World* and Meshchersky, since the latter's distrust of students was well-known in the journalistic world.[64]

At moments in "A Writer's Diary" Dostoevsky is almost able to convince himself of the possibility of counteracting the fragmentation of the postreform era. He sketches the outlines of a regenerative genre that could communicate the potential for spiritual unity represented by the faith of the *narod,* a genre that might draw upon indigenous spiritual and narrative traditions, be redeemed by the Orthodox idea, and depict not the transcendental homelessness of the Russian nobleman or *raznochinets,* but the transfigurative community of the Russian people. This modern epic could, he seems to suggest, replace the novels of alienation and estrangement that have dominated the Russian tradition, a tradition born out of the Petrine fracture. Yet in the ideologically and discursively heterogeneous context of "A Writer's Diary," this generic ideal always appears hazy and indistinct, is continually referred to as a dream or vision, and stands in radical contradistinction to the processes of social and hermeneutic fragmentation represented elsewhere in *The Citizen.*

PART II

Readings

Chapter Three

The Adolescent: Remaking the Noble Family Novel

SINCE THE MOMENT OF ITS FIRST PUBLICATION in the pages of *Fatherland Notes, The Adolescent* has been the subject of critical misunderstanding, condemnation, and neglect. The first negative reviews began to appear in the thick journals and newspapers after the publication of the novel's first installment in January 1875.[1] The work has been marginalized in Dostoevsky scholarship ever since, frequently excluded from studies of Dostoevsky's novels, and treated as the author's least successful work.[2] Among the negative criticism of the novel, one review stands out in its perspicacity, its assessment of the novel's success on its own terms, and its contextualization of the author's creative aims against the backdrop of the contemporary Russian novel. This fictional review, which comments on the "notes" that form the main part of *The Adolescent*, can be found within the frame of the novel itself (13:452–55).

The Adolescent is presented as the autobiographical "notes" (*zapiski*) of Arkady Dolgoruky, the illegitimate son of the landowner Versilov and his former serf Sophia. Ostensibly written a year after the events they relate, the "notes" provide an account of the adolescent's relations with his "accidental family." Abandoned at an early age in a Moscow boarding school, Arkady moves to Petersburg on completion of his studies, is reunited with his family, and becomes embroiled in the plots and subplots of his father Versilov and his various legitimate and illegitimate offspring. *The Adolescent* is thus possessed of a dual structure; it is a work within a work, the "notes" of the adolescent Arkady contained within the novel of Dostoevsky.[3] The autobiographical notes are bounded by a fictional frame that constitutes the novel's hermeneutic key, a letter from the adolescent's Moscow landlord Nikolai Semyonovich containing a critical reading of the adolescent's "notes" and a treatise on the problems of the contemporary Russian novel.

Nikolai Semyonovich sees in the illegitimate Arkady's notes a rejection of the Russian novel's traditional values and preoccupations.[4] He observes that throughout its history the Russian novel has taken for its subject the family life and values of the hereditary nobility, an ideal novelistic subject epitomized in

Pushkin's evocation of the "traditions of the Russian family" in *Eugene Onegin.*[5] By contrast, Arkady has created himself as a new kind of novelistic hero, a "member of an accidental family," who typifies the "general disorder" of the contemporary moment. Nikolai Semyonovich's letter articulates many of the complaints about the Russian novelistic tradition that Dostoevsky had been making in his notebooks and letters since the late 1860s. It also gets to the core of the difficulties facing the novelist who seeks to give artistic form to social "formlessness." Contemplating Arkady's status as "accidental" hero, Nikolai Semyonovich considers the starkly different creative choices open to the contemporary novelist. He can follow in the footsteps of Pushkin and Tolstoy and take for his subject the "finished forms of honor and duty" of the Russian nobility. Or he can take his hero from an accidental family and thus depict the contemporary moment in all its disorder. In the first case, the novelist risks losing fidelity to contemporary reality and falling into the "historical genre," creating "an artistically finished picture of a Russian mirage." In the second, the novel may take on the very formlessness it seeks to represent, collapsing under the weight of its fragmented subject. While such a novel would demonstrate in its very unfinished quality a fidelity to the fragmented reality of the contemporary moment, it might lack artistic shape and in its very disintegration threaten the future of novelistic form itself. The fragmentary nature of Arkady's "notes" demonstrates his commitment to the second path. Conscious of his own nostalgia for the literary certainties of the past enshrined in the works of Pushkin and Tolstoy and anxious to retain the memory of their "beautiful order," Nikolai Semyonovich is troubled by the formlessness of Arkady's disordered narrative. Nonetheless, his reading of Arkady's autobiography forces him to acknowledge that the traditional Russian novel has had its day. In Arkady's notes he sees the seeds of a new kind of novel, one that marks a decisive break with the Russian novel's own generic history.

Nikolai Semyonovich's review of Arkady's autobiography sets the adolescent up as a representative hero for the chaotic historical moment of the 1870s. In his illegitimacy, Arkady represents the degeneration of both his father's noble estate and the family as social and biological unit. His "accidental family" is both the locus and symptom of social disintegration, which loomed so large in the plans for the novel that Dostoevsky even considered calling the work "Disorder" (16:80). As Nikolai Semyonovich points out, it also represents the dissolution of the traditional novelistic subject; it fails to conform to the "beautiful order" that has been the hallmark of the Russian novel since its inception: "I confess, I would not wish to be a novelist whose hero comes from an accidental family! Thankless work and lacking in beautiful forms . . . Major mistakes are possible, exaggerations, oversights" (13:455).[6] He suggests that by faithfully transmitting the image of fractured reality, Arkady's "notes" risk repelling the reader. At the same time, the review posits Arkady as an ideal author for the present moment. Chapter 1 demonstrated how in the late 1860s Dostoevsky had begun to envision the Russian novel not as the open-ended and flexible form described by Bakhtin in his essay "Epic and Novel," a genre that traditionally flourished in times of turbulence and change, but rather as a form that had developed according to a set of thematic and formal limitations connected to its birth in the Westernized culture of post-Petrine Russia.[7] Now through the mouthpiece of Nikolai Semyonovich, Dostoevsky explains his own project of representing the fragmentary nature of contemporary reality within the novelistic form, but he also recognizes the potential risks of such a project. How can fragmented, chaotic modernity be molded into literary form? This paradox of representation lies at the root of *The Adolescent* as a novelistic project and animates the work's narration.

I argue here that in his attempt to answer the conflicting demands of fragmented reality and formal clarity, Dostoevsky directly challenges the traditional forms of the Russian novel, particularly a subgenre I call the "noble family novel," which he saw encapsulated in the works of Tolstoy, Turgenev, and to a lesser extent Goncharov. This challenge brings together the voices of Dostoevsky and his protagonist, each of whom has a different endgame in mind. As well as revealing the central creative dilemma of *The Adolescent,* Nikolai Semyonovich's commentary reveals the parallel existence of two literary projects: Arkady's "notes," of which he is a reader, and Dostoevsky's novel, within which he is a character. Located within the novel's frame, Nikolai Semyonovich's commentary highlights the complex narrative structure of *The Adolescent.* One fictional character's commentary on another's creative choices draws attention to the fictionality of both, thus foregrounding the figure of the implied author. The problem of the relationship between Arkady's "notes" and the larger novel itself moves into focus. Nikolai Semyonovich's comments on Arkady's decision to focus on the formlessness of his own accidental family point the reader toward his creator's choice of hero and in so doing reveal the divergences between *The Adolescent's* two literary projects. Arkady is merely writing his autobiography; he has not chosen himself as an accidental hero. It is Dostoevsky who has embraced the formlessness of this novelistic subject as an alternative to the "finished forms" of the traditional Russian novel, as his "new word" in novelistic representation. As Nikolai Semyonovich explores Arkady's narrative motivation, providing a critical reading far beyond what the notes seem to merit, we are asked to consider Dostoevsky's own creative impulses, the wisdom and daring of his choice of a hero, yet such consideration flouts the text's hermeneutic order, for how can a fictional character comment on the text he himself inhabits? As Nikolai Semyonovich meditates on the differences between Arkady's "notes" and the Russian noble family novel, he reveals the creative potential in the "notes" and argues for their status as the provisional model for a literary project of the future. Speaking through his character, Dostoevsky questions *The Adolescent*'s success as a project, its relationship with traditional Russian novelistic models, and its status as a blueprint for a novel for the present and the future. Arkady's autobiography is revealed to be far more than the story of an adolescent's botched involvement in a series of family plots that he does not completely understand; it emerges as a radical novelistic experiment.

Representing the process of Arkady's formation as a narrator allows Dostoevsky to dramatize his own attempts to find a novelistic form to express the social disintegration of the 1870s, to include within the novel an account of his own authorial motivations. While Arkady examines earlier novelistic models as the means by which he can come to know his father's narrative legacy and his own narrative inheritance, Dostoevsky uses them to inscribe into *The Adolescent* the history of the Russian novel as a genre. He thus explores his own place in the history of the Russian novel as he revisits his own past as a novelist and explores its significance for his current project. Arkady's examination of earlier novels thus allows Dostoevsky to explore the origins and allegiances of the Russian novel, as well as its thematic and formal preoccupations.

Narrating his protagonist's development as an author allows Dostoevsky to lay bare his own novelistic process; the text turns out to be not only an attempt to represent the moment of social transition in all its fragmentation, but also a novelistic meditation on whether and how such representation can be possible within the form of the novel. With their double framing, Arkady's "notes" serve as both an example of fragmented novelistic discourse and an account of the *process* of representing fragmentation. As subject of one text and object of the other, Arkady is both agent and victim of disintegration. At once the embodiment of the disintegrating family and its chronicler, Arkady both symbolizes and narrates social breakdown. This multilayered narrative structure creates the dynamic effect of a work in progress, not merely a narrative *of* transition, but a narrative *in* transition.

A NOVEL OF DISINTEGRATION

The Adolescent emerges out of a profound anxiety over the social reverberations of the Great Reforms of the 1860s; this anxiety informs the novel's thematic concerns and contributes significantly to the work's formal peculiarities. At the very beginning of the notebooks for the novel, Dostoevsky makes the following observation: "The foundations of society are cracking under the pressure of the revolution brought by the reforms. The sea has become troubled. The borderlines of good and evil have disappeared and become obliterated" (16:7). Having already begun to address what he viewed as the social costs of the reforms in his columns for *The Citizen*, Dostoevsky turned next to a novelistic treatment of these social pressures. In *The Adolescent* he is concerned not so much with the social transformation brought by the reforms as with its significance for the novel as a genre. More than any other work by Dostoevsky, *The Adolescent* poses the problem of the postreform era in metaliterary terms; it is concerned with the possible reconciliation of the dynamic of social dislocation and disintegration with the unifying, classifying impulse of novelistic representation.

Like the rest of Dostoevsky's literary projects, *The Adolescent* went through many changes during the process of writing, and the notebooks for the novel reveal many narrative and thematic blind alleys, or novelistic seeds that were never brought to fruition.[8] Of all the ideas and images expressed in the notebooks, perhaps the most tenacious are the images of disintegration (*razlozhenie*) and disorder (*besporiadok*), discussed above. Dostoevsky's earliest notes for the novel show him experimenting with variations on the theme of social disorder, including a children's empire, a predatory type, a set of three brothers, and a parricide.[9] The original hero is the "predatory type." He later becomes Versilov, a figure who belongs to the symbolic line of Stavrogin, the central figure of *Demons,* and of the Great Sinner, the protagonist of Dostoevsky's unfinished project from 1869, "The Confession of a Great Sinner."[10] He dominates the early notes for the novel, and it is his atheism that seems to represent the initial force of disorder in the work. Gradually this "predatory type" cedes the central position in the notes to the character who is variously his younger brother or son, the future Arkady. On July 23, 1874, Dostoevsky decides, "The BOY, not he (the predatory type), is the HERO," and then later reminds himself to write "A LARGER ROLE FOR THE YOUTH" (16:24, 29). As the plans develop, Arkady's formation as a moral individual becomes central to his conception of the novel:

> THE MAIN IDEA
>
> Although the adolescent arrives with a ready-made idea, the whole sense of the novel lies in the fact that he seeks the guiding thread between good and evil, so lacking in our society; he thirsts for this thread. Therein lies the aim of the novel. (16:51)

The adolescent's search for the guiding thread of the knowledge of good and evil soon became the novel's central narrative impetus, and he gradually began to dominate the notes (16:115). His moral journey would take place against the backdrop of the breakdown of traditional social institutions, particularly the family. The adolescent's "education in the world" provided Dostoevsky with the narrative pretext for representing different spheres of postreform Russian society, from the young revolutionaries of the Dergachev organization with which Arkady becomes involved to the high-society circles of Versilov and his legitimate children, from the criminal gang of Arkady's former schoolfriend Lambert to the aristocratic roulette players who associate with the young Prince Seryozha.

His choice of novelistic hero immediately signals Dostoevsky's intention to deal with Russia's contemporary condition. The adolescent Arkady, poised between childhood and adulthood but belonging to neither, troubled by the vicissitudes of awakening sexuality, mystified by the unfamiliar social conventions of the adult world, provided him with the ideal figure through which to represent a society that was itself just emerging into the adulthood of modern capitalist nation-state. His hero's illegitimacy, the pull of an aristocratic father and a peasant stepfather, symbolized Russia's own contradictory changing class structure and its own interrogation of its origins. Arkady's ambition of becoming a Rothschild demonstrated his connection to a whole new set of capitalist values and aspirations coming into existence during this time, as well as the ever-present aping of the more rapid social and economic transformation of the West. Yet it is not merely Arkady who infuses the novel with a sense of the social instabilities of the 1870s: Dostoevsky builds the experience of fragmentation into every level of the novelistic form.

ILLEGITIMACY AND NARRATIVE: ARKADY'S LITERARY EDUCATION

Several scholars have examined *The Adolescent* as a bildungsroman, and the work does share many of that genre's features.[11] It stages the education in the world of both an unformed young protagonist and the reader. Yet I will argue here that it is a particular kind of bildungsroman, one that focuses on the hero's, author's, and reader's narratological educations. The work begins with an account of Arkady's narrative motivation and the establishment of the terms of his literary education. The central stimulus for his autobiographical "notes" is his illegitimacy. His attempt to record his experiences represents the possibility for the child of an accidental family to gain a linguistic and literary legitimacy that can erase the traumatic memory of his neglected childhood. The offspring of a nobleman and his serf, Arkady is fascinated and confused by his own origins; the droit du seigneur that brought him into the world has disappeared along with serfdom, yet his illegitimacy remains an indelible mark on his identity. The circumstances of his birth create narrative potential in the tension between the two social classes he bridges, thereby augmenting the universal narrative potential that illegitimacy traditionally provides within the novel.[12] Yet as he begins his autobiography, Arkady sees his illegitimacy not as increasing his narrative potential but as decreasing it. In describing the burden of his name, which brings with it the unwelcome associations of *Prince* Dolgoruky and to which he is continually forced to respond with the correction "No, *simply* Dolgoruky," he exposes his shame and reveals his narrative motivation (13:7–8).[13] The "simply" is his Achilles' heel; it becomes the vortex of his vulnerability. It marks the end of the story, the exclusion of the traditional narrative possibilities of the Russian novel. Arkady knows only those narratives which concern themselves with the nobility and from which, by virtue of his illegitimacy, he is excluded. A prince has a wide range of narrative paradigms open to him, since all narratives have been about princes. But if he is *simply* Dolgoruky, he has no literary precedents. He learns instead to create his own narrative possibilities from the ambiguities of his origins. Rejecting the narrative closure brought by the word "simply," he begins to respond to questions about his origins by providing complete details of his parentage and social status, anticipating the issue of his illegitimacy. He learns the skills of the realist narrator, mapping his ambiguous identity onto a web of historical and social relations; he is "the illegitimate son of my former master, Mr. Versilov" (13:8). Yet when he is subsequently upbraided by a classmate for boasting of his illegitimacy, he recognizes the need to move beyond this reductive encapsulation of his identity. The whole subsequent development of the novel can be seen as an answer to the problem of being *simply* Dolgoruky, a problem that involves coming up against and ultimately transforming the assumptions of the traditional Russian novel.

The Rothschild idea supplies one answer to the problem of his being *simply* Dolgoruky: the creation of a whole new capitalist narrative paradigm, in which the old narratives about princes will be replaced with new narratives about self-made men. This aspiration represents Arkady's first attempt to create an identity separate from that of his father, to explore his own narrative potentiality, to celebrate the multiplicity of futures that money can bring. Yet the idea itself is reactive; it is predicated on the idea of revenge on the social class from which he is excluded by virtue of his illegitimacy. Though he declares that freedom and isolation motivate him, his insistence that "It's not I who will get in with the aristocracy, but they who will get in with me" testifies to the strength of his desire to turn the tables on his father the aristocrat (13:75). It is not by remaking himself as a capitalist that Arkady will triumph over his social position and its lack of narrative precedent; it is through his own literary undertaking, through his act of opening up the novel to the multiplicity of new narrative paradigms and new codes that have begun to dominate the world he inhabits. His "notes" serve as the means by which he can examine the paradoxical nature of his identity and reflect on the contradictions of his origins.

Versilov dominates the pages of Arkady's autobiography. Arkady confesses, "The appearance of this man in my life, that is, for a moment, in early childhood, was the fateful push with which my consciousness began" (13:62). As his father, Versilov is, along with Dostoevsky, author of Arkady's fate; as the adolescent himself writes, "It's curious that this man, who impressed me so much ever since my childhood, who had such a capital influence on my entire cast of mind, and has maybe even infected my future with himself for a long time to come—this man even now remains in a great many ways a complete riddle to me . . . My whole notebook will be filled with this man" (13:6). Arkady's own role as author allows him to turn the tables on his father and gain power over him. As the author of his own autobiography, Arkady can shape not only his own narrative but also that of his father, and in the process avenge his own childhood humiliations. In order to establish his own narrative identity, chart his own path through life, and write his autobiography, Arkady must first negotiate his relationship with his father. In order to come to know himself, the rootless child of the accidental family must come to know his father, the social class he belongs to, and the historical period he represents. Only by this means can he come to understand his own relationship to the contemporary Russian moment, the role of history in shaping both his own origins and his own, and Russia's, future.

From the novel's very beginning Arkady presents Versilov first and foremost as an aristocrat; indeed, he refers to him as "landowner Versilov" (*pomeshchik*) even before revealing that he is his father (13:6). With his womanizing and spendthrift reputation, Versilov as he is first presented by Arkady seems an amalgam of stock literary images of the early nineteenth-century Russian aristocrat, yet in each aspect he is presented as almost parodically excessive. He has gone through not just one estate, but three (13:7). He has not merely fathered children with one of his peasants, but has fallen in love with her.

Versilov reveals himself as a "man of the '40s" not merely because he reads *Anton Goremyka* and *Polinka Saks,* exemplary works of the Natural School, but also because he bases his behavior on literary stereotypes in the manner of the archetypal superfluous man. If Versilov constructs his behavior in accordance with these literary stereotypes with self-conscious irony, Arkady completely deflates the romance by asking what on earth his mother and Versilov could have had to talk about, adding that Russian literature certainly couldn't have come into it. Arkady's scorn hides a bitter resentment of the narrative certainties available to his father by virtue of his position as an aristocrat, and the knowledge that he himself must follow a different path. Dostoevsky thus sets the stage for a conventional ideological generational conflict, and indeed, he later referred to the novel as his "Fathers and Sons" (22:7). Yet in *The Adolescent* the son's act of rebellion will primarily be not ideological, but narratological.

Learning to negotiate his father's literary heritage in order to overcome it is a crucial part of Arkady's literary and narratological education. For Dostoevsky himself, writing his novel of disintegration, illegitimacy provides the ideal trope for his own tense relationship to the traditional Russian novel. It expresses the genetic hybridity of *The Adolescent.* It conveys both the novel's debt to the Russian novelistic past and its divergence from it. For both Dostoevsky and Arkady, *The Adolescent* becomes a struggle for the present that is played out on the level of novelistic form itself.

Arkady's formation as a narrator involves his measuring of his own work against previous literary models. In a work with such complex narrative framing as *The Adolescent,* assessing the hermeneutic significance of the invocation of previous literary models becomes problematic, located as they are at the intersection of the interwoven narrative perspectives of Arkady, Versilov, and Dostoevsky. The reader of the novel must consistently investigate the reverberations of such models within and between each of these perspectives. Despite his early insistence that he will "avoid literary beauties" and his persistent claims that he is not a literary man, Arkady constantly refers to previous literary works in his autobiographical notes. In describing his father's seduction of his mother, he informs his reader that Versilov had recently read *Anton the Wretch* and *Polinka Saks* (13:10–12).

For Arkady as narrator such previous novelistic models serve both to open his channel of communication with his reader and to allow him mediated access into a world which appears historically and socially distant, and from which he feels himself excluded, yet which has played a crucial role in his own formation. In order to construct his own identity through his autobiography, he must reconstruct the social and emotional origins of his parents' relationship, so typical of the pre-emancipation period and yet so distant and so incomprehensible from his own perspective. He can access the social and historical context of their love only through the mediation of previous novelistic models. Bolstered by his "novelistic" status as a nobleman, Versilov is for Arkady the reference point for the narrative legitimacy that eludes him. In order to uncover and to represent his own identity he must first examine the literary models according to which Versilov defines himself. Overcoming these models is a vital part of Arkady's literary formation.

Dostoevsky as implied author dramatizes in Arkady's narrative insecurity his own fears about writing the family novel anew. He inscribes into Arkady's illegitimacy the sense of his own lack of legitimacy in portraying a character with no usable Russian generic past. But past novelistic models also serve a deeper purpose for Dostoevsky, allowing him to contextualize his work within the history of the Russian novel and, in so doing, make explicit the historical motivation for his own generic choices. Through that contexualization, he identifies the novelistic models against which he is writing and expresses the complex and multifaceted nature of that polemic. Previous literary works were so important to Dostoevsky as he worked on the novel that he made himself a note to "write my 'bibliography'" (16:36). Invoking previous novelistic models, Dostoevsky appeals to what Bakhtin calls genre memory, the impersonal, historical layers of earlier generic strata always present in the novelistic form.[14] *The Adolescent* calls upon the genre memory of the noble family novel that Dostoevsky sees being practiced by his contemporaries Tolstoy, Turgenev, and Goncharov. The palpable presence of those previous models in Dostoevsky's most experimental novel provides a window on the author of *The Adolescent*'s own literary education. Just as Arkady must understand his father's narrative legacy in order to break free of it, so Dostoevsky must explore his own relationship to dominant novelistic models in order to break free of them and write his own experimental novel.

FRAMING VERSILOV: *THE ADOLESCENT* AND THE GENRE MEMORY OF THE NATURAL SCHOOL

The converging and diverging currents in the novel's narrative perspectives and their relationship to previous literary models emerge in a consideration of the two texts Arkady invokes in his account of the circumstances of his parents' first meeting in the very opening of *The Adolescent:* D. V. Grigorovich's *Anton Goremyka* and A. V. Druzhinin's *Polinka Saks.* Recounting Versilov's account of the circumstances of his meeting with Sophia and his return to his estate, Arkady explains,

> He himself told me that he was quite a "silly young pup" then, not that he was sentimental, but *just so,* he had recently read *Anton the Wretch* and *Polinka Saks*—two literary works that had had a boundless civilizing influence on our then rising generation. He added that it was perhaps because of *Anton the Wretch* that he had come to the estate then—and he added it extremely seriously. (13:10)

The peculiar significance of this juxtaposition of two *povesti* with such divergent plots, protagonists, narrative structures, and generic identities is not immediately obvious; the references appear as if randomly out of the explosive bluster of Arkady's narrative voice, with its frequent digressions and contradictions. The verbal layering that distinguishes the narrative structure of *The Adolescent* here already serves to obscure and complicate the function of these two literary models within the text. There is no clear boundary between Arkady's voice and those of Versilov and the implied author, and the reference to the novellas reveals tension between these different voices.

Set on an estate with an absentee landlord, Grigorovich's novella recounts the fate of the serf Anton, who is forced by the pitiless steward Nikita Fyodorych to sell his horse to pay the quitrent. Before he is able to make the sale, Anton is robbed by horse thieves. Anton thus suffers the effective theft of his horse and, after a series of other misfortunes, ends up as a convict.[15] Versilov's reference to the novella suggests an attempt to inscribe his seduction of Makar's wife into a larger context of youthful idealism, liberalism, and paternalism. Along with later hints that he has participated in the emancipation and has been involved with émigrés such as Herzen (which he later denies), the reference to the novella bolsters his identity as a typical gentry liberal of the 1840s. His return to the estate, he seems to be suggesting, was motivated by a desire to save his peasants from the same fate as Anton. But Arkady uses the reference to ground his father's exercising of his droit du seigneur in the context of serfdom. Where Versilov extrapolates out from the novella, inscribing himself into the imagined role of benevolent landlord returning to his roots, Arkady returns to the text and writes him instead into the actual role of the landlord who has married off his mistress to the steward and has apparently fathered the illegitimate vagabond girl, Fatimka. He interprets the landlord as the source of all Anton's woes and transposes the motif of the stolen horse onto the adultery narrative:

> And a man who arrived with *Anton the Wretch* and, on the basis of his rights as a landowner, violated the sacredness of marriage, though it was of his household serf, would be very ashamed in his own eyes, because, I repeat, no more than a few months ago, that is, twenty years later, he spoke extremely seriously of this *Anton the Wretch.* Yet Anton only had a horse taken from him, and here it's a wife! (13:10–11)

Here the peasant Anton stands for Arkady's legal father, the peasant Makar, further emphasizing the illegitimacy of Versilov's claim over Arkady's narrative. Arkady's usurpation of Versilov's original intention concerning Grigorovich's novella carries a deeper significance for his own narrative ambition; it allows him to reframe his representation of Versilov and cast off his father's literary legacy. Once in Arkady's hands, the novelistic model obscures Versilov's narrative identity, plays him off against Makar, and renders him more mysterious rather than less. Breaking down and overcoming this previous literary model not only allows Arkady to interrogate his own paternity but also grants him the freedom to carve out a new narrative identity from the shards of the old; it provides a narrative focus to the adolescent son's contradictory perspectives on his father. It fulfills his need to find both commonality and difference as he measures his own identity against his father's.

The invocation of *Polinka Saks* is at first sight even more puzzling. A

Russian reworking of George Sand's love triangle novel *Jacques,* in which the husband, Saks, meekly accepts his wife Polinka's amorous capitulation to her aristocratic admirer, Prince Galitsky, Druzhinin's novella serves as a cautionary tale both of the imitation of literary models and of the dangers of idealistic pedagogy and its attempts to cultivate the sensibilities of callow young women.[16] Saks's failed attempt to persuade his wife to read *Jacques* foreshadows his own inscription into a plot modeled on that novel, but this plot ends completely differently, with the wife realizing that she loved her husband all along and with her premature death, rather than his. Dostoevsky had already referred to *Polinka Saks* repeatedly in the notebooks for *Demons,* where the figure of Saks is invoked by the character later to become Stepan Verkhovensky as a justification for his marriage to the Ward (later to become Dasha) to cover up "another man's sins" (11:65, 67, 75, 117, 120, 162, 227, 231, 239). *Polinka Saks* thus becomes associated with the contorted reasoning and moral shortcomings of Russian Westernism. Through the reference to the novella in *The Adolescent,* Versilov distances his own love triangle from the droit du seigneur evoked in the model of *Anton Goremyka* and legitimizes it by placing it within the Russian literary-cultural context of the fictional and nonfictional love triangles of the 1840s, triangles that involve many of the figures who hover over the figure of Versilov himself in the notebooks for the novel, those specters of Russian Westernism, Herzen, Turgenev, and Nekrasov.[17]

If Versilov implicitly writes himself into the role of Galitsky, Polinka's lover, Arkady reveals his underlying similarities with Saks, at once suggesting the existence of a pedagogical dimension in Versilov's relationship with Sonya and rendering it ironic as he imagines Versilov explaining the story to her, followed by a furtive and embarrassed flirtation:

> Could he have started explaining *Polinka Saks* to her? And moreover, they couldn't be bothered with Russian literature; on the contrary, according to his own words (he got carried away once), they hid in the corners, waited for each other on stairways, bounced away from each other like rubber balls, red-faced, if somebody passed by, and the "tyrant landowner" trembled before the least washerwoman, despite all his serf-owning rights. (13:11–12)

Imagining Versilov as the earnest pedagogue, Arkady conflates the roles of husband and lover into one: Versilov plays both Saks and Galitsky. Arkady thus deflates his father's literary pretensions and denies the capacity of novelistic models to explain his parents' relationship. Inserting Versilov's voice into his own narrative, he also lends his voice to Versilov's explanation of himself, breaking down the barriers of identity between his father and himself. Taking revenge on his father for his own narrative illegitimacy, Arkady turns Versilov's legitimacy on its head, exposing his script and writing over it. Undermining the novelistic models that have informed Versilov and his behavior, he turns the tables on his father, reconstructing him and their relationship from the novelistic fragments left behind.

The contrasting novelistic models of *Anton Goremyka* and *Polinka Saks* function simultaneously on both mimetic and metaliterary levels. They reveal Versilov's social and psychological origins and Arkady's attitude toward them. They also inscribe Dostoevsky's novel into the generic history of the Russian novel. They illuminate two different sides of the gentry liberal of the 1840s, whose memory is evoked in the character of Versilov himself, but they also evoke two different literary schools whose coexistence in the 1840s and 1850s helped to create the novelistic model which still dominated the Russian literary sphere in the mid-1870s and against which Dostoevsky himself was writing. Grigorovich's novella brings to mind memories of serfdom, opposition to serfdom, and the emancipation itself.[18] At the same time it evokes the genre memory of the Natural School, with its sense of social commitment and its incorporation of the language of the *narod.* Druzhinin's work points toward the social chasms of the period before the emancipation and the Westerners' awkward negotiation of European literary and social models. It evokes the genre memory of what we might call the Sandian strand of Russian literature, with its dependence on the French social novel, a tradition that also incorporates another triangular model hanging heavily but implicitly over *The Adolescent:* Herzen's *Who Is to Blame?* The undermining of these novelistic models prefigures the novel's dual processes of disintegration: the dissolution of Versilov's role as liberal aristocrat and its culmination in his "split" and his breaking of the icon, and the fragmentation of dominant models of the Russian novelistic tradition, no longer able to represent the social, psychological, and historical disintegration of the 1870s.

In a text so intimately concerned with the problem of the Russian contemporary novel, with the problem of novelistic representation in an age of disintegration, these novelistic models bring to mind an earlier and more confident moment in the history of the genre. Both Grigorovich's and Druzhinin's novellas were published in *The Contemporary* in 1847, and the two appear alongside one another in Belinsky's *Survey of Russian Literature for 1847.*[19] Belinsky's long essay, which canonizes the works of the Natural School, represents an originary moment in the construction of a narrative of mid-nineteenth-century Russian literary history and of the Russian novel.[20] In the *Survey,* Belinsky celebrates the generic hegemony of the novel and the *povest',* arguing that the novel unites all other genres of poetry, the lyrical, and the dramatic, a generic hegemony that Dostoevsky will question and interrogate throughout *The Adolescent,* most clearly in the epilogue.[21] The model of Russian literary history Belinsky lays out forms the starting point for the literary debates of the 1860s. Chernyshevsky's *Notes on the Gogol*

Period in Russian Literature will provide the stepping-stone from Belinsky's account to the more radical utilitarian aesthetics of the 1860s.

For Dostoevsky, beginning work on his own experimental novel in 1874, this originary moment serves as a point of departure, which sets the literary context of the contemporary moment within a historical framework. But it also sets it apart, thereby underlining the new literary and historical conditions within which he himself is working. In his explicit invocation of Grigorovich's and Druzhinin's texts, and his implicit gesture toward the Belinskian model of which they form part, Dostoevsky, like Arkady, is evoking the literary moment of 1847. That was of course the year of his own literary debut, when Grigorovich, impressed with *Poor Folk,* took the manuscript to Nekrasov, who in turn brought it to Belinsky.[22] Working in 1874 on *The Adolescent,* he was publishing for the first time in *Fatherland Notes* at Nekrasov's invitation. Invoking the moment of his literary debut, he is casting off from it, but he is also casting it off, breaking free of the narrative of Russian literary history within which he himself was placed at the moment of his own emergence into the world of Russian literature.[23] He is setting the stage for his own literary *Bildung.*[24]

The spectral textual presence of Belinsky's *Survey* brings out the critic's importance for Dostoevsky's sense of his own literary biography. Given that Belinsky, along with Nekrasov, was so intimately connected to the originary moment of his own literary biography, it is perhaps not surprising that Dostoevsky himself might choose to invoke him at a moment when his sense of the uniqueness of his own particular novelistic vision was at its height, and when he felt himself subject to the ire of his contemporaries because of what he himself saw as his fidelity to that vision. Although Dostoevsky had praised Belinsky's literary insight in an article in *Time* in 1861, his opinion of the critic had deteriorated markedly throughout the 1860s, and by 1867 he had written an article (which was unfortunately lost) that seems to have placed Belinsky at the very core of the tradition of Russian Westernism he saw expressed in Turgenev's novel *Smoke* (18:71; 28:II:210, 215, 216, 259, 320, 328).[25] His view had darkened still more by 1870, when his letters to Apollon Maikov and Nikolai Strakhov are filled with diatribes against the critic, and his final letter from Europe, discussed in the first chapter of this book, fuses the fall of the Paris Commune with the culpability of Belinsky and Granovsky before the Russian people and even before Russian literature (29:I:16, 19, 31, 144–47, 206–8, 214–17). That both Belinsky and his own literary debut remained on his mind in 1873–75 is clear from the article "Old People," which he wrote for his column "A Writer's Diary" in *The Citizen* and which takes a more generous view of the critic in its treatment of the circumstances of his "discovery" of Dostoevsky and its analysis of the differences between Herzen and Belinsky (21:8–12).

Although Dostoevsky scholars have highlighted the importance of such figures as Herzen and Chaadaev as sources for Versilov, less attention has been paid to the frequent references to Belinsky in the notebooks for the novel; in the notebooks Versilov is said to "drink champagne a la Herzen. He remembers Herzen, knew Belinsky" (16:50).[26] It is also important to note that the literary analysis of Arkady's autobiography undertaken by his Moscow landlord Nikolai Semyonovich was, in the notebooks for the novel, originally given to Versilov, who appears in several places in the role of the critic (16:277, 414–15). Given Dostoevsky's identification of Belinsky in the early 1870s with what he perceived as the corrupting legacy of Russian Westernism but also with the birth of Russian literary criticism, the association of the critic with the conflicted process of overcoming tradition is far from unexpected. The same combination of nostalgia and judgment that emerges in the implied author's attitude toward Versilov can be found in Dostoevsky's writings about Belinsky in "A Writer's Diary" and elsewhere, and Belinsky's memory hangs almost tangibly over the text.

By linking *Anton the Wretch* and *Polinka Saks* and invoking them at the very outset of his experimental novel, Dostoevsky inscribes into *The Adolescent* the literary moment of the late 1840s, thereby conjuring up its power as the moment when the Russian novel was emerging. Writing in 1874–75, in what he perceives as a moment of turmoil for the novelistic form, he evokes another transitional moment in the history of Russian novelistic representation, the moment of the tradition's formation in the 1840s and 1850s, with its burgeoning confidence, its developing institutions, the thick journals, its debates over the nature of realism and over social engagement, and its soul-searching about the past and present of Russian literature. The references to the Natural School and the memory of Belinsky's model of critical realism form part of a frame around the novel that emphasizes its concern over the future of the novel as a genre and leads into the problems of the contemporary novel as they are presented in the epilogue.

AGAINST "GENTRY LITERATURE": REWRITING THE TOLSTOYAN FAMILY

If *The Adolescent* begins by invoking the originary moment of the Russian novelistic tradition, it soon moves on to engaging the works of Dostoevsky's immediate contemporaries, Tolstoy, Turgenev, and Goncharov. At the turn of the 1870s Dostoevsky had pushed back against the novel as practiced by Tolstoy and Turgenev, first in his correspondence with Strakhov over *War and Peace* and then in *Demons,* his allegory of the alienation of Russian Westernism. *The Adolescent* invokes the genre with which the trio of

Tolstoy, Turgenev, and Goncharov are associated throughout Dostoevsky's letters, notebooks, and journalism from the late 1860s onward: the noble family novel. This novelistic model helps to differentiate between the narrative perspectives of Arkady and the implied author and takes on the central role in the drama of genre that plays itself out formally and symbolically in *The Adolescent.*

The publication circumstances of *The Adolescent* cemented a sense of competition with Tolstoy that significantly shaped both the evolution of the novel itself and Dostoevsky's perception of his own novelistic vision. *The Adolescent* was originally supposed to have been published in *The Russian Messenger,* but Katkov had taken Tolstoy's new family novel, *Anna Karenina,* instead, and the two novels began to be published simultaneously in January 1875. Dostoevsky began to read *Anna Karenina* immediately, and he soon became aware that the reading public was comparing his new novel unfavorably with Tolstoy's (29:II:11). Vladimir Soloviev describes how, at the beginning of 1875, he visited Dostoevsky while the latter was working on *The Adolescent.* Dostoevsky asked him if he thought he envied Tolstoy and proceeded to demonstrate that envy.[27] During the summer of 1875 in Bad Ems, as he struggled with the third part of *The Adolescent,* Tolstoy was clearly on his mind, and there are repeated references to him in the letters and in the notes for the novel (16:360, 390, 424; 29:II:40, 49).[28]

In a famous passage in the notebooks, written on March 22, 1875, Dostoevsky responds to criticisms following the publication of the novel's first installment in *Fatherland Notes* (16:329–30). Accused of crude naturalism by a number of critics in the periodical press, Dostoevsky defends his own representation of a society without foundations, his own underground men and "unfinished people."[29] He compares his own poetics of fragmentation to the creative vision of "our most talented writers, who have been describing, in highly artistic form, the life of our upper middle class (from the vantage point of the family)—Tolstoy, Goncharov—[who] thought that they were describing the life of the majority; in my opinion what they were describing were the lives of some exceptions" (16:329). In the 1871 letter to Strakhov discussed previously, he had complained that what he called the "landowner's literature [*pomeshchich'ia literatura*]" practiced by such luminaries as Tolstoy and Turgenev had nothing left to say, yet the new word that would replace it did not yet exist (29:I:216). At work on his own experimental novel, Dostoevsky insists that Tolstoy, Turgenev, and Goncharov rely on an outmoded concept of the novelistic subject, limiting their novelistic focus to the noble estate and the traditional family, both of which are being washed away by the advancing tide of history. He revels in the intended insult "poet of the underground," arguing that underground characters such as Arkady have more verisimilitude and psychological accuracy than the heroes of *War and Peace:* "Bolkonsky reforms as he sees Anatole's leg being cut off, and we've all been shedding tears over it, but a genuine underground man would never have reformed" (16:330).

It is Tolstoy's bildungsroman, *Childhood. Boyhood. Youth* (1851–57), rather than his *War and Peace,* that frames *The Adolescent.* The trilogy is invoked by Nikolai Semyonovich in his letter, and its memory permeates Dostoevsky's own bildungsroman. The old man writes, "Yes Arkady Makarovich, you are a member of an accidental family, as opposed to our still-recent hereditary types, who had a childhood and a boyhood [*detstvo i otrochestvo*] so different from yours" (13:455). This apparently casual invocation of Tolstoy's trilogy in the novel's closing paragraphs reveals its most richly contradictory and meaningful intertextual relationship, a relationship that plays a crucial role in the process of narrative *Bildung* underlying *The Adolescent.*

As Andrew Wachtel has demonstrated, *Childhood* provided the model for countless accounts of the Russian gentry childhood from Aksakov to Bunin.[30] For Dostoevsky it was the paradigmatic example of the "beautiful order" of the Russian noble family novel, an account of gentry childhood and youth characterized by extraordinary stability and timelessness, the repository of the cultural memory of a bygone age, a work of literature to be cherished and admired, but never emulated. In the July–August 1877 issue of *A Writer's Diary* he complains,

> Never before has there been an era in our Russian life that has offered fewer facts that might be used to gain a sense and a knowledge of our always enigmatic future than the present era. Never has the Russian family been more unsettled, more disarranged and more unformed than it is now. Where could you now find such *Childhood* and *Boyhoods* [*Detstva i otrochestva*] as were recreated so harmoniously and so distinctly by Count Leo Tolstoy, for instance, in depicting *his* era and his family or as he did in *War and Peace*? All these poems are now *no more than historical portraits of the distant past.* Oh, I don't wish at all to say that these are only pretty pictures; by no means do I wish them to be reproduced in our day—that's not what I'm talking about at all. I'm speaking only of their nature, of their literary polish, their accuracy and the explicitness of their character, qualities thanks to which it was possible to have such a clear and distinct portrayal of an era like the one found in both these poems [*poemy*] of Count Tolstoy. Nowadays we have none of this. The modern Russian family is becoming more and more an accidental family. Specifically an accidental family—that's the definition of the modern Russian family. (25:173)

Here, as in the epilogue to *The Adolescent,* Dostoevsky, whether consciously or unconsciously, truncates the title of Tolstoy's trilogy, eliding the third part of the title, *Youth* (*Iunost'*).[31] This truncation conveniently sidelines the section of the trilogy that most closely resembles the phase of life Dostoevsky himself is addressing: adolescence. This elision strongly suggests an anxiety of influence, an awareness that Tolstoy's efforts at representing the adolescent's first tentative, unsteady interactions with the social world might be more relevant to the contemporary moment than Dostoevsky would like to admit, and a fear that his own novel of adolescence might not take its place alongside Tolstoy's trilogy in the Russian novelistic pantheon.

As A. L. Bem points out, in the notebooks for *The Adolescent* Dostoevsky seems to refer to all of Tolstoy's major novels without differentiation, as if to some unitary Tolstoyan text that remains consistent over the decades, and he consistently refers to Tolstoy as "the historian of the Russian nobility."[32] This sense of Tolstoy can be contrasted with Dostoevsky's sense of himself as the biographer of a hero whose social class as yet has no historian, and his growing realization throughout 1875 that his readers have failed to understand his creative mission. While continually measuring himself against Tolstoy, Dostoevsky at times expresses nostalgia for the literary and social certainties the latter seems to represent. By focusing his criticism and nostalgia on Tolstoy's trilogy rather than on *Anna Karenina,* Dostoevsky underlines his own position as chronicler of the accidental family as radically new. At the same time, however, he demonstrates the ambivalence of a novelist who feels intellectually obliged to represent the processes of social change, but who has a palpable sense of anxiety about the future artistic legacy of *The Adolescent.* The complexity of his attitude toward Tolstoy's novels is explicitly represented in *The Adolescent*'s epilogue, but the combination of criticism of the trilogy as having outlived its time and a simultaneous nostalgia for its certainties permeate the novel. The precision, clarity, and completeness of the image of the family in Tolstoy's trilogy represent the antithesis of the accidental family Dostoevsky represents in *The Adolescent.* Yet the representation of the disintegration of the family unit could only be possible if the memory of an integrated family unit was present in the novel. *The Adolescent* can only be understood in relation to *Childhood.*

In *The Adolescent,* Dostoevsky engages with Tolstoy's trilogy in many different ways. He borrows elements of the narrative structure of *Childhood,* and through these structural echoes he both underlines the contrasting qualities of his own novelistic vision, the "accidental" nature of the family that forms his novelistic subject, and reveals its generic history, its relationship to the noble family novel, which plays such a dominant role in the history of the Russian novel. Yet with the exception of the mention of the trilogy in Nikolai Semyonovich's letter, outside the frame of the "notes," Dostoevsky does not embed any direct intertextual references to Tolstoy's works in the final text. This is in marked contrast to the direct invocation of the works of the Natural School discussed previously. And whereas Arkady introduces the genre models of the prose works of the Natural School as prototypes for Versilov's character, there is no evidence to suggest that Arkady evokes Tolstoy in *The Adolescent,* as Perlina points out.[33] Instead, it is Nikolai Semyonovich, in the epilogue, who most directly invokes Tolstoy's trilogy as an intertext. The trilogy functions as an alternative model in Dostoevsky's novel, rather than in Arkady's autobiography, operating within the perspective of the implied author rather than the author. Rather than referring directly to the trilogy, Dostoevsky chooses several of the work's essential structural and thematic features and models them within *The Adolescent* in a radically different hermeneutic context, at a radically different historical and literary moment. Articulating these features, Dostoevsky brings to mind not Tolstoy's work itself, but a memory of it, or, rather, the genre memory of the novel of the Russian noble family, the generic tradition within which Nikolai Semyonovich (and Dostoevsky) places Tolstoy's trilogy. This memory is preserved in the structural fragments of Tolstoy's trilogy still present in Dostoevsky's novel and serves as a double-voiced reminder of the tradition out of which *The Adolescent* emerges and against which it sets itself.

Dostoevsky invokes the memory of Tolstoy's trilogy through the very title of his novel, which points toward another age of man just beyond the three stages Tolstoy describes, an age that had formed part of Tolstoy's original conception.[34] (Dostoevsky's twenty-year-old adolescent is a couple of years older than Tolstoy's youth when the trilogy ends.) But Dostoevsky's title also suggests a reclassification and depoeticization of the states of Tolstoy's trilogy. Dostoevsky's adolescence both supplements and supplants Tolstoy's ages of man. It also shifts the focus from a state or a stage, an age of man, *Childhood,* to a concrete character, the adolescent, whose identity hovers indeterminately between that of an individual and that of a type. Dostoevsky also borrows from the opening of *Childhood* the temporal marker of the exact date without the year. In *Childhood* the date without a year, August 12, the day of Irteniev's first memory of childhood, introduces a model of cyclical time outside of history, which includes the sequence of the seasons but excludes any possibility of social or historical development. This model of cyclical time, as Bakhtin notes, characterizes the chronotope of the idyll, the remnants of which can be found in the noble family novel.[35] It is accompanied by a model of spatial unity that in the case of *Childhood* centers on the estate which has been inhabited by generations of Irtenievs, and on the manor house, where each room is occupied by the shades of Nikolai's ancestors.

Dostoevsky has Arkady begin his autobiography on September 19, but instead of following up with a model of cyclical temporality, he introduces a flurry of activity that takes place over three days, followed by a gap of two months, then another three days of activity.[36] As the novel proceeds, objective temporal markers are replaced by markers of duration as the sense of temporality becomes more subjective, more relational, and more directly centered on Arkady's own experiences. In contrast, duration has no place in Tolstoy's trilogy, where isolated perfective episodes are interspersed with the repeating patterns of an imperfective past.[37]

Whereas Tolstoy's hero spends his childhood on his father's country estate and in Moscow, Arkady has been expelled from both these spaces and finds himself in Petersburg, the refuge of the rootless. If Dostoevsky's novel exhibits any unity of space, it resides only in the alienating urban landscape of Petersburg, in the shadowy taverns where Arkady meets with Versilov. Arkady's illegitimacy manifests itself spatially in his uprootedness, in a sense of homelessness that accompanies him wherever he goes. An outcast even in his own family, he spends his days wandering the city. Arkady's continual wandering through Petersburg, inherited from his two fathers, reflects Makar's journeys through Russia and Versilov's travels in Europe.

Whereas Irteniev's childhood is the idyllic past to which he yearns to return through his act of remembering, Arkady's is a tale of neglect and humiliation best forgotten, recounted patchily through several narrative digressions at the novel's beginning. Irteniev centers his childhood memories on the image of his mother, who appears before her premature death at the end of *Childhood* as a hazy and idealized model of kindness, while his father emerges and remains a distant authority figure to whom the child is never able to relate. Arkady's mother is an equally distant and obscure figure, but his attitude toward her is more ambivalent, characterized by embarrassment, awkwardness, and more than a few echoes of a Freudian family romance.

The problem of fatherhood remains just below the surface of *Childhood,* surfacing only at moments when the father's authority is undermined, such as the moment when the young Nikolai overhears criticism of his father in Moscow.[38] While Nikolai's father is conspicuous by his absence, Arkady's father fills the pages of the adolescent's autobiography with his looming presence. Paternity is not merely the organizing narrative principle of *The Adolescent;* it is also the Holy Grail for which the adolescent spends the whole novel searching. Abandoned in his childhood, Arkady sustains himself with fantasies of the aristocratic father whom he has met only once in his life. His attempts to come to know his father in the novel's main plot ultimately prove futile, and in the closing chapters he finally emerges from under his father's shadow and learns to negotiate the boundaries of his identity on his own terms.

The differences between Tolstoy's trilogy and Dostoevsky's novel are highlighted by their similarities in narrative structure. Tolstoy's trilogy is characterized by a dialogic interplay of different narrative perspectives. The narrator, the adult Nikolai Irteniev, looks back on his childhood from a temporal distance of several decades. He expresses himself mainly in the past tense, sometimes including self-reflective musings that emphasize his act of narration or the mediation of his memory. Episodes of perfective narration are interspersed with passages of imperfective narration that emphasize the distance between the perspective of the narrator and that of his childhood self. In chapter 15 of *Childhood* the narrator moves into the second person, as though directly addressing his childhood self.[39] At times he moves into the present tense, underlining the moment of writing. Sometimes the mediation of memory moves to the background and the voice of Nikolai the child takes over the narration from his adult self.[40] A third narrative voice is occasionally heard in the authoritative statements by the author.[41] The different levels of narrative voice create a sense of the past being irretrievably cut off from the present that does not contradict an awareness of the extent to which the present is suffused with the memory of the past. They demonstrate the dual operations of memory and narration, and the transforming power of the act of narration over the mechanisms of memory. They allow the novel to hover uneasily over the gap between fiction and autobiography.

The merging of the autobiographical and the fictional, the episodic, plotless structure of the *fabula*, and the interplay of the different narrative voices in Tolstoy's trilogy help to transform the narrative from the particular childhood memories of an individual to the lyrical collective nostalgia of a social estate. The nostalgia is strongest in *Childhood*, gradually weakening as the child grows older. It dominates the lyrical episodes that form the central sections of the trilogy's first and third volumes, when the narrator bemoans the impossibility of return. The repeated use of the imperfective aspect creates an impermeable and value-laden absolute past.

In *The Adolescent* Dostoevsky uses a similar tripartite narrative structure, exploiting the dialogic interplay between the perspectives of Arkady as narrator, Arkady as narrated character, and the viewpoint of the implied author. Tolstoy's trilogy is invoked through Arkady's opening statement that he is writing his autobiography. After the opening chapter of the novel, where Arkady makes repeated references to the problem of how to write his autobiography, and his reasons for writing it, the self-referential narration subsides, only to return at the beginning of part III as he wrestles with the question of whether or not he has become "a completely different person" through the act of narration itself (13:280–81). Movements in narrative perspective make themselves felt in the final chapters of the novel through analeptic and proleptic digressions that allow Arkady to alternately narrate events as they took place and events as they were subsequently reported to him. The voice of Arkady the narrator merges with that of the narrated Arkady. Nikolai Semyonovich pronounces judgment on the very manuscript that we are reading, the fictionality of the autobiography is revealed, and the voice of the implied author comes to the fore.

Whereas in Tolstoy's trilogy the adult Irteniev is irrevocably cut off from his past, and the very impermeability of that past is part of what assigns it value, in *The Adolescent* the narrator is much closer to the events he is narrating. The brevity of the interval between his involvement in the plot and his narration of it breaks down the barriers between the narrating and narrated Arkady, as does the interpolation of the narrated Arkady's temporal perspective. Arkady cannot wait until he is old, as Irteniev does, to remember and narrate his youth. He must do so immediately, without delay. His past is the key to understanding his present and the future. His urgent need to narrate reflects Dostoevsky's own sense of urgency regarding the necessity of understanding and narrating Russia's contemporary moment. In *The Adolescent* the multilevel narrative structure emphasizes the present, absorbing the recent past. Instead of an impermeable past, the novel presents an all-pervasive present. This is precisely the sense of presentness that Bakhtin sees as characteristic of the novel as a genre in "Epic and Novel."[42] While Tolstoy's trilogy, like Bakhtin's epic, apotheosizes nostalgia and represents the triumph of the past over the present, Dostoevsky's text takes as its starting point a blank slate, the denial of memory, but gradually acknowledges that without memory form is not possible.

Perhaps the most significant reconfiguration of Tolstoy's trilogy in *The Adolescent* is the narrative displacement enacted through the choice of Arkady as narrator. Although Arkady occupies Irteniev's structural position within the work, it is his father, not the adolescent, who shares Irteniev's symbolic genealogy. Versilov carries the ancient noble pedigree that Irteniev shares with Tolstoy himself, and is around the same age as Irteniev the narrator. Versilov's idealized love for Sophia seems to resemble Irteniev's love for his distant mother more than Arkady's confused and awkward fondness for his. Even Versilov's romanticized vision of the peasant Makar evokes Irteniev's confused wonderment at the peasants who occupy the fringes of his family estate. It is Versilov who shares Irteniev's idealized memories of a childhood on a country estate, memories that consist of the smiling faces of the servant women and the beloved nanny who raised him in lieu of his absent parents (13:86). Dostoevsky twice parodies those nostalgic memories: first by Versilov's own identification of this childhood recollection as the source of his disgust for women working and his abiding love of idleness, and second by Arkady's subsequent account of his own neglected childhood as an angry rejoinder to Versilov's reminiscences (13:91–100). This double parody exemplifies the way *The Adolescent* reframes the trilogy's structural elements. Dostoevsky is simultaneously revealing the illusory and dangerous elements of Tolstoy's vision of the gentry childhood, overcoming them and moving on from them, as demonstrated in the shift from the old hero and symbolic descendant of Irteniev, Versilov, to the new, hybridic hero, Arkady. That symbolic shift from the old aristocratic protagonist to the new socially cross-bred hero occurs during the novel's creative evolution, as the father gives way to the son, but is also narratively present in the novel itself, as Arkady's attempt to take on his father's narrative mantle is gradually replaced by the perception that he can forge a new narrative path independent of past literary models.

Arkady's access to the future is blocked by Versilov and the need to understand his own past. He longs to put together the confused fragments of his own history and understand his own present by accessing the "whole" of his father (13:111). His nostalgia for his father's narrative certainties mirrors Dostoevsky's own inability to reject traditional novelistic family values entirely. The fact that critics almost universally seem to prefer Versilov to Arkady may indicate Dostoevsky's own inability to relinquish his own nostalgia for the Tolstoyan family novel, a nostalgia that we see represented in Nikolai Semyonovich's commentary.[43] But Versilov's novelistic identity is itself fractured; the multiplying dualities within his character form the shards of his psychological and narrative disintegration, which finally materializes in his breaking of the icon, his attempted suicide, and his attempted murder of Akhmakova. As a character, Versilov contains within himself the generic residue of the Russian novel of the noble family, from the shade of the idealistic pedagogue of *Polinka Saks,* through the echoes of the childhood rural paradise of *Childhood,* to his Turgenevian exile in Europe. But these episodes in the novel's history are preserved within him only as the fragments of genre memory, their generic contexts forgotten in the new and dislocated novelistic world Versilov inhabits. The reader of *The Adolescent* can no more reassemble the noble family novel from the generic fragments that remain in Dostoevsky's novel of the accidental family than Arkady can return his father to wholeness. Versilov ultimately disintegrates along with the family he has fathered and the noble family novel he evokes. Arkady is left on the threshold of a new stage in his life, and we as readers are left to contemplate the possibilities of the future artistic work whose vague outlines Nikolai Semyonovich sees in Arkady's notes. In the novel's closing chapters, Dostoevsky projects Versilov's collapse onto a larger national historical screen, inscribing into it a narrative of national and social division. Versilov's disintegration becomes a figure for the social fragmentation of Russia after the Petrine reforms, a symbolic manifestation of the historical culpability of his social estate in this process of fragmentation. Arkady's narratological education is revealed as the figure for Russia's own troubled transition to modernity.

VERSILOV'S CONFESSION

Versilov's symbolic identity, its links to the trilogy, and its position in Arkady's and Dostoevsky's narrative projects are revealed in the dream of the Golden Age and the vision of the thousand Russian noblemen that Versilov reveals to Arkady in the wake of Makar's death (13:373–80), referred to in the notebooks for *The Adolescent* as Versilov's "Confession." The dream and vision rework the same idyllic dream narrated by Stavrogin in his confession to Tikhon in the expurgated chapter of *Demons.* Many critics have emphasized the centrality of atheism to Versilov's dream of the Golden Age, interpreting it as an atheist utopia, which counterbalances Makar's Orthodox spirituality.[44] Without wishing to undermine such a reading, I propose that the dream carries additional symbolic weight by historicizing the problem of disintegration. It inscribes into *The Adolescent* the historical drama of post-Petrine Russia's transition to modernity, providing a deeper historical context for the processes of disintegration represented in the novel. It also points toward the connections between this troubled relationship to modernity and the Russian novelistic tradition. In this sense it provides the formal crystallization of the nexus of associations that had been building in Dostoevsky's creative imagination since the late 1860s. Versilov becomes a purer and more unambiguous representative of Russian Westernism than the ambivalent Stavrogin.

The last creative connection to the "Confession of a Great Sinner," Versilov's "Confession" took on a different meaning as work on the novel progressed, its center of gravity moved to Arkady, and the narration shifted to the first person. The "Confession" became perhaps the only moment in the novel when Versilov is permitted to represent himself, express his own beliefs, and reveal the historical, social, and spiritual contours of his own identity. It is one of the very few instances in *The Adolescent* when Arkady's account of his father is almost completely eclipsed by the implied author's direct narration, a practically unmediated representation of the dialogue between Arkady and Versilov. By loosening Arkady's narrative grip on Versilov, Dostoevsky is able to shift emphasis from Arkady's learning curve to the reader's own hermeneutic field of vision, repositioning the narrative frame and allowing us to see what Versilov represents not in Arkady's autobiography, but in Dostoevsky's novel. This places Versilov and Arkady on the same semantic level, bringing them into structural equivalence and leading to comparisons between them. It reawakens the "fathers and sons" dynamic between them, emphasizing the contrast between the very different generations to which they belong. As Versilov's symbolic identity and literary heritage is revealed, so is the novel's own relationship to the Russian novelistic tradition.

Versilov's "Confession" constitutes his vision of the mission of his own class, "Peter's nobility," the Westernized liberal aristocracy formed by the Petrine reforms. Created in the image of civilized Europeans, the liberal Russian nobility has been sustained by the achievements of the European Enlightenment, eager to replicate them within its own territory, yet aware of the impossibility of such a project: as Versilov explains in the notebooks, "Peter the Great made us citizens of Europe, and we became the bearers of that universal union of ideas" (16:416). Sensitive to his own debt to the historical rupture of the Petrine reforms, without which his class could not exist, the liberal Russian nobleman nonetheless recognizes that this rupture has uprooted him from his native soil. Conscious of the historical distance between the nation of his birth and the European institutions and ideas that inspire him, he has been consigned since his conception to eternal homelessness, belonging neither to Russia nor to Europe.[45] As Versilov tells Arkady, "Europe was just as much our fatherland as Russia. Oh, even more! It's impossible to love Russia more than I do, but I never reproached myself for the fact that Venice, Rome, Paris . . . are dearer to me than Russia" (13:377). Here we see the novelistic flowering of the ideas first expressed in Dostoevsky's May 1871 letter from Europe written in. Sharing the ideals of the Enlightenment, Versilov is horrified by the degeneration of his hopes, the descent of Europe into "the logic of the Tuileries." He sees his liberal aspirations incinerated in the destruction wreaked by the Parisian *pétroleurs* in 1871.[46] Yet he is reluctant to relinquish these hopes, representing as they have for the preceding century the only possible salvation for his homeland. He therefore retreats into a denial of the very historical processes that created him, into a dream of totality, of nostalgia for the image of a prelapsarian, pre-Petrine world, before national, social, and historical differentiation. He retreats into a fantasy in which his ideals of Russia and Europe converge in a perfect figure of historical reconciliation that he calls the "highest Russian thought" (13:375). In this vision, Russia will regain her pre-Petrine totality and will save Europe from itself. The highest ideals of the European Enlightenment, preserved and transformed in the Russian liberal nobility's collective cultural memory, will erase the memory of the burning of the Tuileries (13:469). This dream of the "universal reconciliation of ideas" echoes Dostoevsky's own vision of a salvific Russian universalism in *A Writer's Diary*, yet Versilov believes it to be an explicitly aristocratic dream: "After the Tuileries, a universal reconciliation of ideas. For a Russian nobleman is the universal reconciliation of ideas. The educated Russian is a universal human type, and up to now it has been only the Russian nobleman" (16:432). For Dostoevsky himself reconciliation will be effected through the Russian people.

THE MYTHIC REFUGE FROM HISTORY

Versilov's dream, which ends with "the setting sun of the first day of European civilization," invokes Claude Lorrain's painting of a Golden Age as the image of a world before history, creating a refuge from a historical development that is perpetually founded on rupture. Yet this denial of history is predicated on a denial of his own origins. In his identity as a Russian European, Versilov is himself born out of rupture. The idyllic vision shatters when he awakes and realizes that the sun is setting "on the last day of European mankind." The end of the dream makes clear for the first time the paradox of his identity as a Russian European, and the impossibility of reconciling the historical trajectories of Russia and Europe, an impossibility represented symbolically in Makar's death. The pilgrim stands for the Russia from which Versilov's estate is separated, socially, spiritually, geographically, and historically; it constitutes its Platonic other half.[47] He is identified with the historical epoch brought to an end by the Petrine reforms, the age of Muscovy, and the *narod,* the repository of Russian spirituality.[48] Makar's death leads to Versilov's confession to Arkady, the revelation of his symbolic identity. It offers the possibility of Versilov's marriage to Sophia and seems to clear the way for Arkady's advancement to legitimacy. Yet Makar's passing also marks the end of the dream of totality for Versilov. Without his symbolic other half, reconciliation is impossible: Arkady reveals in the epilogue that "this is only half of the former Versilov" (13:446). Without the two halves, Russia cannot be made one. Europe cannot be saved from the burning of the Tuileries. Without Makar, the symbolic guardian of Orthodoxy's spiritual legacy, which for Dostoevsky himself is central to the reconciliation of Russia's two halves, Versilov's vision lacks a moral rudder.[49] The ultimate failure of Versilov's revelation will be signified in his breaking of the icon, his attempted murder of Akhmakova, and his suicide.

Versilov's embrace of the idea of the salvific, unifying power of the Russian nobility, as E. I. Semenov has pointed out, reflects contemporary debates over the place of the nobility in the future of the Russian state that were triggered by the military of the early 1870s.[50] In his *Russian Society in the Present and the Future,* General Rostislav Fadeev, a prominent opponent of the reforms, thought the nobility played an almost mystical role at the head of the nation, and saw this role as threatened by the reforms.[51] Fadeev's work drew an angry response from the Slavophile Iurii Samarin, who argued that the nobility had always been a service class rather than a "true aristocracy" and that the social group that represented conservative Russia's salvation and reconciliation was not the nobility but the *narod.*[52] Dostoevsky mentions both Fadeev and Samarin in the notebooks for *The Adolescent* as he is working on the articulation of Versilov's idea: "Our best men are lost, many men, many minds. Samarin, Fadeev, communism" (16:367).[53] The dispute between Fadeev and Samarin is mirrored in the gap between Versilov's vision of a social and spiritual reconciliation of Russia led by his own Westernized noble estate, represented in the novel as the victim of its own internal contradictions, and Dostoevsky's own idealized vision of Russian social and religious regeneration, which appears only fleetingly in *The Adolescent* in Arkady's attraction to his legal father, Makar.

There is a crucial metaliterary significance to Versilov's identity as a Westernized liberal nobleman, his vision of the Russian nobility's mission, and his dream of the Golden Age. The notes referring to the Golden Age are interspersed with the meditations on the Russian noble family novel that are eventually incorporated into the epilogue as the paradigmatic novelistic model Arkady rejects in his notes (16:414–39). Significantly, Versilov's "Confession," which was originally the novel's semantic center of gravity, was gradually eclipsed by Arkady's perspective.[54] Versilov represents at once the socially divided historical legacy of the post-Petrine epoch, the remnants of which were disintegrating under the pressure of the Great Reforms of the 1870s, and the literary archetype of the Westernized liberal novelistic hero, scion of a noble family, protagonist of the novels of Goncharov, Turgenev, and above all Tolstoy; he is, as Perlina puts it, a Tolstoyan character in a Dostoevskian novel.[55] He shares with Tolstoy and his novelistic double, Konstantin Levin, a regard for the "blessed order" of Russian peasant wisdom and a belief in the Russian nobility as the moral conscience of the nation.[56] As a liberal Russian nobleman sustained by a dream of escaping history, he shares the nostalgic vision of Tolstoy's Irteniev, the mythic refuge from history that represents the Russian novel's own culpability, its attempted escape from the post-Petrine historical fragmentation that is the legacy of the Petrine reforms. In the notebooks the principal site of his wandering is Venice, which is explicitly described as "Prince Vronsky's Venice" (16:417).

The generic drama of *The Adolescent* finds its symbolic climax on the level of plot with the fragmentation and collapse of Versilov. Versilov comes to symbolize both the Russian realist novelistic tradition and the historical period that gave rise to it. Associated by Nikolai Semyonovich with "a multitude of Russian-European civilizers of the Petersburg period of Russian history," he becomes identified with the epoch of Russian history that began with the Petrine reforms and ended with the Great Reforms of the 1860s (13:455). This is the epoch that has given rise to the Russian novel, yet its contradictions are rarely confronted by the genre. The Russian novel's resistance to change is juxtaposed to Russia's own modernization within Versilov's final act of self-sabotage. His breakdown represents the disintegration of the Russian novelistic tradition and the collapse of the dream of totality that has animated both Russian fantasies of progress and the history of the Russian novel itself. It symbolizes the end of the "St. Petersburg period of Russian history" and the end of the genre that has in many ways defined it.

The symbolic climax of *The Adolescent* is Versilov's psychological collapse, which begins with his smashing of Sophia's icon and ends with his frustrated attempt to shoot both Katerina and himself. The breaking of the icon is central to the novel's overall scheme, as is evident from the frequency with which it occurs in the notebooks for the novel. There it serves as a watershed moment in Versilov's character trajectory; events occur before or after the smashing of the icon (16:33, 45, 57).[57] The act itself is rich with multilayered allegorical meaning, the significance of which is only emphasized by Versilov's initial disavowal: "Don't take it as an allegory, Sonya, it's not Makar's inheritance I've broken . . . Why not take it as an allegory; it certainly must have been" (13:409). It represents the cracking open of the fissure within, the symbolic realization of Versilov's historical burden.

The icon Versilov breaks in two is an Old Believer icon depicting two saints. Kasat'kina convincingly proposes that it represents the saints Makarii and Andrei, two sides of a single image of Russian sanctity, the only true image of Sophia's husband.[58] The two saints also represent the ideal images of Arkady's two fathers, the two halves of post-Petrine Russian society: the Westernized rootless itinerant nobleman (*skitalets*) Versilov, and the Russian peasant wanderer (*strannik*) Makar. Separated by the institution of serfdom, they are opposites defined by their relation to one another.[59] *Strannik* and *skitalets,* they are also doubles of one another, one wandering through the capitals and spas of Western Europe, the other wandering through the monasteries and hermitages of Rus'.[60] Polar opposites, they are also interchangeable: as Kasat'kina points out, the saints associated with the name Makarii are frequently princely, whereas among those named Andrei can be found holy fools.[61] Unbroken, the icon is the repository of the memory of Russian spiritual unity before the Nikonian reforms, but also of the image of a prelapsarian Rus,' the dream of a Russia that knows neither the social, cultural, spiritual, and historical differentiation of the Petrine reforms nor the ideological, social, and historical disintegration of the Great Reforms, a dream that suffuses *A Writer's Diary.* Its split symbolizes the ruptures of those three schisms of modern Russian history, the three sets of reforms Dostoevsky identifies with one another in the notebooks for the novel, and the end of the dream of totality that is figured in Versilov's vision of a Golden Age. It demonstrates that historical and social differentiation and dislocation are inevitable and reveals Versilov's vision as itself fragmented, lacking the spiritual and religious integrity of the Orthodox legacy that is Makar's true inheritance. It is the tangible manifestation of the fallen, fragmented world of the 1870s.

Versilov's collapse also dramatizes *The Adolescent*'s break with the "Petersburg" chapter of the Russian novel's literary history. In the figure of the alienated nobleman Versilov, Dostoevsky has created a prototype novelistic hero, a composite of literary fragments from the works of Herzen, Turgenev, Goncharov, and Tolstoy, the embodiment of the genre memory of the Russian noble family. As Versilov collapses, so too does the integrated memory of the traditional Russian novel. Figured in Versilov's disintegration is the end of the literary historical epoch baptized by Belinsky. An alternative non-novelistic generic principle exists in embryonic form in Makar, who expresses himself using the generic norms and patterns of medieval genres such as the *zhitie;* this represents the beginning of a generic path that Dostoevsky will follow in *The Brothers Karamazov.*

Versilov's collapse clears the way for the triple liberation of Arkady, Dostoevsky, and the reader. Arkady's narratological emancipation from Versilov's legacy is expressed in his declaration "I'm sorry that I have neither time nor space to say more about him" (13:446). Despite Versilov's claims to nobility and social order, it is he, ultimately, who is the source of the disintegration that fragments the characters and multiple plots of *The Adolescent.* And it is Arkady, whose illegitimacy, dislocated family history, and lack of narrative precedent seem the epitome of disorder, who yearns above all for order and who finally learns how to create an ordered narrative out of the chaotic flotsam and jetsam of his life. Versilov in all his disorder reveals what was for Dostoevsky the dark underbelly of the idyllic vision of the Russian noble family novel: the Westernized nobility's responsibility for the social dislocation of the 1870s. Arkady's yearning for order, his openness to the ideals of Makar, and his final liberation from his obsession with his illegitimacy suggest the new ideals and earnest curiosity about Russia's national identity that Dostoevsky identified in the younger generations of populists who made up the novel's first generation of readers on its first publication in *Fatherland Notes.*[62]

The Adolescent constitutes Dostoevsky's most significant attempt to represent in novelistic form the embryonic, transitional social forms of the postreform period. By means of the twin tropes of youth and illegitimacy, *The Adolescent* plays out on the level of novelistic form the uncertainties and tensions of Russia's transition to modernity. The figure of the adolescent, experimenting with different ideas, exploring the inner and outer limits of his personality, developing his relationships with his family, negotiating between his own new, hybridic and unprecedented social position and the old social, spiritual and narratological paradigms of the nobility, represents Russia's own modernization, the troubling coexistence of the old and the new in the period following the Great Reforms. Versilov symbolizes within his own divided self the self-contradictory legacy of the Westernized nobility born out of the Petrine reforms and historically dominant throughout the Petersburg period of Russian history. His final disintegration signifies the curtain call of that epoch, the Great Reforms themselves, which have given rise to a new historical moment, the time of the adolescent.

As an actor in his own plot, Arkady explores the nature of his relationship to his family, his father, his society, his nation, but as author of his own autobiography, he is always also exploring the problem of how to narrate it. Arkady's narrative choices become the primary arena of his formation, his complex negotiations and compromises with his father's literary legacy. Arkady's invocation of previous novelistic models provides Dostoevsky with the formal pretext to explore the history of the Russian novel, to reveal its generic predilections and elisions, its nostalgia for the "finished forms" of the Russian noble family and its resistance to the representation of the "accidental" social bonds of the new historical moment. In the process Dostoevsky reveals the contours of his own novelistic project and the complex genealogy of its own generic past. Arkady's obsession with his own narratological illegitimacy allows Dostoevsky to invest in the figure of Versilov the ideological, spiritual, and aesthetic power of the Russian noble family novel even while he insists that the era of its generic hegemony has passed. The genre memory of the Tolstoyan novel is preserved within *The Adolescent* as formal and thematic fragments. The figure of Versilov becomes the ultimate arena of Dostoevsky's authorial self-definition, the site of his own ambivalent negotiation of the social, spiritual, and literary legacy of the Westernized Russian nobility and of his own ultimate insistence on the birth of a new social and literary moment.

In its dual status as "notes" and novel, *The Adolescent* seeks to represent the contingent, open, unformed nature of the contemporary moment while also answering the demands of narrative form and narrative closure. In his youth, inexperience, and narrative insecurities, Arkady symbolizes a present which is not yet determined yet which Dostoevsky insists must be narrated. The act of representing the inchoate forms of the moment of transition is a complex balancing act, and its successful outcome is far from self-evident, even for Dostoevsky himself, as we see in Nikolai Semyonovich's ambivalent commentary on the "notes." Yet *The Adolescent's* interrogation of the novel as a genre represents a crucial and unsung moment in both Dostoevsky's own career as a novelist and the evolution of the Russian novel; the questions it raises and the solutions it proposes seem to represent a turn we might even call protomodernist.[63] In *The Adolescent* Dostoevsky has created a novel that is not so much an object as a process; the novel's structure itself undergoes development and change, with which we, as readers, are forced to actively engage. Through that act of engagement, we gain privileged access to the paradoxes of representation within Dostoevsky's own creative process. Sadly, the novel has rarely received the critical or readerly engagement it so richly deserves.

Chapter Four

Between Babel and a New Word: *A Writer's Diary* as Monojournal

IN THE SHORT STORY "DREAM OF A RIDICULOUS MAN," published in the April 1877 issue of *A Writer's Diary,* Dostoevsky provides a powerful account of narrative collapse in the face of an ineffable transcendent ideal. The ridiculous man is saved from suicide by a redemptive vision, yet he is unable to communicate that vision to those around him. The gulf between the transcendent ideal of his vision and the disordered chaos of the world he inhabits is expressed in terms of a communication breakdown: "But how we are to build paradise I do not know, because I do not have the words to express it. I lost the words after my dream. At least all the main words, the most essential ones. But never mind: I shall go off and keep talking tirelessly" (25:118).[1]

Faced by this verbal inadequacy, he hovers between hope and despair, between the need for narration and the awareness of its shortcomings. He resolves to keep on talking, to churn out an endless stream of words in an attempt to express his vision, the image of a prelapsarian world, an insight into the time before the social and metaphysical fragmentation brought by the differentiation of language itself.

As he contemplated mid-1870s Russia, with its processes of social, intellectual, and spiritual breakdown, Dostoevsky shared the ridiculous man's dream of a world where linguistic unity still reigned. The era of social transition, the age of *razlozhenie* and *obosoblenie,* had given rise to a new Babel as political polarization brought with it an increased sense of social differentiation, a proliferation of languages, worldviews, and belief systems as foreign to each other as to the traditional intellectual and spiritual institutions they opposed. In this reincarnation of *A Writer's Diary* as a freestanding autonomous work, a monojournal, Dostoevsky hoped to bring a messianic "new word" to the dissociated intellectuals whose rootless secular ideologies he saw as undermining the core spiritual values of the Russian nation, a "new word" that would unify these disparate groups and reignite their faith in the

Russian people and the Orthodox faith.[2] Yet even as he sought to defy history with his prophetic vision, he could not ignore the cacophony of voices around him. As he attempted to understand the cultural undercurrents of the social ferment he read about every day in the Petersburg press, he tried to represent the full spectrum of the divergent discourses that existed in the Russian Empire's newspapers, courtrooms, and lecture halls. In *A Writer's Diary* he represented these dissonant voices in the full chaotic glory of their diversity, demonstrating the multiplicity of languages that existed in this new Babel.

Even more than his columns in *The Citizen,* the monojournal incarnation *A Writer's Diary* tries to reconcile two creative visions that are ideologically and formally incompatible: on the one hand, the conception of a multilingual, heterogeneric heteroglossia that seeks to compensate for the fragmentation of the postreform era through a diverse combination of voices and perspectives and through the sheer power of narration; on the other, a utopian dream of overcoming communication breakdown and uniting the diffuse elements of Russian society through the Word of the Orthodox Christ. Dostoevsky seeks simultaneously to represent these divergent discourses and to counteract them with his own unifying discourse. The incompatibility of these two endeavors creates a hermeneutic tension that is present from start to finish and pulls the reader in radically different directions. If *The Adolescent* depicts a narratological education and *The Brothers Karamazov* models a trial of genres, then *A Writer's Diary* constitutes a verbal battleground, the clash of two different approaches to the word.

A continuation of the columns he had written in 1873–74 for *The Citizen, A Writer's Diary* was another incarnation of the project he had described in the notebooks and epilogue to *The Adolescent,* an attempt to convey in literary form the discrete phenomena of the new social reality he saw unfolding around him in the streets of Petersburg, in the far-off capitals of Western Europe, on the battlefields of the Balkans, and in the peasant villages of central Russia. Journalism served as a platform from which Dostoevsky could engage more directly with contemporary life, providing him with a different set of generic demands and code of representation from those offered by the novel.[3] The formal demands of the novel had restricted his encyclopedic ambition; journalism allowed him to work on a massive scale, to engage more directly both with his subject matter and with his readers.

Yet this was to be a unique type of journalism, one that would commandeer an entire arsenal of literary and journalistic genres, modes, contracts, and devices. It would involve a complex merging of levels of authorial identity and shifts in temporal perspective between past, present, and future. It would combine a concern with the everyday events of the Petersburg street with messianic nationalism, sociological and journalistic enquiry with prophecy, and a focus on the particular with a universalizing tendency. Above all, it was to be a journalism that flaunted its ambivalent relationship to the genre of the novel, a relationship at once deeply dependent and subtly confrontational.

The plurality of social discourses within the postreform era, the multiplicity of voices clamoring to be heard, and the new kinds of narratives appearing in newspapers and journals all called for new kinds of literary forms that would be maximally open to the flux of life. Having tried somewhat unsuccessfully in *The Adolescent* to adapt the novel form to convey these processes of fragmentation, Dostoevsky wanted to find a genre that could more effectively respond to these social and historical circumstances. In *A Writer's Diary* he attempted to portray the process of social fragmentation both thematically, taking for his subject matter the streets, orphanages, courtrooms, and slums of Petersburg, and formally, as he incorporated the process of narrative breakdown into works of fiction and semi-fiction such as "The Meek One," "Bobok," and "The Sentence."

A Writer's Diary occupies a peculiar place within the field of Dostoevsky criticism. Like *The Adolescent,* it has been consistently neglected by scholars both because of its ideological agenda, which combines prophetic nationalism, antisemitism, and populism, and because of its status as "mono-journal," which makes it difficult to categorize. With a dazzlingly complex hierarchy of narrators, modes, and genres, it has to be subjected to a rigorous formal analysis before its "message" can be decoded. With the exception of a few scholars who have attempted the Herculean task of decoding the complex poetics of the *Diary,* the majority of critics have treated the work either merely as the creative laboratory for themes and ideas given novelistic representation in *The Brothers Karamazov,* or else as a semi-literary behemoth infected by journalistic polemic, more valuable as a historical artifact than as a work of art.[4] Yet the *Diary* is no isolated generic anomaly: it is a work that was born out of a rich literary and hermeneutic exchange between the novel and journalism and that everywhere reflects the troubled symbiosis between novelistic and journalistic systems of representation.

How can such a heterogeneric work be categorized? Since its first appearance, readers of the *Diary* have been troubled by a tension between its poetic, artistic, or literary sections, and its prosaic *nauchnyi,* scholarly or scientific sections, with their tendency toward abstract theoretical arguments, arguments that are seen to have a place within journalistic discourse but not within literary discourse.[5] How are we to react to this mixing of genres? Should we read the *Diary* as a work of literature or a work of journalism, or both? Literature and journalism sit together uncomfortably, and their dissonance tends to impede our ability to read the *Diary* systematically, to make out the shape of a master genre within the multiplicity of genres that make up this vast and complex work.

This generic conflict can be connected to a duality of vision that goes to the very core of *A Writer's Diary:* the tension between irony and utopianism. Critics have highlighted the coexistence in the *Diary* of the voices of the ironist and the metaphysician, the anti-utopian and the utopian.[6] On the one hand Dostoevsky challenges the utopian prescriptive formulas of the radical intelligentsia by presenting an alternative view of reality, based not on one point of view claiming ultimate authority, but on a diversity of perspectives and on a "poetics of the topical."[7] On the other he seeks to find his own "guiding thread through chaos" and imposes his own utopian vision of an idealized transcendent future onto the heterogeneous reality about which he writes. For the reader of the *Diary*, this dialogue between Dostoevsky as critic of the philosophical and stylistic foundations of "linearity" and Dostoevsky the utopian is deeply problematic and has led to accusations of stylistic inconsistency, even failure.[8]

This conflict at the heart of *A Writer's Diary* takes place alongside the collision of two different systems of representation: the novelistic and the journalistic. Each generates its own generic repertoire, narrative contract, narrative perspective, intertextual relationships, relation to reality, rhetorical strategies, attitude toward representation. What happens when they coexist within one work? Can the work withstand the friction and contradictions between their often very different sets of hermeneutic assumptions? How can the reader negotiate the relationship between their differing perspectives? How can she recognize the shift from one system to the other? What happens if she mistakenly applies some of the generic assumptions associated with the journalistic system to the novelistic sections, or reads the journalistic sections as she would the fictional pieces?

Central to my study of the *Diary* is an examination of the role and image of the Diarist himself. Resembling at times a novelistic narrator, at others a journalistic one, sometimes coinciding with Dostoevsky's own voice and sometimes clearly distinct from it, the Diarist remains the key to the work's dissonant poetics. The textual fluidity of his narrative identity enlivens and complicates the work as he tries sometimes to undermine any monolithic reading of the whole work, sometimes to insist on a particular interpretation. Similarly central to the clash of the novelistic and journalistic modes is the contradictory role of dialogue within the *Diary*. I use Bakhtin's theories of heteroglossia and dialogue within the novel to investigate the attitude of the Diarist toward the voices of others. Is he open to other perspectives, or insistent on maintaining his own point of view at all costs?

I conclude by examining the relationship between this twin set of conflicts, the representational and poetic, and the ideological and philosophical. What effect does the clash of the novelistic and journalistic systems of representation have on the work's overall shape? I argue that although this clash of representational systems subverts his utopian aims and breaks the guiding thread, leaving the reader to find his own way in darkness through the chaotic labyrinth of Dostoevsky's prose, at the same time this bewildering combination of broken narrative contracts, of contradictory generic conventions, of differing narrative perspectives, constitutes a profoundly appropriate literary response to the diverse social discourses that clamored for attention in mid-1870s Russia.

THE *DIARY* AS PROJECT: THE GUIDING THREAD THROUGH CHAOS

The coexistence of literary and journalistic genres is characteristic of the publication circumstances of nineteenth-century Russian literature. In periodicals and newspapers, serialized novels, poems, and short stories rubbed shoulders with feuilletons and physiological sketches, treatises on political economy and current affairs, columns on high-society life and literary criticism. Readers were used to turning their attention from the high seriousness of a lyric poem to the polemical force of an economic treatise, from the light-hearted ribaldry of a feuilleton to news of the latest events in the Balkans. Works of radically different genres were separated by minimal textual or typographic boundaries; they faced each other, followed one another, and often, through this typographic arrangement, seemed placed into implicit dialogue with each other.[9] The reader was thus trained to quickly move from one genre to another.

As well as coexisting on the page, "high" literature and journalism connected in the lives and careers of their practioners. Novelists and poets on the left and right of the political spectrum alternated between works of belles lettres and articles, polemics, or columns for journals.[10] Dostoevsky's relationship to the world of journalism spanned his entire literary career. Mere months after being "discovered" as a novelist by Nekrasov and Belinsky, the author of *Poor Folk* was turning his hand to the feuilletons of *The Jester* and *Petersburg News.*[11] From 1860 to 1863 and then again from 1864 to 1865, along with his brother Mikhail he edited the journals *Time* and *Epoch,* contributing both nonfiction articles and novels. On the death of his brother and the closure of *Epoch,* Dostoevsky left the journalistic fray to devote his time to writing novels full time, but he continued to contemplate different kinds of journalistic projects, as is clear from his correspondence (28:II:141, 224, 233; 29:I:11). A plan for a periodical publication, first mentioned in a letter of 1865, has crystallized by 1867, when he writes to his niece Sonya, "When I return [to Russia] I would certainly like to publish something like a newspaper (I even recall mentioning it to you in passing, but here both the form and the aim have become completely clear)" (28:II:224). All his projected publications were encyclopedic and heterogeneous in form and content.

For the novelist, the appeal of such a project is clear. Journalism, so often belittled by literary critics as the lucrative last resort for the starving writer of belles lettres, also provides a creative outlet for the novelist for whom the constraints of literary form have become burdensome. Although the "Writer's Diary" columns in *The Citizen* allowed for some generic mixing, they nonetheless followed the norms of newspaper or journal columns; it was not until he reconceived the project as a "monojournal" that Dostoevsky's generic ambitions could take on their full heterogeneity.

Even for a writer so steeped in the interactions between journalism and "high" literature as Dostoevsky, *A Writer's Diary* was a revolutionary project on both a macrocosmic and a microcosmic level. Though contemporary readers were used to the coexistence of fiction and nonfiction within journals, they were able to shift their mode of reading with the shift in author, from economist to novelist. The editor of a "thick journal" such as *The Russian Messenger*'s Mikhail Katkov chose his material based on the general ideological tendency of his publication and tried to maintain a certain degree of political consistency, but his publication did not seek the status of literary or ideological totality.[12] He did not look for resonance between the anthologized works of individual authors. The *Diary*, on the other hand, was conceived of as a unitary heterogeneric work in which a series of themes were expressed through different modes and genres. Though each issue was divided into two or three chapters, and each of those chapters was divided into several sections, the boundaries between these sections did not coincide with those of the work's diverse genres. The genres seeped into one another, journalistic commentary melding into fiction, literary criticism transforming into autobiography, and semi-fictional speculation taking on the coloration of nationalist prophecy. This new relationship to genre made complex demands on Dostoevsky's readers; it required them to enter into a wholly new kind of generic contract, one that included generic shifts within a single entry and shifts in the hierarchy of narrative voices. Most significantly, it sought to combine modes of representation that were sometimes irrevocably opposed to one another in their structures and worldviews.

Each chapter and chapter section of each issue of the *Diary* contains many different genres, which together filter a single theme or set of themes. The January 1876 issue takes the theme of the future. In "In Place of a Foreword," the Diarist begins by looking ahead, in the light-hearted fragmentary tone of the feuilletonist, but he never gets around to writing a proper foreword because he is too preoccupied by the social chaos that surrounds him. The path to the future is blocked by the disintegration of the present (22:5–7). Challenged by a reader to explain himself, he moves first into autobiography and then into a projected novel in "A Future Novel" (22:7–8). The projected novel centers on children, who serve as a metaphor for Russian society's uncertain future. He shifts into journalistic commentary on a story he has read about in the newspaper, which flows apparently seamlessly into the next section, "The Christmas Tree at the Artists' Club," which combines the genres of feuilleton, literary criticism, autobiography, and dialogue to tell a story of the plight of Russian youth, sacrificed on the altar of Russian Westernism (22:9–12). The lapsarian present leads him to contemplate the alternative, his own utopian vision of Russia's future. In "The Golden Age in One's Pocket," the Diarist creates a kind of feuilletonistic utopia, a meditation on the nature and possibility of a utopian outlook that borrows the irony, self-contradiction, and self-referentiality of the feuilletonistic mode (22:12–13).[13] In the second part he begins by recounting a factual episode, a boy he saw begging, but journalism gives way to semi-fictional speculations and then finally to fiction in "The Boy at Christ's Christmas Party" (22:14–17). In "The Colony of Young Offenders," he presents his visit to a children's penal colony as straightforward reportage (22:17–25). In the 1873 columns he shifted voices and perspectives within a single genre, but in the monojournal each new section offers a new generic perspective, a new lens to help perceive the outlines of Russia's future.

The difference between the *Diary* as column and as monojournal should be seen more broadly in terms of the evolution of Dostoevsky's thinking about genre. In 1876, after his experimentation with novelistic form in *The Adolescent,* his attitude toward genre was even more radical and more complex than it had been in 1873–74. As we have seen in the previous chapter, the meditations on the novel in both the notebooks for *The Adolescent* and the work itself demonstrate his ambition to rework the structure of the novel to make it more open to the expression of contemporary transitional social forms. Following his experimentation on a single genre, it was perhaps natural that he would conduct his next formal experiment on several genres simultaneously.

Dostoevsky's dual aims for his new literary genre can be found in the *Diary* itself, in an entry from January 1877. Reflecting on a letter he has received about the suicide of a twelve- or thirteen-year-old boy, ostensibly because of bad grades at school, he is reminded, significantly, of Tolstoy's *Childhood* (25). Tolstoy describes a similar torment taking place in the mind of his young hero, Irteniev. Acknowledging the enigmatic nature of the schoolboy's suicide, Dostoevsky wonders if he was subject to the same psychological torment described by Tolstoy, yet he suggests that the changed social and historical circumstances of this boy's suicide require a new kind of artist, one whose vision goes beyond that of the "historian of the aristocracy." Returning to the topic of the epilogue and notebooks for *The Adolescent,* Dostoevsky renews his plea for a new kind of historian of the contemporary condition, a chronicler of the dissociated and fragmented corners of Russian life:

> One senses that something is not quite right here, that an enormous part of the Russian order of life has remained entirely without any observer and without any *historian.* At least it is clear that the upper-middle level of our nobility, so vividly described by our writers, is already an insignificant and "dissociated" corner of Russian life generally. Who then, will be the historian of the other corners, of which, it seems, there are so awfully many? (25:35)[14]

In the March 1876 entry "Dissociation" ("Obosoblenie"), Dostoevsky refers to the present as the "the epoch of universal dissociation" (23:80). He describes the process by which individual members of the intelligentsia and educated class are isolating themselves, rejecting their spiritual and cultural heritage in favor of hazy concepts of originality and individuality embodied in grand social and political theories. This dissociation manifests itself most strikingly in the many ideological suicides that Dostoevsky examines throughout the *Diary,* particularly at the end of 1876. While dissociation takes on the appearance of social breakdown in crises such as the perceived epidemic of ideological suicides, it interests Dostoevsky primarily as an intellectual, linguistic, and even hermeneutic phenomenon: "All are dissociating themselves, isolating themselves from everyone else, everyone wants to invent something of his own, something new and unheard of. Everybody sets aside all those things that used to be common to our thoughts and feelings and begins with his own thoughts and feelings. Everyone wants to begin from the beginning" (22:80). The *Diary* aimed to counteract this process, to return traditional common institutions and social forms to a central position within the new world order. It was the thought processes of the intelligentsia, their readings of the situation, and the form of their expression of their dilemmas and solutions that Dostoevsky sought to take on. Thus he presents the *Diary* as a series of hermeneutic filters through which the phenomena of everyday life pass. These filters differ in their ideological and generic assumptions, thus yielding different images of man and his spiritual makeup. We are frequently encouraged to examine the material of these filters and the nature and extent of their subjectivity. Reading becomes the major theme of the work itself.

Yet in spite of, or perhaps because of, its critique of the intelligentsia's utopian mind-set, and their need for reductive, totalizing systems, the *Diary* partakes in its own brand of dissociation. Dostoevsky too wants to find a "new word," a new word that he claims more than once is the "last word." The assumption of a guiding thread itself suggests the existence of a master narrative, an explanatory system that can lead us through the labyrinth of discrete elements. But as the Diarist teaches us to read the underlying assumptions of these hermeneutic filters, he also provides us with the tools necessary to interpret his own filters, and thus opens up his own explanatory systems to critical scrutiny.

We find here the same kind of reservations that had troubled Nikolai

Semyonovich as he had struggled to read the adolescent's account of a life lived against the backdrop of rapid social transition. Artistic representation relies on the possibility of signification, on finding an image that can stand for more than merely itself. He conceives of the possibility of artistic representation as akin to a normative law or a guiding thread the true artist picks out of the formless chaos that surrounds him. Yet he wonders whether the dissociation and the fragmentation have not reached such proportions that this image remains indistinct, even for the greatest artist:

> And if, within this chaos that has gone on for so long and that is particularly prevalent in the life of our society now—a life in which, perhaps, even an artist of Shakespearean proportions cannot find a normative law and a guiding thread—who, then, will illuminate even a little part of this chaos, never mind dreaming of some guiding thread? The main thing it seems is that no one is capable of doing this; it is as if it were still too early, even for our greatest artists. One cannot deny that a way of life in Russia is disintegrating; consequently, family life disintegrates as well. (25:35)

This sense of universal dissolution and disintegration is accompanied by its opposite: an awareness of the new social forms that are coming into being, which he must learn to represent.

The continual vacillation between acknowledgment of the extreme difficulty, even impossibility, of representing the processes of social and intellectual diffusion taking place all around him and the absolute imperative of trying to find connections between the disparate phenomena of day-to-day social reality is central to the literary and ideological dynamism of the *Diary*. It deals with the problem of how to represent narrative collapse. In the earnest and hesitant soul-searching of the passage above, Dostoevsky's acknowledgment of the irresolvable nature of his paradox is expressed through the form of unanswered questions, which remain in our minds as we read on in the *Diary*. Yet such truly dialectical moments are rare: the Diarist usually prefers to foreground either the chaos or the guiding thread, attempting to sidestep the complex hermeneutic paradox that underlies his entire project.

THE NARRATIVE CONTRACT

The narrative contract for the 1876–77 monojournal is laid out in the journal's announcement to subscribers, published at the end of 1875. The announcement reads,

> In the coming year F. M. Dostoevsky's publication, *A Writer's Diary*, will appear monthly in separate issues.

> Each issue will be composed of sixteen to twenty-four pages of small print in the format of our weekly newspapers. But this will not be a newspaper; all twelve issues (for January, February, March, etc.) will form a whole, a book written by a single pen. It will be a diary in the literal sense of the word, an account of impressions actually experienced each month, an account of what was seen, heard, and read. Of course, some stories and tales may be included, but pre-eminently it will be about actual events. (22:136)

This contract brings out the generic ambiguities in the very title of Dostoevsky's new journalistic enterprise. On the one hand it is a diary "in the literal sense of the word," the record of an individual's impressions and thoughts. The social and historical background of a diary reveals itself only in relation to the individual's particular story. The individual seeks to unfold the multiplicity of events of his or her life through remembering and recording them. Unlike memoirs, diaries tend to be written directly after the events they describe, so that the diarist does not normally portray them against the broad sweep of time. He or she is still living out the direct consequences of the events being recorded. The structural principle of the diary is chronological; by recording events in the order in which they took place, the Diarist hopes to be able to detect the pattern behind the flow of events, to decipher the meaning behind a seemingly random event through its connection to other events. The contract refers to another potential generic peculiarity: it may include some stories and tales. How will these fictional works adapt to fit the *Diary*'s chronological structure?

The problem of the *Diary*'s genre was one that caught the attention of its readers right from the moment of its first publication. P. Boborykin complained, in the pages of the *Saint Petersburg News*, "How should one look at 'A Writer's Diary,' thought up by Mr. Dostoevsky? As a journal in literary form or as a real diary that expresses all the particularities of his physiognomy as a writer?"[15] Indeed, the fact that this is a *writer's* diary transforms our expectations. It ceases to be the private record of an individual's life and takes on a wider literary and cultural significance. It moves from the private to the public sphere. It becomes enmeshed within a web of literary connections, as it can be seen as a source for, and a commentary on, the writer's other works. Extraliterary factors such as the writer's image within his society enter into the equation, obscuring the boundaries of the text and complicating the task of reader and critic alike. The many faces of Dostoevsky, from former *katorzhnik* to political obscurantist and supporter of the autocracy, from man of the '40s to ambivalent defender of idealistic youth, all consciously came into play, both on the part of the author himself and on the part of his readers.[16] *A Writer's Diary* offered the possibility of setting the record straight, yet its literary form complicated the reconstruction of

Dostoevsky's public image. Internal textual dynamics competed with external political considerations, creating the complex generic cross-fertilization suggested by the concept of a *writer's diary*.

The *Diary* also borrows generously from the generic repertoire of another genre: the feuilleton. As Dostoevsky himself pointed out in a January 1876 letter to Soloviev: "Without doubt, *A Writer's Diary* will resemble a feuilleton, with the difference that a monthly feuilleton naturally cannot resemble a weekly feuilleton" (29:II:73). In its poetics and system of representation the feuilleton borrows both from journalism and from fiction. Almost every Russian novelist of the nineteenth century from Pushkin onward tried his or her hand at writing feuilletons, first for the "thick" journals and later for the newspapers, which began to compete for a growing readership in the second half of the century and especially following the explosion in newspaper publication following the Great Reforms of the 1860s. Thus novelistic techniques entered the feuilleton through its practitioners, and feuilletons in their turn informed the novels of the period in a continual process of creative exchange.[17]

Central to the poetics of the feuilleton is the image and self-fashioning of the feuilletonist, who occupies an ambiguous position between fiction and reality. Taking on a pseudonym, the feuilletonist immediately distanced himself from his real persona. His literary identity emerged within the parameters of the feuilleton and developed gradually over a period of time, just like the identity of narrator or characters in a serialized novel. Yet donning this fictional mask did not prevent the author from bringing his own political beliefs or biographical details into the realm of the feuilleton, and he often gave accounts of real events in the life of the city or the country. Thus the world created by the feuilletonist stood in uneasy relation to the real world; the reader of the feuilleton found himself before a distorting mirror whose reflection he knew to be determined by the genre's foibles, yet he was sometimes unable to tell precisely where the mirror image departed from the original. The January 1876 *Diary* opens in the playful voice of the feuilletonist, who declares his intention to write a foreword to the publication but is too distracted by current events to be able to make any large opening statement (22:3–5). Significantly, it also opens in medias res, with an ellipsis and a reference to Gogol's Khlestakov, the protagonist of *The Government Inspector.* The Diarist compares his contemporaries unfavorably to Khlestakov; the latter is at least capable of feeling some shame. The literary reference, double-voiced feuilletonistic tone, and ellipsis insert the Diarist's opening volley into what seems to be an ongoing journalistic conversation.

The feuilleton is one of many different genres to bring its conventions and assumptions to the *Diary.* A fruitful example of the work's genre play can be found in its autobiographical sections, such as "The Peasant Marey"

(22:46–50). The autobiographical mode, as Lejeune has shown, relies on a particular generic contract between author and reader, central to which is the tacit assumption that the events being narrated have taken place in the life of the author.[18] Hybrid genres, such as the autobiographical novel, can incorporate autobiographical elements into themselves but are not bound by this autobiographical contract; the novelistic or fictional contract supersedes it. In a work made up of many different genres, what contractual obligations bind author and reader? When we read "The Peasant Marey," should we treat it as a piece of autobiographical reading that can stand alone and is structured according to a standard autobiographical contract, the events narrated having actually taken place in the life of the author? Or does its location within the *Diary* fictionalize a narrative whose authenticity we know only from the extratextual evidence of diaries and letters? Does "The Peasant Marey" have its own generic contract, or is it subject to the generic contract of the larger work, of the *Diary* itself?

These questions are particularly pertinent in the case of "The Peasant Marey," since it recapitulates within the *Diary* a narrative which had earlier been fictionalized within *Notes from the House of the Dead* but which Dostoevsky now frames as a reminiscence of a reminiscence (22:46–50). While in Siberian exile the twenty-nine-year-old Dostoevsky is accosted by a fellow convict, a Polish political prisoner, who expresses his hatred for their fellow peasant prisoners. The Pole's comments trigger a memory, an incident from his childhood, when, alone in the fields and fearing the presence of a wolf, he was comforted by a peasant who was plowing. In its location within the February *Diary,* it functions as a "proof" of the Russian peasant's redemptive moral potential, forming part of a polemical argument on the Russian people's historical mission. This autobiographical element, while central to Dostoevsky's own narrative of his Siberian conversion experience, does not define the episode in its location within the *Diary.* Dostoevsky stresses both the peasant's actions as a typical instantiation of the Russian people's native compassion and the episode's status as a recollection of a recollection. The *Diary*'s self-referential quality dominates the episode, and it becomes a Proustian meditation on recollection itself. Meanwhile, the mediating layers of memory undercut the article's didactic thrust. Within the *Diary* the narrative exists at the meeting point of various different generic contracts and modes of representation, several of which come into play as we read, extending and complicating its meaning.

THE NOVELISTIC

Although the *Diary* is not a novel and does not contain any novels, several critics have written of a *novelizing tendency* within it.[19] The idea that the novel is more than a set of formal features constituting a generic structure—that it projects its own particular view of humankind and the world and contains a particular kind of generic filter, a novelizing drive—has developed within several schools of twentieth-century novel theory. Taking their cue from the Aristotelian roots of genre theory itself, where the perspectives of particular genres, along with their corresponding subjects, were seen to provide each genre with its own conventionalized view of man, thus making a difference between the tragic and the epic hero, twentieth-century novel theorists have brought differing theoretical assumptions to their task but have explored the relationship between the novel and its worldview in similar ways. Though their conclusions diverge markedly, Lukács, Bakhtin, José Ortega y Gasset, and Ian Watt all develop theories of the novelistic rather than of the novel.[20] All argue for a novelistic worldview that came into being within a particular set of historical conditions, alongside analogous developments in the field of philosophy.[21] They explore the narrative implications of humans' increasing awareness of themselves as individuals and social beings and of the resulting tensions. If we subscribe to this view of novelistic narrative as part of a sequence of larger historical and intellectual processes rather than merely the sum of the defined structural features of a prescribed literary form, then it becomes possible to argue that it can exist outside the novel form. While the novelistic form is usually the carrier of novelistic narrative, it is not its exclusive property. As Bakhtin points out in "Epic and Novel," "In an era when the novel reigns supreme, all the remaining genres are, to a greater or lesser extent, 'novelized' . . . In an environment where the novel is the dominant genre, the conventional languages of strictly canonical genres begin to sound in new ways."[22] For the novelist who writes in other genres, the novelizing drive is even more likely to dominate. My use of the concept of the novelistic drive derives from this critical tradition. It should not be confused with the fictional, the literary, or the artistic, although within the *Diary* it can be found most frequently in the fictional and semi-fictional sections, and less frequently within the journalistic articles.[23]

But what constitutes a novelistic worldview, and how can we detect its presence in another kind of text? I shall argue that the novel's particular structural configurations, its construction of a fictional cross-section of a projected fictional world, its attempt to balance the demands of biography, the narrative of the life of an individual, with those of sociology, the narrative of the life of an entire society, create a particular philosophy of representation. Integral to this philosophy of representation is an awareness of the novelistic subject as simultaneously individual and universal, unique and typical. When these attitudes toward representation spill over into other genres, those genres become novelized.

Comparative studies of novelistic and journalistic representation have rarely been undertaken. While scholars are beginning to study the serialization of novels and the institutions of journalism, closer analyses of the poetics of these modes and their relation to one another remain comparatively rare.[24] Examinations of novelistic discourse, especially in the Russian tradition, usually refer to its relation to other genres within the sphere of "high" literature, such as lyric poetry, but rarely deal with its relation to nonliterary or semi-literary rhetorical structures. Something of an exception to this generalization is the stylistic analysis performed by Vinogradov. The Soviet scholar, whose work on literary language includes stylistic analysis of some journalistic passages in *A Writer's Diary*, complements Bakhtin's short exposition on the difference between dialogue in novelistic and journalistic discourse with an examination of the rhetorical strategies Dostoevsky uses against the speech of the prosecuting attorney in the Kroneberg case (*Diary*, March 1876).[25] Yet Vinogradov undertakes an analysis not of novelistic prose, but of artistic prose in general. I combine the approaches of Bakhtin and Vinogradov to compare some of the underlying assumptions of novelistic and journalistic representation.

Systems of novelistic and journalistic representation differ from one another in their attitudes toward the relationship of the part to the whole. The novel is structured around a central paradox: the novelistic subject is both novel, that is, out of the ordinary, yet representative, expected to signify more than just itself. Novels continually vacillate between the claim to novelty and individuality and the claim to typicality and generality. Dostoevsky tackles this paradox of novelistic representation in the preface to *The Brothers Karamazov* as the implied author anticipates the objections his readers might have to his hero, who is simultaneously remarkable (*primechatelen*), eccentric (a *chudak*), and somehow universal, carrying within himself the heart of the whole (*sertsevinu tselogo*) (14:5). We may note here the etymology of *primechatelen*, or "noteworthy," from *primechat'*, "to make a mental note of something," and *primechanie*, "annotation or literary note," which points toward the literary significance of this preface (Dal'). The impled author defends his hero's eccentricity, yet insists he has not broken the novelistic narrative contract: Aleksei Fyodorovich signifies, yet his signification remains obscure and opaque (14:5). Dostoevsky locates the anticipated failure of his hero to signify within a familiar context: the age of *obosoblenie*, when social forms and discourses are in flux. In order for him to fulfill his novelistic contractual obligations, he must not only show the subject of his novel to be "novelistic"; he must also redefine the "novelistic," beginning with the novelistic hero.

The vacillation between typicality and individuality gives rise to what might even be called the novelistic function: continual deliberation over the possibility of representing. The primary question every novel raises is whether the narrative it represents stands for many other similar narratives, or whether it stands alone; whether it was chosen for its typicality or its uniqueness.

In journalistic discourse there is no place for individual consciousness. The individual's experience merely provides material for the journalist's larger assertions about the life of a social class or the whole society. Similarly in journalism there is no ambivalence about the typicality of the represented subject. Universal signification is a cornerstone of the journalistic contract. If a journalist writes about a beggar, then it is assumed that that beggar's story can stand in for the stories of all the beggars of that particular street, or city, or country. He must be symptomatic of a place and a time. A news item must always reflect a larger phenomenon; otherwise it ceases to deserve our attention. Every newspaper, taken as a totality, seeks to represent the whole life of a society. If we doubt the typicality of a particular narrative or image, then the journalistic contract is broken. Hybrid journalistic genres such as the feuilleton and the physiological sketch frequently explore the boundaries of typicality, concerning themselves with the phantasmagoria that lies beneath the surface of the everyday, the unique and fantastic aspects of the city's life. Because of the challenge they represent for the journalistic contract, they are always separated from the straightforwardly journalistic articles in newspapers by a solid typographic boundary.

The feuilleton projects a complex and ambivalent attitude toward its own system of representation. On the one hand, it partakes of the same careful decoding of the urban social landscape as the physiological sketch, alighting on a tiny, seemingly accidental, unique detail of Petersburg reality, and drawing from it evidence of a larger social design. On the other, it continually interrogates its own concepts of the typical, undercutting them and injecting them with irony.

Dostoevsky refers to another paradox of novelistic representation in the preface to *The Brothers Karamazov:* the novel's troubled simultaneous existence as fragment and totality. While purporting to provide a kind of temporal cross-section of an imagined parallel universe, it strives to achieve the status of an aesthetic totality. Although the fictional world stretches no further than the beginning and end of the work presented by the author, it creates a million possible narrative threads in its reader's imagination, threads that lead on into infinity. Every novelistic event is simultaneously isolated, accidental, and self-contained, and connected to the whole, significant only in relation to the totality.

We experience novelistic structure as simultaneously open and closed. As Morson points out, as we read we have the impression that the novel's characters are free and that the future of the plot is open to any or all possibilities, yet we also know that the novel has been written, the plot determined; the characters are the pawns of the author.[26] Novelistic narrative has thus evolved to exhibit freedom and determinism simultaneously. The combination of the demands of structure and the demands of the novelistic worldview create a balance between open-endedness and closure at the novel's ending.

Bakhtin's "Discourse in the Novel" argues for the existence of a novelistic worldview, a vision of a world based on a multiplicity of voices and narrative perspectives, where meaning comes into being through the interaction of coexisting narratives, through the resonances of their differing social, cultural, and linguistic contexts as they enter the arena of the novel. He argues for a revolution in the theory of the novel, a rejection of traditional stylistics in favor of examination of the novel in all its heterogeneric, multivoiced, multilingual open-endedness. He argues that traditional stylistics has ignored the diversity of social speech types and of individual voices that exist within the novel. It has thus read the novel as a stylistic unity, a misconception Bakhtin rejects in the strongest possible terms.

The novel, argues Bakhtin, constitutes an artistic, generic, and linguistic hybrid. It differs from all other literary genres in its encyclopedic nature; rather than a form with a set of constituent structural features, it is a way of organizing and representing languages to create a fictional model of reality. Within life, languages are stratified and differentiated. Each sphere of life, each profession, each institution creates its own language. In periods of intense and rapid social transition this stratification becomes even more intensive:

> Various tendencies, circles, journals, particular newspapers, even particular significant artistic works and individual persons are all capable of stratifying language, in proportion to their social significance; they are capable of attracting its words and forms into their orbit by means of their own characteristic intentions and accents, and in so doing to a certain extent alienating these words and forms from other tendencies, parties, artistic works and persons.[27]

The novel has the unique ability to model this linguistic stratification, or heteroglossia, and therein lies its literary and social importance. Novelists build the social fabric of our world in literary form by representing the relationship between these stratified languages. As it incorporates these languages, the novel becomes colored by their original social, historical, and professional contexts. Entering the novelistic frame, they each project different assumptions and images of humans and their behavior onto the background of the novel. They make up the novel's social fabric, determining even the plot itself.[28] Novelization in Bakhtin's conception, realizes itself as a process of democratic dialogue between the worldviews of these diverse languages. They enter into dialogue with one another and, in so doing, fuel the novel's internal social, ideological, and artistic dynamic. The novelistic worldview is thus a dialogic one, a blending of differing and often contradictory assumptions and visions of humans and their world. On entering the novel these languages lose their ultimate self-contained authority, since they are continually engaged in the struggle with each other for the creation of meaning. The semantic echoes of their original context combine with the complex resonances of their new context within the polymorphous verbal texture of the novel, and they become integrated into the novelistic worldview.

All utterances are simultaneously old and new: old syntactic constructions in new semantic contexts. For Bakhtin novelistic narratives differ in their awareness of this duality, in their manipulation of the tensions between old and new meanings. Thus they also reflect the divided consciousness of the novelistic hero, with his simultaneous awareness of himself as an individual, as a wholly unique self, and as part of a larger social body.

Often these narratives take the shape of genres incorporated within the novel: the confession, the diary, the memoir. These bring their own generic conventions and assumptions to the novel but are also transformed, revivified through their interaction with each other and with other kinds of narratives within the structure of the novel.

Meaning is generated by the dialogue of these narratives through the author's demonstration of hierarchies among them. The worldviews of some narratives are shown to be superior to others: more complete, or more truthful. The author reveals his attitude toward these languages through the mode in which he represents them, through the orientation of his own voice toward these voices of others. He can represent them parodically or ironically, revealing their weaknesses and deficiencies through double-voiced discourse, as Pushkin does through his representation of Romantic lyric poetry's excesses, in the voice of Lensky in *Eugene Onegin.* Or he can ventriloquize them neutrally, underlining them as the truth and forcing the reader to accept them, as Tolstoy frequently does with the voice of Levin in *Anna Karenina.* Most of the time we experience these narratives simultaneously on a syntagmatic level, as part of the novel's fabric, as subjects, and on a paradigmatic level, as represented discourses, as objects.

Bakhtin also identifies another kind of language, authoritative discourse, which resists dialogic interactions with other narratives within the novel.[29] Authoritative discourse insists on its own monopoly on the truth. It brooks no opposition and enters into no compromises. It enters the novel as a quotation with no speaker and no context. As an utterance with no social or historical location, it lays claim to universal authority. Kinds of authoritative discourse include the biblical command and the prophecy, political propaganda and pedagogy, journalistic and legal discourses. For Bakhtin this kind of discourse is profoundly antinovelistic. Its presence in novels such as Tolstoy's *Resurrection* disrupts the novelistic paradigm, providing the hermeneutic equivalent of a bone that sticks in the reader's throat.[30]

In "From the Prehistory of Novelistic Discourse," Bakhtin argues that the "Galilean perception of language" that is found in novelistic narrative has flourished in very different geographical areas during several very different periods in history: in Greek literature during the Hellenistic period as Rome's influence on linguistic culture weakened; and during the age of Pushkin when the Russian literary language rejected the solidified forms it had inherited from French and German (428–30, 415–18). Such periods are united by the emergence of a sudden diversity of languages following the long ascendancy of one dominant language. In the fervor of their sudden liberation, each clamors for its place and finds expression in the novel's rich verbal texture. The 1870s in Russia provides a loosely parallel situation, as the Great Reforms and their legacy suddenly opened up a Pandora's box of new discourses—perhaps not languages in the strict sense of the word, but nonetheless distinctive systems of thought and expression that sought to reject the ideological, moral, and linguistic assumptions of the preceding systems. Dostoevsky participates in just such a Galilean revolution, though he frequently recants his participation and denies that it is necessary.

Bakhtin's formulations provide a useful framework for examining the relationship of *A Writer's Diary* to the novel. Like Bakhtin's conception of the novel, the *Diary* is a heterogeneric structure that incorporates different kinds of narratives with different social contexts. Dostoevsky takes his narratives from newspapers and journals, from his own life, from other literary texts, from the courtroom, and from the street. Yet if his novels constitute textbook examples of heteroglossia, of different kinds of discourses entering into productive and meaningful dialogue with each other, then what of the *Diary*? If in his novels Dostoevsky functions as the ultimate novelistic choirmaster, conducting his multiplicity of voices with the finesse of a maestro, how does his authorial voice operate within *A Writer's Diary*? Bakhtin sees the novel and journalism as implacably opposed to one another in their treatment of the embedded narratives in the worlds they create. *A Writer's Diary* presents a challenge to his lifelong tripartite project of tracing the philosophically liberating effects of dialogism, of celebrating Dostoevsky's status as the architect of the polyphonic novel, and of creating a grand theory of the novel. That Bakhtin himself was aware of its complex and problematic textual identity is testified to by the references in his *Notes of 1971–1972* to a project he was planning on authorial voice in which the *Diary* would play a central role.[31] It offers a unique case study in the complex relations between the novel and journalism. By examining it within the paradigm of Bakhtin's dialogic theory, we can begin to answer the question as to whether it upholds, or opposes, a novelistic worldview.

Although fluid authorial identity and dialogue are both integral to the structure of the *Diary*, they take a very different form from that envisaged by Bakhtin. Here the coexistence of different narratives does not bring the liberating dialogization of meaning that Bakhtin conceives of as taking place within the novel; here the novelistic mode is embroiled in a continual, often torturous and exasperating duel of meaning with other modes with different conceptions of humans and the world. This duel often creates confusion in the reader and breakdown in the text's overall meaning rather than an open-ended multiplicity of meaning. We frequently find heteroglossia without dialogue, and dialogue without heteroglossia. *A Writer's Diary* represents the dark side of the dialogic imagination. Yet for this reason it is a crucial text for those concerned with the novelistic and its instantiation in Dostoevsky's literary universe. The Diarist's own voice, and his approach to the voices of others, becomes the central arena of the conflict between journalistic and novelistic principles of representation.

THE DIARIST

The Diarist's problematic identity is the key to the constantly shifting textual parameters of *A Writer's Diary*. In both the 1873 columns and the 1876–81 monojournal, we can identify a narrative persona who functions as the Diarist. He makes his presence felt from the beginning of the monojournal, his feuilletonistic voice first sounding in "In Place of a Foreword." Here he has three main duties: First, he writes the *Diary*'s primary material, its frame narrative. Second, he functions as reader and editor of its secondary material, the interpolated narratives contained within it, whether they are fictional or taken from the newspapers, journals, and works of literature that provide the *Diary*'s source material. The narrative contract defines his editorial duties, and he continually focuses on the problem of the *Diary*'s poetics; even his breaking of the narrative contract is calculated, intended to spur the reader into active engagement with the *Diary* itself.[32] Where he includes interpolated narratives written by other fictional narrators, he usually provides some kind of introduction explaining his reasons for including it, as in the frame for the May–June 1877 entry, "From the Book of Predictions of Johann Lichtenberg, 1528" (25:122–25). He also chooses the genre of a particular entry of the *Diary* and orders and arranges the material. Third, he functions as a flaneur and conversationalist, recording dialogues he has engaged in during his fictionalized life outside the imaginary offices of "Writer's Diary."[33] The Diarist records his conversations with a series of different interlocutors; some of them provide him with an entire interpolated narrative, such as the woman in "A Hundred-Year-Old Woman," while others act as the vehicles for social or political views the Diarist wishes to examine, such as the "paradoxicalist" who appears in April 1876, again in the July–August issue, and then again in 1877 (22:122–26; 23:84–102; 25:206–9).

Hermeneutic problems arise with the Diarist's simultaneous existence within two different schemes of representation. In order to highlight this duality, we must first turn our attention to the structure of narration within the novel. In *The Rhetoric of Fiction,* Wayne Booth develops the concept of the implied author to show how authors position themselves in relation to "unreliable" narrators.[34] We have already seen how the dialogic interaction between Arkady as character and narrator, Nikolai Semyonovich as commentator, and Dostoevsky as implied author and historical author generates an interrogation of novelistic representation. The meaning of a novel is frequently determined in the space between narrator and implied author; an ability to differentiate between the two is vital for the novel's reader, who is always on guard against an unreliable narrator. The novel's narrative contract allows for any kind of misrepresentation by the narrator; in the process of reading the reader learns how to translate out of and into the narrator's version of events.

The narrative contract of most newspaper or journal articles is very different. There is no differentiation between the text's implied author and the narrator of the article's contents. The narrator and the implied author completely coincide, and the author takes full responsibility for the opinions laid out in the article. Certain journalistic genres do differentiate between the narrator and the implied author. Feuilletons rely on the concept of a stylized narrator, who may share some of the author's biographical features and political views but who is predominantly a fictionalized persona, with an analogous structural relationship to the author as a novelistic narrator.[35] The author establishes the feuilletonist's fictionalized status primarily by using a pseudonym that differentiates him from the author writing as himself, perhaps elsewhere in the same journal or newspaper. Thus the journalist Gradovsky would publish his feuilletons in *The Voice* under the pseudonym Gamma, and his straight journalism under his own name.[36] Dostoevsky maintained a similar kind of differentiation in *The Citizen* between the columns published within the frame of "A Writer's Diary" and the articles he wrote as "Dostoevsky."

In the *Diary,* Dostoevsky moves back and forth between these two antithetical types of narration. Sometimes there is ironic distance between the implied author and the Diarist, and we sense his fictional quality, experience him as representation. At other times he merges with Dostoevsky himself, and we are forced to read him referentially, prevented from questioning the context and form of his discourse. As novelistic narrator he is open to a multiplicity of voices and opinions; he raises a myriad of rhetorical questions that are answered only through the fictional embodiment of different possible outcomes and scenarios. He listens to the voices that oppose him, open to their points of view, sensitive to the form of their arguments, the nuances of their language. He is hesitant rather than forthright, his every narrative either fragmenting into hermeneutic shards realized typographically through ellipses, or floundering on the rocks of a paradox. In articles such as the June 1876 entry, "The Utopian Conception of History," as journalistic narrator, as an emboldened Dostoevsky holding forth, he trumpets an absolute language and ideological structure that brooks no opposition, opts out of dialogue, and demands to be understood only in those terms he himself has set (23:46–51). Irony is banished, and as Bakhtin puts it, he demands his "right to the serious word."[37] He ventriloquizes the opinions of others only in order to reveal them as straw men. The hierarchy of his values is clear and unambiguous.

These two approaches to narration are conceptually, stylistically, linguistically, and ideologically opposed to one another. As novelistic narrator the Diarist is infinitely pluralist; as journalist he is monologic. Their coexistence results in the profound textual dissonance that characterizes the *Diary*.

We see this dissonance in the entries for July and August 1876. In the first entry the Diarist records his conversation with a Moscow acquaintance (25:172–75). On his way to a much-loved childhood haunt, he wonders what memories contemporary children will carry with them from this enigmatic Russian present. The childhood memories are Dostoevsky's own, and the geographical space in which the Diarist finds himself is the very province where Dostoevsky was spending the summer. The notes to the Academy Edition tell us that the acquaintance may have been Ivan Aksakov. Yet once it is represented within this context, their conversation becomes fictionalized. The thoughts the conversation leads to, the idea of the disintegration of the Russian family into an accidental family, are Dostoevsky's own, yet here they are represented in a language that is recognizably that of the Diarist's meditating mode. His thoughts are represented as conjectures and speculations, questions without answers. His voice is continually expanding, contracting, metamorphosing, as it takes on the verbal tones of others, exploring their perspectives. Attempting to understand the disintegrating present, he sees only a profoundly enigmatic future (25:173:13–19). This kind of narration, with its open-endedness of perspective and its real and fictional dialogues, gives rise to and reflects a particular view of the world, which the Diarist acknowledges:

> Oh of course there will be all kinds of answers, maybe even more than there are questions—good and bad answers, foolish and wise answers; but the principal character of the answers will be, I think, that each of them will give rise to three new questions, and it will go on and on crescendo. The result will be

> chaos, but chaos would not be so bad: half-baked solutions are worse than chaos. (25:174)

The multiplicity of perspectives engenders hermeneutic chaos, but also shapes the Diarist's sense of how the present must be expressed.

Yet these conjectures give way to the single-minded monologism of the journalist, especially in the subsection "Confessions of a Slavophile" in the second section of the entry. Here narrator, implied author, and author merge as Dostoevsky admits, "Here I am compelled to express some of my feelings," his lengthy explanation testifying to his awareness of this authorial intrusion's problematic effect on the literary dynamics of the work he is creating (25:195). The grammar and syntax of this voice underline its monopoly on a truth it demands we accept: future perfectives replace the conditional and subjunctive clauses we find in the novelistic narrator's discourse. A tendency toward classification and generalization provides the rhetorical ballast for his authority. He anticipates the objections of the reader, demonstrating his rights over his opponents' points of view as well as his own. Perhaps most importantly of all, he claims the right to a "new word" which will be the "last word," seemingly unaware that he is falling into precisely the same trap as those dissociated intellectuals whose declared monopoly on truth he attacks in "The Very Last Word on Civilization" (23:61–63).

This conflation of perspectives and levels of narration into the single-minded voice of the journalist-prophet takes place most frequently in the subsections of the *Diary* that deal with the Balkan war, and these escalate along with the war itself, so that the novelistic narrator seems almost completely forced out of the work by the end of 1877.

DIALOGUE IN THE DIARY

Closely connected to this movement between novelistic and journalistic narration, there is an analogous movement between different attitudes toward dialogue, and in particular different orientations toward the speech of others. The Diarist interweaves his narratives with the voices of others: fellow journalists, writers, his readers, lawyers, jurors, criminals, beggars, shopkeepers, children, suicides, foreign politicians, newspaper editors. He co-opts them, incorporates them, parodies them, includes them as neutral third parties, and polemicizes with them, weaving them into a complex verbal panorama. But how does this multiplicity of voices function? Do we see the egalitarian democratic dialogic interaction that Bakhtin sees as central to the novel? Or do we find the kind of monologic need to dominate characteristic of rhetorical discourses?

The novel's relationship toward dialogue is multifaceted and polysemic. Intertextuality, the invocation of the semantic echoes of the previous literary and cultural contexts of quotations, is a central dynamic of all literary texts, especially the novel, and serves to identify the particular text with a generic or intellectual tradition, locate it within a canon of great works, and assure it a place within a history of literature. An example of this would be Dostoevsky's polemic with Goncharov and Tolstoy in the epilogue of *The Adolescent.* Yet also central to novelistic structure is intratextual dialogue: dialogue between characters or between different narratives within the same text, narratives with opposed worldviews. An archetypal example would be the dialogue between Ivan and Alyosha in the "Rebellion" chapter of *The Brothers Karamazov* or the opposition of the poem of the Grand Inquisitor and the notes on the life of the Elder Zosima. As we have seen, for Bakhtin this kind of dialogue characterizes the novelistic worldview, which seeks to balance and integrate differing points of view rather than to silence opposing voices.

The *Diary* combines two diametrically opposed attitudes toward dialogue. The Diarist starts out by maintaining the dialogic principle of the introduction to the 1873 columns, representing a diverse set of voices and opinions. In "In Place of a Foreword," his readers chime in, questioning him on his editorial decisions, and he quotes from rival publications such as *The Voice* (22:5–7). Even when the Diarist allows free reign to his utopianism, as in "The Golden Age in Your Pocket," he cheerfully welcomes the laughter of those who disagree (22:12–13). He questions his own motives and reminds the reader of his role as novelist, inviting a skeptical view of his own claims. Although there are voices the Diarist disagrees with, he nonetheless allows them to be heard.

Yet often dialogue functions as nothing more than a rhetorical device; the Diarist apes his opponents' voices only to reveal the flaws in their arguments, folding them into his own monologic perspective. A primary example is the treatment of Spasovich's speech in the Kroneberg case (22:57–63). The Diarist quotes from the speech extensively, revealing the lawyer's rhetorical strategies, the assumptions underlying his discourse, and the liberties he has taken with the truth. As Vinogradov points out in a detailed analysis of Dostoevsky's rhetorical treatment of this speech, this is dialogue as a device rather than dialogue as a principle.[38] Refusing to allow his opponents' speech any context outside the one he himself creates, the Diarist subsumes them into his own argument, and the utterance loses all contextual coloration. In the June 1876 entry, "The Utopian Conception of History," he uses the external structure of dialogue, including a quotation from his imagined opponent, who objects to his vision of an all-powerful Russia at the head of a union of Orthodox Slavs that will reclaim Constantinople (23:50). But like the profusion of rhetorical questions in the *Diary*'s prophetic journalism, the quotations are merely a foil for Dostoevsky's ready-made responses, responses that are forged from that very authoritative discourse which Bakhtin sees as the dominant mode of journalistic polemic. Entering the textual universe of the *Diary*, the voices of his opponents are manipulated by the Diarist: they are no longer autonomous voices of the kind instantiated within Dostoevsky's novels. In his critique of the linearity of the narratives of his opponents, the Diarist, now Dostoevsky, commits the very fault for which he has excoriated them: the desire to have the last word.

In the July–August 1876 articles "Russian or French" and "What Language Should a Patriot Speak?" Dostoevsky tackles the question of language head-on (23:77–80, 80–84). Though he begins with a sophisticated discussion of the way languages shape ideas and reflect the cultures that they represent, what has the potential to become a powerful description of how history affects language degenerates into a nationalist rant. He argues that while European literature can be conveyed adequately in Russian, Russian literature remains ineffable, untranslatable. The idea of linguistic hierarchy is profoundly nondialogic. If the Russian language conveys a greater spiritual truth, it cannot engage with the lesser languages and remains enthroned, or trapped within a monologic system. The Russian language becomes the vehicle for universal enlightenment, the master language that can repair linguistic differentiation and, in so doing, reverse the process of cultural fragmentation.

A CASE STUDY: OCTOBER, NOVEMBER, DECEMBER 1876

The October and November 1876 issues of *A Writer's Diary* most clearly exemplify Dostoevsky's novelistic preoccupations. Focusing on the actual suicides of two women, Herzen's illegitimate daughter Liza and a young seamstress who threw herself out of a Petersburg window holding an icon, the Diarist explores an ongoing theme: the phenomenon of ideological suicide ("Two Suicides," 23:144–46). Young *raznochintsy*, torn between sense of self and enslavement to the grand narratives of historical determinism, are driven to take their own lives. For Dostoevsky, they are casualties of Russia's transition to modernity. In the May 1876 entry, "One Unconnected Idea," he had written about the death of Pisareva, a young radical who had killed herself, leaving a suicide note full of ressentiment (23:24–27). Despite their very different psychological contexts, the deaths of Liza and the seamstress both lead him to continue his May meditations. Quintessentially modern heroines, Pisareva and Liza suffer from the same atrophied consciousness as the underground man.[39] Seeking in death the freedom they had failed to find in life, they sacrifice the self that is so dear to them on the altar of brute causality. In their double-voiced suicide notes, they attempt to assign themselves meaning by audaciously asserting the emptiness of their deaths. Like the novelistic subject, they are at once unique individuals, the psychological and metaphysical circumstances that led to their suicides irreducible to any common mean, and types, universal signifiers of a psychic disintegration that is all-embracing.

The seamstress's suicide is at once more straightforward than that of the other women, since the icon testifies to her faith, and more enigmatic, since the mode of her death belies it. Despite the Diarist's insistence on the difference between their deaths, their juxtaposition suggests affinity. Indeed, he himself admits that Liza's death reminds him of the seamstress.

The Diarist explores the phenomenon of the suicide note, seeing in it the ultimate example of the collapse of narrative, and connecting it to his task of exploring the narrative implications of *obosoblenie.* The suicide note finalizes its author, fixes her identity forever at the moment before death. Only by bringing Pisareva and Liza Herzen back to life in narrative can one defer the terrible finality of their suicide notes. The Diarist seeks the meaning behind these women's deaths by exploring the final moments of their lives, examining the circumstances that led up to their fatal decisions. In so doing, he defies determinism, showing through the multiplicity of possible narrative threads that it could have been otherwise, that the brute causality they perceive to be leading their every move is in fact an illusion. Thus, within the *Diary,* the suicides are resurrected as novelistic heroines.

In "The Sentence" Dostoevsky composes a fictional suicide note that forcefully expresses the dilemma of ideological suicide (23:146–48). Reminiscent of Ippolit Terentyev's anguished meditations on his own imminent death in *The Idiot* and foreshadowing Ivan Karamazov's arguments on the suffering of children, N. N.'s confession centers on his agonizing awareness of his autonomy, his overpowering sense of self, and his consciousness of a harmony of the whole that he cannot access.[40] He describes his consciousness as dissonance (*disgarmonia*) (146). N. N. stands as the very image and likeness of Lukács's idea of novelistic heroes as problematic individuals on the cusp of modernity, hopelessly out of step with the world they inhabit.[41] Here there is no reconciliation. Dissonance, the *Diary*'s underlying theme, motivation, and structural principle, so often abandoned in favor of a monotonic harmony, wins out. Thus "The Sentence" functions as a crucial formal and thematic key to one of the work's conflicting worldviews, the novelistic one. Significantly, it was the source of one of the best-known and most widespread misunderstandings on the part of Dostoevsky's readers.[42]

In the fictional work "The Meek One: A Fantastic Story," which takes up the *Diary*'s entire November issue, Dostoevsky provides the most complete representation of the kind of narrative breakdown about which he writes so often in the *Diary* (24:5–35). The story is structured in the same way as the *Diary*'s other sections; it is divided into two parts, each of which is subdivided into four or five sections. It thus blends seamlessly into the structure of the *Diary* and invites comparisions with the work's other issues. The story begins with a foreword explaining that the work's subtitle, "A Fantastic Story," refers to its form, a chaotic transcription of the fractured internal thoughts of its pawnbroker protagonist (24:5–6). The author of the foreword, presumably the Diarist, heads off any possible criticism of the form as unrealistic by declaring it to be fantastic. By inviting comparisons with Victor Hugo's *The Last Day of a Man Condemned,* which he calls "among the most real and most truthful of his writings," the Diarist implies that this fantastic story reveals something true about contemporary Russian society and thus shares some of the *Diary*'s broader preoccupations (24:6). Indeed, the foreword suggests that the story can be seen as another kind of diary, albeit one that deals with private, rather than public, impressions (24:5). Inspired by the suicide of the seamstress he had discussed in "Two Suicides," Dostoevsky writes the fictional narrative of the events leading up to her death. "The Meek One" takes the form of the confession of the pawnbroker whose wife lies dead on the table before which he paces, the victim of a suicide that came about as a result of the sadistic power relationship he enacted with her. Motivated by a need to provide his own explanation and the urge to take refuge from the plot he has created, he constructs his own narrative, seeking to absolve himself of responsibility for her death, to blame it on fate, the "blind inertia [*mrachnaia kosnost'*]" which he claims has destroyed what is dearest to him (24:35).[43]

The pawnbroker's narrative relies on maxims and generalizations to give it the appearance of truth. His organizing discourse forms a kind of code of laws of human behavior according to which he judges everyone with whom he comes into contact. Like the underground man, he anticipates every response from those around him. What he calls his "system," his attempt to tame the girl and bend her to his will, is based on both those fundamental maxims and his reductive assumptions about the girl's preconceptions: the girl, with all the idealistic fantasies of youth, must despise her pawnbroker husband, whom she must perceive as "revenging" himself on society, yet she is forced to marry him due to her unfortunate situation. But through the psychological "duel" that finally allows the pawnbroker to "fight" the aborted duel of his past and prove himself to the girl, he will show her his own high-mindedness and courage and she will love him for himself. However, the "system" goes wrong. She is strong-minded; she goes and meets his former accuser. She is tempted to kill the pawnbroker but does not. Instead she falls ill. When she is well again, her spirit is broken and she forgets the pawnbroker's existence. She cannot bear the strain of their reconciliation and throws herself out of the window. The pawnbroker blames Fate for the failure of his system, and his narrative attempts to show its cruelty. He tries to create the impression that his is the one true story, drawing an imaginary dotted line onto an imagined parallel existence where eventually happiness would have assuaged his guilt.

The work draws its dynamism from the contradiction between the organized, ordered certainty of the pawnbroker's narrative, and the horrific incomprehensibility of the act of suicide itself. His narrative attempts to "re-write" the story of what should have happened. It attempts both to assuage his guilt and to find comfort in the security of form. It offers the pawnbroker security; the chaos around him can be ordered into a coherent and rational narrative structure. He takes comfort in the linearity of beginning, middle, and end. Using structural devices to give his "system" the appearance of reliability, he continually reaffirms the need to tell the story in the correct order. He clings to the structural supports of the narrative process itself, detailing the first, second, and third times he particularly noticed the girl.

However, there are chinks in the ordered certainty of the pawnbroker's narrative that reveal the turmoil underneath. These chinks become more frequent as the narrative progresses. The ellipses, which hint at doubt and the failure to articulate some deeper repressed feeling, are accompanied by admissions of misunderstanding and a gradual creeping awareness that his is not the only perspective. Doubts about his point of view are compounded by more and more questions, self-laceration, and an increased awareness of his imagined reader. His anguished reproaches are increasingly directed at himself as the "shroud fell." In the second part of the text the dialogue between the narrative certainty and uncertainty becomes more intense still. His narrative speeds up and becomes more confused as the pawnbroker nears his conclusion. He stops his self-flattery; his tone becomes more frantic, his narrative more punctured by frenzied adjectives. He changes from his own voice to the indirect speech of Lukeria the maid, to her direct speech, in a desperate attempt to formulate a narrative capable of expressing the inexpressible, of explaining the inexplicable, of comprehending the incomprehensible.

However, as we see from the final paragraph, the narrative process has not provided the pawnbroker with the comfort of a simple, linear solution. Instead, he moves from a dogged faith in the success of his "system" to a despairing rejection of all laws: "What are all your laws to me now? What use to me now are your customs, your morals, your life, your state, your faith?" (24:35). Finally all narrative certainty is gone. His narrative is his last defense against the appalling reality of his wife's death and the evidence of his own culpability, but finally even that breaks down into incoherence. His attempt to formulate a coherent story has broken down, leaving him with the prospect of either silence, which dominated his relationship with his wife, or the incessant repetition of the word *bred* (delirium). His narrative account has become disembodied, devoid of signifier and signified, bereft of addressee, existing only to fill the vacuum left by her body. Just as the laws on which the pawnbroker has based his worldview collapse, so does his narrative itself.

The image of the pawnbroker's dead wife serves as the source and the representation of narrative collapse. It continually breaks into his narrative, subverting his attempts at self-justification. First introduced in the foreword, the body remains on the table throughout the pawnbroker's confession. It intrudes into his explanations: "That's still a question? What kind of question? And you don't understand that: the answer lies on the table and you talk about a 'question'!" (24:12). Its invisible presence makes itself felt through the ellipses. In chapter 4 we again see the power of the image to subvert the linearity of the pawnbroker's narrative as it undermines his generalizations and stereotypes. He asserts, "There's no originality in women, that's an axiom, even now, even now it's an axiom. What does it prove that she's lying out there in the anteroom? Truth is truth, and even Mill himself can do nothing about it" (24:15). We see here his lack of repentence, how he even tries to incorporate the corpse into his argument. But the image merely underlines his guilt, and he sinks into an incoherent and despairing wail as it seeps back into his thoughts. Just as the story has emerged from the image, so it retreats back into it, the pawnbroker's narrative dissolving into the dead girl's image.

Yet even while it represents his culpability, the dead girl's image also carries within it the seeds of an alternative worldview. Even as it functions as an icon of death, breaking down language with its indomitable silence, the body is holding an icon, offering the possibility of redemption, of life after death. It serves as the counterargument that Dostoevsky raises implicitly in the October issue in answer to the suicidal narratives of the women and N. N., and explicitly in the December issue as he responds to the confusion provoked in his readers by "The Sentence." The pawnbroker's final oblique fumbling toward a Christian vision of love, "'People, love one another,' who was it who said that?," as well as the Diarist's claim that his narrative reveals the truth, suggests an entirely different perspective on his wife's death, the possibility of a transcendent ideal that can rise above the tragic outcome of their marriage (24:35).

The Diarist's claim in the foreword that the pawnbroker has seen the truth yields many possible interpretations. Does he finally come to believe in the redemptive power of his wife's life and death? Does the intrusion of the image into his narrative represent his gradual enlightenment? Or does it merely represent his despairing realization of his own culpability? Are those closing words merely an ironic mocking parody of belief? Does irony underlie the Diarist's own claim that the pawnbroker has seen the truth? This story's open-endedness, its refusal to be reduced to an illustration of any belief system, its ability to sustain multiple hermeneutic possibilities, and its refusal to be reduced to any one of these scenarios all testify to its novelistic nature.

The foreword of "The Meek One" frames the story within the poetics of the *Diary* itself. The voices of the pawnbroker and the Diarist are brought into the larger work's hermeneutic field, and tensions between them emerge. Even as the confessional form draws us in, the foreword allows us another perspective, enables us to look in at the pawnbroker's narrative from the outside, to witness its disintegration from the sidelines. The pawnbroker's story becomes one of the *Diary*'s many accounts of narrative breakdown in the face of Russian modernity. As we witness the collapse of his narrative, we are reminded of the *Diary*'s other exemplary stories detailing the limitations of all linear narrative in the face of dissociation, disintegration, and death, such as "The Sentence." We are also reminded of the Diarist's own retreats into linear narrative. His utopian pronouncements sound the same note of delusion as those of the pawnbroker, and, having shown us the building blocks of linear narrative in the pawnbroker's monologue, he involuntarily turns our attention onto himself.

In the astonishing virtuosity of its portrayal of narrative breakdown, "The Meek One" lies at the heart of the *Diary*'s vision. It is both profoundly typical and atypical of the larger work within which it is embedded: typical in its embodiment of a central theme of the *Diary*, the problem of how narrative responds to death, particularly death by suicide, atypical in the success of its execution, in the way Dostoevsky creates a narrative that is both open and closed, subject and object, representing and represented. It is a "fantastic story" based on a real incident, a story that conveys through its fantastic form both the delusions of the pawnbroker's fantasy and the reality of the seamstress's religious belief even at the moment of suicide. This belief could strike the reader as fantastic, but Dostoevsky is at pains to show that it is real. "The Meek One" simultaneously models the chaos of a broken relationship and the guiding thread of renewal, conveyed through the meek one's icon. Just as we believe we can make out the image of the guiding thread, the faith that has sustained it even in death, it is subsumed back into the chaos out of which it came. Just as we begin to believe we perceive nothing but chaos, the outline of the guiding thread appears.

In the December 1876 *Diary*, underlining his ownership of the Diarist's voice, Dostoevsky is determined to have the last word on the story. Annihilating the space between his own voice and that of his narrator, he attempts to rein in the open-endedness of his novelistic explorations of suicide and doubt in the October and November issues. It should be noted that the second half of the October issue constitutes a journalistic commentary on the war in the Balkans, followed by a historical narrative that seeks to explain the Russian Idea and a prophetic interpretation of the Russian volunteer movement (23:148–62). It reads as a profoundly jarring sequel to the narratives of suicide in the first half and exemplifies the problems of combining novelistic and journalistic narratives within a single issue. In December, the Diarist continues in the same doctrinaire journalistic voice he had employed in the second half of the October issue. Launching into an analysis of "The Sentence," he takes on the voice of the prophet-pedagogue, explaining how the whole work is intended to illustrate the impossibility of living without the idea of immortality (24:43–54). By means of authoritative discourse that assigns a single meaning to the story, he reduces not only "The Sentence" but the entire October issue to a dogmatic sermon. Having teased out the idiosyncratic and individual identities of the suicides, he fixes them as uncompromisingly as their own suicide notes had done. Dissonance is replaced by a rigidly enforced harmony. He insists that the social and lingustic fragments of the postreform era, the rich mélange of narratives that have inspired the encyclopedic canvas of the *Diary,* can be made whole again through his master narrative of Orthodox spirituality and a return to the soil. In its monologic domination over the novelistic narratives of October, this prophetic mode confuses the reader and generates a hermeneutic collapse. The rift between these two radically different ways of looking at the world was to become ever wider in 1877, as the *Diary* began to disintegrate along with the social and religious forms it sought to uphold.

As he looked for new ways to embody in literary form the changing social landscape of mid-1870s Russia, Dostoevsky turned from the novelistic form back to journalism. Journalism offered new ways of looking at the world, the possibility of greater engagement with the present, dialogue with his readers, and liberation from the novel's formal constraints. *A Writer's Diary* was perhaps his boldest generic experiment, an encyclopedic work that sought to model the heterogeneous narratives of the postreform era within its very structure. A journal born of a struggle with novelistic form, it shares many of the novel's formal devices: a tension between particular and universal perspectives, a dynamic hierarchy of narrative voices, and an ability to embody social transition within narrative. Yet combining different genres with their often contradictory structures and worldviews carries the inherent risk of narrative breakdown.

In the final reckoning *A Writer's Diary* does not rank alongside Dostoevsky's novels. Yet it occupies an important place in the history of generic experimentation, testifying to both the richness and the problematic nature of combining genres with different sets of assumptions within a single work. Its final collapse into messianic nationalism illustrates some of the less appealing aspects of Dostoevsky's own ideology. The *Diary* is a defining example of the perils of generic cross-fertilization. Literary texts are enlivened and enriched by generic mixing, yet this mixing is not endlessly productive and meaningful, as postmodernists would claim. Through its mixing of novelistic and journalistic narratives, the autobiographical and the feuilletonistic mode, history and prophecy, the *Diary* often induced confusion in its readers, projecting contradictory sets of hermeneutic assumptions and resulting in textual lacunae and sometimes narrative collapse. Despite, perhaps even because of, its artistic flaws, the *Diary* constitutes a profoundly appropriate response to the chaotic cacophony of discordant social, cultural, and literary discourses of the age of disintegration.

Chapter Five

The Novel and Legend: Religious Narrative in *The Brothers Karamazov*

IN THE CHAPTER OF *THE BROTHERS KARAMAZOV* entitled "Cana of Galilee" Dostoevsky presents the novel theorist with a rich web of problems of interpretation.[1] Returning to the monastery after the death and subsequent putrefaction of Elder Zosima have challenged his faith, Alyosha Karamazov hears Father Paissy reading the parable of the miracle of the wedding at Cana. Pondering the parable's meaning, he suddenly seems to hear the voice of his departed Elder, and then all at once he feels his soul become one with the universe as he falls down to embrace the earth:

> It was as if threads from all those innumerable worlds of God all came together in his soul, and it was trembling all over, "touching other worlds" . . . With each moment he felt clearly and almost tangibly something as firm and as immoveable as this heavenly vault descend into his soul. Some sort of idea, as it were, was coming to reign in his mind—now, for the whole of his life, and unto ages of ages. He fell to the earth a weak youth, and rose up a fighter, steadfast for the rest of his life, and he knew it and felt it suddenly, in that very moment of his ecstasy. Never, never in all his life would Alyosha forget that moment. "Someone visited my soul in that hour," he would say afterwards, with firm belief in his words. (14:328)[2]

This representation of Alyosha's sudden epiphanic transformation challenges many of the core genre assumptions of novel theory. In this moment the gulf between the problematic individual and his or her world, which for Lukács was the defining generic principle of the novel, is suddenly closed, as novel gives way to epic.[3] For Bakhtin this scene represents the only moment in the whole work when the narrator breaks through the novelistic frame, taking on the tone of the hagiographer.[4] Here Dostoevsky seems to move out of the traditional realm of novelistic narrative into a world of silence, unity, and myth. Narrative is no more, and the novel must end. Yet it does not.

The kairotic moment notwithstanding, Alyosha returns to the world, Fyodor Karamazov is murdered, and Dmitry is arrested; the novelistic machinery continues to turn.

"Cana of Galilee" places in sharp relief the dilemmas facing the author who seeks to represent religious experience in novelistic narrative. What happens to the novel when it has closed the gap within which narrative exists, when it appears to disregard that uncertainty of identity on which novels themselves are predicated, that need to determine, through narrative, exactly where one's individuality begins and ends? How will the reader react when, expecting a detective story, she is confronted with a novelistic world that is unashamedly dualistic, balanced precariously between a tangible heaven and hell? At the heart of the generic project of *The Brothers Karamazov* is Dostoevsky's attempt to overcome this creative paradox, to find a way of expressing religious experience within novelistic narrative.[5]

Faced with a novel that insists on the possibility of representing religious experience, critics of *The Brothers Karamazov* have traditionally chosen to focus on one or the other side of the equation, preferring either to examine it as a novel much like any other while ignoring the generic transgressions, or to focus on it as a theodicy, a confession of the author, or a philosophical treatise while turning a blind eye to the issue of novelistic form.[6] Recently a rich vein of criticism has begun to address the work's complex generic status, exploring the relationship between its religious message and the novel's generic demands. Scholars such as Nina Perlina and Diane Oenning Thompson have examined how the novel's engagement with the authoritative sacred texts of Scripture and high religious genres fits with the ambivalence and open-endedness of the novelistic form.[7] Like these scholars, I see the question of genre as primary for an understanding of the aesthetic and ethical worldview of *The Brothers Karamazov,* a work that occupies a key position in the generic experimentation of Dostoevsky's last decade. I argue that the writer moves away from the fragmentary, centrifugal model of the novel that he had used in 1875 in *The Adolescent* and leaves aside the contemporary modes of secular biography and sociology, instead returning to the aesthetic and ethical values of an earlier, more traditional genre system. *The Brothers Karamazov* constitutes an attempt to reveal, transform, and extend the novel's own genre possibilities by engaging with, and borrowing from, the rich generic heritage of Christian legend. Dostoevsky recasts the problem of the reconciliation of the Christian moral paradigm and novelistic narrative within the framework of a trial of genres. *The Brothers Karamazov* serves as the final fulfillment of the dream of reconciliation first conceived of in *Time.* It provides that dream with a formal and narrative structure.

The Brothers Karamazov engages with many different traditions of Christian legend, from the high canonical genre of hagiographic legend to the oral, popular genre of folk legend, from the medieval apocrypha, with their roots in early Christian doctrinal anxieties, to nineteenth-century popular legends that unite Christian motifs with the social and political concerns of the Russian peasantry. While previous scholars have discussed the novel's use of hagiographic and apocryphal legend and of different kinds of popular folkloric narrative, there has never been a systematic study of either the function of these references, their relation to one another, or their connection to the literary, textological, and philological debates of Dostoevsky's time.[8] I argue here that Dostoevsky does not merely borrow isolated elements from these genres of the legend, but models them as authentic worldviews, building their aesthetic and ethical differences and dialogic interactions into his novel. An examination of the generic hierarchy of the different legends allows us to trace how their aesthetic and ethical reverberations impact the novel's narrative structure.

In all its many incarnations, Christian legend has traditionally carried out the function of narrating the spaces between the Scriptures, of contextualizing biblical narratives within the popular imagination, of demonstrating how Christian moral law affects the life of an ordinary believer, and of exploring the narrative implications of Christianity itself.[9] Combining the canonical and noncanonical, high and low, written and oral genres, the generic landscape of legend shares much with the heterogeneous and nonhierarchical generic territory of the novel.

Unlike *The Adolescent, The Brothers Karamazov* has a clearly centripetal plot dynamic: both *sjuzhet* and *fabula* are structured around the murder of Fyodor Karamazov. Yet it is a vacant center, the break in the narrative represented by the novel's only set of ellipses, the moment of indeterminacy during which the murder takes place. At the novel's core is an absence, a space for which a narrative must be found. The narrative first builds up to this moment, as we learn about the relationships between the brothers, the relationship each has with his father, and their respective ethical-religious worldviews, and then proceeds from it, as we follow the events of the arrest, interrogation, and trial, and the psychological effects these events have on each brother. Though the novel's true center is modeled as absent, we are offered a conflicting set of narratives to stand in for the missing one, the narration and explanation of the murder. These competing accounts, which include "Grand Inquisitor" and the "Life of Zosima," as well as a host of less celebrated inserted narratives of varying genres, do not address the question of who killed Fyodor Karamazov head-on. Instead they embed the murder within a broader aesthetic and metaphysical context. They offer contradictory worldviews that propose divergent models of humans' ethical identity. The novel structures this conflict in diverse ways.

As the title suggests, the relation of brotherhood is the novel's central artistic organizing principle. Having grown up apart, the brothers have never had the chance to explore their shared identity. With the death of their father and the revelation of their different relationships to him and to each other, they are brought into a single narrative orbit. Their brotherhood functions as a point of structural equivalence that reveals difference as well as similarity. The novel uncovers what is essential in Mitya, Ivan, and Alyosha, their "Karamazov spirit," but simultaneously reveals how they differ, each following a different belief system, each exhibiting profoundly different character traits. Dostoevsky offers a series of fraternal oppositions as Mitya is played against Ivan, Ivan against Alyosha, Alyosha against Mitya. Each of these oppositions on a formal level generates a new perspective on the murder as well as on the motives and ethical makeup of each brother. Each brother has a book of the novel named after him, which serves as an axis for the representation of that particular brother, so that the novel seems to contain not one center, but many.[10]

In this complex play between form and content, structure and ideology, genre takes on a vital role. Alongside the trial of Dmitry Karamazov and the novelistic investigation into the question of who is to blame for Fyodor Karamazov's murder, Dostoevsky proposes another trial: a trial of genre. Which genre can most fully account for and explain what happened at the Karamazov house that night? The relationship between the brothers is expressed in terms of genre. The central opposing narratives, Ivan's "Grand Inquisitor" and Alyosha's "Life of Zosima," are set against each other as antithetical moral anatomies of humankind. Each authored by a different brother, each depicting an alternative father figure, each endorsing a different ethical system, these narratives meditate on similar themes: on the problems of sin, temptation, expiation, and redemption. Just like the Karamazovs, the genres of these narratives both resemble and differ from one another. They are all constructed from the building blocks of Christianity, yet they draw opposite conclusions as to humans' ethical nature. Representing the brothers' worldviews within hagiographic, apocryphal, and folk legend allows Dostoevsky to reveal their similarities and differences. Like the brothers themselves, the genres of Christian legend emerge from the same source, the canonical biblical texts, yet have grown apart from one another, fed by the contradictory assumptions of antithetical intellectual, cultural, and literary systems. Within the novel's structure they are brought back into a single textual orbit and tested against one another. Which genre can offer the most penetrating account of human moral contradictions? Which most closely follows the assumptions of the novel itself?

THE LEGEND AS GENRE

The legend is a hybrid genre that exists at the meeting point of official hagiography, the saints' lives of the Orthodox collections of the *Prolog* and the

Chet'i Minei, apocryphal literature, and folklore. Even a brief examination of the etymology and nineteenth-century usage of the term *legenda* demonstrates the complicated patchwork of textual traditions and religious and national affiliations that attached themselves to this genre designation. The word entered the Russian language at the turn of the nineteenth century through either French or German from the medieval Latin *legenda,* becoming frequently used by the first quarter of the century.[11] Its first dictionary appearance was in Kirillov in 1845.[12] By the 1850s the word had begun to be used interchangeably with the older genre designations *predanie* and *skazanie,* its Church Slavic equivalents, which had previously been used to translate the Latin *legenda* as well as the Greek equivalents. The entry in Dal' includes the definition "sacred legend [*sviashchennoe predanie*]." We see the interchangeability of the genre designations *legenda, predanie,* and *skazanie* in Kushelev-Bezborodko's 1860–63 *Monument to Old Russian Literature,* edited by N. Kostomarov, which is subtitled *Skazaniia, legendy, povesti, skazki i pritchi.*[13]

The genre territory of the legend in the second half of the nineteenth century includes at least three distinctive groups: the hagiographic, the apocryphal, and the folk legend. Although each group is derived from the doctrines of the Orthodox Church, each maintains a different relationship toward the canonical texts and is governed by a different set of narrative conventions. The hagiographic legend, the *zhitie,* is a high religious genre contained within the Orthodox canon. In the Orthodox tradition it refers to those lives of saints included in the canonical collections of the *Prolog* and the *Chet'i Minei* and arranged according to where the saints' days fell in the Orthodox calendar. The Lives within the *Chet'i Minei* were intended to be read to oneself, those from the *Prolog* to be read out loud.[14] The most influential hagiographic collection, that compiled by the sixteenth-century Metropolitan of Moscow Makarii, was the subject of renewed scholarly interest in the 1860s onward, and a critical edition was undertaken in 1868.[15] Dostoevsky had in his library an 1860–61 selection of the Lives in twelve volumes.[16]

The second group of works comprises the so-called apocryphal legends, written texts that were rejected by the ecclesiastical authorities and thus remained outside the Orthodox canon. They include Old and New Testament apocrypha, translations from Greek, South Slavic borrowings, and apocrypha that originated within the Russian lands. Alongside the "Gospels" of Thomas, Jacob, and Nicodemus and "The Legend of How God Created Adam" can be found narratives about the journeys of the Virgin, Christ, and the Apostle Paul into hell. The main collections of apocrypha, edited by Nikolai Tikhonravov and Alexander Pypin, were both published in 1863.[17] The 1860s and 1870s saw a flood of interest in the apocrypha on the part of scholars, writers, and even the educated public.[18] Dostoevsky's knowledge of and interest in apocryphal legend is demonstrated through his many references to apocryphal narratives in *The Brothers Karamazov.*

The third kind of legend is the folk legend, the *narodnaia legenda.* This differs from the other two groups through its oral transmission; it was in circulation much later, in the eighteenth and nineteenth centuries. In the folk legend, motifs, plots, and characters from canonical Orthodox texts including the Bible, the *Prolog,* and the *Chet'i Minei* coexist both with supernatural and fantastic elements from the wonder tale and other folk genres and with social themes taken from the lives of its peasant narrators. The first and most important collection of legends was Alexander Afanasiev's 1859 *Russian Folk Legends,* collected by the folklorist in northern and western Russia and in the Ukraine.[19] The coexistence of pagan and Orthodox beliefs as well as the anticlerical nature of many legends led to its banning on the orders of the Holy Synod. The ban notwithstanding, Afanasiev's collection was read extremely widely in intellectual and literary circles, and many other collections followed in its wake. Dostoevsky's knowledge of Afanasiev's work is demonstrated by his use of one of the folklorist's Ukrainian folk legends as the prototype for Grushenka's tale of the onion.

Folklorists distinguish the folk legend from the wonder tale first of all by virtue of its religious elements, which tend to vary a lot from Orthodox doctrines.[20] A common theme is that of Christ as *strannik,* wandering the earth in the guise of a beggar in the company of his apostles or saints, coming into contact with peasants and setting them some kind of moral test. Folk legend deviates from the doctrines of organized religion through its dependence on motifs from apocryphal legend, and also through its irreverent portrayals of heaven and hell. A common theme the folk legend takes from apocrypha is a journey into heaven or hell, sometimes both, often undertaken by a conscript on his way back from military service. Heaven becomes tedious because of its lack of alcohol and tobacco, while the conscript is frequently thrown out of hell for building a chapel to worship in.[21]

In the mid-nineteenth-century literary landscape, the legend was thus located within the flow of the two great religious and cultural rivers: the Catholic legacy of Western Europe, and the customs and traditions of Byzantium and Orthodox Slavdom. Within its territory the waters of these rivers converged. *The Brothers Karamazov* exploits this heterogeneous flow, and its complex literary structure celebrates the rich narrative traditions of early and medieval Christianity while recasting them according to the literary and cultural values of the second half of the nineteenth century. The narrative of the "Life of Zosima" is littered with references to the Lives of Saints such as Aleksey the Man of God and Mary of Egypt, whose humility and penitent self-sacrifice have granted them a central position in the Orthodox tradition. Yet Alexey and Mary are also early Christian martyrs who represent a religious and cultural heritage that Orthodoxy shares with Catholicism.[22] Even Ivan's discourse exploits this common birthright: his "Rebellion" and his "Grand Inquisitor" poem borrow motifs from both Russian and Western apocryphal legend, but relocate them in a post-Enlightenment world.

THE NOVEL, LEGEND, AND LITERARY SCHOLARSHIP

Dostoevsky's use of the genres of the legend in *The Brothers Karamazov* should be viewed in the context of a surge of interest in the 1860s through 1880s in the relationship between the verbal culture of early Christianity and the medieval period on the one hand, and the genre of the novel on the other. The nineteenth-century philologist Fyodor Buslaev first pointed out the similarities in function and structure between different genres of Christian legend in the medieval period and the novel in his own century. Uniting adventure narratives, family memoirs, and important historical events, hagiographic legends were the novels of their day, claimed Buslaev.[23] Alexander Veselovsky, perhaps the greatest Russian philologist of the nineteenth century, wrote extensively on the connections between medieval Byzantine and Russian Christian legends and apocrypha, most notably in a series of articles he wrote for the journal of the Ministry of National Enlightenment titled "Studies in the History of the Development of Christian Legend."[24] In works such as "Monuments of Narrative Literature," he traced a link between medieval narrative genres and the modern novel.[25] This interest resulted in his treatise *From the History of the Novel and the Novella,* a work of historical poetics and embryonic theory of the novel.[26]

Dostoevsky's contemporaries had begun to understand the generic peculiarities of the novel in terms of its heterodox ancestry, which could be found neither in the classical genres of antiquity nor in the stratified eighteenth-century genre system, but in the complex interplay between the written and oral genres of the Middle Ages, between the strict doctrines of the church and the heterogeneous beliefs of the people. It was a line of research that would be enthusiastically pursued by many novel theorists in the following century, including Bakhtin.[27] The philological debates on these diverse kinds of legend taking place in the 1860s and 1870s provide not only the background but also a significant motivating force behind the generic and religious dynamism of *The Brothers Karamazov.* Dostoevsky takes part in contemporary genre debates within the novelistic form and, in that process, structures within his own novel the prehistory of its genre, its first tentative steps through the richly heterogeneric verbal culture of medieval Russia.[28]

Like the legend, the novel takes the form of a compilation, a container genre. The medieval hagiographic legend frequently took the form of a series of narratives of differing liturgical and hagiographic genres, which were placed together in an anthology.[29] The Bakhtinian view of the novel as an overarching genre carrying within itself a multiplicity of interpolated genres borrows more from medieval textual tradition than Bakhtin himself ever admitted. *The Brothers Karamazov* makes explicit the parallels between these two apparently different textual traditions. By placing the hagiographic legend of the Life of Zosima alongside the apocryphon of the "Grand Inquisitor," the folk legend of the onion alongside the sacral narrative of Alyosha's moral resurrection, Dostoevsky creates his own novelistic compilation in the manner of medieval legend.

Dostoevsky also exploits similarities in the intertextual relationships of legend and the novel. Both novel and legend engage in a continuous dialogue and draw on a repository of shared themes, motifs, and paradigms. Whereas hagiographic legends explore theoretical models of Christianity laid out in Scripture and test out ways of living according to the moral precepts of the Bible, apocrypha provide a fresh perspective on stories from the Bible and hagiographic legends themselves, and folk legends rework apocryphal visions and recontextualize figures from the Bible and hagiographic legend in a contemporary rural Russian setting. The canonized Saint Georgii is reconceived as the folk hero Yegor the Brave, while the Old Testament apocryphal narratives of Solomon the Wise were updated by peasants in the nineteenth century and passed down through the oral tradition.[30] Novels share this process of narrative recycling, taking part in a broader social dialogue, refracting within their own structure previous literary formulations of the themes they address.[31] *The Brothers Karamazov* borrows quotations and motifs from Goethe, Schiller, and Rousseau; reworks plots from George Sand and Émile Zola; and takes part in contemporary debates over crime, biology, church-state relations, education, and legal and governmental reforms.[32] Dostoevsky supplements these parallels, highlighting the similarities in the two genres' preoccupation with the tension between scriptural moral paradigms and the chaotic and contradictory worlds they themselves represent.

Dostoevsky structures these differing models into the novel through the generic identities of the three Karamazov brothers. Each brother is steeped in the textual tradition of the kind of legend he represents; his perspective on the world is shaped by that legend, and he is the author of an interpolated narrative structured according to that legend's narrative principles. Alyosha, the author of the hagiographic work, the "Life of Zosima," experiences a moment of transfiguration modeled according to the conventions of hagiographic legend, and hagiographic discourse flows into the novel itself in the chapter "Cana of Galilee." Ivan borrows from diverse forms of apocryphal legend for the ideological and aesthetic underpinnings of his "Rebellion" and "Grand Inquisitor." And after his arrest and during his incarceration Dmitry takes on the ambivalent moral dimensions of the hero of folk legend.

Each brother is also the hero of a narrative being manipulated by the implied author, a narrative that takes the form of his particular type of legend but is juxtaposed to other kinds of legend and to the novel itself. The implied author lays bare the aesthetic and ethical assumptions of each legend and, in that process, opens up each brother's character. In short, genre functions as worldview, as characterization, even as an engine of plot. The legends begin as interpolated genres within the novel but permeate the novel's deeper structure, carrying with them semantic echoes that reverberate throughout the novel, as Dostoevsky offers a novelistic demonstration of how each brother's aesthetic, ethical, and generic assumptions play out on the level of plot. Interrogation of these different kinds of legends and their worldviews reveals a new perspective not only on the relationships between the Karamazovs, but also on the genre assumptions of the novel itself and its own representation of religious experience.

IVAN AND APOCRYPHAL LEGEND

Ivan Karamazov identifies with the literary form and many of the spiritual and philosophical assumptions of apocryphal legend. His rebellion and *poema* borrow from several different Old Russian apocryphal traditions: the apocalyptic tradition; the tradition of God's questioner; the journey through hell; and, finally and most obviously, the apocryphal variant of the biblical wilderness temptation narrative. Though often perceived by critics as an essentially modern nihilist-existentialist vision, Ivan's rebellion borrows from a rich tradition of popular religious dissent and heresy dating back to the medieval period.

Ivan's rebellion consists in his refusal to accept the construction of a world predicated on human suffering. As an expression of spiritual discontent and a plea for an explanation of the ways of God, it borrows not only from the canonical book of Job, but also from the generic tradition of the frequently heretical medieval apocrypha that seek to fill in the spiritual or narrative gaps in canonical biblical texts.[33] These apocrypha present a biblical character, such as the Mother of God, an apostle, or a prophet, who addresses questions either to God or to the devil. To this group belong apocrypha such as "St. Bartholomew's Questions to the Mother of God," "St. Bartholomew's Questions to Jesus," "The Questions of John the Theologian to God on Mountain Tabor," "The Questions of John the Theologian to Abraham about Righteous Souls," and "The Questions of John the Theologian to Abraham on Mount Elyon."[34] These apocrypha are often apocalyptic, hence their attribution to John the Theologian, the apostle traditionally perceived as the author of Revelation, the only apocalyptic text in the canonical New Testament.[35] By framing his rebellion within the terms of these medieval apocrypha, Ivan confers upon it a powerful spiritual, intellectual, and emotional legitimacy. He expresses the same doubts Christians have been grappling with for well over a thousand years: what kind of accounting will there be in the afterlife for injustices on earth?

As Murav points out, Ivan's narration of anecdotes on children's suffering as an explanation of his decision to "return his ticket" provides a symbolic representation of another subgenre of apocryphal narrative, that of the tour of hell.[36] With his graphic description of the children's suffering, Ivan leads Alyosha through the circles of hell just as the Archangel Michael leads the Mother of God in *Mother of God Visits the Torments,* a crucial reference narrative for "Grand Inquisitor."[37] Byzantine in origin, this apocryphon was transmitted to the Russian lands in a South Slavic translation in the early medieval period and was included in the collections of both Tikhonravov and Pypin.[38] The legend recounts how the Mother of God is led through hell by the Archangel Michael. Touched by the fate of the sinners, especially those who have been consigned to a burning lake and "forgotten by God," she asks pardon from God for all those whose suffering she has witnessed. God refuses to release them, pointing to Christ's wounds and asking how he can forgive what has been done to his Son. The Mother of God then asks all the saints and apostles to pray with her for their absolution, and God agrees to a cessation of their torments once a year for the period from Good Friday to Pentecost.

Ivan places the legend as a biblical thematic motif before his *poema,* implying that both in its ethical and in its generic foundations the *Mother of God* prefigures his own *poema.*[39] With its presentation of the sufferings of sinners in hell, the apocryphon provides an interesting segue from Ivan's refusal to accept the sufferings of the innocent and his denial of the necessity of suffering as atonement for original sin in "Rebellion," to the Grand Inquisitor's complete negation of suffering, and his subsequent inversion of the Christian moral paradigm. Ivan's narrative stresses God's intransigence, his merciless insistence on the continued sufferings of the sinners in hell as atonement for their persecution of Christ, which finds both its mirror and its antagonist in the obduracy of the Grand Inquisitor. As he paraphrases the plot of the apocryphon for Alyosha, he dwells on those forgotten by God. God's plea "How can I forgive his tormentors" echoes Ivan's plea to Alyosha on behalf of the tortured children. The legend illustrates a suffering that will no longer exist under the rule of the Grand Inquisitor.

In the novel as a whole, however, the legend carries altogether different resonances. When we read it alongside the novel's other narratives of sin, expiation, and redemption, such as Grushenka's tale of the onion and the folk legend about hell told to Dmitry by his coachman, then the meaning of the apocryphon is transformed, as though suddenly lit from behind. It illustrates the infinite mercy of God and the continuing possibility of moral regeneration, even after the last possible moment, and even from within the flames of hellfire itself. The clash of the apocryphon's two framings immediately throws into question the ethical and narrative implications of Ivan's own apocryphal legend.

The *poema* "Grand Inquisitor" is scattered with references to apocryphal narratives, as well as to the book of Revelation, which, though it is canonical, retains affinity with apocrypha because of its apocalyptic tone. As he nears the climax of his own prophetic narrative, the Grand Inquisitor spews out a verbal battery of the central motifs of Revelation, including the Whore and the Beast (14:230, 231, 234, 235, 236; 15:559–63). He identifies with the "great prophet" John and his intoxication with the wisdom and insight of his own revelation. Though its central metaphor, the devil's three temptations of Christ in the wilderness, is taken from the Synoptic Gospels, the *poema* locates itself outside the biblical canon. The Grand Inquisitor's retelling and analysis of the temptation narrative is structured as an apocryphal Gospel in its own right. It restructures the meaning of the temptations in light of the subsequent history of humans and their suffering; it revisits the biblical events from a retrospective perspective.[40] With its vision of a world where the church has thrown in its lot with the devil, "Grand Inquisitor" evokes one of the most revolutionary of medieval heresies, that of the Bogomils, which itself played a significant role in shaping many medieval Russian apocrypha.[41]

If Ivan starts out as the author of an apocryphon, he ends up as the protagonist of his own apocryphal narrative. The aesthetic and ethical implications of the *poema* he himself has written determine his subsequent development within the novel. Through his appropriation of humans' freedom, the Grand Inquisitor, and through him Ivan, forecloses all temporality and choice, and thus all narrative potentiality. If humans have been deprived of their freedom of choice, then there remains nothing to narrate. Through this attack on the concept of individual moral freedom, Ivan lays siege not only to the foundations of the Christian moral paradigm, but also to the foundations of novelistic narrative. Since he himself is a novelistic creation, this denial of narrative potentiality would be disastrous. Dostoevsky carries the implications of his vision to their ultimate conclusion: madness. Though Ivan criticizes Christianity for the inevitable universal cycle of suffering that it imposes on his followers, the alternative he offers suffers from the same blind determinism. While Dostoevsky the Orthodox believer sees Ivan's negation of humans' moral freedom as that which undermines their metaphysical vision, Dostoevsky the novelist sees his rejection of narrative possibility as that which will lead him into madness.

Dostoevsky administers the ultimate poetic justice to Ivan in his confrontation with the devil. With the appearance of the "dread spirit," apocryphal legend permeates the novel's own structure, flouting the conventions of the realist novel. Denying the narrative freedom on which the realist novel relies, Ivan is condemned to wander through his own philosophical hell, to inhabit the fictional world of apocryphal legend, and to lose his sanity along with his individual autonomy. The confrontation with the devil also marks the final unraveling of Ivan's critique of Christianity. Both the devil's appearance and the apocryphal parodies he recounts to Ivan undermine the authority of Ivan's earlier apocryphal visions, for this is not the wise and heretical figure of apocryphal legend, whose insightful questions point to the ambiguities in the divine plan and whom we find embodied in the figure of the Grand Inquisitor, but rather his burlesque double, a Francophile sponger of low cunning, fallen on hard times. The devil's parodic Enlightenment tics expose Ivan's true ideological lineage. It is not the authors of medieval Christian apocrypha who are Ivan's intellectual forebears; rather, it is the Enlightenment apocryphers, Descartes and Voltaire. The devil's revelations also relocate Ivan's rebellion in the novel's chain of ironic references to the Enlightenment, revealing their echoes in the farcical rebellions of Smerdyakov and Fyodor, both of whom tell their own scabrous tales about Enlightenment philosophers.

While the novel recoils from the genre implications of Ivan's apocryphon and his rebellion is parodied as Enlightenment vaudeville, semantic fragments from the borrowed apocryphal legends lodge themselves within the novel. His adoption of the form of the apocryphal legend to question the Christian doctrines of original sin, suffering, and expiation is upheld in the novel; it is his answers which are rejected. His apocryphal questions are answered instead within the novel's frame, in the form of a very different genre of legend.

ALYOSHA AND HAGIOGRAPHIC LEGEND

Alyosha is characterized within the terms of a different kind of legend: hagiography. Just as Ivan is transformed from author to subject of his own apocryphal narrative, Alyosha begins as hagiographer but ends up as hagiographic hero.[42] Writing the "Life of Zosima," a hagiographic legend that becomes incorporated into the novel's narrative structure, Alyosha begins to model his worldview according to hagiographic convention, and his faith is challenged as he observes the gap between the novelistic world he inhabits and the hagiographic world he produces in his own work.

Like all hagiographic legends, the "Life" is structured not by *chronos,* but by *kairos;* it assumes the existence of a kairotic moment, a point of conversion located outside ordinary temporal experience.[43] In this moment, the saint ceases to inhabit the fallen world of flux and fragmentation. Past, present, and future fuse in the experience of oneness with God. This temporal rupture proves problematic for the hagiographer, who must find a way of narrating a life that has been touched by the sacred, invested with a higher significance. Up to the moment of conversion, the future saint is not conscious of the imminence of that transformative moment; the hagiographer reorders the events of the saint's life in the light of the kairotic moment.

The moment of conversion in the "Life of Zosima" takes place on the morning when the future elder is preparing to fight his duel. Remembering his violence toward his manservant Afanasy, he recalls his brother Markel's teachings and "suddenly the whole truth appeared to me in its full enlightenment" (14:20). His conversion is marked by the bridging of the gap between himself and others, and between himself and God. The sudden revelation that all men are made in the image and likeness of God strips Zosima utterly of the consciousness of the difference between self and other. Those present at the duel witness his transformation and forgive him for withdrawing his challenge as they quickly realize that he has ceased to inhabit the social world in any ordinary sense, for he has taken on his monastic vocation.

The difference between the hagiographic and novelistic modes is evident if we compare the narrative of Zosima's duel and the narrative of the mysterious stranger.[44] Even as Zosima describes the events leading up to the challenge, the moment of conversion intrudes. His behavior seems to follow a predetermined pattern, a path toward enlightenment. There is no narrative suspense, no identifiable moment of moral choice, when his conscience could have led him either one way or another. The mysterious stranger, on the other hand, continually defers his admission of guilt, demonstrating his moral choice.

Hagiography operates according to a set of assumptions that could not be further from those of the novel. Within a novel's complex structure every description, every event is subject to multiple possible interpretations, whereas in hagiography every event corresponds to a single stable interpretation. In the novel, repetition implies connection: characters share a trait or an experience not by accident, but to provide a structural connection that must affect the interpretation of the whole work. Yet at the same time, each character must also be perceived as the arbiter of his or her own individual fate. Family and social identifications continually circumscribe individual autonomy; individual intellectual or moral developments and environmental factors balance out biological or genetic motivations. Novelistic representation provides a balance between individuality and sameness. If each event in each individual human biography can be interpreted simultaneously as the result of genetic predisposition, social or environmental factors, and individual choice, each event in hagiographic discourse is subject to a particular law of hagiographic representation and plays a stable and predictable role in the artistic and ideological structure of the whole.

Dostoevsky models the clash between the assumptions of hagiographic and novelistic representation on the level of novelistic structure in the failure of Zosima's body to escape decomposition.[45] As a reader and writer of hagiographic legend, Alyosha anticipates the miracle of bodily preservation, and when it fails to take place, his faith is shaken. His expectations are shaped by hagiographic narrative not merely as a literary and philosophical system, but as lived experience. When life fails to emulate literary convention, he is forced to reassess his entire belief system.

THE ONION

In the chapters "The Onion" and "Cana of Galilee," Dostoevsky offers two models of moral resurrection. One, Alyosha's conversion experience, unfolds according to the conventions of hagiography; the inclusion of a miracle, suggesting transcendence of the space of incomprehension separating man from God, shows that we have gone beyond the realm of novelistic narrative. The other, the complex mutual conversion of Grushenka and Alyosha, which finds expression in the folk legend of the onion, suggests a model of resurrection that takes place *within* narrative, that can be expressed in narrative, and that is fully compatible with the laws of the novelistic universe.

Alyosha's spiritual resurrection is a complex process that extends beyond the boundaries of hagiographic representation. His and Grushenka's moral transformations occur simultaneously, and it is impossible to identify which of them instigates the conversion process. As the narrator announces, Alyosha's grief for the elder provides him with his greatest defense against seduction. Grushenka's discovery of the elder's death induces shame in her at her own behavior, yet seduction never appears likely. The complexity and multiplicity of motivations and the impossibility of predicting either Grushenka's or Alyosha's behavior foreground an ambiguous kind of conversion, a process rather than a moment, which follows a novelistic rather than hagiographic trajectory.

The onion legend provides the metaphor for the apparent "miracle" of Grushenka's decision not to seduce Alyosha, which displaces the failed miracle of Zosima's bodily preservation. In the legend a wicked old woman is given the chance to escape from a fiery lake in hell by her guardian angel, who, remembering her one good deed, digging up an onion for a beggar woman, offers her the onion to pull herself out of hell. When her fellow sinners try to hold onto her legs, she kicks them back into the lake, the onion breaks, and she plunges back down into hell. The legend models the novel's central theme: the continuing possibility of moral resurrection at the last possible moment, even from within hell. The onion narrative bears remarkable similarity to one of the variants of a legend published by Afanasiev in *Russian Folk Legends,* "Christ's Brother."[46]

The onion, a characteristic motif of the folk legend, functions as a familiar symbol of the sustenance and protection offered by the earth. The possibility of escape from hell testifies to an ethical-religious outlook that offers more compassion and second chances than that of canonical Orthodoxy, but the woman's failure to grasp the moral principle of the onion or to spread her good fortune among the denizens of hell suggests a worldview in which religious principles are tempered by bitter social experience. The onion narrative offers two different conclusions: in the legend the old woman fails the moral test set by her guardian angel, but in the novel itself Grushenka takes the onion, refuses to seduce Alyosha, and thus begins her moral regeneration.[47] This "novelistic" miracle is dualistic, suggesting alternative narrative outcomes.

Dostoevsky juxtaposes the onion narrative and its novelistic incarnation to the transcendent miracle of Alyosha's spiritual regeneration. Whereas Alyosha's miracle seems to stop narrative in its tracks, Grushenka's miracle regenerates it, opening up a number of alternative plot scenarios. Grushenka has sinned, yet she is on one of many paths to redemption. Far from circumscribing her narrative possibilities, the onion legend reveals narrative vistas for her. It underlines her moral potentiality as it is realized within the structure of the novel: the onion stands as symbol of her redemption, possible yet not inevitable. Unlike Alyosha's kairotic moment, it is a miracle realized *within* narrative, enabled by the narration of the legend itself.

In the chapter "Cana of Galilee" Alyosha at last experiences the kairotic moment denied him in the hours following Zosima's death. This miracle of oneness with the universe in fact follows precisely the pattern which the narrator has already laid out in the chapter "Elders": the miracle follows the faith, rather than the other way round (14:24–25). Grushenka's transformation proves to be the spiritual and narrative peripetaeia leading to the moment of conversion. And since Grushenka's own moral potentiality is conveyed through the legend of the onion, it follows that what appears at first to be an affirmation of the hagiographic perspective is in fact mediated by the folk legend.

This redemptive narrative climax is structured by a multilayered hagiographic perspective, by hagiography as popular legend rather than as literary or spiritual system. The novel's brief opening onto the transcendent simultaneously carries within itself a return to the earthly, which we see mirrored in the mechanism of spatial perspective: after Alyosha has looked up into the heavens, he immediately returns his gaze to the earth and throws himself down onto the ground. Thus what has begun as a movement away from the earth, a retreat into the divine, turns into the opposite, an embrace of the earth and of the human. In the end it is the onion narrative, rather than the "Life" or "Cana of Galilee," which provides the aesthetic and ethical momentum for the rest of the novel, and it is Mitya, rather than Alyosha, who plays the role of novelistic hero.

MITYA AND FOLK LEGEND

Dmitry Karamazov appears in the first half of the novel as what Morson has called a generic refugee, a hero in search of a genre.[48] This search is modeled in the structure of the novel itself in the three confessional chapters devoted to Mitya, "Confessions of an Ardent Heart." In the chapter "Confessions of an Ardent Heart in Verse," he locates himself in a world modeled primarily according to Romantic convention, identifying his own "insect sensuality" in Schiller's "Ode to Joy."[49] Yet his understanding of Romanticism is a limited one; he identifies with its outer form—its portrayal of extreme states, the abyss, and beauty's duality—but he is unable to grasp its inner content.

He relates his first meeting with Katerina Ivanovna in the following chapter using the terms of the debased romanticism of the French boulevard novel, thereby invoking the sickly intensity of cheap melodrama. Yet even this generic universe he inhabits only for a second, before inscribing himself into a tragedy: "You understand the first half: it's a drama and took place there. The second half is a tragedy, and will take place here" (14:103). Mitya occupies the role of tragic hero for much longer, and the novel itself seems to sanction this role, as it is one which suggests that it is he who will murder Fyodor. Zosima's bow to him in the monastery and his own continual references to the abyss over which he is poised, also serve to bolster the idea that he stands at the center of a tragedy beginning to unfold.

The tragic momentum builds to a climax in book 8, which provides an account of Dmitry's frantic attempts to procure the three thousand rubles he must return to Katerina Ivanovna so that he can clear his name and win Grushenka. Following the chapter "Cana of Galilee" and Alyosha's moment of revelation, when the narrative perspective breaks free of novelistic time and space and enters the realm of hagiographic legend, in book 8 the narrative moves back in time, covering the same two days from Dmitry's perspective. Repetitions of the word "fate" and its variants (*sud'ba, rokovoi*) alert us to the fact that we are in the realm of tragedy, the governing principle of which is the unstoppable machine of fate. The tragic mode is invoked initially either by Dmitry himself or by the narrator's free indirect discourse: "And he, in those two days, had literally been rushing in all directions, 'struggling with his fate and trying to save himself,' as he put it" (14:329). The narrator seemingly apes Dmitry's view of himself as trapped within a fated downward spiral, presenting all roads as leading to the inevitable catastrophe: "Here we shall outline only the most necessary facts of those two terrible days of his life, which preceded the horrible catastrophe that broke so suddenly upon his fate" (14:329). Yet the narrator's tendency to indulge in proleptic narration also undercuts the tragic mode, warning us against being taken in by the apparently irrevocable forward motion of the fatal mechanism. The narrative bifurcates into two alternative possibilities for Dmitry and Grushenka's future: Mitya's dream of a completely new virtuous life, in which Grushenka helps him remove himself from the "vile bog" that threatens to drown him, or a fatal outcome that hangs, unspoken yet tangible, over the narrative. Pulling us in and out of the tragic spiral, the narrator builds narrative tension by continually shifting perspective between his own point of view and that of Dmitry and by the liberal use of ellipses within free indirect discourse, a favorite Dostoevskian device for expressing the worst possible scenario, the most secret, unspeakable fears:

> That would be only in the case of the first, *happy* solution to the question. There was another solution; he imagined a different and terrible ending. She suddenly says to him: "Go, I've just reached an agreement with Fyodor Pavlovich and shall marry him, you're no longer needed" . . . and then . . . but then . . . (14:330)

The reduction of all narrative possibilities to two mutually exclusive scenarios is the prerequisite of the tragic mode, the narrative preparation for the subsequent narrowing to one single inescapable path.

In his appeal to Kuz'ma Kuz'mich, Mitya continues to assert the existence of only two narrative possibilities: "And here three men are at loggerheads, if you like, because fate is a grisly thing, Kuz'ma Kuz'mich! Realism, Kuz'ma Kuz'mich, realism! And since you should have been counted out long ago, there are two heads left . . . Everything is in your hands now—three fates and two lots" (14:335). Without subverting the buildup of tragic atmosphere, the comic tone and repetition serve an estranging function, revealing the tragic fatalistic perspective to be Mitya's own and reminding us, through his uncomprehending reference to realism, of the novelistic context. Like the narrator's prolepsis, this allows us to remain partially outside the tragic mode and thus to examine it as a worldview, as a set of assumptions about the moral makeup of human beings that reduce them to pawns in the implementation of some grand design.

The spatial-temporal configuration of tragedy is movement against the grain, rapid motion through space toward a goal that turns out to be a mirage, an uphill climb up an unending series of false summits. This is the spatiotemporal pattern of book 8 up to Mitya's return to his father's house in chapter 4 as he tries to obtain enough money to tempt Grushenka away from his father. His failure to convince Kuz'ma Samsonov to lend him the money, followed by his excruciating wild-goose chase in search of Lyagavy, and finally the painful absurdity of his meeting with Madame Khokhlakov, all contribute to the quicksand of tragedy, an ever-expanding space where no movement is fast enough to cover the rapidly shifting terrain.

The narrator explicitly develops the themes of fatalism and tragedy made explicit in his digression on Othello and the theme of jealousy (14:343–44). Othello is the generic archetype of the tragic hero: possessed of an ideal that is destroyed as a result of his own self-delusion, he smashes himself against its broken shards. The narrator invokes Othello in opposition to Mitya's "truly jealous man." Unlike Othello, who, once deceived into jealousy, is carried by the unstoppable momentum of the tragic mechanism, Mitya is capable of extreme jealousy one minute and complete trust the next. His loftiness contains his jealousy within it, and, caught between these two extremes, he remains utterly unpredictable. By this comparison the narrator subtly pulls away from the characterization of Mitya as a tragic hero and suggests that he belongs to a different generic system altogether.

Chapter 4, "In the Dark," brings what we assume will be the moment of tragic apotheosis, the murder of Fyodor Karamazov. The tragic buildup continues with the narrator's description of Mitya's thoughts: "'The whole intrigue, the whole deception is obvious now . . .' All this flew like a whirlwind through his head" (14:352). The language of excess and turbulence used to describe Mitya's headlong run to Fyodor Pavlovich's, his bated breath and his pounding heart, all seem to point toward the murder as a certainty.

Coming face to face with his father at last, he is filled with uncontainable anger. The narrator reminds us at that moment of his conversation with Alyosha the day before:

> "I don't know, I don't know," he had said then. "Maybe I won't kill him, and maybe I will [*mozhet, ne ub'iu, a mozhet ub'iu*]. I'm afraid [*Boius'*] that *his face at that moment* will suddenly become [*stanet*] hateful to me. I hate his Adam's apple, his nose, his eyes, his shameless sneer. I feel a personal loathing. I'm afraid of that, I may not be able to help myself." (14:355)

Mitya's words here convey on a microcosmic scale the struggle between tragedy's fatalistic, deterministic, downward spiral, and the novel's free, open-ended play of potentialities. Mitya's continuing freedom to act, or not to act, is expressed through the alternating possibilities, "maybe I won't kill him, and maybe I will [*mozhet, ne ub'iu, a mozhet ub'iu*]," two options separated only by a comma and a negative article, their connection concretized by the repetition of the word *mozhet,* two mutually exclusive narrative scenarios locked in a single syntactic embrace. The sense of possibility is then seemingly undermined by the fatalistic future perfective *stanet,* which, used after *boius',* conveys a hypothetical rather than an inevitable scenario, thereby functioning as an indicator of inevitable future completion. This play between open and closed narrative development thus comes to a climax at the moment of the murder.

The ellipses that represent the murder of Fyodor Karamazov signify the turn from tragic inevitability to novelistic potentiality. The moment Mitya utters the words "God was watching over me then," the irrevocable downward spiral of fate is resisted, the tragic mode broken (355). Yet what replaces it? Are we to view this as a second miracle, akin to the one experienced by Alyosha in the previous chapter? Grigory Vasilievich immediately wakes up, goes to investigate, and is knocked down by Mitya. If this does not immediately negate the miracle of Mitya's retreat from the act of murder, it reminds us at least that we are in the dominion of the novel, rather than in the realm of salvation literature. The either/or of the tragic mode has been replaced not by the kairotic time of a conversion narrative but by the novelistic open field, and all narrative possibilities are in play.

With the collapse of the tragic mode, Mitya is again forced to seek out the genre within which he belongs. Mitya's generic affiliation is revealed through the coachman Andrei's narration of a folk legend. As an ex-soldier, womanizer, and drunkard with a predisposition for violence, Mitya wholeheartedly resembles the archetypal hero of folk legend. Yet until the murder he is never explicitly connected with the genre.

The second half of the novel serves as a trial not merely of Mitya, but also of genre itself, the search for a form which can explain that missing narrative and, in doing so, provide us with a literary model for the representation of man and his manifest moral contradictions. In the chapters following the murder, when we are already aware of Mitya's innocence, the novel demands that we reassess our reading of human potentiality, that we open ourselves up to a very different image of humankind from that offered by epic and tragedy. The folk legend that Andrei tells Mitya is thus located at a crucial moment in the novel, after the collapse of the previous genre models offered to us. In the light of this collapse, it is able to offer a very different worldview and image of humankind from those of the "high" literary genres that precede it.

Andrei tells Mitya the folk legend as he drives him to Mokroye to look for Grushenka. The frenzied atmosphere of the last few hours is dispersed by the journey, which refreshes Mitya (14:369). The sky is clear, the stars visible, and the narrator reminds us, "This was the same night, perhaps the same hour, when Alyosha threw himself to the earth, 'vowing ecstatically to love it for ages unto ages'" (14:369). The narrator thus places Mitya and Alyosha within structural equivalence, suggesting the possibility of Mitya's spiritual rebirth. Andrei asks Mitya's permission to ask him a question about his guilt, but the latter responds with a partial confession of his guilt toward Grigory and an anguished if ambivalent plea for punishment.

Mitya asks Andrei whether he believes Mitya will go to hell, and Andrei tells him the folk legend:

> You see sir, when the Son of God was crucified on the cross and died, he went straight from the cross to hell and freed all the sinners suffering there. And hell groaned because it thought it wouldn't have any more sinners coming. And the Lord said to hell: "Do not groan, O hell, for all kinds of mighty ones, rulers, great judges and rich men will come to you from all parts, and you will be as full as ever, unto ages of ages, till the time when I come again." (14:372)

The editors of the Academy Edition reference the legend first of all in terms of the "harrowing of hell" apocrypha, where, following the Crucifixion but before the Resurrection, Christ frees sinners from hell.[50] Such apocrypha include "Pilate's Epistle to the Emperor Tiberius" (part of the apocryphal gospel of Nicodemus) and "Saint Bartholomew's Questions," both included in Pypin's collection.[51] They further suggest that the source may be a piece of religious folk poetry (15:575).[52] Yet Mitya's response, "a folk legend [*narodnaia legenda*], wonderful," makes the narrative's genre clear. The motif of a newly resurrected Christ setting the sinners free from hell can be found in one of the folk legends in Afanas'iev's collection: no. 15, "Solomon the Wise."[53] Solomon the Wise is a common character in folk legends, primarily because of his presence in so many apocrypha.[54] In Afanas'iev's legend, Christ releases all the other sinners from hell but leaves Solomon there, since he is wise enough to get out on his own initiative. Asked by a devil why he is measuring hell, Solomon replies that he intends to build a monastery and a church right there in hell. The frightened devil runs to tell Satan, who releases Solomon forthwith.

The legend demonstrates an unexpectedly dualistic attitude toward miracles. Hell is anthropomorphized, groaning as it is emptied of sinners. God here is forced to sympathize with hell, to promise it recompense in the form of the authority figures that will be sent there in the released sinners' stead. And what is the significance of the emptying of hell? On the one hand it testifies to the infinite compassion of Christ, who, even during the Passion, before his Resurrection, redeems sinning humanity. On the other it demonstrates the enduring existence of hell, the continuation of sin, and the unchanging nature of the earth's occupants. This is a profoundly ambivalent model of sin, expiation, and redemption. God releases the sinners not because they have repented, but because of Christ's compassion. The miracle of the "harrowing of hell" in its folk legend incarnation is built on novelistic rather than eschatological foundations.

The genre of the folk legend fuses the earthly with the divine; though inspired by apocryphal motifs and biblical images, it is grounded in the earth and projects an image of humans as greedy and generous, wily and naive, selfish and selfless: as broad as the Karamazovs. Despite its spatial and temporal configurations, its frequent representations of heaven and hell, the folk legend is concerned not with beginnings and ends, but with the essentially unchanging cycle of life. It thus provides a way to narrate religious experience within the novel's generic terms, without impinging on the novelistic hero's ability to carry on the endless process of self-definition through narrative.

The folk legend provides the model for Mitya's subsequent moral and spiritual development within the novel. The vision of hell instantiated in the folk legend permeates the novelistic structure, just as the appearance of Ivan's devil infuses it with the generic conventions of apocryphal legend. Identifying with the worldview expressed in Andrei's legend, Mitya enters into his own process of redemption. His cross-examination is played out against the background of the legend's model of hell. The three chapters that recount his interrogation are entitled "The Soul's Journey through the Torments" after the forty days of torments the soul endures after death according to popular Orthodox belief.[55] As Dostoevsky himself points out in a letter to Liubimov, "He experiences a purification of the heart and conscience under the storm of misfortune and false accusation. He accepts with his soul punishment not for what he did, but for the fact that he was so hideous that he could and did want to commit the crime of which he will be falsely accused through a judicial error" (30:I:130). He then explains this behavior within the terms of a Russian folk proverb: "It's a thoroughly Russian personality: if the thunder doesn't rumble, the peasant won't cross himself."[56]

Just like the forty days of torments, the interrogation serves as a moral test for Dmitry, forcing him to undergo diverse kinds of suffering and humiliation, from insults to Grushenka, to being forced to undress and to disclose his "great secret." With the revelation of the great secret, the interplay of genres ends at last as Mitya's aesthetic and ethical worldview becomes fully delineated, modeled within the generic foundations of the so-called legend of the *ladonka*.

LEGEND AND THE RESURRECTION OF NOVELISTIC NARRATIVE

In the novel's closing books, the ethical model of humankind proposed both by the folk legend and by the novel undergoes a completely different kind of critique. Here it is not other kinds of religious legend that counterpose the folk legend, but the secular discourses of the trial lawyers. The trial effectively reminds us of the novel's historical and ideological context. Having been carried along by the novel's internal aesthetic and ethical currents and drawn into its metaphysical conflicts, we now return to the problem of contemporary reality, of how the novel's ethical dilemmas can be understood and represented within the social and political discourses of 1870s Russia. Throughout much of the novel the themes of sin, temptation, expiation, and redemption have been represented within the symbolic terms of Christian legend, within genres that reflect the narrative traditions of a thousand years of Russian religious culture. In the final chapters they are recontextualized, materializing as problems of a particular time and place, problems that lie within the jurisdiction of the law. The novel's interpretative systems collide as judgment of Mitya's moral potentiality falls to the peasant jury and commentary is taken over by the lawyers.

The court case provides the pretext for two more accounts of the events leading up to Fyodor Karamazov's murder. Located at the novel's end, when the narrative reverberations of the brothers' generic worldviews have already made themselves felt—after Ivan has descended into madness, Mitya has succeeded in not murdering his father, and Alyosha has regained his faith, it fulfills an important function in the novel. Though the gaps in the fabula have already been explained, and we know the circumstances of the murder, the court case provides a forum for the final showdown, the clash of secular legal discourses with the ethical landscape of legend. It also plays a somewhat programmatic role, as Dostoevsky lays his cards on the table, making explicit the ethical model he himself proposes in answer to the Grand Inquisitor. Juxtaposed to the speeches of both lawyers, who seek to explain Mitya's behavior from the standpoint of family, society, or history, is the so-called legend of the *ladonka,* Mitya's claim that he kept some of the money given to him by Katerina Ivanovna in a bag made from his landlady's old cloth cap, in order to show that, although a scoundrel, he is not a thief (15:131).[57] Though the prosecutor's description of the cloth bag narrative as a legend represents an attempt to discredit it as evidence, the description is double-voiced. Mitya's account of his motivation in keeping the money in a cloth bag as a symbol of his moral potentiality is perfectly expressed within the generic terms of folk legend.

The banal and plain quality of the *ladonka* itself, a scrap of fabric taken from Mitya's landlady's old hat, already suggests that we are within the realm of folk legend. The idea of moral potentiality being contained within such a humble object fits perfectly into that genre's symbolic system. Just like Grushenka's onion tale and Andrei's legend of the sinners in hell, the cloth bag narrative offers a profoundly dualistic vision, an ambiguous and complex proof of Mitya's moral freedom. It gives rise to a contradictory set of narrative scenarios, a contradictory set of interpretations. The cloth bag contains only half the money Mitya has taken from Katerina Ivanovna and thus brings to mind the moral depths to which he has sunk, for it stands for the money he has already squandered. Thus it reminds us of his moral weakness, impulsiveness, and passion. However, although the *ladonka* is half empty, at the same time it is half full. While the money remains around his neck he retains on his person the tangible proof of the possibility of moral resurrection, the means by which he can go to Katerina Ivanovna and show her that he is not beyond repair; that though fallen, he can still be resurrected. How we view this set of interpretations is determined by the context of the legend.

Dostoevsky juxtaposes the legend of the *ladonka* to the lawyers' speeches, contrasting it with them. The speeches themselves, which are closely modeled on legal discourses of the time, exemplify the kinds of linear thought that Dostoevsky had attacked in *A Writer's Diary*.[58] They are composed in relation to a preordained final goal, that is, to prove the guilt or innocence of Mitya Karamazov, which must continually define their structure, content, and philosophical underpinnings. In their attempt to explain the case, the lawyers work back from the murder in order to "deduce" what "must have" taken place. As they retell the murder for the jury, they rewrite what might have taken place as a linear narrative, a path of certainty in which gaps and anomalies are ignored. The chronological order of the telling gives an illusory authority to their speculations, an authority bolstered by the use of self-referential, organizing discourse. Both lawyers emphasize the linearity of their accounts, telling events (*po poriadku* [128]) as if the chronology of the events depicted exactly replicated the chronology of the narrative. Both lawyers repeatedly assure jurors of their account's veracity using phrases such as "I assert," "this fact," and "without a doubt" (15:123–76).

This linearity also defines the lawyers' attitude toward Mitya and his moral freedom. The lawyers' narratives differ profoundly in their approach to human moral freedom. Ippolit Kirillovich sees the process that leads up to and proceeds from the murder as a straight line leading from cause to effect to aftermath. Like the pawnbroker in "The Meek One," who blames his wife's death on the blind force of fate, he clings to the idea that human beings are subject to the laws of what he calls *kosnost'* (inertia or immutability).[59] The prosecution lawyer maintains that once Mitya has threatened to kill his father, he has set in motion a process that must run its bloody course. Ippolit Kirillovich repeatedly claims that the murder took place "as it was written" (15:133; 142), thereby implying that the moment Mitya wrote that he wished to kill his father, he set in motion the inevitable unfolding of the crime, but also invoking the idea of fate, making a pawn of Mitya and denying him the possibility of moral freedom. His narrative progresses linearly from probability to certainty, the automatic movement from the conditional to the perfect tense, from the theoretical to the actual, from the abstract and generalized to the particular and individual. "Probably" becomes "without a doubt," while generalizations about how the typical criminal would behave in a certain situation explain the particular behavior of Mitya in this particular case: "Oh, in such cases the criminal often becomes amazingly shallow and credulous" (15:148).

Instead of creating a linear narrative that refuses to acknowledge the validity of any other perspective and that portrays Mitya as caught in an end-determined, "inert [*kosnyi*]" murderous momentum, the defense lawyer creates an altogether different narrative, one that constitutes a movement into a Borgesian labyrinth of parallel possible narratives, in which the truth becomes illusory. Beginning with his observation that "psychology is a stick with two ends" (15:155), the defense lawyer shows that every piece of evidence referred to by Ippolit Kirillovich can be read in many different ways, thus revealing many possible narratives to explain the murder. If Ippolit Kirillovich assumes that what is probable must be true, Fetyukovich takes the opposite line: unless something is definite, it cannot be true. If Ippolit Kirillovich turns the dotted lines of possibility into the black lines of certainty, Fetyukovich negates those dotted lines altogether, or rather draws so many other dotted lines that truth and reality are invariably lost in a maze of possibilities. He questions fact after fact, and the lack of evidence as to the money's whereabouts leads him to conclude that there was no robbery at all, although he then points out that there may have been. His throwaway comment "I do not contradict myself: the money could have existed" (15:166) reveals that his technique lies not in a single consistent interpretation of the case, but in creating a web of possible scenarios. When he declares that there has been no parricide because Fyodor Karamazov forfeited his claim to the title of father, we feel he has gone a step too far. If Ippolit Kirillovich, as a linear thinker, peppers his narrative with received wisdom, with unquestioned, unfounded assumptions about human nature, Fetyukovich allows for no "prejudices," undermining the idea that there are certain sacred truths or values. Not even the blood ties between father and son are sacrosanct: a father must earn his son's love rather than receive it unconditionally. The defense lawyer's narrative rejects the possibility of any eternal truths about human beings.

As we become conscious of the linearity of the lawyers' speeches, their failure to grant Mitya moral freedom, and their failure to take into account anything that lies on either side of the straight line they draw to their preconceived goal, we are naturally drawn to what they reject: the legend of the *ladonka*. This worldview begins where the lawyers' speeches end, rooted in that which they exclude: the fantastic, the extraordinary, the contradictory, and the transcendent. This "legend" fundamentally differs from both legal narratives in terms of its construction, subject matter, concept of the hierarchy of reality, relationship with other narratives, and underlying assumptions about human nature.

The legend of the *ladonka* is structured more like a dream or allegory, for it relies on a central image from which we gain a kind of revelation. It is neither linear nor chronological, but fractured and splintered. It is first introduced during Mitya's initial interrogation, but is told in fits and starts due to Mitya's own reluctance to reveal the inner motives of his behavior toward Katerina Ivanovna (14:441). It is then reintroduced by the lawyers during the trial. The "legend" differs from the legal narratives in terms of its spatiotemporal configurations: Mitya cannot pinpoint the story's time sequence, nor can he remember when or where he opened the bag. Such details of time and space, which are vitally important to the legal narratives, are sidelined by the central image of the cloth bag, out of which the whole narrative unfolds.

Just as the court case serves as the forum for the unveiling of the generic foundations of legend, as embodied in the aesthetic and ethical contours of the cloth bag narrative, it also allows Dostoevsky to demonstrate the similarity between the narrative implications of the legend and the novel itself. As before, Ippolit Kirillovich is the ironic and unwitting herald of this revelation, so crucial to Dostoevsky's own novelistic mission. The prosecution calls Mitya a "novelist [*romanist*]," the cloth bag narrative a "novel [*roman*]," and launches into an unprecedented attack on the novelistic worldview, as exemplified by the "legend." Fetyukovich, the defense lawyer, in turn denounces the "novel" he accuses Ippolit Kirillovich of creating. Here again Dostoevsky's own voice is audible over the pejorative overtones of the lawyers. The *ladonka* legend is a novelistic narrative not because it opposes truth with fantasy, as the lawyers contend, but because of the complexity of its representation of truth and because of its ability to represent human morality in all its contradictory nature.

The cloth bag narrative reveals the novelistic hero's ambivalent relationship toward the Christian moral paradigm. Mitya's actions demonstrate his awareness of a higher spiritual ideal, his sense of himself as an ethical being bound by moral law. Yet this awareness is tempered by his continuing need to fight against that ethical system, to feel out its limits, and to prove his individuality through transgression. In this he stands apart from both Ivan, who denies absolutely the authority of the Christian moral code, and Alyosha, who accepts it wholeheartedly. It is precisely his ability to embody these two antithetical instincts that accords him his status as novelistic hero. The novel finds its narrative energy in the tension between the absolute precepts of Christian moral law and the unruly and chaotic scenes of individual human life. Like Christian legend, it occupies that ambiguous space between Scripture and human life, providing the narrative foreground and background for biblical narratives that often seem far distant from the concerns and dilemmas of human society.

Dostoevsky thus opposes the lawyers' discourses with a miracle that unfolds within the generic contours of the novel itself. In epic and biblical texts, the miracle marks the end of narration. In hagiographic legend it marks a narrative shift, whereby the hero begins to occupy a completely different temporal space. In the folk legend and the novel, it marks a new beginning, but one that continues to generate narrative and produces its own new problems, which in turn generate new plots. Like the hero of folk legend, the novelistic hero lies at the nexus of narrative possibility, always poised to undergo some new and entirely unexpected development. Through the structured multiplicity of its plots, the novel projects a world where absolute moral judgment is deferred by the continuing process of narration; wherever narration is still possible, the final moral reckoning cannot take place.

The novel's epilogue leaves the fate of many of the characters wide open.[60] Though Mitya has been sentenced to Siberian exile, Alyosha, Katerina Ivanovna, and Mitya himself discuss his possible escape. Though Ivan has lost his mind, it is not clear whether or not he will regain consciousness, or even whether he will live or die. Katerina Ivanovna and Grushenka undergo an ambivalent reconciliation, in which it is unclear whether vengeance and forgiveness will ultimately prevail. Only Ilyusha's funeral functions as a symbol of closure, and even that seems to point outward, beyond the events of the novel, into a web of possible future scenarios, as Alyosha and the boys pledge to hold Ilyusha in their memory even as they disperse across space and time.[61]

Dostoevsky structures into the novel's ending an unambiguous answer to the question as to whether the novelist should concern himself with the representation of religious experience, whether an ethical-spiritual vision can be reconciled with novelistic narrative. To Kolya Krasotkin's question as to whether they will all rise from the dead and be reunited with Ilyusha, Alyosha asserts, "Certainly we shall rise again, certainly we shall see and gladly, joyfully *tell* one another all that has been" (15:197, italics mine). In this statement, Dostoevsky combines both the resurrection narrative and the resurrection *of* narrative. *The Brothers Karamazov* embraces the Christian eschatological vision, yet insists that this does not mean renouncing its novelistic status. Christian legend offers a blueprint of how to build a novelistic universe on Christian metaphysical foundations.

Writing like Monk Parfeny in an age resistant to the idea of miracles, Dostoevsky decided to look to the genres of the past to reconcile religious experience with novelistic narrative. He found in the literary form and metaphysical landscape of legend an alternative to the secular subgenres of the novel within which he had been working in the 1870s. In its use of the diverse genres of the legend, *The Brothers Karamazov* achieves the status of a work of religious polyphony that navigates the normally tense spaces between doctrinal/canonical Orthodoxy and popular religion. It celebrates Orthodox Christianity not as canon law, as an established set of moral laws that must be followed, but as a rich repository of narrative forms. Legend demonstrates the creativity and literary potentiality contained in religious narrative, its ability to continually generate new variants. Taking its building blocks from the canonical models of scriptural narrative forms, it fills in the gaps in the biblical accounts, explores the narrative reverberations that result from the transposition of Scripture into an idiomatic key. Whether through the Byzantine Lives of Saints, which made sacred virtue tangible through its instantiation within the life of an individual; the medieval apocrypha, which sought to illuminate the darker corners of the Christian doctrines; or the nineteenth-century folk legends, which recast the values of the biblical accounts in the light of the peasantry's social values, legend has always provided the narrative means by which Christianity has become intelligible to the majority of its followers.

Through its celebration of this narrative potentiality, the legend functions as a genre metaphor for the novel itself. Like the legend, the novel takes as its subject the problematic realm between divine law and earthly freedom. It finds its raw materials in the gap between the ideal and the real, in the sphere of the all-too-human impediments to the application of the Christian moral paradigm: in temptation, self-doubt, ambition, and love. *The Brothers Karamazov* is concerned with moments of moral suspense—narrative scenarios where characters must measure themselves against absolute moral standards—and with how they will respond to this moment of reckoning. Structuring into his novel the generic interplay between hagiography, apocrypha, and folk legend through the central characters of the Karamazov brothers, Dostoevsky provides three competing models of sin, expiation, and redemption. It is the spirit of the folk legend, crystallized within the novel in the narrative of Dmitry Karamazov, that most closely approaches the ethical and aesthetic assumptions of the novel as a genre.

Conclusion

THIS STUDY HAS ARGUED that Dostoevsky's works of the 1870s are characterized by two contradictory formal impulses. The first is expressed in Dostoevsky's choice of an illegitimate half-peasant, half-noble adolescent for his hero in *The Adolescent,* a choice that represents a direct challenge to the aristocratic heroes of Tolstoy and Turgenev. It is an impulse toward fragmentation, a recognition of the necessity of representing chaotic postreform Russian reality in literary form. This impulse defines *The Adolescent*'s ambiguous generic identity as "notes" and determines its hermeneutically ambivalent epilogue, which simultaneously defends and polemicizes with the work's hesitant generic claims. It is equally present in the diverse stories of modern life that appear in the monthly column Dostoevsky wrote for Prince Meshchersky's journal *The Citizen,* "A Writer's Diary," particularly in the disparate voices permitted to speak for themselves. This formal impulse is foreshadowed in the generic hybridity of *Demons,* with its ideological ambiguities and its open-endedness to multiple readings. It is present in the multilingual, heterogeneric heteroglossia of the monojournal version of *A Writer's Diary,* which seeks to represent the linguistic differentiation of the postreform era. Its open-ended structure and forms seek to replicate a vision of the world as unpredictable, as continually being shaped and reshaped by the capricious forces of modernity in its many shapes and forms.

This acceptance of fragmented modernity's formal implications is reflected in Dostoevsky's pride in being called "the poet of the underground" by mocking critics, expressed in the notebooks for *The Adolescent* and in his identification with his "accidental hero" even as he expresses through the voice of Arkady's Moscow landlord his own misgivings about the risks of writing a novel that seeks to represent the amorphous forms of the age of transition. It is present in *A Writer's Diary* in his fidelity to the new Babel that is postreform Russia in all its social and spiritual differentiation, and in his creation of the dark visions of "Bobok," "The Meek One," and the "Dream of a Ridiculous Man."

The other approach to form that we find in the works of the 1870s understands the world to be maximally interconnected and the text to be closed and self-contained. Form becomes the means by which a fragmented world can be made whole again. It embraces narrative totality and holds up the image of Christ as the transcendental sign of harmonious ideal form. It seeks to overcome linguistic differentiation with the transcendent power of the word. We see this formal impulse as early as Dostoevsky's generic fantasy of a historical epic pitched to Maikov in 1867, an epic that seeks to move beyond the temporal horizons of the post-Petrine era, which Dostoevsky sees as restricting the traditional Russian novel. It inspires Dostoevsky's ambition of blending hagiographic conventions with the traditional bildungsroman structure in his *Life of a Great Sinner* and his attempt to create a Russian aristocratic hero who could become transfigured by the power of the Russian Idea in the notebooks for *Demons.*

This impulse finds its clearest expression in his aim of redeeming the novelistic form, of transfiguring a genre associated with the Petrine schism and making it reflect the experience of the section of Russian society who have been excluded from the Russian novel throughout most of its history. Even *The Adolescent* projects a version of this aspiration. Its appeal to the genre memory of the noble family novel expresses not merely the desire to overcome it, but also a dream of reintegrating the fragments of Russian literature and art shattered and dispersed by the pressures of modernization and of returning to what Dostoevsky imagines as the perfect forms of the pre-Petrine, pre-Nikonian era. But it comes closest to realization in *The Brothers Karamazov,* where Dostoevsky finally creates a generic landscape that can bring into the novel both religious experience and the social and cultural values of the soil, which he has been hoping to reintegrate into the Russian literary landscape since the reconciliatory program of *Time.*

There is a parallel movement toward formal reintegration in Dostoevsky's journalism. We see it in the 1873 columns of "A Writer's Diary" in the criteria used for picking the stories Dostoevsky shares with his readers. He seeks out any signs of the utopian future that he sees as the imminent inevitable result of the national embrace of the ideal image of the Russian Christ. More and more, and above all in the monojournal, this approach demands a monologic voice that brooks no authority, that denies the polysemic nature of many of the images he chooses to highlight. Here we find an insistence on the absolute power of the final word Dostoevsky is offering to the world, a word that will overcome the linguistic and social differentiation of the modern age.

This approach represents a denial of modernity and its implications, a desire to return to the imagined unity of the Russian nation before the Petrine fall. It forswears recognition of the diversity and complexity of modern experience in favor of a blinkered utopian nationalist vision that sees the future as already determined, as closed off. This is the very vision Dostoevsky himself criticizes so harshly in the trial of Dmitry Karamazov, yet he is peculiarly blind to the tendency of his own journalism to fall into the very same pitfalls of determinism that lead the prosecution lawyer to insist so vociferously on Dmitry's guilt. It is only in Dostoevsky's journalism, as well as in his letters and notebooks, that this denial of modernity is ever allowed to have the final word. In his novels, open-endedness is almost always allowed to win out; even a creative vision as unashamedly polemical as *Demons* is tempered by textual ambiguities and mixed messages that obscure the dogmatic conclusion.

All of the works of Dostoevsky's last decade display both of these formal impulses and adopt both of these contradictory perspectives on modernity. But it was in *The Brothers Karamazov,* his greatest novelistic achievement, that Dostoevsky was able to combine both impulses and create a work that re-created within the novel both the generic and metaphysical landscape of legend and the religious experience of the Russian people and revealed the potentiality of the genre itself as a vehicle for representing human moral freedom. It marks the glorious rehabilitation of the novel in Dostoevsky's creative universe and the triumphal last act of his literary career. It is *The Brothers Karamazov,* rather than Dostoevsky's nationalist Pushkin Speech, that marks the ultimate return of the dream of reconciliation which had sustained him ever since his return from Siberia.

The two visions of modernity that helped to shape Dostoevsky's thinking about genre seem at first sight to be absolutely antithetical to one another, yet by the end of the nineteenth century they became profoundly typical expressions of Russian modernity. Anxieties about disintegration, breakdown, and collapse, coupled with dreams of building on the ashes of the old, revolutionary rupture, and sudden universal transformation, coexisted with ease in Russian symbolism at the turn of the twentieth century and strengthened still more in Russian modernism. Dostoevsky's experience of and response to modernity became not anomalous, but typical. Even the two approaches to form that Dostoevsky takes in the works of the 1870s, the coexistence of an impulse toward fragmentation and nostalgia for lost unity and dreams of unity and totality, can be seen as the two formal impulses of modernist art. The 1860s and 1870s mark a crucial moment not just for Dostoevsky's literary trajectory but also for the experience of Russian modernity and its reverberations in the literary world. After *Demons* and *The Adolescent* the Russian novel could never be the same again.

In his last decade Dostoevsky remade the novel not once but twice, the first time seeking to open up the form to represent new forms of social life, the second to redeem it, to open it up to a broader spectrum of narrative traditions. In both cases he was seeking to make it more fully representative of the whole range of Russian social experience, which had been opened up by the processes of modernization. The formal impulse of fragmentation is stronger in *The Adolescent* and weaker in *The Brothers Karamazov*. The opposing impulse toward formal unity dominates *The Brothers Karamazov* but remains within *The Adolescent* as a brake on the poetics of disintegration. Both of these works, as well as both incarnations of *A Writer's Diary*, are structured by the clash of these competing dynamics. And Dostoevsky is caught in a dilemma that would define modernism: the problem of how to overcome old forms and structures. Often, especially in *Demons* and *The Adolescent*, his novelistic art is built out of the fragments of older, more traditional forms, which continue to exert their power over the novelist and his narrators even as he seeks to overcome them. At times of transition the field of genre, seemingly the most conservative and parochial of all hermeneutic concerns, proves to be the central laboratory of experiments in how to confront the modern.

Notes

INTRODUCTION

1. F. M. Dostoevskii, "Zapisnaia Tetrad' (1872–1875)," in *Neizdannyi Dostoevskii: Zapisnye knizhki i tetrad 1860–1881 gg, Literaturnoe Nasledstvo* 83 (Moscow: Nauka, 1971), 290. The Academy Edition editors include most of this passage (up to "The Citizen must present the picture") in the preparatory notes for the conclusion of *Demons,* perhaps because of the mention of Kirillov, but the last two sentences appear in volume 21, alongside the rest of the notes on *The Citizen:* Dostoevskii, *Polnoe sobranie sochinenii v tritsati tomakh* (*Complete Works,* hereafter cited as *CW*), ed. V. G. Bazanov et al., 30 vols. (Leningrad: Nauka, 1972–90), 11:308, 21:252. The task of deciphering the chronology and ordering of Dostoevsky's notebooks, especially those from this period, has presented scholars with formidable challenges, as Lidia Rosenblium pointed out in her introduction to the volume of *Literaturnoe Nasledstvo* which first introduced the notebooks to the reading public. The notes rarely contain dates and deal with a wide variety of topics. See L. M. Rosenblium, "Tvorcheskie dnevniki Dostoevskogo," *Literaturnoe Nasledstvo* 83 (Moscow: Nauka, 1971), 9–92, and *Tvorcheskie dnevniki Dostoevskogo* (Moscow: Nauka, 1981). Here and throughout the rest of the book, unless stated otherwise, translations of passages from Dostoevsky's notebooks are taken from Fyodor Dostoevsky, *The Unpublished Dostoevsky,* ed. Carl Proffer, trans. Arline Boyer and Carl Proffer, 3 vols. (Ann Arbor, Mich.: Ardis, 1975).

2. On the reforms of Alexander II, sometimes called the "Great Reforms," see W. B. Lincoln, *The Great Reforms: Autocracy, Bureaucracy and the Politics of Change in Imperial Russia* (DeKalb: Northern Illinois University Press, 1990). For a recent study of the cultural significance of the reforms, see Olga Maiorova, *From the Shadow of Empire: Defining the Russian Nation Through Cultural Mythology, 1855–1870* (Madison: University of Wisconsin Press, 2010).

3. "Heteroglossia," or *raznorechie,* is of course Mikhail Bakhtin's term, taken from his "Discourse in the Novel." The unstable social dynamics of postreform Russia provided the perfect breeding ground for the linguistic stratifica-

tion which Bakhtin sees as the novel's primary material: Bakhtin, "Slovo v romane," in *Voprosy literatury i estetiki* (Moscow: Khudozhestvennaia literatura, 1975), 72–88. For discussion of the term "heteroglossia," see Gary Saul Morson and Caryl Emerson, *Mikhail Bakhtin: Creation of a Prosaics* (Stanford, Calif.: Stanford University Press, 1990), 139–45.

4. For Bakhtin, monologism is the countervailing force to dialogized heteroglossia. When an author takes on a monologic voice, he often makes use of "authoritative discourse" or "internally persuasive language." See Bakhtin, "Slovo v romane," 72–88; Morson and Emerson, *Mikhail Bakhtin,* 218–23.

5. The reforms of Alexander II are generally seen by historians as beginning with the emancipation of the serfs in 1861 and ending with the Universal Military Service Statute of 1874, which held all Russian men, no matter what their social estate, equally responsible before the law to defend their country, meaning that all men between sixteen and twenty had to register for military service. Before this the nobility had been exempt from military service.

6. J. W. Kipp and W. B. Lincoln, "Autocracy and Reform: Bureaucratic Absolutism and Political Modernization in Nineteenth Century Russia," in *Imperial Russian History II: 1861–1917,* vol. 3 of *Articles on Russian and Soviet History 1500–1991* (New York: Garland, 1992), 1–21.

7. Lincoln, *The Great Reforms,* 163–64.

8. See Richard Wortman, *The Crisis of Russian Populism* (Cambridge: Cambridge University Press, 1967), 1–34, and Adam B. Ulam, *In the Name of the People: Prophets and Conspirators in Pre-Revolutionary Russia* (New York: Viking, 1977), 269–96.

9. Richard Wortman, *The Development of a Russian Legal Consciousness* (Chicago: University of Chicago Press, 1976), 28.

10. W. B. Lincoln, *In the Vanguard of Reform: Russia's Enlightened Bureaucrats, 1825–1861* (DeKalb: Northern Illinois University Press, 1982).

11. Louise McReynolds, *The News Under Russia's Old Regime: The Development of a Mass Circulation Press* (Princeton, N.J.: Princeton University Press, 1991), 11–29.

12. Ibid., 41–43.

13. Harriet Murav, *Russia's Legal Fictions* (Ann Arbor: University of Michigan Press, 1998), 57–59. See the most notable trial commentary in *A Writer's Diary:* 21:13–23; 22:50–73; 23:5–20, 136–41; 24:36–43; 25:182–93.

14. See the notes to M. E. Saltykov-Shchedrin, *Sobranie sochinenii,* ed. A.S. Bushmin et al., 20 vols. (Moscow: Khudozhestvennaia Literatura, 1970–76), 13:655–56.

15. For a modern take on and a summary of the arguments about the perceived social threats presented by modernization, see Johan Galtung, "On the Social Costs of Modernization: Social Disintegration, Atomie/Anomie, and Social Development," *Development and Change* 27, no. 2 (Apr. 1996): 379–413.

16. For a discussion of this notebook passage, see Sarah Hudspith, *Dostoevsky and the Idea of Russianness* (London: Routledge-Curzon, 2004), 59–61.

17. The idea that modern social democratic societies produce isolated, atomized individuals who have lost the ability to engage with their community can be attributed to, among others, Alexis de Tocqueville, whose *Democracy in America* was widely read in Russia on its first publication in 1835. This work enjoyed a renewed popularity in the 1860s after the publication of his *The Ancient Regime and Revolution* (1856). See G. J. Thurston, "Alexis de Tocqueville in Russia," *Journal of the History of Ideas* 37, no. 2 (Apr.–June 1976): 289–306.

18. The idea of *sobornost'* was a central pillar of Slavophile thought. For a discussion of its meaning and context in Slavophilism, see Hudspith, *Dostoevsky and the Idea of Russianness,* 8–12.

19. Fyodor Dostoevsky, *A Writer's Diary,* trans. Kenneth Lantz, intro. Gary Saul Morson, 2 vols. (Evanston, Ill.: Northwestern University Press, 1993). Translations from both the 1873 columns of "A Writer's Diary" and the 1876–77 monojournal will be taken from this edition unless otherwise indicated.

20. Abbott Gleason remarks, "A crucial goal of virtually all the communitarian experiments of the last one hundred and fifty years has been the ending of 'alienation,' the 'reintegration' of the shattered and fragmented faculties of modern man." He points to the Slavophile Ivan Kireevsky's vision of human reintegration based on communalism and on a reconnection with the principles of Orthodox Christianity. Abbott Gleason, *Young Russia: The Genesis of Russian Radicalism in the 1860s* (New York: Viking, 1980), 23–24.

21. Katkov's refusal to publish the chapter meant that the first generation of readers of *Demons* never got the chance to appreciate the fuller characterization of the novel's protagonist that is provided by the dream.

22. For two recent summaries and treatments of the relationship between the ways in which Dostoevsky expresses ideas in his fiction and in his journalism, see Susan McReynolds, *Redemption and the Merchant God: Dostoevsky's Economy of Salvation and Antisemitism* (Evanston, Ill.: Northwestern University Press, 2008), 207–9, and Robin Feuer Miller, *Dostoevsky's Unfinished Journey* (New Haven, Conn.: Yale University Press, 2007), 13–21.

23. In fact, as Benjamin points out, the newspaper article is itself a response to the process of fragmentation through its attempt to split its subject off from the reader's experience, to isolate each separate aspect of life and to consign it to its own corner. Walter Benjamin, "On Some Motifs in Baudelaire," in *Illuminations,* trans. H. Zohn (New York: Harcourt, Brace, Jovanovich, 1968), 158–59.

24. Georg Lukács, *The Theory of the Novel: A Historico-philosophical Essay on the Forms of Great Epic Literature,* trans. Anna Bostock (Cambridge, Mass.: MIT Press, 1971), 56.

25. Unless otherwise specified, all translations from the notebooks for *The*

Adolescent are taken from *The Notebooks for "A Raw Youth,"* ed. and trans. Edward Wasiolek (Chicago: University of Chicago Press, 1969).

26. V. Dal', *Tolkovyi slovar' zhivogo velikorusskogo iazyka* (St. Petersburg, 1881–82), s.v. "Razlozhenie."

27. Mikhail Bakhtin, *Problemy poetiki Dostoevskogo,* in *Sobranie sochinenii v semi tomakh,* ed. S. G. Bocharov, 7 vols. (Moscow: Russkie slovari, 1996), 6:115–202. For an English translation, see *Problems of Dostoevsky's Poetics,* ed. and trans. Caryl Emerson (Minneapolis: University of Minnesota Press, 1984). For discussion of the context of genre memory in Bakhtin's thinking, see Morson and Emerson, *Mikhail Bakhtin: Creation of a Prosaics,* 295–97.

28. Bakhtin, "Slovo v romane," 124–36.

CHAPTER ONE

1. Quoted in Ulam, *In the Name of the People,* 65.

2. For the most comprehensive account of the journal's ideology and the involvement of its founders, see Wayne Dowler, *Dostoevsky, Grigor'ev and Native Soil Conservatism* (Toronto: University of Toronto Press, 1982).

3. Translations of the announcements and articles from *Time* are, unless otherwise indicated, taken from Fyodor Dostoevsky, *Dostoevsky's Occasional Writings,* ed. and trans. David Magarshack (Evanston, Ill.: Northwestern University Press, 1997).

4. On the emancipation timeline, see Lincoln, *The Great Reforms,* 61–90. See also Daniel Field, "The Year of Jubilee," in *Russia's Great Reforms, 1855–1881,* ed. Ben Eklof, John Bushnell, and Larissa Zakharova (Bloomington: Indiana University Press, 1994), 40–57. On the cultural significance of the emancipation, see Irina Paperno, "The Liberation of the Serfs as a Cultural Symbol," *Russian Review* 50, no. 4 (Oct. 1991): 418–36.

5. F. M. Dostoevskii, *Biografiia, pis'ma i zamet'ki iz zapisnoi knizhki F. M. Dostoevskogo,* ed. O. Miller and N. Strakhov (St. Petersburg, 1883), 177. See also Dostoevskii, *CW,* 18:229.

6. On the Nechaev affair, see Franco Venturi, *Roots of Revolution: A History of the Populist and Socialist Movements in Nineteenth Century Russia,* trans. Francis Haskell (New York: Grosset and Dunlap, 1966), 354–88.

7. This comes from an 1863 article entitled "A Necessary Literary Explanation on Various Questions Involving Bread and Not Involving Bread." "Neobkhodimoe literaturnoe ob'iasnenie po povodu raznyikh khlebnikh i nekhlebykh voprosov," *Vremia 1,* Jan. 1, 1863, sec. II: 29–38. I am grateful to Olha Tytarenko for this reference.

8. Translations from the notebooks for *Demons* are, unless otherwise noted, taken from Fyodor Dostoevsky, *The Notebooks for "The Possessed,"* trans. Victor Terras, ed. Edward Wasiolek (Chicago: University of Chicago Press, 1968).

9. English translations from Dostoevky's letters are taken, unless otherwise noted, from *Fyodor Dostoevsky, Complete Letters*, ed. and trans. David A. Lowe, 5 vols. (Ann Arbor, Mich.: Ardis, 1988–91).

10. *Time* and *Epoch* are available online on the website of the Philological Faculty, University of Karelia, "Zhurnal M. M. i F. M. Dostoevskikh 'Vremia,' Teksty," http://www.philolog.ru/filolog/vremtext.htm (01/18/2013), and "Zhurnal M. M. i F. M. Dostoevskikh 'Epokha', Teksty," http://www.philolog.ru/filolog/epotext.htm (01/18/2013). References here will be given to the paper versions. On the journal and its contents, see V. S. Nechaeva, *Zhurnal M. M. i F. M. Dostoevskikh "Vremia," 1861–1863* (Moscow, 1972). For a recent comprehensive reappraisal of the movement and its ideas, see Andrzej de Lazari, *V krugu Fedora Dostoevskogo: Pochvennichestvo*, trans. M. V. Leskinen (Moscow: Nauka, 2004). On Grigor'ev specifically, see Wayne Dowler, *An Unnecessary Man: The Life of Apollon Grigor'ev* (Toronto: University of Toronto Press, 1995). On Strakhov's involvement with the journal, see Linda Gerstein, *Nikolai Strakhov: Philosopher, Man of Letters, Social Critic* (Cambridge, Mass: Harvard University Press, 1971).

11. Nechaeva puts the number of new journals that opened between 1856 and 1860 at 150. V. S. Nechaeva, *Zhurnal*, 5, cited in Dowler, *An Unnecessary Man*, 62.

12. *Time* was the subject of a rigorous critique by Antonovich in *The Contemporary* in December 1861. The following year it launched into a fierce debate with Mikhail Katkov's *The Russian Messenger* over women's emancipation. In 1863 it was the subject of a vituperative attack by Ivan Aksakov, the de facto leader of the Slavophiles. See Dowler, *Dostoevsky, Grigor'ev and Native Soil Conservatism*, 130–51.

13. On *Time's* interpretation of the Petrine reforms and on its relationship to Slavophilism, see Hudspith, *Dostoevsky and the Idea of Russianness*, 44–46.

14. "Vysochaishii manifest," *Vremia* 3, March 1861, sec. III, 1–10.

15. Nikolai Strakhov, quoted in Dowler, *Dostoevsky, Grigor'ev and Native Soil Conservatism*, 78. See also de Lazari, *V krugu Fedora Dostoevskogo*, 62.

16. "Riad' statei o russkoi literature. I. Vvedenie," *Vremia* 1 (Jan. 1861), sec. II, 1–34; "II. G-n –bov i vopros ob iskusstve," *Vremia* 2 (Feb. 1861), sec. II, 165–205; "III Knizhost' i gramotnost'. Stat'ia pervaia," *Vremia* 7 (July 1861), sec. II, 35–52; "Knizhost' i gramotnost'. Stat'ia vtoraia," *Vremia* 8 (Aug. 1861), sec. II, 91–130; "V. Poslednie literaturnye iavlenie. Gazeta "Den'," *Vremia* 11 (Nov. 1861), sec. II, 64–104.

17. On the literary debates of the 1860s, see Charles A. Moser, *Esthetics as Nightmare: Russian Literary Theory, 1855–1870* (Princeton, N.J.: Princeton University Press, 1989).

18. For a detailed analysis of the arguments on aesthetics which Dostoevsky makes in response to Dobroliubov, see Robert Louis Jackson, *Dostoevsky's Quest*

for Form: A Study of His Philosophy of Art (New Haven, Conn.: Yale University Press, 1966), 138–51; James P. Scanlon, *Dostoevsky the Thinker* (Ithaca, N.Y.: Cornell University Press, 2002), 118–57.

19. Dowler, *Dostoevsky, Grigor'ev and Native Soil Conservatism*, 116–29.

20. A. A. Grigor'ev, "I. S. Turgenev i ego deiatel'nost': Po povodu romana 'Dvorianskoe Gnezdo,'" *Literaturnaia Kritika* (Moscow, 1965), 322–27.

21. A. A. Grigor'ev, "Vzgliad na russkuiu literaturu so smerti Pushkina: Stat'ia pervaia: Pushkin-Griboedov-Gogol'-Lermontov," *Literaturnaia Kritika* (Moscow, 1965), 166–67.

22. A. A. Grigor'ev, "Peterburgskii sbornik," *Finskii vestnik* 9 (1846): 5–7. See also Dowler, *An Unnecessary Man*, 49–50. On the centrality of the Varyngian myth to Russian national consciousness in this period, see Maiorova, *From the Shadow of Empire*, 53–93.

23. A. A. Grigor'ev, "Narodnost' i literatura," *Vremia* 2 (Feb. 1862), sec. II, 83–112. See also Dowler, *An Unnecessary Man*, 172–74.

24. A. A. Grigor'ev, "Vgliad na russkuiu literature so smerti Pushkina. Stat'ia pervaia: Pushkin-Griboedov-Gogol'-Lermontov," *Literaturnaia Kritika*, 162–69. See also Dowler, *An Unnecessary Man*, 150–52.

25. A. A. Grigor'ev, "I. S. Turgenev i ego deiatel'nost'. Po povodu romana *Dvorianskoe gnezdo*," *Literaturnaia Kritika*, 240–366.

26. On Dostoevsky's Pushkin speech, see Marcus C. Levitt, *Russian Literary Politics and the Pushkin Celebration of 1880* (Ithaca, N.Y.: Cornell University Press, 1989).

27. On the usage and meanings of the words *narod* and *narodnost'*, see de Lazari, *V krugu Fedora Dostoevskogo*, 47–59.

28. N. I. Pirogov was an educational administrator who angered the radicals by arguing that corporal punishment was occasionally justified. Dostoevsky berated the radicals for their moralizing absolutism and their failure to accept the necessity of social gradualism. On the "Pirogov affair" as a turning point in Dostoevsky's attitudes toward the radicals, see Dowler, *Dostoevsky, Grigor'ev and Native Soil Conservatism*, 135–36.

29. Quoted in J. Frank, *Dostoevsky: The Stir of Liberation* (Princeton, N.J.: Princeton University Press, 1986), 146. On the nature of the *Young Russia* movement, see Venturi, *Roots of Revolution*, 285–302.

30. Dowler, *Dostoevsky, Grigor'ev and Native Soil Conservatism*, 140–41.

31. Ibid., 163–67.

32. On *Epoch*, see V. S. Nechaeva, *Zhurnal M. M. i F. M. Dostoevskikh "Epokha" 1864–1865* (Moscow: Nauka, 1975).

33. Strakhov, "Zametki letopistsa," *Epokha* 12 (Dec. 1864), 15–25. See also Dowler, *Dostoevsky, Grigor'ev and Native Soil Conservatism*, 163–64.

34. On Dostoevsky's trip to Europe and his account of the trip in *Winter Notes*, see Hudspith, *Dostoevsky and the Idea of Russianness*, 47–55.

35. On Dostoevsky's view of the problem of fragmentation in West European bourgeois liberal democracy, see Bruce K. Ward, *Dostoevsky's Critique of the West* (Waterloo, Ontario: Wilfrid Laurier University Press, 1986), 87–91.

36. On the Slavophile definition of *sobornost'*, see Hudspith, *Dostoevsky and the Idea of Russianness*, 8–12.

37. For two different analyses of this passage, see J. Frank, *Dostoevsky: The Stir of Liberation*, 296–308, and Steven Cassedy, *Dostoevsky's Religion* (Stanford, Calif.: Stanford University Press, 2005), 115–23.

38. For a discussion of this notebook passage, see Hudspith, *Dostoevsky and the Idea of Russianness*, 60–61.

39. Joseph Frank provides an excellent reading of *Notes from Underground* as a fictionalized critique of *What Is to Be Done?* in *Dostoevsky: The Stir of Liberation*, 310–47. See also A. S. Skaftymov, "*Zapiski iz podpolia* sredi publitsistiki Dostoevskogo," in *Nravstvennye iskaniia russkikh pisatelei* (Moscow: Khudozhestvennaia Literatura, 1972), 88–133.

40. J. Frank, *Dostoevsky: The Stir of Liberation*, 328–31.

41. For an account of *Dawn*, see Gerstein, *Nikolai Strakhov*, 73–76.

42. N. Ia. Danilevskii, *Rossiia i Evropa* (Saint Petersburg: Obshchestvennaia pol'za, 1871).

43. Robert McMaster, *Danilevsky: A Russian Totalitarian Philosopher* (Cambridge, Mass.: Harvard University Press, 1967), 228–50.

44. Ibid., 242–43.

45. Danilevskii, *Rossiia i Evropa*, 54–91.

46. Ibid., 76–79.

47. Ibid., 91–113.

48. Nikolai Strakhov, "Voina i mir, t. I,II, III, i IV: Stat'ia vtoraia," *Kriticheskiia Stat'i ob I. S. Turgeneve i L. N. Tolstom, 1862–1885* (St. Petersburg, 1887), 179–310. Also see Gerstein, *Nikolai Strakhov*, 80–89, and Lina Steiner, *For Humanity's Sake: The Bildungsroman in Russian Culture* (Toronto: Toronto University Press, 2011), 149–51.

49. Strakhov, "Voina i mir," 221–68.

50. Nikolai Strakhov, "Poslednie proizvedenie Turgeneva," in *Kriticheskiia stat'i ob I. S. Turgeneve I L. N. Tolstom*, 98–131. Also see Gerstein, *Nikolai Strakhov*, 96–98.

51. In *The Adolescent* it becomes the "St. Petersburg period of Russian history." Dostoevskii, *CW*, 13:455.

52. On the history and background of the European *Bildungsroman*, see Franco Moretti, *The Way of the World: The* Bildungsroman *in European Culture*, trans. A. Sbragia (London: Verso, 1987).

53. Lukács, *The Theory of the Novel*.

54. Linda Ivanits, *Dostoevsky and the Russian People* (Cambridge: Cambridge University Press, 2008), 53–55.

55. For more on folk legend and its generic characteristics, see chapter 5.

56. See chapter 3.

57. Lina Steiner has persuasively argued that *Atheism* and *The Life of a Great Sinner* can be seen as the products of Dostoevsky's ambition to create a genuinely Russian national epic to compete with Tolstoy's *War and Peace,* an ambition that helps shape *The Adolescent* and finally achieves fruition in *The Brothers Karamazov.* Steiner, *For Humanity's Sake,* 135–73.

58. On the concept of *translatio imperii* see Dmitri Stremoukhoff, "Moscow the Third Rome: Sources of the Doctrine," *Speculum* 8 (1953): 84–101, and Donald Treadgold, *The West in Russia and China, 1472–1917,* 2 vols. (Cambridge: Cambridge University Press, 1973), 2:20–22.

59. Dostoevsky referred to himself proudly as a "poet of the underground" in the notebooks for *The Adolescent,* borrowing the phrase from a negative review of the novel's first installment. Dostoevskii, *CW,* 16:329.

60. On the evolution of the *Demons* project from *The Life* to the completed novel, and in particular on the changing image of Stavrogin, see A. L. Bem, "Evoliutsia obraza Stavrogina," in *Besy: Antologiia russkoi kritiki,* ed. L. I. Saraskina (Moscow: Soglasie, 1996), 638–62. See also Joseph Frank, "The Masks of Stavrogin," *Sewanee Review* 77, no. 4 (Autumn 1969): 660–91, and *Dostoevsky: The Miraculous Years* (Princeton, N.J.: Princeton University Press, 1990), 396–412.

61. The relations between characters, rather than plot, are the basic currency in creative circulation in the notebooks for *Demons.* Where plots are continually transmogrifying, and individual characters change names and personality, the character constellations stay remarkably constant. The ideological or ethical doubling or filiation between characters that is found at the beginning of the notebooks tends to remain remarkably consistent and make its way into the completed work. This is a complete contrast from the notebooks for *The Idiot,* where, as Wasiolek points out, "the relationships between characters fluctuate from plan to plan: sisters are and are not sisters, nephews become sons, and fathers become uncles." Fyodor Dostoevskii, *The Notebooks for "The Idiot,"* trans. Katharine Strelsky, ed. and intro. Edward Wasiolek (Chicago: University of Chicago Press, 1967).

62. Valentino notes that these clusters remain almost unchanged within the completed novel. Russell Scott Valentino, *Vicissitudes of Genre in the Russian Novel* (New York: Peter Lang, 2001), 109–10.

63. On the textual history of the section "At Tikhon's," see Vladimir Seduro, "The Fate of Stavrogin's Confession," *Russian Review* 25, no. 4 (Oct. 1966): 397–404. On the structural significance of the section to the novel, see A. S. Dolinin, "Ispoved' Stavrogina," in Saraskina, *Besy: Antologiia russkoi kritiki,* 534–59.

64. J. Frank, "The Masks of Stavrogin," 681–86.

65. Ibid.

66. W. J. Leatherbarrow, *A Devil's Vaudeville: The Demonic in Dostoevsky's Major Fiction* (Evanston, Ill.: Northwestern University Press, 2005), 116–39.

67. Valentino, *Vicissitudes of Genre,* 87–126.

68. Ibid., 107.

69. On Stavrogin's absence within the novel, see R. M. Davison, "*The Devils:* The Role of Stavrogin," in *New Essays on Dostoyevsky,* edited by Malcolm V. Jones and Garth M. Terry (Cambridge: Cambridge University Press, 1983), 95–114.

70. This links him closely to the figure of Versilov in *The Adolescent,* whose status as nobleman is so emblematic that his illegitimate son refers to him as *pomeshchik.*

71. Like Russia, Stavrogin has a "Petersburg period" in the novel's prehistory. This period is the source of his corruption, a mysterious period during which he lost his beliefs.

72. Ivanits, *Dostoevsky and the Russian People,* 111–12.

73. Ibid., 117.

74. Frank argues that this unconsummated false marriage proves that no true union is possible between the *narod* and representatives of Russian Westernism. I would counter that even in its failure, it shows the potentiality of a true union. Surrounded as she is by implications of heresy, Maria can hardly be seen as an uncorrupted representative of the *narod.* J. Frank, "The Masks of Stavrogin," 678–79.

75. Ivanits, *Dostoevsky and the Russian People,* 123–27.

76. Leatherbarrow sees the two epigraphs as introducing two different models of demonic possession into the novel. The first, introduced by Pushkin's poem, is the carnivalistic chaos embodied by Petr Verkhovensky and his minions. The second, introduced by the biblical passage, is the redemptive or apocalyptic theme that emerges in the plotlines of Stavrogin and Stepan Verkhovensky.

77. Valentino, *Vicissitudes of Genre,* 103.

78. Harriet Murav, *Holy Foolishness: Dostoevsky's Novels and the Poetics of Cultural Critique* (Stanford, Calif.: Stanford University Press, 1992), 99–123.

79. Ibid., 118–19.

80. Danilevskii, *Rossiia i Evropa,* 170–71. See McMaster, *Danilevsky,* 200–208.

81. The term "novel-tragedy" is Viacheslav Ivanov's: V. I. Ivanov, *Freedom and the Tragic Life,* ed. and trans. Robert L. Jackson (New York: Noonday, 1952).

82. Dostoevsky's engagement with contested genre definitions was of course not limited to the period of the 1870s. His first novel, *Poor Folk* (1846), was a parody and reworking of Gogol's *Petersburg Tales,* as Yury Tynianov shows: Iu. N. Tynianov, *Dostoevskii i Gogol': K teorii parodii* (Petrograd: Opoiaz, 1921).

CHAPTER TWO

1. A full-text version of all the issues of *The Citizen* edited by Dostoevsky is available online on the website of the Philological Faculty, University of Karelia, "Zhurnal F. M. Dostoevskogo 'Grazhdanin,' Bibliograficheskaia spravka, Teksty," http://www.philolog.ru/filolog/grajdanin.htm. References given here are to the paper version.

2. See the introduction for an explanation and citation of these notes.

3. "Zhelanie," *Grazhdanin* 1 (Jan. 1, 1873), 28. Translation mine.

4. The laboratory metaphor has of course been commonly used in Dostoevsky scholarship to refer to the writer's notebooks, letters, and even *A Writer's Diary,* most notably by A. S. Dolinin and L. M. Rosenblium. Nevertheless, it seems particularly apt here, since the failed experiments as well as the experimental procedures are also present in *Grazhdanin.* See A. S. Dolinin, *V tvorcheskoi laboratorii Dostoevskogo: Istoria sozdaniia romana* Podrostok (Moscow: Sovetskii Pisatel', 1947); L. M. Rosenblium, "V tvorcheskoi laboratorii Dostoevskogo," *Literaturnoe Nasledstvo* 77 (Moscow: Nauka, 1965).

5. I use quotation marks here to differentiate between the column and the monojournal of the same title published by Dostoevsky in 1876–77 and 1880–81. The latter work will be indicated with the use of italics.

6. V. P. Meshcherskii, *Vospominania* (Moscow: Zakharov, 2001), 297.

7. On the reception of *Demons* among the radicals, see Dostoevskii, *CW,* 12:257–72. Mikhailovsky's February 1873 review of the novel is typical of the radicals' reaction to the novel; see N. K. Mikhailovskii, "Literaturnye i zhurnalnye zametki," *Otechestvennye Zapiski,* February 1873, no. 2, 317–43, and *Sochinenia,* 6 vols. (St. Petersburg: Tipografiia V. M. Vol'fa, 1896–97), 1:856–88.

8. I. Zohrab, "The First Thirty Issues of Meshchersky's *The Citizen* (*Grazhdanin*) During Dostoevsky's Editorship (in English Translation). Uncovering the Authorship of Unsigned Contributions," *New Zealand Slavonic Journal* 38 (2004): 181–225.

9. See, for instance, the lengthy series of articles on the reforms ten years on, published in 1871–72 in *Vestnik Evropy:* G., "Desiat' let reform': 1860–1870," *Vestnik Evropy,* 1871, no. 2, 778–801, no. 3, 332–72, no. 4, 771–813, no. 5, 386–402, no. 6, 812–30, no. 7, 346–82, no. 9, 352–83, no. 10, 830–47, no. 11, 345–68; 1872, no. 2, 296–325, no. 3, 289–323, no. 5, 327–362. See also N. A. Demert, "Vnutrennee obozrenie: Iz reform poslednego desiatiletie, sudebnaia okazyvaestsia vse prochnee," *Otechestvennye Zapiski,* 1873, no. 3, 69–93.

10. The very first issue of *The Citizen* edited by Dostoevsky marked the anniversary with a brief review of the published collection of Sergei Solov'iev's series of public lectures on the effects of the Petrine reforms on Russian society, which Dostoevsky had previously called a panegyric to Peter: "Publichniia chtenia o Petre Velikom," *Grazhdanin* 1 (Jan. 1, 1873), 23. Radical journals and

newspapers such as *Fatherland Notes* used the bicentennial to point out how little social progress had been made during the previous two centuries: N. A. Demert, "Vnutrennee Obozrenie. Pered samym prazdnykom dvukhsotiletia so dnia rozhdenia Petra Velikogo my nachinaem soznovat,' chto u nas ne khvataet to togo, to drugovo, i chto my v dvesti let sdelalili ne osobenno mnogo," *Otechestvennye Zapiski*, 1872, no. 4, 244–272.

11. Dostoevsky devotes several pages of his notebooks for 1873–74 to a discussion of the relationship between the Great Reforms and the Petrine reforms, 21:265–73.

12. Despite publishing several protestations about the obsession of the Petersburg press with the Nechaev trial, the *Citizen* republished an extensive description of the trial from the *Government Messenger:* see "Peterburgskoe Obozrenie," "Moskovskie Zametki," and "Nechaevskii protsess," *Grazhanin* 4 (Jan. 22, 1873), 91–93, 93–96, 105–8. Dostoevsky himself reflected on Nechaev and Nechaevism in the column of *A Writer's Diary* entitled "One of Our Contemporary Falsehoods": "Odna iz sovremennykh fal'shei," Dostoevskii, *CW*, 21:125–36.

13. *The Citizen* enthusiastically covered the debates over the reform of secondary education, mostly in support of the increased emphasis on the classics: V. Meshcherskii, "Etiudy Peterburgskogo bol'shogo sveta: Otvet pedagoga i moralista grafine Dlinnorukovoi," *Grazhdanin* 2 (Jan. 8, 1873), 40–43; "Pis'ma vol'nodumtsa: Gde luchshe, v selenii gde est' shkola, no mertvaia, ili tam gde net shol'y," *Grazhdanin* 28 (July 9, 1873), 774–78; "Oblastnoe obozrenie: Nechto o skol'nom dele," *Grazhdanin* 35 (Aug. 27, 1873), 942–45. Dostoevsky himself was also strongly in favor of the return to classical education, as is revealed in his notebook entries: Dostoevskii, *CW*, 21:268–70. *Vestnik Evropy* was vehemently opposed to the reforms: P. N., "Novaia reglamentatsiia gimnazii"; D. E., "Tsvety na psevdoklassicheskoi pochve," *Vestnik Evropy* 1873, 5:377–81, 451–63. For further discussion, see Dostoevskii, *CW*, 21:45, 458.

14. The *Citizen* published several articles broadly critical of the military reforms: "Nechto o razriadakh v proekte novogo pokolenia o voennoi povinnosti," *Grazhdanin* 49 (Dec. 3, 1873), 1300–1302; "O russkom dvorianstve pered voennoi reforme," *Grazhdanin* 51 (Dec. 17, 1873), 1360–61.

15. Like the rest of the press, the *Citizen* covered the famine extensively and also campaigned for donations for its victims: "O golode v Samarskoi gubernii," *Grazhdanin* 50 (Dec. 10, 1873), 1354–55; 51 (Dec. 17, 1873), 1361–63; 52 (Dec. 29, 1873), 1388–89. In December 1873 it published an article, probably by Pobedonostsev, on the question of whether the *zemstvo* was legally responsible for the failure to prevent the famine: "Podlezhit' li zemstvo po zakonu otvetstvennosti za nepriniatie mer protiv goloda?" *Grazhdanin* 52 (Dec. 29, 1873), 1397–98.

16. "Ot redaktsii," *Grazhdanin* 40 (Oct. 1, 1873), 1059. See also Dostoevskii, *CW*, 21:285–86, 537.

17. "Ot redaktsii," *Grazhdanin* 42 (Oct. 15, 1873), 1087. See also Dostoevskii, *CW*, 21:537.

18. E. Ambler, *Russian Journalism and Politics, 1861–1881: The Career of Aleksei S. Suvorin* (Detroit: Wayne State University Press, 1972), 121. For a synthetic account of Dostoevsky's relations with Meshchersky, see Joseph Frank, *Dostoevsky: The Mantle of the Prophet* (Princeton, N.J.: Princeton University Press, 2002), 38–65.

19. For an extensive list of contributors to *Grazhdanin,* see Zohrab, "The First Thirty Issues of Meshchersky's *The Citizen (Grazhdanin)* During Dostoevsky's Editorship," 182–84.

20. "Desiat' let reform: 1861–1871," *Grazhdanin* 4 (Jan. 22, 1873), 118–23.

21. A. A. Golovachev, *Desiat' let reform: 1861–1871* (St. Petersburg, 1872).

22. On Golovachev's role in the emancipation movement, see Lincoln, *In the Vanguard of Reform,* 178. For the memorandum on the necessity of emancipation written by Golovachev and A. M. Unkovskii, see "Zapiska A. A. Golovacheva i A. M. Unkovskogo," 1858, TsGAOR, fond 109, opis' 1, delo no. 1960. For an English translation, see Terence Emmons, *The Russian Landed Gentry and the Peasant Emancipation of 1861* (Cambridge: Cambridge University Press, 1968), 427–43.

23. "Desiat' let reform: 1861–1871," 120. Translation mine.

24. On the military reforms, see Forrestt A. Miller, *Dmitrii Miliutin and the Reform Era in Russia* (Nashville, Tenn.: Vanderbilt University Press, 1968), 182–230.

25. R. V. Fadeev, *Russkoe obshchestvo v nastoiashchem i budushchem, Sobranie sochinenii,* 3 vols. (St. Petersburg, 1889–90), 3:1–224. On Fadeev's ideas see Andrzej Walicki, *The Slavophile Controversy: History of a Conservative Utopia in Nineteenth Century Russian Thought* (Oxford: Clarendon, 1975), 487–88.

26. "O russkom dvorianstve pered voennoi reforme," *Grazhdanin* 51 (Dec. 17, 1873), 1360–61. In October 1873 the *Citizen* had included a highly favorable review of an earlier collection of articles by Fadeev on military and political topics: "Kritika i bibliografia. Nash voenniyi vopros," *Grazhdanin* 44 (Oct. 29, 1873), 1180–81.

27. For references to Fadeev in the notebooks, see Dostoevskii, *CW,* 21:264–271. On the significance of Fadeev for *The Adolescent,* see E. I. Semenov, "U istokov *Podrostka,*" *Russkaia Literatura* 3 (1973): 107–16, and *Roman Dostoevskogo* Podrostok (Leningrad: Nauka, 1979), 3–35; and Dostoevskii, *CW,* 17:257–58.

28. "Since the time of Peter's reform (formative period) those brought up during the period learned only to disdain Russia and crap on her, they too got atheism in accordance with their degree of education." Dostoevskii, *CW,* 21:266.

29. See V. I. Meshcherskii, "O russkom dvorianstve pered voennoi reformoi," *Grazhdanin* 51 (Dec. 17, 1873), 1360–61; Fadeev, *Russkoe obshchestvo v nastoiashchem i budushchem,*

30. The two-hundred-year anniversary of Peter's birth provided an opportunity for Dostoevsky to reflect on this, not that he really needed one. In the note-

books he writes, "Where did this society come from? O, you, historians of ours, celebrating the two-hundredth jubilee, tell me whose work this is, whatever caused or contributed to the uprooting of the soil" (Dostoevskii, *CW,* 21:255).

31. "Fadeev forgot what Orthodoxy stipulates. If one power betrays Orthodoxy then the *narod* will choose another power. Orthodoxy, i.e., a form of religious belief in Christ, is the beginning of our morality and our conscience and therefore the beginning of social strength, of science, of everything" (ibid., 266).

32. Dostoevsky's discussion of the *narod* in "A Writer's Diary" can be placed within the context of several different journalistic debates of the early 1870s. In his series of articles "The Characteristics of Literary Thought from the 1820s to the 1850s," published in 1872–73, Alexandr Pypin had included an article highly critical of the ideas of the Slavophiles. He argued that the Slavophile vision of the Kireevskys and Konstantin Aksakov was based on the naive and flawed assumption that before the Petrine reforms the Russian peasantry lived in an undifferentiated state of religious harmony and social unity. In fact, argued Pypin, such a unity never existed. He also argued that the Slavophiles' view of the West as increasingly beset by social and cultural struggles had in the subsequent decades been shown to be demonstrably false. Pypin's criticism of the Slavophiles was greeted with outrage by Dostoevsky and his colleagues at the *Citizen:* Dostoevsky's notebooks for 1873 contain a number of references to Pypin's article, and the journal commissioned a pair of articles on the Slavophiles by no lesser an individual than the historian Mikhail Pogodin, who had himself belonged to the Slavophile circle, in which he refuted the charges leveled by Pypin. See A. Pypin, "Kharakteristiky literaturnikh mnenii ot dvatsatikh do piatidesiatikh godov: Istoricheskie ocherki," *Vestnik Evropy* 1872, no. 11, 47–97; no. 12, 618–78. For Dostoevsky's comments, see Dostoevskii, *CW,* 21:91, 254, 438. For Pogodin's response, see M. Pogodin, "K voprosu o slavianofilakh," *Grazhdanin* 11 (Mar. 12, 1873), 347–52; and 12 (Mar. 18, 1873), 415–20.

33. This is a continuation of his interpretation of the reforms in the announcement for the publication of *Time.* In "Vlas," he writes, "The Petrine period of Russian history was truly ended by the 19th February" (Dostoevskii, *CW,* 21:41). In the notebooks he writes, "All reforms of the present reign are the direct antithesis (in essence) of the reforms of Peter the Great and the nullification of them in all respects" (Dostoevskii, *CW,* 21:268).

34. F. M. Dostoevskii, "Dnevnik pisatelia," *Grazhdanin* 1 (Jan. 1, 1873), 14–15, 15–16; 2 (Jan. 8, 1873), 32–26; 3 (Jan. 15, 1873), 61–64; 4 (Jan. 22, 1873), 96–100; 6 (Feb. 5, 1873), 162–66; 8 (Feb. 19, 1873), 224–26; 10 (Mar. 5, 1873), 285–89; 13 (Mar. 26, 1873), 423–26; 18 (Apr. 30, 1873), 533–38; 21 (May 21, 1873), 606–8; 25 (June 18, 1873), 705–6; 29 (July 16, 1873), 806–9; 32 (Aug. 6, 1873), 877–79; 35 (Aug. 27, 1873), 955–58; 50 (Dec. 10, 1873), 1349–53; Dostoevskii, *CW,* 21:5–136.

35. See Gary Saul Morson, *The Boundaries of Genre: Dostoevsky's Diary of a Writer and the Traditions of Literary Utopia* (Austin: University of Texas

Press, 1981), 28, and introduction to *A Writer's Diary* (Evanston, Ill.: Northwestern University Press, 1993), 1:7–8.

36. I. L. Volgin, *Dostoevskii—zhurnalist* (Moscow: Izdatel'stvo Moskovskogo Universiteta, 1982), 24.

37. V. V. Vinogradov, *Problema avtorstva i teoria stilei* (Moscow: Khudozhestvennaia literatura, 1961), 567.

38. Zohrab, "The First Thirty Issues of Meshchersky's *The Citizen* (*Grazhdanin*) During Dostoevsky's Editorship," 186–89.

39. V. Tunimanov, "Publitsistika Dostoevskogo," in *Dostoevskii: Khudozhdnik i myslitel': sbornik statei,* ed. A. L. Grishunin (Moscow: Khudozhestvennaia literatura, 1972), 165–209.

40. P. Fokin, "Struktura i obraz avtora v Dnevnike pisatelia 1876–1877 gg. F. M. Dostoevskogo," avtoreferat dissertatsii, Institut russkoi literatury, St. Petersburg, 1995, 8.

41. Morson, *The Boundaries of Genre,* 191, note 38.

42. A. K. Dostoevskaia, *Vospominaniia* (Moscow: Khudozhestvennaia Literatura,1971), 244–45.

43. Benjamin, "On Some Motifs in Baudelaire," 158–59.

44. Morson, Introduction to *A Writer's Diary,* 82–93.

45. Morson, *The Boundaries of Genre,* 65–66.

46. Bakhtin, *Problems of Dostoevsky's Poetics,* 147.

47. Robert Louis Jackson, *The Art of Dostoevsky: Deliriums and Nocturnes* (Princeton, N.J.: Princeton University Press, 1981), 303.

48. Ilya Vinitsky, "Where Bobok Is Buried: The Theosophical Roots of Dostoevskii's 'Fantastic Realism,'" *Slavic Review* 65, no. 3 (2006): 523–43. See also his *Ghostly Paradoxes: Modern Spiritualism and Russian Culture in the Age of Realism* (Toronto: University of Toronto Press, 2009), 119–35.

49. I do not by this mean to imply that Dostoevsky was a heretic, merely that the Nikonian reforms also mark a movement away from what he and the Slavophiles saw as the undifferentiated spiritual unity of the *narod.*

50. See Jackson, *Dostoevsky's Quest for Form,* 71–91, 99–101.

51. See for instance, the passage, "More scope must be given to the idea, and the ideal should not be feared. A portraitist, for example, seats his subject to paint its portrait; he prepares; he studies the subject carefully . . . Because he knows from experience that a person does not always look like himself, and therefore he seeks out 'the principal idea of his physiognomy,' that moment when the subject most resembles himself. The portraitist's gift consists in the ability to seek out and capture that moment. And so what is the artist doing here if not trusting first his own idea (the ideal) more than the reality before him," Dostoevskii, *CW,* 21:75. Also see Jackson on the distinction between Dostoevsky's use of the term in a Hegelian aesthetic context versus a moral-spiritual one: Jackson, *Dostoevsky's Quest for Form,* 100.

52. See Jackson, *Dostoevsky's Quest for Form,* 122.

53. For a discussion of "Apropos of the Exhibition" as a programmatic statement of Dostoevsky's understanding of "presentness" and its importance for art, see G. S. Morson, *Narrative and Freedom: The Shadows of Time* (New Haven, Conn.: Yale University Press, 2006), 180–82.

54. The story had been previously sent by Leskov for publication in *The Citizen,* but had been rejected by Dostoevsky. It was published instead in *Russkii Vestnik.*

55. "Ob'iavlenie o podpiske na zhurnal 'Vremia,' na 1861 god," 18:36. For further discussion of this passage, see J. Frank, *Dostoevsky: The Stir of Liberation,* 37.

56. See *Grazhdanin* 31 (Dec. 4, 1872), 460; 5 (Jan. 29, 1873), 129–30; 31 (July 30, 1873), 845.

57. J. Frank, *Dostoevsky: The Mantle of the Prophet,* 109.

58. "Malen'kie kartinky (v doroge)," *Skladchina: Literaturnyi sbornik sostavlyonnyi iz trudov russkikh literatorov v pol'zu postradavshikh ot goloda v Samarskoi gubernii* (St. Petersburg: Tipografia Kostomina, 1874), 455–78. See Dostoevskii, *CW,* 21:469–73.

59. I. A. Goncharov, *Sobranie sochinenii.* 8 vols. (Moscow, 1955), 8:457.

60. Ibid., 8:460. Fallout from the dispute with Goncharov figures prominently in Dostoevsky's letters and notebooks for 1873–75 and in the conception and development of the novelistic project of *The Adolescent.* See chapter 3.

61. As early as February he had written to Pogodin that "the shapes of stories and novels swarm in my head and take shape in my heart. I think them up, jot them down, add new traits every day to the plan that has been sketched out, and at that point I see that all my time has been taken up by the journal, that I cannot write any more—and I am driven to repentance and despair." Dostoevskii, *CW,* 29:1:262.

62. For some examples of these clashes, see J. Frank, *Dostoevsky: The Mantle of the Prophet,* 53–64.

63. See I. Zohrab, "Dostoevsky's Editorship of Meshchersky's *The Citizen* (*Grazhdanin*): Issues nos 31–52. Uncovering the Authorship of Unsigned Contributions," *New Zealand Slavonic Journal* 39 (2005), 216–35; J. Frank, *Dostoevsky: The Mantle of the Prophet,* 59–60; and Dostoevskii, *CW,* 29:I:308.

64. See Joseph Frank's discussion of Dostoevsky's disapproval of Meshchersky's support for student surveillance, in *Dostoevsky: The Mantle of the Prophet,* 59–60; and Dostoevskii, *CW,* 29:I:308.

CHAPTER THREE

1. For a summary of the novel's reception in the periodical press during and shortly after its serialization in *Fatherland Notes,* see the Academy Edition commentary: Dostoevskii, *CW,* 17:345–60.

2. Leonid Grossman's assessment of *The Adolescent* as testament to "the crisis of Dostoevsky's novelistic form" has provided a critical paradigm for negative evaluations of the work by subsequent generations of critics up to Joseph Frank, who argues that "the consensus of critical opinion . . . is surely right in maintaining that here Dostoevsky sinks below the level of his masterpieces." Grossman, "Dostoevskii—khudozhnik," in *Tvorchestvo F. M. Dostoevskogo* (Moscow, 1959), 392; Joseph Frank, "Dostoevsky's Trojan Horse: *A Raw Youth,*" in *Literary Imagination, Ancient and Modern,* ed. T. Breyfogle (Chicago: University of Chicago Press, 1999), 312–33. See also J. Frank, *Dostoevsky: The Mantle of the Prophet,* 171–96.

3. Surprisingly, many commentators have ignored the dual structure of the novel. Exceptions include Hans-Jurgen Gerigk, *Versuch über Dostojewski's "Jüngling," ein Beitrag zur Theorie des Romans* (Munich: Wilhelm Fink, 1965); E. A. Ivanchikova, "*Podrostok:* Povestvovanie s liricheskim rasskazchikom," *Voprosy iazykoznaniia* 3 (1995): 70–76; Nina Perlina, "Rethinking Adolescence," in *Celebrating Creativity: Essays in Honour of Jostein Börtnes,* ed. Knut Andreas Grimstad and Ingunn Lunde (Bergen: University of Bergen, 1997), 216–26; Aage Hansen-Löve, "Diskursivnye protsessy v romane Dostoevskogo *Podrostok,*" in *Avtor i tekst,* ed. V. M. Markovich and Vol'f Schmid (St. Petersburg, 1996), 229–67; P. A. Jensen, "Paradoksal'nost' avtorstva (u) Dostoevskogo," in *Paradoksy russkoi literatury: Sbornik stat'ei,* ed. V. M. Markovich and Vol'f Schmid (St. Petersburg: INAPress, 2001), 219–33; and three works by Susanne Fusso: "Dostoevsky's Comely Boy: Homoerotic Desire and Aesthetic Strategies in *A Raw Youth,*" *Russian Review* 59, no. 4 (2000): 576–96; "The Weight of Human Tears: The Covetuous Knight and a Raw Youth," in *Alexander Pushkin's Little Tragedies: The Poetics of Brevity* (Madison: University of Wisconsin Press, 2003), 229–42; and *Discovering Sexuality in Dostoevsky* (Evanston, Ill.: Northwestern University Press, 2006).

4. For a detailed discussion of the aesthetic implications of Nikolai Semyonovich's letter for the novel, see Hansen-Löve, "Diskursivnye protsessy v romane Dostoevskogo *Podrostok,*" 261–67.

5. Here Dostoevsky has Nikolai Semyonovich ventriloquize Strakhov's views on *The Captain's Daughter,* expressed in his 1869 review of Tolstoy's *War and Peace.* Lina Steiner has seen in this passage evidence that *The Adolescent* constitutes an important stage in Dostoevsky's attempt to create an authentic Russian epic to challenge *War and Peace.* As will become clear, while I agree with Steiner that Dostoevsky was engaged in such a project in the late 1860s, culminating in *The Life of a Great Sinner,* I believe that he conceived of *The Adolescent* in novelistic rather than epic terms. Tolstoy's *Childhood* trilogy is here a far more important antimodel for Dostoevsky. Steiner, *For Humanity's Sake,* 135–73.

6. Unless otherwise indicated, quotations from the novel are from Fyodor Dostoevsky, *The Adolescent,* trans. Richard Pevear and Larissa Volokhonsky (New York: Everyman Library, 2003). Quotations from the notebooks are from

Fyodor Dostoevsky, *The Notebooks for "A Raw Youth,"* trans. Victor Terras, ed. Edward Wasiolek (Chicago: University of Chicago Press, 1969).

7. M. M. Bakhtin, "Epos i roman," in *Voprosy literatury i estetiki* (Moscow: Khudozhestvennaia literatura, 1975), 447–84.

8. The notebooks for *The Adolescent* are more detailed and give a greater insight into Dostoevsky's working practices than any of his other plans. For discussion of the notebooks and commentary on the writing process, see Rosenblium, "Tvorcheskie dnevniki Dostoevskogo"; Dolinin, *V tvorcheskoi laboratorii Dostoevskogo*; *Poslednie romany Dostoevskogo: Kak sozdavalis'* Podrostok *i* Bratia Karamazovy (Moscow: Sovetskii pisatel', 1963); and Jacques Catteau, *La Création littéraire chez Dostoïevski* (Paris: L'Institut des études slaves, 1978).

9. The "predatory type," of course, refers back to the two fundamental Russian cultural types described by Apollon Grigor'ev. See chapter 1.

10. On the connections between the "Confession of a Great Sinner" and the early plans for *The Adolescent*, see Dolinin, *V tvorcheskoi laboratorii*, 17–20.

11. On *The Adolescent* as a *Bildungsroman*, see E. I. Semenov, *Roman Dostoevskogo* Podrostok (Leningrad: Nauka, 1979); Elena Krasnoshchekova, "Pamiat' zhanra v romane 'Podrostok,'" in *Roman Dostoevskogo Podrostok: vozmozhnosti prochteniia*, ed. V. A. Viktorovich (Kolomna: Kolomenskii gosudarstvennyi pedagogicheskii institut, 2003), 137–58. For a recent examination, see Steiner, *For Humanity's Sake*, 135–73.

12. As Joseph Frank points out, the specter of illegitimacy also hovers over the character that would become Prince Myshkin in the notebooks for *The Idiot*. J. Frank, *Dostoevsky: The Miraculous Years*, 266. See also Dostoevskii, CW, 9:187–89. For an extensive discussion of the relationship of illegitimacy and narrative, see Peter Brooks's discussion of *Le Rouge et le noir* in *Reading for the Plot* (Cambridge, Mass.: Harvard University Press, 1984). For a broader perspective on the function of the illegitimacy motif in the development of the novel, see Marthe Robert, *Roman des origines et origines du roman* (Paris: Gallimard, 1972). The Freudian family romance paradigm, which Robert sees as underlying the evolution of novelistic structure, seems a particularly clear motivator of narrative in the case of *The Adolescent*. Whereas Freudian studies usually focus on *The Brothers Karamazov*, I would argue that the earlier novel offers a more dynamic subject for a study of symbolic relationships and their role in novelistic structure.

13. It is clear that the name Dolgoruky ironically invokes a well-known Russian aristocratic family, the Dolgorukovs. For two commentaries on the significance of this invocation, see N. G. Pustygina, "O familii Dolgorukov v romane F. M. Dostoevskogo 'Podrostok,'" *Uchenye zapiski Tartuskogo gosudarstvennogo universiteta* 654 (1985): 37–53; T. Kasat'kina, "Roman F. M. Dostoevskogo 'Podrostok': 'Ideia' geroia i ideia avtora," *Voprosy Literatury* 1 (2004): 181–212; Perlina, "Rethinking Adolescence," 224–25.

14. Bakhtin writes: "A genre lives in the present, but always remembers its past, its beginning. Genre is a representative of creative memory in the process of literary development": *Problemy,* 121. Also see Morson and Emerson, *Mikhail Bakhtin: Creation of a Prosaics,* 295–97. Elena Krasnoshchekova invokes the concept of genre memory in her discussion of *The Adolescent* as *Bildungsroman.* See Krasnoshchekova, "Pamiat' zhanra v romane 'Podrostok,'" 137–58.

15. D. V. Grigorovich, *Sochinenia v trekh tomakh,* 3 vols. (Moscow: Khudozhestvennaia Literatura, 1988), 1:141–247.

16. A. V. Druzhinin, *Polinka Saks. Dnevnik* (Moscow, 1989). On the novel as reworking of *Jacques,* see Emily Klenin, "On the Ideological Sources of *Čto delat'?* Sand, Družinin, Leroux," *Zeitschrift für Slavische Philologie* 51, no. 1 (1991): 367–407.

17. On the love triangles of the men of the 1840s, see Irina Paperno, *Chernyshevsky and the Age of Realism* (Stanford, Calif.: Stanford University Press, 1988).

18. This association is explicitly alluded to in the notebooks, where Versilov is given the lines "Serfdom. Why, weren't we the emancipators, didn't we abolish serfdom, Anton Goremyka" (Dostoevskii, *CW,* 16:424).

19. V. G. Belinskii, "Vzgliad na russkuiu literature, 1847 goda," in *Polnoe sobranie sochinenii,* 13 vols. (Moscow: Izdatel'stvo Akademii Nauk SSSR, Institut russkoi literatury, 1953–59), 10:347.

20. On the importance of Belinsky as architect of a model of Russian literary history that Dostoevsky himself drew upon, see Victor Terras, *Belinskij and Russian Literary Criticism: The Heritage of Organic Aesthetics* (Madison: University of Wisconsin Press, 1974); "Belinsky the Journalist and Russian Literature," in *Literary Journals in Imperial Russia,* ed. Deborah Martinsen (Cambridge: Cambridge University Press, 1997), 117–28.

21. Belinskii, "Vzgliad na russkuiu literature, 1847 goda," 10:315–16.

22. Dostoevsky refers to the story of his debut in a "Writer's Diary" entry entitled "Old People," published in the *Citizen* in 1873. Annenkov provides the standard account of Dostoevsky's "discovery" in his memoirs, *Literaturnye vospominaniia* (Leningrad: Akademia, 1928).

23. It is also worth pointing out that 1847 is the year of Gogol's *Vybrannye mesta iz perepiski s druziami* and Belinsky's own *Pis'mo k Gogoliu,* a work that would carry an ominous significance in Dostoevsky's own life. It was for the act of reading this work out at the Mikhailovsky circle that Dostoevsky was arrested. See Joseph Frank, *Dostoevsky: The Seeds of Revolt, 1821–1849* (Princeton, N.J.: Princeton University Press, 1977), 239–91. It should also be pointed out that Dostoevsky emphatically broke free of Belinsky's grip on his literary debut with *The Double* (1847), which Belinsky renounced as a betrayal of its author's early promise.

24. Nathan Rosen has made the argument that in *The Adolescent* Dostoevsky was regenerating himself, a line of reasoning which Susanne Fusso has

taken further, arguing convincingly that Dostoevsky engages with his own younger self and that *The Adolescent* provides a reframing of several of his own earlier works. See Nathan Rosen, "Breaking Out of the Underground: The Failure of *A Raw Youth*," *Modern Fiction Studies* 4, no. 3 (1958): 225–39; and three works by Fusso: "Dostoevsky's Comely Boy," 576–96; "The Weight of Human Tears," 229–42; *Discovering Sexuality in Dostoevsky*, 65–68.

25. See J. Frank, *Dostoevsky: The Miraculous Years*, 227–30.

26. On Herzen and Chaadaev as prototypes, see A. S. Dolinin, *Poslednie romany Dostoevskogo: Kak sozdavalis' The Adolescent i Brat'ia Karamazovy* (Moscow: Sovetskii pisatel', 1963), 95–126.

27. V. V. Grigorenko et al., *F. M. Dostoevskii v vospominaniakh sovremennikov* (Moscow: Izdatel'stvo Khudozhestvennaia literatura, 1964).

28. Dostoevsky's later high praise of *Anna Karenina* in the 1877 *Diary*, his criticism of part 8 notwithstanding, once *The Adolescent* was behind him, suggests that he was well aware of the evolution that had taken place in Tolstoy's style in that novel: Dostoevskii, *CW*, 25:198–202.

29. The populist critic A. M. Skabichevskii found the first installment of *The Adolescent* excessively naturalistic. See his article "Mysli po povodu tekushchei literatury: Nechto o romanakh g. F. M. Dostoevskogo voobshe. 'Podrostok,' roman g. F. M. Dostoevskogo, chast' pervaia," *Birzhevye Viedomosti*, no. 35 (Feb. 6, 1875). For commentary, see Dostoevskii, *CW*, 17:349–50, 421.

30. Andrew Wachtel, *Battle for Childhood: Creation of a Russian Myth* (Stanford, Calif.: Stanford University Press, 1990).

31. I would like to thank Michael Heim for drawing my attention to this elision. Nina Perlina has argued that *The Adolescent* demonstrates a strong intertextual relationship with the third section of the trilogy. Perlina, "Rethinking Adolescence," 216–26.

32. A. L. Bem, "Khudozhestvennaia polemika s Tolstym: K ponimaniu 'Podrostka,'" in *O Dostoevskom: Sbornik stat'ei pod redaktsiei A. L. Bema*, 3 vols. (Prague: Petropolis, 1936), 3:192–214.

33. Perlina, "Rethinking Adolescence," 221–22.

34. On Tolstoy's original conception, see Boris Eikhenbaum, *Molodoi Tolstoi: Vospominaniia, pis'ma, dnevniki*, ed. A. G. Ostrovskiĭ (Moskva: Agraf, 1999).

35. M. M. Bakhtin, "Formy vremeni i khronotopa v romane," in *Voprosy literatury i estetiki* (Moscow: Khudozhestvennaia literatura, 1975), 234–407; and "Forms of Time and Chronotope in the Novel," in *The Dialogic Imagination: Four Essays by M. M. Bakhtin*, ed. Michael Holquist, trans. Michael Holquist and Caryl Emerson (Austin: University of Texas Press, 1981), 224–36.

36. On the representation of time in *The Adolescent*, see Tat'iana V. Tsivian, "O structure vremeni i prostranstva v romane Dostoevskogo *Podrostok*," *Russian Literature* 4, no. 3 (1976): 203–47.

37. Lukács writes of *War and Peace,* "The great moments which offer a glimpse of an essential life, a meaningful process, remain mere moments, isolated from the other two worlds [those of social convention and of nature] and without constitutive reference to them. Thus the three concepts of time are not only mutually heterogeneous and incapable of being united with one another, but moreover none of them expresses real duration, real time, the life-element of the novel" (*Theory of the Novel,* 151). This might be more persuasively argued of the trilogy.

38. L. N. Tolstoi, *Detstvo, Sobranie sochinenii v 20 tomax,* 20 vols. (Moscow: Nauka, 1960), 1:77–78.

39. "Sometimes, when you were tired of running about, you'd sit down on a high armchair at the tea table; it would be late already, you'd long since finished your sugared milk and your eyes were beginning to close, but you did not move an inch, you sat and listened" (ibid., 1:62).

40. An example from the hunting scene in *Childhood* can illustrate this point: "When I heard this I froze at my post. I riveted my eyes on the spot where the trees ended and grinned idiotically. The sweat poured off me and although the drops tickled me as they ran down my chin, I did not wipe them off. It seemed to me that there could never be a moment more crucial than this" (ibid., 1:41).

41. An example of this voice can be found near the end of the work: "Vanity is the feeling that is most incompatible with genuine sorrow, yet at the same time this feeling is so firmly grafted onto human nature that it is very rarely that even the greatest grief succeeds in driving it out" (ibid., 1:117).

42. Bakhtin, "Epos i roman," 447–84. See also Morson and Emerson, *Mikhail Bakhtin: Creation of a Prosaics,* 419–23.

43. Joseph Frank writes, "Versilov is far and away the most interesting character in the book, and after Part I Dostoevsky is unable to prevent him from taking center stage" (*Dostoevsky: The Mantle of the Prophet,* 176).

44. Konstantin Mochulsky's reading of the novel is a paradigmatic example of such an interpretation. K. V. Mochulski, *Gogol', Soloviev, Dostoevskii* (Moscow: Respublika, 1995), 464–88. Joseph Frank also provides such a reading in *Dostoevsky: The Mantle of the Prophet,* 188–91.

45. The notebooks make reference to "unfinished people (as a consequence of the Petrine reforms in general)" (Dostoevskii, *CW,* 16:330). Versilov states, "A Russian nobleman cannot live without Weltschmerz, and so I too had to suffer from it" (ibid., 16:416). He also asks, "How did it happen that we have developed this curious type of a universally suffering man, from Peter the Great's nobility? And why say that he is good for nothing but wandering from place to place? Why, could it not be true that Weltschmerz is also a great thing?" (ibid., 16:417).

46. In the notebooks he declares, "Don't I know that this is what's going to

happen, everything is going to perish in this conflagration (The Tuileries). But I don't want this to happen. I love my past" (ibid.).

47. Kasat'kina, "Roman F. M. Dostoevskogo 'Podrostok,'" 201–2.

48. Ibid., 202.

49. The notebooks include multiple repetitions of the lines "As a Russian nobleman I was an atheist" (Dostoevskii, *CW,* 16:416–17).

50. E. I. Semenov, "U istokov *Podrostka,*" *Russkaia Literatura* 3 (1973): 107–16. See Dostoevskii, *CW,* 17:257–58.

51. Fadeev, *Russkoe obshchestvo v nastoiashchem i budushchem,* 3:1–224.

52. Iurii Samarin, *Revoliutsionnyi konservatizm* (Berlin, 1875). Also see Walicki, *The Slavophile Controversy,* 487–89.

53. Also see Dostoevsky's notes on Fadeev's ideas made in 1873 (Dostoevskii, *CW,* 22:265–66), discussed in chapter 2 of the present volume.

54. Dolinin, *Poslednie romany Dostoevskogo,* 95–133. The "confession" is ubiquitous in the notebooks, the subject of meditations from the very beginning to the very end of the period of writing.

55. Perlina, "Rethinking Adolescence," 222.

56. Ibid., 220.

57. The image of the smashed icon first appears at the very beginning of the notebooks, in the very early stages of work on the novel: Dostoevskii, *CW,* 16:12.

58. Kasat'kina, "Roman F. M. Dostoevskogo 'Podrostok,'" 201.

59. Perlina writes that for Versilov, "*dvoriane* and *dvorovye* (the gentry and the serfs) are concepts sharing both origin and root" ("Rethinking Adolescence," 220).

60. The *strannik* is explicitly a pilgrim, a wanderer devoted to God, whose wanderings are motivated by a preexisting faith. The word *skitalets* carries subtly different connotations; the word *skit* was used to denote the monasteries of Old Believers. The contemporary usage of *skitalets* reflects a complex web of implications. It has certainly has intimations of schismatics, but it also has the sense of wandering without aim, without God, without destination. Makar inherits the resignation but also the certitude of the Orthodox hermit. Versilov conversely inherits both the life-destroying obsession of excessive belief of the Old Believer and the aimlessness of the total absence of belief. The spatial equivalence between these two wanderers reveals their difference: Makar's desert is charged with God's presence, Versilov's with his absence. Dal', *Tolkovyi slovar' zhivovo velikorusskogo iazyka* (1881–82).

61. Kasat'kina, "Roman F. M. Dostoevskogo 'Podrostok,'" 201.

62. Joseph Frank argues that the publication of *The Adolescent* in the populist *Fatherland Notes* helped shape the novel's aesthetic and ideological structure. J. Frank, "Dostoevsky's Trojan Horse," 312–33.

63. A number of critics have identified protomodernist features in the novel. Gerigk has argued that in its experiments with time and space, *The Adolescent* anticipates Proust's modernist experiments in *In Search of Lost Time.*

Hansen-Löve argues that Arkady's rejection of conventional literary style and the novel's complex narrative framing form part of a refutation by Dostoevsky of what he sees as the artifices of traditional realism, an attempt to resist the reductive structuring impulse of closure, which prevents the novel from truly being able to represent the flow of life. Gerigk, *Versuch über Dostojewski's "Jüngling,"* 191–93; Hansen-Löve, "Diskursivnye protsessy v romane Dostoevskogo *Podrostok,*" 229–67.

CHAPTER FOUR

1. Unless otherwise indicated, translations are taken from Fyodor Dostoevsky, *A Writer's Diary,* trans. Kenneth Lantz, intro. Gary Saul Morson, 2 vols. (Evanston, Ill.: Northwestern University Press, 1994).

2. Volgin coined the term "monojournal." Volgin, *Dostoevskii—zhurnalist.*

3. In his letters of 1876 and 1877, Dostoevsky wrote extensively on the reasons behind his return to journalism and his ambitions for the design of *A Writer's Diary.* See Dostoevskii, *CW,* 29:72–73, 74, 77–78, 101–2, 178.

4. Analysis of the poetics of the *Diary* began with V. A. Sidorov's groundbreaking article, "O Dnevnike pisatelia," in *Dostoevkii: Stat'i materialy,* ed. A. S. Dolinin, 2 vols. (Leningrad, 1924), 2:109–16. Sidorov's lead was followed first by V. Tunimanov in "Publitsistika Dostoevskogo," in *Dostoevskii—khudozhnik i myslitel': Sbornik stat'ei,* ed. A. L. Grishunin (Moscow: Khudozhestvennaia literatura, 1972), 165–209, and then by Igor Volgin in his "Dnevnik pisatelia: Tekst i kontekst," in *Dostoevskii: Materialy i issledovaniia,* vol. 3 (1978), 151–58, and later in his *Dostoevskii—zhurnalist.* Also noteworthy is T. V. Zakharova's excellent essay, "Dnevnik pisatelia kak original'noe zhanrovoe iavlenie i ideino-khudizhestvennaia tselostnost'," in *Tvorchestvo F. M. Dostoevskogo: Iskusstvo sinteza,* ed. N. M. Iurkova (Ekaterinburg: Izdatel'stvo Ural'skogo Universiteta, 1991), 251–84. On the structure of the *Diary* see also Pavel Fokin's 1995 dissertation: "Struktura i obraz avtora v Dnevnike pisatelia 1876–1877 gg. F. M. Dostoevskogo," avtoreferat dissertatsii, Institut russkoi literatury, St. Petersburg, 1995. The Western scholar who has dealt most significantly with the question of the poetics of the *Diary* is Gary Saul Morson, in his "Dostoevsky's *Diary of a Writer:* Threshold Art," Ph.D. diss., Yale University, 1974, and *The Boundaries of Genre: Dostoevsky's "Diary of a Writer" and the Traditions of Literary Utopia* (Austin: University of Texas Press, 1981). He has a slightly different take on the *Diary*'s poetics in his introduction to *A Writer's Diary,* vol. 1 (Evanston, Ill.: Northwestern University Press, 1993), 1–117. For a recent monographic treatment of the *Diary* that focuses on Dostoevsky's interactive relationship with his readers, see Raffaella Vassena, *Reawakening National Identity: Dostoevsky's "Diary of a Writer" and Its Impact on Russian Society* (Bern: Peter Lang, 2007).

NB: On the translation of *publitsistika, zhurnalistika,* and other permutations: I have used the terms "journalism" and "journalistic discourse" to cover both of these Russian terms, rejecting the frequently used "publicistic" as clumsy and unnatural in English.

5. A. A. Potebnia, "Chernovnye zametki o L. N. Tolstom i Dostoevskom," *Voprosy teorii i psikhologii tvorchestva* (Kharkhov, 1914), 279.

6. Morson, Introduction to *A Writer's Diary,* 72–101; A. Kelly, "Irony and Utopia in Herzen and Dostoevsky: *From the Other Shore* and *Diary of a Writer,*" *Russian Review* 50, no. 4 (1991): 397–416.

7. Morson, Introduction to *A Writer's Diary,* 57–72.

8. In the introduction to *A Writer's Diary,* Morson expresses his view of how the so-called prophetic journalism begins to hold sway over the critique of prescriptive formulas and embrace of multiple perspectives that characterizes the first few months of the 1876 *Diary* (ibid., 28–30).

9. Comparatively little work has been done on the effect of these typographic arrangements on the original readers' responses to literary works presented in this way. For an exploration of the effects of serialization and other related publication circumstances on the form of the nineteenth-century novel, see much of the work of W. M. Todd, especially "*The Brothers Karamazov* and the Poetics of Serial Publication," *Dostoevsky Studies* 7 (1986): 87–97.

10. See C. A. Moser, "Dostoevsky and the Aesthetics of Journalism," *Dostoevsky Studies* 3 (1982): 27–41.

11. See V. L. Komarovich, "Peterburgskie fel'etony Dostoevskogo," in *Fel'etony sorokovykh godov,* ed. Iurii Oksman (Leningrad: Academia, 1930), 89–124.

12. See A. I. Reitblat, *Ot Bovy k Bal'montu: Ocherki po istorii chteniia v Rossii vo vtoroi polovine XIX veka* (Moscow: Izd. MPI, 1991), 32–47.

13. See Morson's discussion of the meta-utopian theme in the January 1876 issue: Introduction to *A Writer's Diary,* 62–65.

14. Significantly, instead of the word for "novelist," *romanist,* he uses the more condescending and potentially ironic *belletrist,* invoking literature rather than the novel. This may well be because he was already developing a conception of the novel as more able to deal with the emerging forms of contemporary life than other literary genres.

15. P. Boborykin, *Sankt-Peterburgskie Viedomosti,* January 11, 1876. For other contemporary reactions to the *Diary* see Volgin, *Dostoevskii—zhurnalist,* 23–40, and Dostoevskii, *CW,* 22:288–306.

16. On the many public faces of Dostoevsky see the final volume of Joseph Frank's exhaustive autobiography, *Dostoevsky: The Mantle of the Prophet.* On the relevance of these for the *Diary,* see Vassena, *Reawakening National Identity,* 43–80.

17. On the place of the feuilleton in nineteenth-century Russian literary

culture, see Katia Dianina, "The Feuilleton: An Everyday Guide to Public Culture in the Age of the Great Reforms," *SEEJ* 47, no. 2 (2003): 186–208. See also Konstantine Klioutchkine, "Russian Literature and the Press, 1860–1914," Ph.D. diss., University of California, Berkeley, 2002, 1–49.

18. Philippe Lejeune, *Le Pacte autobiographique* (Paris: Seuil, 1975).

19. Volgin, *Dostoevskii-zhurnalist,* 66; V. N. Zakharov, *Sistema zhanrov Dostoevskogo: Tipologiia i poetika* (Leningrad: Leningrad University Press, 1985), 204. Also see Fokin, "Struktura i obraz avtora v Dnevnike pisatelia 1876–1877 gg. F. M. Dostoevskogo," 10.

20. Jose Ortega y Gasset, *Meditations on Quixote,* trans. E. Rugg and D. Marin (New York: Norton, 1961); Lukács, *Theory of the Novel;* Mikhail Bakhtin, especially "Epos i roman" and "Slovo v romany," in *Voprosy,* 72–233, 447–84; Ian Watt, *The Rise of the Novel* (Berkeley: University of California Press, 1957).

21. Obviously the historical and geographical focuses of these theorists of the novel differ: Ortega y Gasset examines the intellectual shift in sixteenth-century Spain, Lukács focuses on the shift that took place in Continental Europe in the Romantic period, Bakhtin is concerned primarily with the age of the great European Realist novels, and Watt looks at the literary evolution of eighteenth-century England; but all see the development of the novelistic as part of a manifestation of the modern mind-set.

22. Bakhtin, "Epos ili roman," in *Voprsoy,* 451–52. Translation from Bakhtin, "Epic and Novel," in *The Dialogic Imagination,* 5–6.

23. Here my focus differs from that of Morson, who uses the categories of the literary and the fictional, but does not apply the idea of the novelistic to the *Dnevnik* (see Morson, *The Boundaries of Genre,* 39–48).

24. On serialization see the recent work of W. M. Todd, especially "*The Brothers Karamazov* and the Poetics of Serial Publication." On journals, newspapers, and other literary institutions and their mechanisms, see Reitblat, *Ot Bovy k Bal'montu,* and Deborah Martinsen, ed., *Literary Journals in Imperial Russia* (Cambridge: Cambridge University Press, 1997).

25. V. Vinogradov, *O khudozhestvennoi proze* (Moscow, 1930), 146–75.

26. G. S. Morson, *Narrative and Freedom: The Shadows of Time* (New Haven, Conn.: Yale University Press, 1994), esp. 43–45.

27. Bakhtin, "Slovo v romane," in *Voprosy,* 103. Translation from Bakhtin, "Discourse in the Novel," in *The Dialogic Imagination,* 290.

28. Bakhtin, "Slovo v romane," in *Voprosy,* 176–77.

29. Ibid., 154–56. Authoritative discourse is similar to what Bakhtin calls centripetal language earlier in the essay, where novelistic discourse is closer to centrifugal discourse. Authority provides the center toward which the first kind of language is oriented, whereas novelistic narrative resists movement toward this center, resists a single unambiguous definition.

30. Morson calls such discourse "absolute language" and has explored its

ubiquity in the works of Tolstoy. See Gary Saul Morson, *Hidden in Plain View: Narrative and Creative Potentials in "War and Peace"* (Stanford, Calif.: Stanford University Press, 1987), 9–36.

31. Bakhtin, "Iz zapisei 1970–1971 godov," in *Estetika,* 408.

32. Morson, *The Boundaries of Genre,* 61–63.

33. My use of quotation marks here is intended to designate the fictionalized journal written by the literary persona of the Diarist rather than the concrete text with which we are dealing.

34. Wayne Booth, *The Rhetoric of Fiction* (Chicago: University of Chicago Press, 1961). Also see Boris Uspensky, *A Poetics of Composition* (Berkeley: University of California Press, 1984).

35. See E. Zhurbina, *Teoriia i praktika khudozhestvenno-publisticheskikh zhanrov, ocherk, fel'eton* (Moscow: Mysl', 1969), 22.

36. See *Golos* 39 (Feb. 8, 1876) and 67 (Mar. 7, 1876).

37. Bakhtin, *Estetika,* 352.

38. Vinogradov, *O khudozhestvennoi proze,* 166–67.

39. On the suicides in the *Diary,* see Irina Paperno, *Suicide as a Cultural Institution in Dostoevsky's Russia* (Ithaca, N.Y.: Cornell University Press, 1997), 162–84.

40. Paperno shows that "The Sentence" was based on a real letter which Dostoevsky had received from a man contemplating suicide (ibid., 168–72).

41. Lukács, *Theory of the Novel,* 70–83.

42. Dostoevsky's response in the December 1876 Diary, as well as the memoirs of Simonova-Khokhryakova, make it clear that this article was interpreted by his readers not as the fictionalized confession of a fictional character, but as his own authentic confession (Dostoevskii, *CW,* 24:44). Instead of switching into the novelistic mode, as the Diarist required them to do, they continued to read "The Sentence" within the journalistic mode, assuming the thoughts to be those of the Diarist. Also see Paperno, *Suicide as a Cultural Institution,* 172–73.

43. For a more detailed discussion of the story and its context, see Kate Holland, "The Fictional Filter: 'Krotkaia' and *The Diary of a Writer,*" *Dostoevsky Studies,* n.s., 4 (2000): 95–116.

CHAPTER FIVE

1. This is an extended version of a reading of the novel I first put forward in "Novelizing Religious Experience: The Generic Landscape of *The Brothers Karamazov,*" *Slavic Review* 66, no. 1 (Spring 2007): 63–81.

2. Unless otherwise noted, translations are taken from Fyodor Dostoevsky, *The Brothers Karamazov,* trans. Richard Pevear and Larissa Volokhonsky (New York: Farrar, Straus and Giroux, 2002).

3. Lukács, *Theory of the Novel,* 56–69.

4. Bakhtin, *Problemy poetiki Dostoevskogo,* 335.

5. Dostoevsky was of course not the first author to try to bring religious experience into the secular genre of the novel. This was a prominent feature of the early Romanticism that Dostoevsky had embraced in his youth. E. T. A. Hoffmann and Victor Hugo, both longtime literary heroes of Dostoevsky's, grappled with the same problem in their "Der Magnetiseur" and *Notre Dame de Paris,* respectively. For more on this, see J. Frank, *Dostoevsky: The Seeds of Revolt,* 101–26.

6. In the first group I have in mind such critics as V. L. Komarovich, B. G. Reizov, and Robert Belknap, in the second Vasilii Rozanov, Nikolai Berdyaev, and a host of contemporary Russian and Western critics writing under their influence. V. L. Komarovich, *F. M. Dostojewskij: Die Urgestalt der Brüder Karamasoff: Dostojewskijs Quellen, Entwürfe und Fragmente* (Munich: R. Piper, 1928); B. G. Reizov, "K istorii zamysla *Brat'iev Karamazovykh,*" *Zven'ia* 6 (1936): 545–73; Robert Belknap, *The Structure of "The Brothers Karamazov"* (The Hague: Mouton, 1967); V. V. Rozanov, *Legenda o velikom inkvizitore F. M. Dostoevskogo* (1891); N. Berdiaev, *Novoe religioznoe soznanie i obshchestvennost'* (St. Petersburg: Izdatel'stvo M.V. Pirozhkova, 1907); Ellis Sandoz, *Political Apocalypse: A Study of Dostoevsky's Grand Inquisitor* (Baton Rouge: Louisiana State University Press, 1971).

7. Nina Perlina, *Varieties of Poetic Utterance: Quotation in "The Brothers Karamazov"* (New York: University Press of America, 1985); Diane Oenning Thompson, *"The Brothers Karamazov" and the Poetics of Memory* (Cambridge: Cambridge University Press, 1991).

8. For previous discussions of the role of hagiography in *The Brothers Karamazov,* see V. E. Vetlovskaia, *Poetika Romana "Bratia Karamazovy"* (Leningrad: Nauka, 1977); Jostein Børtnes, "The Function of Hagiography in Dostoevskij's Novels," *Scando-Slavica* 24 (1978): 27–33; Margaret Ziolkowski, *Hagiography and Modern Russian Literature* (Princeton, N.J.: Princeton University Press, 1988); A. Opul'skii, *Zhitiia sviatykh v tvorchestve russkikh pisatelei XIX veka* (East Lansing, Mich.: *Russian Language Journal,*1986); and Thompson, *"The Brothers Karamazov" and the Poetics of Memory,* 74–107. On the significance of apocryphal legend, see Murav, *Holy Foolishness,* 140–42; and Perlina, *Varieties of Poetic Utterance,* 82–87. For accounts of Dostoevsky's uses of folk legend in *The Brothers Karamazov,* see George Gibian, "Dostoevsky's Use of Russian Folklore," in *Slavic Folklore: A Symposium,* ed. A. B. Lord, Special Series of the American Folklore Society 6 (1956), 230–45; L. M. Lotman, "Romany Dostoevskogo i russkaia legenda," in *Realizm russkoi literatury 60-kh godov XIX veka* (Leningrad, 1974), 285–315; Faith Wigzell, "Dostoevskii and the Russian Folk Heritage," in *The Cambridge Companion to Dostoevsky* (Cambridge: Cambridge University Press, 2002), 21–46; Thompson, *"The Brothers Karamazov" and the Poetics of Memory,* 108–16; and Shawn Kate Elliott, "The Aesthetics

of Russian Folk Religion and *The Brothers Karamazov,"* Ph.D diss., University of California, Berkeley, 1997. For a recent study on the role of popular religion in the novel, including the folk legend, see Ivanits, *Dostoevsky and the Russian People,* 159–88.

9. For discussion on the sociological and narrative functions of Christian legends see Hippolyte Delahaye, *Les Légendes hagiographiques* (Brussels: Bureaux de la Société des Bollandistes, 1905), and Andrei Jolles, *Einfache Formen* (Halle: Max Niemeyer Verlag, 1929).

10. In his letters to Liubimov, Dostoevsky continually refers to different books of the novel as "the culminating point" (Books 5 and 6), "the spirit and sense of the whole" and "the most essential section of the novel" (Book 7), and the "key to the whole work" (Book 8). Dostoevskii, *CW,* 30:I:63, 66, 75, 102, 103, 126.

11. Dal', *Tolkovyi slovar' velikogo russkogo iazyka* (1881–82), s.v. "Legenda"; Vasmer, *Etimologocheskii slovar' russkogo iazyka,* trans. Trubachev, 4 vols. (Moscow: Progress, 1986–87), s.v. "Legenda."

12. Chernykh notes an early attribution to Pushkin, in a letter to Pletnev, in which he advises Pushkin to read the *Chet'i Minei,* "especially the legends (*legendy*) about the Kievan wonderworkers": P. Chernykh, ed., *Istoriko-etimologicheskii slovar' sovremennogo russkogo iazyka* (Moscow, 1993), s.v. "Legenda."

13. *Pamiatniki starinnoi russkoi literatury,* 4 vols., vols. 1, 2, and 4 ed. N. Kostomarov, vol. 3 ed. A. Pypin (St. Petersburg: Count Kushelev-Bezborodko, 1860–63).

14. Ziolkowski, *Hagiography and Modern Russian Literature,* 19.

15. This period also saw the publication of Vasilii Kliuchevskii's groundbreaking work on the historical importance of hagiography, *Drevnerusskiie zhitiia sviatikh kak istoricheskii istochnik* (Moscow, 1871), Nikolai Kostomarov's *Russkaia istoria v zhizneopisaniiakh ee glavnykh deiatelei* (St. Petersburg, 1874), and Archmandrite Ignatii's *Kratkie zhizneopisaniia russkikh sviatykh* (St. Petersburg, 1875).

16. *Izbrannye zhitiia sviatykh, kratko izlozhennye po rukovodstvu Chet'ikh-Minei* (Moscow, 1860–61). See Leonid Grossman, *Biblioteka Dostoevskogo* (Odessa: Izdatel'stvo A. A. Ivasenko, 1919). This work is number 185 of Grossman's inventory.

17. N. Tikhonravov, ed., *Pamiatniki otrechennoi literatury* (Moscow, 1863); A. Pypin, ed, "Lozhnye i otrechennye knigi russkoi starinnoi," in *Pamiatniki starinnoi russkoi literatury,* III.

18. See for instance, A. Pypin, "Drevniaia russkaia literatura: I: Starinnye apokrify. II: Skazanie o khozhdenii bogoroditsy po mukam," *Otechestvennye zapiski* 115, no. 2 (1857); I. I. Sreznevskii, "Khozhdenie bogoroditsy po mukam" (St. Petersburg, 1863); I. Smirnov, "Apokrifichiskie skazaniia o Bozhiei Materi

i deianiiakh apostolov" (St. Petersburg, 1873); F. Kerenskii, "Drevnerusskie otrechennye verovaniia i kalandar' Briusa" (St. Petersburg, 1874).

19. A. N. Afanas'iev, *Narodnye russkie legendy, sobrannye Afananasievym* (Moscow: Tipografia V. Gracheva i Komp., 1859).

20. Jack Haney, "Legends," in *The Complete Russian Folktale* (Armonk, N.Y.: Sharpe, 1999), 1:106–108.

21. See, for instance, the variants of the folk legend "Soldat i smert'" in Afanas'iev, *Narodnye russkie legendy*, 122–30.

22. On these saints in the Orthodox and Catholic tradition, see Ziolkowski, *Hagiography and Modern Russian Literature*, 73–83.

23. Fedor Buslaev, *Istoricheskye ocherki russkoi narodnoi slovesnosti* (St. Petersburg, 1861), 172.

24. A. Veselovskii, "Opyti po istorii razvitiia khristianskoi legendy," *Zhurnal Ministerstva Narodnogo Prosveshcheniia* (St. Petersburg, 1875–77).

25. A. Veselovskii, "Pamiatniki literatury povestvovatel'noi," in *Istoriia russkoi slovesnosti*, ed. A. Galakhov, 2nd ed. (St. Petersburg, 1880).

26. A. Veselovskii, "Istoriia ili teoria romana?" and "Iz istorii romana i povesti," in *Izdanie otdeleniia russkogo iazyka i slovesnosti* (St. Petersburg, 1886).

27. Mikhail Bakhtin, "Iz predistorii romannogo slova," in *Voprosy literatury i estetiky* (Moscow, 1975), 408–46. Its subtitle, "Towards a Historical Poetics," itself seems to invoke Veselovskii's work. Of all the Russian philologists of the previous generation, only Vesėlovskii impressed Bakhtin. See I. Shaitanov, "Aleksandr Veselovskii's Historical Poetics: Genre in Historical Poetics," *New Literary History* 32 (2001): 429–43.

28. Though there is no concrete evidence to show that Dostoevsky read the works of Buslaev, Veselovskii, and Pypin, one work in his library does show similar concerns and preoccupations, namely Evstafiev's *Drevniaia ruskaia literatura: Do-petrovskii period*, subtitled "Ustnaia narodnaia slovesnost'." See Grossman, vol. 115 of the inventory; P. V. Evstafiev, *Drevniaia ruskaia literatura: Dopetrovskii period: Ustnaia narodnaia slovesnost'* (St. Petersburg, 1877). Evstafiev's survey discusses the unique cross-breed of medieval oral literature, engendered by the fertile verbal culture of *dvoeverie*, nourished alike by the narrative traditions of Christianity and pre-Christian beliefs. He draws a line to the oral literature of the nineteenth century, the folk legends and religious poetry still being narrated in villages all the way across the Russian Empire. He discusses the heterogeneous nature of folk legend, quoting at length from one of Afanas'iev's legends. The academic discussion in Evstafiev's book may well have resonated with Dostoevsky's own sense of the rich artistic and spiritual sensitivity of the Russian peasantry and their innate feeling for their own religious and cultural heritage.

29. Vasmer's definition highlights this aspect of the legend: "a collection of liturgical extracts for the daily service." Vasmer, *Etimologicheskii slovar'*, s.v. "Legenda."

30. See the discussion of the appropriation and reworking of Christian legend in folkloric contexts in E. V. Anichkov, "Khristianskie legendy v narodnoi peredache," in *Istoria russkoi literatury*, ed. Anichkov et al., 2 vols. (Moscow, 1908).

31. See Bakhtin's discussion of the novel's emergence from the low parodic versions of high literary genres: Bakhtin, "Iz predystorii romannogo slova," 424–32.

32. On the breadth of the novel's intertextual references, see Robert Belknap, *The Genesis of "The Brothers Karamazov": The Aesthetics, Ideology, and Psychology of Making a Text* (Evanston, Ill.: Northwestern University Press, 1990), and Reizov, "K istorii zamysla *Brat'iev Karamazovykh*," 559–73.

33. On the book of Job in *The Brothers Karamazov*, see Richard C. Miller, "The Biblical Story of Joseph in Dostoevskii's *The Brothers Karamazov*," *Slavic Review* 41, no. 4 (Winter 1982): 653–65.

34. Tikhonravov, *Pamiatniki otrechennoi literatury*, 18, 173, 193, 197; Pypin, "Lozhnye i otrechennye knigi russkoi starinnoi," 109, 113.

35. Pypin, "Legendy i apokrify v drevnei russkoi pis'mennosti," *Vestnik Evropy* (1894): 314, 325.

36. Murav, *Holy Foolishness*,139–40. Also see Pypin, "Drevniaia russkaia literatura."

37. Dostoevskii, *CW*, 14:225.

38. Tikhonravov, *Pamiatniki otrechennoi literatury*, 2:23; Pypin, "Lozhnye i otrechennye knigi russkoi starinnoi," 18.

39. See V. E. Vetlovskaia, "Apokrif 'Khozhdenie bogoroditsy po mukam' v *Brat'iakh Karamazovykh* Dostoevskogo," *Dostoevsky i mirovaia kul'tura* 11 (1998): 35–47.

40. In fact, Tikhonravov includes two apocryphal accounts of the temptation narrative in his collection, entitled "God's Debate with the Devil" (Tikhonravov, *Pamiatniki otrechennoi literatury*, 282), and several of the other apocrypha make references to the same events.

41. The Bogomils, medieval dualistic dissenters, believed that the material world was the creation of the devil himself. On the role of the Bogomil heresy in the development of Slavic apocrypha, see see V. Mil'kov, *Drevneruskie apokrify* (St. Petersburg: Izdate'lstvo russkogo Khristianskogo Gumanitarnogo instituta, 1999), 92.

42. For a very different analysis of the significance of hagiography in the generic hierarchy of the novel, see Thompson, *"The Brothers Karamazov" and the Poetics of Memory*, 74–106.

43. For discussion of the conflict between kairotic and chronological time and its significance for novelistic narrative, see Frank Kermode, *The Sense of an Ending* (Oxford: Oxford University Press, 1967), 46–54.

44. Caryl Emerson sees the episode with the mysterious stranger as a powerfully unresolved moment in the "Life" and a key stage in the transposition of

hagiographic to novelistic discourse. Caryl Emerson, "Zosima's 'Mysterious Visitor': Again Bakhtin on Dostoevsky, and Dostoevsky on Heaven and Hell," in *A New Word on "The Brothers Karamazov,"* ed. Robert L. Jackson (Evanston, Ill.: Northwestern University Press, 2004), 155–79.

45. As he indicates in a letter to his editor Liubimov, Dostoevsky took the corruption motif from Monk Parfeny's travelogue: Dostoevskii, *CW,* 30:II:126. See R. Pletnev,"Dostojevskij und der Hieromonach Parfenij," *Zeitchrift für slavische Philologie* 14 (1937).

46. Afanas'iev, *Narodnye russkie legendy,* 130–31. The origins of the legend are consciously or unconsciously hidden by Dostoevsky. Grushenka calls the onion narrative a tale *(basnia)*, and Dostoevsky claims in a letter to Liubimov that it was told to him by a peasant woman: Dostoevskii, *CW,* 14:319, 30:I:126–27. His claim to have heard it for the first time is not backed up by any evidence, and the similarities with Afanas'iev's version are undeniable. Ivanits suggests that Dostoevsky may have been trying to distance himself from Afanas'iev's collection because it was banned: Ivanits, *Dostoevsky and the Russian People,* 160.

47. Gary Saul Morson makes a similar point in "The God of Onions: *The Brothers Karamazov* and the Mythic Prosaic," in Jackson, *A New Word on "The Brothers Karamazov,"* 107–24. Also see Sara Smyth, "The "Lukovka" Legend in *The Brothers Karamazov," Irish Slavonic Studies* 7 (1986): 41–53.

48. Morson coined this term in an essay on *Fathers and Sons,* but uses it in relation to Alyosha's role in *The Brothers Karamazov.* Although all of the Karamazov brothers can be seen as refugees from other kinds of legend, I feel that this description is particularly appropriate for Mitya. Morson, "The God of Onions," 112, 123; see also his "Genre and Hero/Fathers and Sons: Intergeneric Dialogues, Generic Refugees, and the Hidden Prosaic," in *Literature, Culture, and Society in the Modern Age,* ed. Edward J. Brown, Lazar Fleishman, Gregory Freidin, and Richard Schupbach, *Stanford Slavic Studies* 4, no. 1 (1991): 336–81.

49. Dostoevskii, *CW,* 14:98.

50. Ibid., 15:575.

51. Pypin, "Lozhnye i otrechennye knigi russkoi starinnoi," 109, 106.

52. For the apocrypha, see *Pamiatniki starinnoi russkoi literatury,* vol. 3. The folk poetry mentioned is one of the "Dream of the Virgin" prototypes, of Christ's dialogue with hell. The "Visit of the Mother of God through the Torments" can also obviously be seen as another variant of the "harrowing of hell" narrative.

53. Afanas'iev, *Narodnye russkie legendy,* 53.

54. Pypin, "Lozhnye i otrechennye knigi russkoi starinnoi," 51–71; Tikhonravov, *Pamiatniki otrechennoi literatury,* 254–72. The inclusion of motifs from many different types of apocrypha in folk legends is very characteristic. Old and

New Testament apocrypha provided the inspiration for a significant number of the legends recorded by Afanas'iev.

55. In fact, Dostoevsky's notebooks for 1877 testify to the fact that one of his creative projects was a *poema* on the subject of the *sorokovina,* these forty days of torments (17:14).

56. The use of this proverb is hardly accidental; like the folk legend, it suggests the duality of Russian popular Christianity, the continuing coexistence of Christian codes and folk superstitions that reflect a belief in nature's primeval power.

57. For an extended treatment of the role of the cloth bag narrative in the novel, see Kate Holland, "The Legend of the *Ladonka* and the Trial of the Novel," in Jackson, *A New Word on "The Brothers Karamazov,"* 192–200.

58. On *The Brothers Karamazov* as a product of the historical context of the 1867 legal reforms and the intellectual debates of the time, see D. Keily, *The Brothers Karamazov and the Fate of Russian Truth,* Ph.D. diss., Harvard University, 1996.

59. For a discussion on inertia in Dostoevsky, see Liza Knapp, *The Annihilation of Inertia: Dostoevsky and Metaphysics* (Evanston, Ill.: Northwestern University Press, 1996).

60. We know from Suvorin and others, as well as from the preface, that Dostoevsky was intending to write a sequel to the novel, and this can be posited as one reason for the openness of the ending, but I would argue that Dostoevsky is also exploiting the projection outward that is structured into the novel's own generic perspective. On the critical debate over the intended sequel, see Volgin, *Poslednyi god Dostoevskogo* (Moscow: Sovetskii pisatel', 1986), 23–37.

61. On the tension in the final scene between the jubilant tone of Alyosha and the boys and the tragic events of the novel itself, see Jackson, "Alyosha's Speech at the Stone," in Jackson, *A New Word on "The Brothers Karamazov,"* 234–54.

Bibliography

WORKS BY DOSTOEVSKY

Dostoevskii, F. M. *The Notebooks for "The Idiot."* Translated by Strelsky, edited by Edward Wasiolek. Chicago: University of Chicago Press, 1967.

———. *The Notebooks for "The Possessed."* Translated by Victor Terras, edited by Edward Wasiolek. Chicago: University of Chicago Press, 1968.

———. *The Notebooks for "A Raw Youth."* Edited and translated by Edward Wasiolek. Chicago: University of Chicago Press, 1969.

———. *The Notebooks for "The Brothers Karamazov."* Edited and translated by Edward Wasiolek. Chicago: University of Chicago Press, 1971.

———. *Neizdannyi Dostoevskii: Zapisnye knizhki i tetrad 1860–1881 gg. Literaturnoe Nasledstvo* 83. Moscow: Nauka, 1971.

———. *Polnoe sobranie sochinenii v tridtsati tomakh.* Edited V. G. Bazanov et al. 30 vols. Leningrad: Nauka, 1972–90.

———. *The Unpublished Dostoevsky: Diaries and Notebooks, 1860–81.* Edited by Carl Proffer; translated by Arline Boyer and Carl Proffer. 3 vols. Ann Arbor, Mich.: Ardis, 1973–76.

———. *Fyodor Dostoevsky, Complete Letters.* 5 vols. Edited and translated by David A. Lowe. Ann Arbor, Mich.: Ardis, 1988–91.

———. *The Brothers Karamazov.* Translated by Richard Pevear and Larissa Volokhonsky. New York: Farrar, Strauss and Giroux, 1990.

———. *A Writer's Diary.* 2 vols. Edited and translated by Kenneth Lantz. Introduced by Gary Saul Morson. Evanston, Ill.: Northwestern University Press, 1993.

———. *Demons.* Translated by Richard Pevear and Larissa Volokhonsky. New York: Vintage Classics, 1994.

———. *Dostoevsky's Occasional Writings.* Edited and translated by David Magarshack. Evanston, Ill.: Northwestern University Press, 1997.

———. *The Adolescent.* Translated by Richard Pevear and Larissa Volokhonsky. New York: Knopf, 2003.

OTHER WORKS

Afanas'iev, A. N. *Narodnye russkie legendy, sobrannye Afananasievym.* Moscow: Tipografia V. Gracheva i Komp., 1859.

———. *Narodnye russkie skazki.* Leningrad: Nauka, 1984.

Ambler, E. *Russian Journalism and Politics, 1861–1881: The Career of Aleksei S. Suvorin.* Detroit: Wayne State University Press, 1972.

Anderson, Nancy K. *The Perverted Ideal in Dostoevsky's "The Devils."* New York: Peter Lang, 1997.

Anichkov, E. V. "Khristianskie legendy v narodnoi peredache." In *Istoria russkoi literatury,* edited by E. V. Anichkov et al., 2:109–34. Moscow: Mir, 1908.

Annenkov, P. V. *Literaturnye vospominaniia.* Leningrad: Akademia, 1928.

Arkhangelskaia, V. *Ocherki narodnicheskoi fol'kloristiki.* Saratov: Saratov University Press, 1976.

Auerbach, E. *Mimesis: The Representation of Reality in Western Literature.* Princeton, N.J.: Princeton University Press, 1953.

Bakhtin, M. M. *Voprosy literatury i estetiki.* Moscow: Khudozhestvennaia literatura, 1975.

———. *Estetika slovesnogo tvorchestva.* Edited by S. G. Bocharov. Moscow: Iskusstvo, 1979.

———. *The Dialogic Imagination: Four Essays by Mikhail Bakhtin.* Edited by Michael Holquist; translated by Caryl Emerson and Michael Holquist. Austin: University of Texas Press, 1981.

———. *Problems of Dostoevsky's Poetics.* Edited and translated by Caryl Emerson. Minneapolis: University of Minnesota Press, 1984.

———. *Speech Genres, and Other Late Essays.* Edited by Caryl Emerson. Austin: University of Texas Press, 1986.

———. "Roman vospitaniia i ego znachenie v istorii realizma (fragmenty prospekta)." In "Mikhail Bakhtin i teoriia vospitaniia," by Brian Poole. In *M. M. Bakhtin i perspektivy gumanitarnykh nauk,* edited by V. I. Makhlin, 62–72. Vitebsk: N.A. Pan'kov, 1994.

———. *Sobranie sochinenii v semi tomakh.* Edited by S. G. Bocharov. Moscow: Russkie slovari, 1996.

Balashov, N. "Put' Dostoevskogo ot *Besov* k *Podrostku.*" *Kontekst,* 1985, 21–48. Moscow: Nauka, 1985.

Belinskii, V. G. *Polnoe sobranie sochinenii.* 13 vols. Moscow: Izdatel'stvo Akademii Nauk SSSR, Institut russkoi literatury, 1953–59.

Belknap, Robert L. *The Structure of "The Brothers Karamazov."* The Hague: Mouton, 1967.

———. "The Rhetoric of an Ideological Novel." In *Literature and Society in Imperial Russia, 1800–1914,* edited by William Mills Todd, 173–201. Stanford, Calif.: Stanford University Press, 1978.

———. *The Genesis of "The Brothers Karamazov": The Aesthetics, Ideology, and Psychology of Making a Text.* Evanston, Ill.: Northwestern University Press, 1990.

Bem, A. L. "Khudozhestvennaia polemika s Tolstym: K ponimaniu 'Podrostka.'" In *O Dostoevskom: Sbornik stat'ei pod redaktsiei A. L. Bema,* 3:192–214. Prague: Petropolis, 1936.

———. "Evoliutsiia obraza Stavrogina." In *Besy: Antologiia russkoi kritiki,* edited by L. Saraskina, 638–62. Moscow: Soglasie, 1996.

Benjamin, Walter. *Illuminations.* Translated by H. Zohn. New York: Harcourt, Brace, Jovanovich, 1968.

Berdiaev, N. *Novoe religioznoe soznaniie i obshchestvennost'.* St. Petersburg: MV Pirozhkov, 1907.

Bessonov, P. V. *Kaleki perekhozhie.* 6 vols. Moscow: A. Semen, 1861.

Booth, Wayne. *The Rhetoric of Fiction.* Chicago: University of Chicago Press, 1961.

Bortnes, J. "The Function of Hagiography in Dostoevskij's Novels." *Scando-Slavica* 24 (1978): 27–33.

Brooks, Jeffrey. *When Russia Learned to Read: Literacy and Popular Literature, 1861–1917.* Princeton, N.J.: Princeton University Press, 1985.

Brooks, Peter. *The Melodramatic Imagination.* New York: Columbia University Press, 1984.

———. *Reading for the Plot.* Cambridge, Mass.: Harvard University Press, 1984.

Bulgakov, S. "Ivan Karamazov v romane Dostoevskogo 'Bratia Karamazovy' kak filosofskii tip." In *O velikom inkvizitore: Dostoevskii i posleduiushchie,* edited by Iu. Seliverstvov, 193–217. Moscow: Molodaia gvardiia, 1991.

Buslaev, F. *Istoricheskie ocherki russkoi narodnoi slovesnosti i isskustva.* 2 vols. St. Petersburg: Obshchestvennaia pol'za, 1861.

———. "Znachenie romana v nashe vremia." St. Petersburg, 1877.

Cassedy, Steven. *Dostoevsky's Religion.* Stanford, Calif.: Stanford University Press, 2005.

Catteau, Jacques. *La Création littéraire chez Dostoïevski.* Paris: L'Institut des études slaves, 1978.

———. "The Paradox of the Legend of the Grand Inquisitor in *The Brothers Karamazov.*" In *Dostoevsky: New Perspectives,* edited by Robert L. Jackson, 243–54. Englewood Cliffs, N.J.: Prentice Hall, 1983.

Chances, Ellen. "Literary Criticism and the Ideology of Pochvennichestvo in Dostoevsky's Thick Journals *Vremia* and *Epokha.*" *Russian Review* 34, no. 2 (Apr. 1975): 151–64.

Chernykh, P., ed. *Istoriko-etimologicheskii slovar' sovremennogo russkogo iazyka.* Moscow: Russkii iazyk, 1993.

Dal', V., ed. *Tolkovyi slovar' zhivogo velikorusskogo iazyka.* 4 vols. St. Petersburg, 1881–82. Reprint: Moscow: Russkii iazyk, 1989.

Danilevskii, N. Ia. *Rossiia i Evropa.* St. Petersburg: Obshchestvennaia pol'za, 1871.

Davison, R. M. "*The Devils:* The Role of Stavrogin." In *New Essays on Dostoyevsky,* edited by Malcolm V. Jones and Garth M. Terry, 95–114. Cambridge: Cambridge University Press, 1983.

Delehaye, H. *Les Légendes hagiographiques.* Brussels: Bureaux de la Société des Bollandistes, 1905.

———. *The Legends of the Saints.* Translated by D. Attwater. Dublin: Four Courts, 1998.

Desnitskii, V. A. "Publitsistika i literatura v 'Dnevnike pisatelia' F. M. Dostoevskogo." In F. M. Dostoevskii, *Polnoe sobranie sochinenii,* 13 vols., 11:3–26. Leningrad: Gosudar'stvennoe izdatel'stvo, 1926–30.

Dianina, Katia. "The Feuilleton: An Everyday Guide to Public Culture in the Age of the Great Reforms." *Slavic and East European Journal* 47, no. 2 (2003): 186–208.

Dmitrieva, L. S. "O zhanrovom svoeobrazii *Dnevnika pisatel'a* (k probleme tipologii zhurnala)." *Vestnik Moskovskogo Universiteta,* Seria 11, Zhurnalistika, 6 (1969): 23–25.

Dolinin, A. S. *V tvorcheskoi laboratorii Dostoevskogo: Istoria sozdaniia romana* Podrostok. Moscow: Sovetskii pisatel', 1947.

———. *Poslednie romany Dostoevskogo: Kak sozdavalis'* Podrostok *i* Bratia Karamazovy. Moscow: Sovetskii pisatel', 1963.

———. "Ispoved' Stavrogina." In *Besy: Antologiia russkoi kritiki,* edited by L. Saraskina, 534–59. Moscow: Soglasie, 1996.

Dostoevskaya, A. G. *Vospominaniia.* Edited by L. P. Grossman. Moscow: Gosudarstvennoe izdatel'stvo, 1925.

Dowler, Wayne. *Dostoevsky, Grigor'ev and Native Soil Conservatism.* Toronto: University of Toronto Press, 1982.

———. *An Unnecessary Man: The Life of Apollon Grigor'ev.* Toronto: University of Toronto Press, 1995.

Druzhinin, A. V. *Polinka Saks.* Moscow: Dnevnik, 1989.

Eikhenbaum, B. *Molodoi Tolstoi.* Munich: W. Fink, 1968.

Emerson, Caryl. "Zosima's 'Mysterious Visitor': Again Bakhtin on Dostoevsky, and Dostoevsky on Heaven and Hell." In Jackson, *A New Word on "The Brothers Karamazov,"* 155–80.

Emmons, Terence. *The Russian Landed Gentry and the Peasant Emancipation of 1861.* Cambridge: Cambridge University Press, 1968.

Engel'gardt, B. "Ideologicheskii roman Dostoevskogo." In *Dostoevskii: Stat'i i materialy (sbornik vtoroi),* edited by A. S. Dolinin. Leningrad, 1924.

Esin, B. I. *Russkaia zhurnalistika 70-kh i 80-kh XIX veka.* Moscow: Izdatel'stvo Moskovskogo Universiteta, 1963.

Evstafiev, P. V. *Drevnaia russkaia literatura: Do-petrovskii period.* St. Petersburg, 1877.

Fadeev, R. V. *Russkoe obshchestvo v nastoiashchem i budushchem, Sobranie sochinenii.* 3 vols. St. Petersburg, 1889–90.

Fedorenko, B. V. "K istorii gazety-zhurnala 'Grazhdanin.'" In *Dostoevskii: Materialy i issledovaniia* 11 (1994): 246–59.

Fedotov, G. *The Russian Religious Mind.* Cambridge, Mass.: Harvard University Press, 1946.

Field, Daniel. "The Year of Jubilee." In *Russia's Great Reforms, 1855–1881,* edited by Ben Eklof, John Bushnell, and Larissa Zakharova, 40–57. Bloomington: Indiana University Press, 1994.

Fokin, P. "K voprosu o genezise 'Dnevnika pisatel'ia' 1876–1877 gg. (biografi cheskii aspekt)." *Dostoevkii i mirovaia kul'tura* 2 (1994): 119–26.

———. "Struktura i obraz avtora v *Dnevnike pisatelia* 1876–1877 gg. F. M. Dostoevskogo." Avtoreferat dissertatsii, Institut russkoi literatury, St. Petersburg, 1995.

Frank, Joseph. "The Masks of Stavrogin." *Sewanee Review* 77, no. 4 (Autumn 1969): 660–91.

———. *Dostoevsky: The Seeds of Revolt.* Princeton, N.J.: Princeton University Press, 1976.

———. *Dostoevsky: The Years of Ordeal.* Princeton, N.J.: Princeton University Press, 1983.

———. *Dostoevsky: The Stir of Liberation.* Princeton, N.J.: Princeton University Press, 1986.

———. *Dostoevsky: The Miraculous Years.* Princeton, N.J.: Princeton University Press, 1990.

———. "Dostoevsky's Trojan Horse: *A Raw Youth.*" In *Literary Imagination, Ancient and Modern: Essays in Honor of David Grene,* edited by Todd Breyfogle, 312–33. Chicago: University of Chicago Press, 1999.

———. *Dostoevsky: The Mantle of the Prophet.* Princeton, N.J.: Princeton University Press, 2002.

Frank, S. "Legenda o Velikom inkvizitore." In *O velikom inkvizitore: Dostoevskii i posleduiushchie,* edited by Iu. Seliverstov, 243–50. Moscow: Molodaia gvardiia, 1991.

Fridlender, G. *Realizm Dostoevskogo.* Leningrad: Nauka, 1964.

———. "Estetika Dostoevskogo." In *Dostoevskii—Khudozhnik i myslitel': Sbornik stat'ei,* edited by A. L. Grishunin, 97–164. Moscow: Khudozhestvennia literatura, 1972.

Frus, P. *The Politics and Poetics of Journalistic Narrative.* Cambridge: Cambridge University Press, 1994.

Fusso, Susanne. "Dostoevsky's Comely Boy: Homoerotic Desire and Aesthetic Strategies in *A Raw Youth.*" *Russian Review* 59, no. 4 (2000): 576–96.

———. "The Weight of Human Tears: The Covetuous Knight and a Raw Youth." In *Alexander Pushkin's Little Tragedies: The Poetics of Brevity,* edited by Svetlana Evdokimova, 229–42. Madison: University of Wisconsin Press, 2003.

———. *Discovering Sexuality in Dostoevsky.* Evanston, Ill.: Northwestern University Press, 2006.

Gachev, G. "Ispoved', propoved', gazeta i roman." *Dostoevskii v kontse XX veka.* Moscow: Klassika-plius', 1996.

Galtung, Johan. "On the Social Costs of Modernization: Social Disintegration, Atomie/Anomie, and Social Development." *Development and Change* 27, no. 2 (Apr. 1996): 379–413.

Gerbel', N. *Poeziia slavian.* St. Petersburg, 1871.

Gerigk, H.-J. *Versuch über Dostojewski's "Jüngling," ein Beitrag zur Theorie des Romans.* Munich: Wilhelm Fink, 1965.

Gerstein, Linda. *Nikolai Strakhov: Philosopher, Man of Letters, Social Critic.* Cambridge, Mass: Harvard University Press, 1971.

Gibian, G. "Dostoevsky's Use of Russian Folklore." In *Slavic Folklore: A Symposium,* edited by A. B. Lord, 230–45. Philadelphia: American Folklore Society, vol. 6. 1956.

Ginzburg, L. *On Psychological Prose.* Translated by Judson Rosengrant. Princeton, N.J.: Princeton University Press, 1991.

Girard, René. *Deceit, Desire and the Novel.* Translated by Yvonne Freccero. Baltimore, Md.: Johns Hopkins University Press, 1961.

Gleason, Abbott. *Young Russia: The Genesis of Russian Radicalism in the 1860s.* New York: Viking, 1980.

Goethe, J. W. *Werke.* Edited by Erich Trunz et al. Hamburg: Christian Wegner Verlag, 1948–60.

Golovachev, A. A. *Desiat' let reform: 1861–1871.* St. Petersburg, 1872.

Goncharov, I. A. *Sobranie sochinenii.* 8 vols. Moscow: Khudozhestvennaia literatura, 1952–55.

Gorelov, A. A., et al., eds. *Russkaia literatura i fol'klor: Pervaia polovina XIX veka.* Leningrad: Nauka, 1976.

———. *Russkaia literatura i fol'klor: Vtoraia polovina XIX veka.* Leningrad: Nauka, 1982.

———. *Russkaia literatura i fol'klor: Konets XIX veka.* Leningrad: Nauka, 1987.

Griffiths, Frederick, and Stanley Rabinowitz. *Novel-Epics.* Evanston, Ill.: Northwestern University Press, 1990.

Grigorenko, V.V. et al. *F. M. Dostoevskii v vospominaniakh sovremennikov.* 2 vols. Moscow: Khudozhestvennaia literatura, 1964.

Grigor'ev, A. A. *Literaturnaia Kritika.* Moscow: Khudozhestvennaia literatura, 1967.

Grigorovich, D. V. *Sochinenia v trekh tomakh.* 3 vols. Moscow: Khudozhestvennaia literatura, 1988.

Grishin, D. *Dnevnik pisatelia F. M. Dostoevskogo.* Melbourne: University of Melbourne, 1966.

Grossman, L. *Biblioteka Dostoevskogo*. Odessa: Izdatel'stvo A. A. Ivasenko, 1919.

———. *Tvorchestvo Dostoevskogo*. Odessa: Vseukrainskoe gosudarstvennoe izdatel'stvo, 1921.

———. *Poetika Dostoevskogo*. Moscow: Gosudarstvennaia akademia khudozhestvennykh nauk, 1925.

———. "Poslednii roman Dostoevskogo." In *Bratia Karamazovy*. Moscow: Izdatel'stvo Khudozhestvennaia literatura, 1935.

Haney, J. V., ed. *The Complete Russian Folktale*, vol. 1: *An Introduction to the Russian Folktale*. Armonk, N.Y.: Sharpe, 1999.

———. *The Complete Russian Folktale*, vol. 5: *Russian Legends*. Armonk, N.Y.: Sharpe, 2003.

Hansen-Löve, A."Diskursivnye protsessy v romane Dostoevskogo *Podrostok*." In *Avtor i tekst*, edited by V. M. Markovich and Vol'f Schmid, 229–67. St. Petersburg: Izdatel'stvo St. Peterburgskogo universiteta, 1996.

Holland, Kate. "The Fictional Filter: 'Krotkaia' and *The Diary of a Writer*." *Dostoevsky Studies*, n.s., 4 (2000): 95–116.

———. "The Legend of the *Ladonka* and the Trial of the Novel." In Jackson, *A New Word on "The Brothers Karamazov,"* 192–200.

———. "Novelizing Religious Experience: The Generic Landscape of *The Brothers Karamazov*." *Slavic Review* 66, no. 1 (Spring 2007): 63–81.

Holquist, Michael. *Dostoevsky and the Novel*. Princeton, N.J.: Princeton University Press, 1977.

Hudspith, Sarah. *Dostoevsky and the Idea of Russianness*. London: Routledge-Curzon, 2004.

Ivanchikova, E. "*Podrostok:* Povestvovanie s liricheskyn rasskazchikom." *Voprosy iazykoznaniia* 3 (1995): 70–76.

Ivanits, Linda. *Russian Folk Belief*. Armonk, N.Y.: Sharpe, 1989.

———. *Dostoevsky and the Russian People*. Cambridge: Cambridge University Press, 2008.

Ivanov, Viacheslav. *Freedom and the Tragic Life*. Edited and translated by Robert L. Jackson. New York: Noonday, 1952.

Jackson, Robert L. *Dostoevsky's Quest for Form: A Study of His Philosophy of Art*. New Haven, Conn.: Yale University Press, 1966.

———. *The Art of Dostoevsky: Deliriums and Nocturnes*. Princeton, N.J.: Princeton University Press, 1981.

———. *Dialogues with Dostoevsky: The Overwhelming Questions*. Stanford, Calif.: Stanford University Press, 1983.

———. "Alyosha's Speech at the Stone: 'The Whole Picture.'" In *A New Word on "The Brothers Karamazov,"* 234–54.

———, ed. *A New Word on "The Brothers Karamazov."* Evanston, Ill.: Northwestern University Press, 2004.

Jensen, P. A. "Paradoksal'nost' avtorstva (u) Dostoevskogo." In *Paradoksy russkoi literatury: Sbornik stat'ei,* edited by V. M. Markovich and Vol'f Schmid, 219–33. St. Petersburg: INAPress, 2001.

Jolles, André. *Einfache Formen.* Halle: Max Niemeyer Verlag, 1929.

Jones, Malcolm. *Dostoyevsky After Bakhtin: Readings in Dostoyevsky's Fantastic-Realism.* Cambridge: Cambridge University Press, 1990.

Kabat, Geoffrey. *Ideology and Imagination: The Image of Society in Dostoevsky.* New York: Columbia University Press, 1978.

Karlova, T. S. *Dostoevskii i russkii sud.* Kazan: Izdatel'stvo Kazanskogo Universiteta, 1975.

Kasat'kina, T. "Roman F. M. Dostoevskogo 'Podrostok': 'Ideia' geroia i ideia avtora." *Voprosy Literatury* 1 (2004): 181–212.

Keily, D. *The Brothers Karamazov and the Fate of Russian Truth.* Ph.D. diss., Harvard University, 1996.

Kelly, Aileen. "Irony and Utopia in Herzen and Dostoevsky: *From the Other Shore* and *Diary of a Writer.*" *Russian Review* 50, no. 4 (Oct. 1991): 397–416.

Kermode, Frank. *The Sense of an Ending.* Oxford: Oxford University Press, 1967.

Kipp, J. W., and W. B. Lincoln. "Autocracy and Reform: Bureaucratic Absolutism and Political Modernization in Nineteenth Century Russia." In *Imperial Russian History II: 1861–1917,* vol. 3 of *Articles on Russian and Soviet History 1500–1991,* pp. 1–21. New York: Garland, 1992.

Kirpotin, V. Ia. "Roman Dostoevskogo *Podrostok.*" In F. M. Dostoevskii, *Podrostok,* 583–609. Moscow: Goslitizdat, 1961.

———. *Dostoevskii v shestidesiatye gody.* Moscow: Khudozhestvennaia literatura, 1966.

Klenin, Emily. "On the Ideological Sources of *Čto delat'?* Sand, Družinin, Leroux." *Zeitschrift für Slavische Philologie* 51, no. 1 (1991): 367–407.

Klioutchkine, K. "Russian Literature and the Press, 1860–1914." Ph.D. diss., University of California, Berkeley, 2002.

Kliuchevskii, V. *Drevnerusskie zhitiia sviatykh kak istoricheskii istochnik.* Moscow, 1871.

Knapp, Liza. *The Annihilation of Inertia: Dostoevsky and Metaphysics.* Evanston, Ill.: Northwestern University Press, 1996.

Kolesnitskaia, I. M. "Russkie predaniia i legendy v publikatsiakh 1860–1870-kh godov." *Russkii fol'klor* 13 (1972): 20–39.

Komarovich, V. "Roman *Podrostok* kak khudozhestvennoe edinstvo." In *Dostoevskii: Stat'i i materialy (sbornik vtoroi),* edited by A. S. Dolinin, 31–68. Leningrad: Mysl', 1924.

———. "Genezis romana *Podrostok.*" *Literaturnaia Mysl'* 3, no. 1 (1925): 366–86.

———. *F. M. Dostojewskij. Die Urgestalt der Brüder Karamasoff. Dostojewskijs Quellen, Entwürfe und Fragmente.* Munich: R. Piper, 1928.

Krasnoshchekova, Elena. "Pamiat' zhanra v romane Podrostok." In *Roman Dostoevskogo Podrostok: Vozmozhnosti prochteniia,* edited by V. A. Viktorovich,

137–58. Kolomna: Kolomenskii gosudarstvennyi pedagogicheskii institut, 2003.

Lazari, Andrzej de. *V krugu Fedora Dostoevskogo: Pochvennichestvo.* Translated by M. V. Leskinen. Moscow: Nauka, 2004.

Leatherbarrow, W. J., ed. *The Cambridge Companion to Dostoevskii.* Cambridge: Cambridge University Press, 2002.

———. *A Devil's Vaudeville: The Demonic in Dostoevsky's Major Fiction.* Evanston, Ill.: Northwestern University Press, 2005.

Lejeune, P. *Le Pacte autobiographique.* Paris: Seuil, 1975.

Leontiev, K. *Sobranie sochinenii.* Moscow, 1912–14.

Levitt, Marcus C. *Russian Literary Politics and the Pushkin Celebration of 1880.* Ithaca, N.Y.: Cornell University Press, 1989.

Likhachev, D. *Poetika drevnerusskoi literatury.* Moscow: Nauka, 1967.

Lincoln, W. B. *In the Vanguard of Reform: Russia's Enlightened Bureaucrats, 1825–1861.* DeKalb: Northern Illinois University Press, 1982.

———. *The Great Reforms: Autocracy, Bureaucracy and the Politics of Change in Imperial Russia.* DeKalb: Northern Illinois University Press, 1990.

Linner, S. *Dostoevskij on Realism.* Stockholm: Almquist and Wiksell, 1967.

———. *Starets Zosima in "The Brothers Karamazov": A Study in the Mimesis of Virtue.* Stockholm: Almquist and Wiksell, 1975.

Lotman, L. M. "Romany Dostoevskogo i russkaia legenda." In *Realizm russkoi literatury 60-kh godov XIX veka,* 285–315. Leningrad: Nauka, 1974.

Lukács, G. *Die Theorie des Romans.* Berlin: Cassirer, 1920.

———. *Goethe und seine Zeit.* Berlin: Aufbau Verlag, 1950.

———. *The Theory of the Novel: A Historico-philosophical Essay on the Forms of Great Epic Literature.* Cambridge, Mass.: MIT Press, 1971.

———. *The Historical Novel.* Lincoln: University of Nebraska Press, 1983.

———. *Dostojewski: Notizen und Entwürfe.* Budapest: Akadémiai Kiadó, 1985.

Maiorova, Olga. *From the Shadow of Empire: Defining the Russian Nation Through Cultural Mythology, 1855–1870.* Madison: University of Wisconsin Press, 2010.

Martinsen, Deborah A. "Dostoevsky's *Diary of a Writer:* Journal of the 1870s." In *Literary Journals in Imperial Russia,* edited by Deborah Martinsen, 150–68. Cambridge: Cambridge University Press, 1997.

———, ed. *Literary Journals in Imperial Russia.* Cambridge: Cambridge University Press, 1997.

———. *Surprised by Shame: Dostoevsky's Liars and Narrative Exposure.* Columbus: Ohio State University Press, 2003.

Matlaw, Ralph. *The Brothers Karamazov: Novelistic Technique.* The Hague: Mouton, 1957.

McMaster, Robert. *Danilevsky: A Russian Totalitarian Philosopher.* Cambridge, Mass.: Harvard University Press, 1967.

McReynolds, Louise. *The News Under Russia's Old Regime: The Development of a Mass Circulation Press.* Princeton, N.J.: Princeton University Press, 1991.

McReynolds, Susan. *Redemption and the Merchant God: Dostoevsky's Economy of Salvation and Antisemitism.* Evanston, Ill.: Northwestern University Press, 2008.

Meerson, Olga. *Dostoevsky's Taboos.* Dresden: Dresden University Press, 1998.

Meijer, J. M., and J. Van der Eng. *"The Brothers Karamazov" by F. M. Dostoevskii.* Dutch Studies in Russian Literature. The Hague: Mouton, 1971.

Merezhkovskii, D. S. *L. Tolstoi i Dostoevskii: Khristos i antikhrist v russkoi literature.* St. Petersburg, 1901.

Meshcherskii, V. P. *Vospominania,* Moscow: Zakharov, 2001.

Mikhailovskii, N. *Sochinenia.* 6 vols. St. Petersburg: Tipografiia V. M. Vol'fa, 1896–97.

Mil'kov, V. *Apokrify Drevnei Rusi: Teksty i issledovaniia.* St. Petersburg: Nauka, 1997.

———. *Drevnerusskie apokrify.* St. Petersburg: Izdatel'stvo russkogo Khristianskogo Gumanitarnogo instituta, 1999.

Miller, Forrestt A. *Dmitrii Miliutin and the Reform Era in Russia.* Nashville: Vanderbilt University Press, 1968.

Miller, Richard C. "The Biblical Story of Joseph in Dostoevskii's *The Brothers Karamazov.*" *Slavic Review* 41, no. 4 (1982): 653–65.

Miller, Robin Feuer. *The Brothers Karamazov: Worlds of the Novel.* New York: Twayne, 1992.

———. *Dostoevsky's Unfinished Journey.* New Haven, Conn.: Yale University Press, 2007.

Mochulskii, Konstantin. *Gogol', Soloviev, Dostoevskii.* Moscow: Respublika, 1995.

Moretti, Franco. *Signs Taken for Wonders: Essays in the Sociology of Literary Forms.* Translated by S. Fischer, D. Forgacs, and D. Miller. London: Verso, 1983.

———. *The Way of the World: The* Bildungsroman *in European Culture.* Translated by Alberto Sbragia. London: Verso, 1987.

———. *Modern Epic.* London: Verso, 1996.

Morson, Gary Saul. "Dostoevsky's *Diary of a Writer:* Threshold Art." Ph.D. diss., Yale University, 1974.

———. *The Boundaries of Genre: Dostoevsky's Diary of a Writer and the Traditions of Literary Utopia.* Austin: University of Texas Press, 1981.

———. *Hidden in Plain View: Narrative and Creative Potentials in "War and Peace."* Stanford, Calif.: Stanford University Press, 1987.

———. Introduction to *A Writer's Diary,* 1:1–117. Evanston, Ill.: Northwestern University Press, 1993.

———. *Narrative and Freedom: The Shadows of Time.* New Haven, Conn.: Yale University Press, 1994.

———. "The God of Onions: *The Brothers Karamazov* and the Mythic Prosaic." In Jackson, *A New Word on "The Brothers Karamazov,"* 107–25.

Morson, Gary Saul, and Caryl Emerson. *Mikhail Bakhtin: Creation of a Prosaics.* Stanford, Calif.: Stanford University Press, 1990.

Moser, C. A. "Dostoevsky and the Aesthetics of Journalism." *Dostoevsky Studies* 3 (1982): 27–41.

———. *Esthetics as Nightmare: Russian Literary Theory, 1855–1870.* Princeton, N.J.: Princeton University Press, 1989.

Muller, L. *Dostojewskij.* Munich: Erich Wewel Verlag, 1982.

Murav, Harriet. "Representations of the Demonic: Seventeenth Century Pretenders and *The Devils.*" *Slavic and East European Journal* 35, no. 1 (Spring 1991): 56–70.

———. *Holy Foolishness: Dostoevsky's Novels and the Poetics of Cultural Critique.* Stanford, Calif.: Stanford University Press, 1992.

———. *Russia's Legal Fictions.* Ann Arbor: University of Michigan Press, 1998.

Nechaeva, V. S. *Zhurnal M. M. i F. M. Dostoevskikh "Vremia," 1861–1863.* Moscow: Nauka, 1972.

———. *Zhurnal M. M. i F. M. Dostoevskikh "Epokha," 1864–1865.* Moscow: Nauka, 1975.

New Testament Apocrypha. Compiled by E. Henneke. Edited by W. Schneemelcher. Translated by R. Wilson. London: SCM, 1963.

Oksman, Y. I. *Fel'etony sorokovykh godov.* Moscow: Akademia, 1930.

Opul'skii, A. *Zhitiia sviatikh v tvorchestve russkikh pisatelei XIX veka.* East Lansing, Mich.: Russian Language Journal, 1986.

Ortega y Gasset, José. *Meditations on Quixote.* Translated by E. Rugg and D. Marin. New York: Norton, 1961.

Pamiatniki otrechennoi literatury. Edited by N. Tikhonravov. Moscow, 1863.

Pamiatniki starinnoi russkoi literatury. 4 vols. Vols. 1, 2, and 4 edited by N. Kostomarov, vol. 3 edited by A. Pypin. St. Petersburg: Count Kushelev-Bezborodko, 1860–63.

Paperno, Irina. *Chernyshevsky and the Age of Realism.* Stanford, Calif.: Stanford University Press, 1988.

———. "The Liberation of the Serfs as a Cultural Symbol." *Russian Review* 50, no. 4 (Oct. 1991): 418–36.

———. *Suicide as a Cultural Institution in Dostoevsky's Russia.* Ithaca, N.Y.: Cornell University Press, 1997.

Parfeny, Monk. *Skazanie o stranstvii i puteshestvii po Rossii, Turtsii i Sviatoi Zemle, postrizhenika Sviatye Gory Afonskiia inoka Parfeniia.* Moscow: A. Semen, 1856.

Peace, R. *Dostoyevsky: An Examination of the Major Novels.* Cambridge: Cambridge University Press, 1971.

Perlina, N. *Varieties of Poetic Utterance: Quotation in "The Brothers Karamazov."* New York: University Press of America, 1985.

———. "Rethinking Adolescence." In *Celebrating Creativity: Essays in Honour of Jostein Börtnes.* Edited by Knut Andreas Grimstad and Ingunn Lunde, 216–26. Bergen: University of Bergen, 1997.

Pletnev, R. "Dostojevskij und der Hieromonach Parfenij." *Zeitchrift für slavische Philologie* 14 (1937): 30–46.

———. "La légende chrétienne dans l'œuvre de Dostoïevsky." *Études slaves et est-européenes* 6 (1961): 131–57.

Poole, B. "Mikhail Bakhtin i teoriia romana vospitaniia." In *M. M. Bakhtin i perspektivy gumanitarnykh nauk,* edited by V. L. Makhlin, 62–72. Vitebsk: N. A. Pan'kov, 1994.

Potebnia, A. A. "Chernovnye zametki o L. N. Tolstom i Dostoevskom." *Voprosy teorii I psikhologii tvorchestva.* Kharkhov, 1914.

Prendergast, C. *The Order of Mimesis.* Cambridge: Cambridge University Press, 1986.

Propp, V. "Legenda." *Russkoe narodnoe poeticheskoe tvorchestvo.* Vol. 2, book 1, 378–86. Moscow, 1955.

———. *Morphology of the Folktale.* Austin: University of Texas Press, 1968.

———. *Theory and History of Folklore.* Translated by Ariadna and Richard Martin and edited by Anatoly Liberman. Minneapolis: University of Minnesota Press, 1984.

Pustygina, N. G. "O familii Dolgorukov v romane F. M. Dostoevskogo 'Podrostok.'" *Uchenye zapiski Tartuskogo gosudarstvennogo universiteta* 654 (1985): 37–53.

Pypin, A. "Drevniaia russkaia literatura: I: Starinnye apokrify. II: Skazanie o khozhdenii bogoroditsy po mukam." *Otechestvennye zapiski* 115, no. 2 (1857): 335–60.

———. *Istoriia russkoi etnografii.* 4 vols. St. Petersburg: Tip. M. M. Stasiulevicha, 1891.

———. "Legendy i apokrify v drevnei russkoi pis'mennosti." *Vestnik Evropy* 3 (1894): 291–339.

Reitblat, A. I. *Ot Bovy k Bal'montu: Ocherki po istorii chteniia v Rossii vo vtoroi polovine XIX veka.* Moscow: Izd. MPI, 1991.

Reizov, B. G. "K istorii zamysla *Brat'ev Karamazovykh.*" *Zvenia* 6 (1936): 545–73.

Rice, J. L. *Dostoevsky and the Healing Art.* Ann Arbor, Mich.: Ardis, 1985.

Robert, Marthe. *Roman des origines et origines du roman.* Paris: Gallimard, 1972.

Rosenblium, L. M. "V tvorcheskoi laboratorii Dostoevskogo." *Literaturnoe Nasledstvo* 77. Moscow: Nauka, 1965.

———. "Tvorcheskie dnevniki Dostoevskogo." *Literaturnoe Nasledstvo* 83. Moscow: Nauka, 1981.

Rousseau, Jean-Jacques. *Confessions*. Paris: Gallimard, 1973.
Rozanov, V. *Legenda o Velikom Inkvizitore F. M. Dostoevskogo*. Moscow: Respublika, 1996.
Saltykov-Shchedrin, M. E. *Sobranie sochinenii*. Edited by A. S. Bushmin et al. 20 vols. Moscow: Khudozhestvennaia literatura, 1970–76.
Samarin, Iurii. *Revoliutsionnyi konservatizm*. Berlin, 1875.
Sandoz, E. *Political Apocalypse: A Study of Dostoevsky's Grand Inquisitor*. Baton Rouge: Louisiana State University Press, 1971.
Saraskina, L. *Besy: Roman-predubezhdenie*. Moscow: Sovetskii pisatel', 1990.
———, ed. *Besy: Antologiia russkoi kritiki*. Moscow: Soglasie, 1996.
———. *Fedor Dostoevskii: Otdolenie Demonov*. Moscow, 1996.
Savchenko, N. "Kak postroen roman Dostoevskogo 'Podrostok.'" *Russaia Literatura* (1964): 41–57.
Scanlon, James P. *Dostoevsky the Thinker*. Ithaca, N.Y.: Cornell University Press, 2002.
Seduro, Vladimir. "The Fate of Stavrogin's Confession." *Russian Review* 25, no. 4 (Oct. 1966): 397–404.
Sekirin, P. "Text Unity and Cohesion of Dostoevsky's *Writers's Diary*." Ph.D. diss., University of Toronto, 1999.
Semenov, E. I. "U istokov '*Podrostka*.'" *Russkaia Literatura* 3 (1973): 107–16.
———. *Roman Dostoevskogo* Podrostok. Leningrad: Nauka, 1979.
Shaitanov, I. "Aleksandr Veselovskii's Historical Poetics: Genre in Historical Poetics." *New Literary History* 32 (2001): 429–43.
Sidorov, V. A. "O *Dnevnike pisatelia*." In *Dostoevkii: Stat'i materialy*, edited by A. S. Dolinin, 2:109–116. Leningrad: Mysl' 1924.
Skabichevskii, A. Review of *The Adolescent*. *Birzhevye Vedomosti*, 1876, 8.
Skaftymov, A. S. *Nravstvennye iskaniia russkikh pisatelei*. Moscow: Khudozhestvennaia Literatura, 1972.
Smirnov, V. *Literaturnaia istoriia "Otechestvennykh zapisok," 1864–1884*. Perm: Permskii gosudarstvennyi institut, 1974.
———. *F. M. Dostoevskii i russkaia demokraticheskaia zhurnalistika 70- 80-kh godov*. Volgograd, 1996.
Smyth, S. "The 'Lukovka' Legend in *The Brothers Karamazov*." *Irish Slavonic Studies* 7 (1986): 41–53.
Soloviev, V. "Tri rechi v pamiat' Dostoevskogo (1881–1883)." *Sobranie sochinenii*. St. Petersburg, 1901.
Steiner, Lina. *For Humanity's Sake: The Bildungsroman in Russian Culture*. Toronto: Toronto University Press, 2011.
Strakhov, N. N. *Kriticheskiia Stat'i ob I. S. Turgeneve I L. N. Tolstom, 1862–1885*. St. Petersburg: Tip. brat. Panteleevykh, 1887.
———. *Iz istorii literaturnago nigilizma, 1861–1865*. St. Petersburg: Tip. brat. Panteleevykh, 1890.

Stremoukhoff, Dmitri. "Moscow the Third Rome: Sources of the Doctrine." *Speculum* 8 (1953): 84–101.

Swales, M. *The German Bildungsroman from Wieland to Hesse.* Princeton, N.J.: Princeton University Press, 1978.

Terras, V. *Belinskij and Russian Literary Criticism: The Heritage of Organic Aesthetics.* Madison: University of Wisconsin Press, 1974.

———. *A Karamazov Companion.* Madison: University of Wisconsin Press, 1981.

———. "The Art of Fiction as a Theme in *The Brothers Karamazov.*" In *Dostoevsky: New Perspectives,* edited by Robert L. Jackson, 193–205. Englewood Cliffs, N.J.: Prentice Hall, 1983.

———. "Belinsky the Journalist and Russian Literature." In *Literary Journals in Imperial Russia,* edited by Deborah Martinsen, 117–28. Cambridge: Cambridge University Press, 1997.

———. *Reading Dostoevsky.* Madison: University of Wisconsin Press, 1998.

Thompson, D. *The Brothers Karamazov and the Poetics of Memory.* Cambridge: Cambridge University Press, 1991.

Thurston, G. J. "Alexis de Tocqueville in Russia." *Journal of the History of Ideas* 37, no. 2 (Apr.–June 1976): 289–306.

Tihanov, G. *Lukács, Bakhtin, and the Ideas of Their Time.* Oxford: Oxford University Press, 2000.

Todd, W. M. "*The Brothers Karamazov* and the Poetics of Serial Publication." *Dostoevsky Studies* 7 (1986): 87–97.

———. "Contexts of Criticism: Reviewing *The Brothers Karamazov* in 1879." *Stanford Slavic Studies* 4, no. 1 (1991): 293–310.

Tolstoi, L. *Polnoe sobranie sochinenii.* Edited by V. Chertkov. Moscow: Gosudarstvennoe izdatel'stvo, 1928–59.

Torop, P. *Dostoevskii: Istoria i ideologia.* Tartu: Tartu Ulikooli Kirjastus, 1997.

Treadgold, Donald. *The West in Russia and China, 1472–1917.* 2 vols. Cambridge: Cambridge University Press, 1973.

Tsivian, T. "O structure vremeni i prostranstva v romane Dostoevskogo *Podrostok.*" *Russian Literature* 4 (1976): 203–55.

Tunimanov, V. "Publitsistika Dostoevskogo." In *Dostoevskii—khudozhnik i myslitel': Sbornik stat'ei,* edited by A. L. Grishunin, 165–209. Moscow: Khudozhestvennaia literatura, 1972.

———. *Tvorchestvo Dostoevskogo.* Leningrad: Nauka, 1980.

Tynianov, Iu. N. *Dostoevskii i Gogol': K teorii parodii.* Petrograd: Opoiaz, 1921.

———, ed. *Fel'eton.* Leningrad: Akademia, 1927.

———. *Poetika, istoria literatury, kino.* Moscow: Nauka, 1977.

Ulam, Adam B. *In the Name of the People.* New York: Viking, 1977.

Uspensky, Boris. *A Poetics of Composition.* Berkeley: University of California Press, 1984.

Valentino, R. S. *Vicissitudes of Genre in the Russian Novel.* New York: Peter Lang, 2001.

Vasmer, M. *Etimologocheskii slovar' russkogo iazyka.* Translated by O.N. Trubachev. 4 vols. Moscow: Progress, 1986–87.

Vassena, Raffaella. *Reawakening National Identity: Dostoevsky's* Diary of a Writer *and Its Impact on Russian Society.* Bern: Peter Lang, 2007.

Venturi, F. *Roots of Revolution: A History of the Populist and Socialist Movements in Nineteenth Century Russia.* Translated by F. Haskell. New York: Grosset and Dunlap, 1966.

Veselovskii, A. N. "Opyti po istorii razvitiia khristianskoi legendy." *Zhurnal Ministerstva Narodnogo Prosveshcheniia.* St. Petersburg: Ministry of National Enlightenment, 1875–1877.

———. "Zametki po istorii i narodnoi slovesnosti." *Izdanie otdelenia russkogo iazyka i slovesnosti.* St. Petersburg: Academy of Sciences, 1880.

———. "Istoriia ili teoria romana? Iz istorii romana i povesti." *Izdanie otdeleniia russkogo iazyka i slovesnosti.* St. Petersburg: Academy of Sciences, 1886.

Vetlovskaia, V. "Literaturnye i fol'klornye istochniki 'Brat'ev Karamazovykh': Zhitie Alekseia cheloveka bozhiia i dukhovnye stikhi o nem." In *Dostoevkii i russkye pisateli: Traditsii, novatorstvo, masterstvo,* edited by V. Ia. Kirpotin, 325–54. Moscow: Sovetskii pisatel', 1971.

———. *Poetika Romana "Brat'ia Karamazovy."* Leningrad: Nauka, 1977.

———. "F. M. Dostoevskii." *Russkaia literatura i fol'klor (Vtoraia polovina XIX veka),* edited by A. A. Gorelov, 12–75. Leningrad: Nauka, 1982.

———. "Alyosha and the Hagiographic Hero." In *Dostoevsky: New Perspectives,* edited by Robert L. Jackson, 206–26. Englewood Cliffs, N.J.: Prentice Hall, 1984.

———. "Apokrif 'Khozhdenie bogoroditsy po mukam' v 'Brat'iakh Karamazovykh.'" *Dostoevskii i mirovaia kul'tura* 11 (1998): 35–47.

Viktorovich, V. *Roman Dostoevskogo* Podrostok: *Vozmozhnosti prochteniia.* Kolomna, 2003.

Vinitsky, I. "Where Bobok Is Buried: The Theosophical Roots of Dostoevskii's 'Fantastic Realism.'" *Slavic Review* 65, no. 3 (Fall 2006): 523–43.

———. *Ghostly Paradoxes: Modern Spiritualism and Russian Culture in the Age of Realism.* Toronto: University of Toronto Press, 2009.

Vinogradov, V. *O khudozhestvennoi proze.* Moscow, 1930.

———. *Problema avtorstva i teorii stil'ei.* Moscow: Khudozhestvennaia literatura, 1961.

Vlaskin, A. "Zaochnyi dialog N. S. Leskova i F. M. Dostoevskogo po problemam religioznosti i narodnoi kul'tury." *Russkaia Literatura* 1 (2003): 16–48.

Volgin, I. L. "Dostoevskii i tsarskaia tsenzura (k istorii izdaniia *Dnevnika pisatelia*)." *Russkaia Literatura* 4 (1970): 106–20.

———. "Dnevnik pisatelia: Tekst i kontekst." In *Dostoevskii: Materialy i issledovaniia* 3 (1978): 151–58.

———. *Dostoevskii—zhurnalist.* Moscow: Izdatel'stvo Moskovskogo Universiteta, 1982.

———. *Poslednii god Dostoevskogo.* Moscow: Sovetskii pisatel', 1986.

Voloshinov, V. *Marxism and the Philosophy of Language.* Translated by L. Matejka and I. Titunik. Cambridge, Mass.: Harvard University Press, 1986.

———. *Marksizm i philosofia iazyka.* Moscow: Labirint, 1994.

Wachtel, A. *The Battle for Childhood: Creation of a Russian Myth.* Stanford, Calif.: Stanford University Press, 1990.

Walicki, Andrzej. *The Slavophile Controversy: History of a Conservative Utopia in Nineteenth Century Russian Thought.* Oxford: Clarendon, 1975.

Ward, Bruce K. *Dostoevsky's Critique of the West.* Waterloo: Wilfrid Laurier University Press, 1986.

Wasiolek, E. *Dostoevsky: The Major Fiction.* Cambridge, Mass.: MIT Press, 1964.

Watt, Ian. *The Rise of the Novel.* Berkeley: University of California Press, 1957.

Wellek, R., and A. Warren. *Theory of Literature.* New York: Harcourt, 1956.

Wigzell, Faith. "Dostoevskii and the Russian Folk Heritage." In *The Cambridge Companion to Dostoevskii,* edited by W. J. Leatherbarrow, 21–46. Cambridge: Cambridge University Press, 2002.

Wortman, Richard. *The Crisis of Russian Populism.* Cambridge: Cambridge University Press, 1967.

———. *The Development of a Russian Legal Consciousness.* Chicago: University of Chicago, 1976.

Zaionchkovskii, P. *Krizis samoderzhaviia na rubezhe 1870–1880-kh godakh.* Moscow: Izdatel'stvo Moskovskogo Universiteta, 1964.

Zakharov, V. N. *Sistema zhanrov Dostoevskogo: Tipologiia i poetika.* Leningrad: Leningrad University Press, 1985.

Zakharova, T. V. "*Dnevnik pisatelia* kak original'noe zhanrovoe iavlenie i ideino-khudozhestvennaia tselostnost'." In *Tvorchestvo F. M. Dostoevskogo: Iskusstvo sinteza,* edited by N. M. Iurkova, 251–84. Ekaterinburg: Izdatel'stvo Ural'skogo Universiteta, 1991.

Zapadov, A. P., ed. *Russkii fel'eton.* Moscow: Politicheskaia literature, 1958.

Zenkovsky, S. *Medieval Russia's Epics, Chronicles and Tales.* New York: Meridian, 1974.

Zhurbina, E. *Iskusstvo fel'etona.* Moscow: Khudozhestvennaia literatura, 1965.

———. *Teoriia i praktika khudozhestvenno-publisticheskikh zhanrov, ocherk, fel'eton.* Moscow: Mysl', 1969.

———. *Povest' s dvum'iami siuzhetami.* Moscow: Sovetskii pisatel', 1974.

Ziolkowski, M. *Hagiography and Modern Russian Literature.* Princeton, N.J.: Princeton University Press, 1988.

Zohrab, I. "Dostoevsky as Editor of *The Citizen* (*Grazhdanin*)." In *Polyfunktion und Metaparodie. Aufsätze zum 175. Geburtstag von Fedor Michajlovic Dostoevskij*, 211–37. Dresden: Dresden University Press, 1998.

———. "The First Thirty Issues of Meshchersky's *The Citizen* (*Grazhdanin*) During Dostoevsky's Editorship (in English Translation): Uncovering the Authorship of Unsigned Contributions." *New Zealand Slavonic Journal* 38 (2004): 181–225.

———. "Dostoevsky's Editorship of Meshchersky's *The Citizen* (*Grazhdanin*): Issues nos 31–52. Uncovering the Authorship of Unsigned Contributions." *New Zealand Slavonic Journal* 39 (2005): 216–35.

Index

About the Author

Kate Holland is an assistant professor in the Department of Slavic Languages and Literatures at the University of Toronto.